"What a blessing it would be to sit down with the perfect person to answer every last question you have about the true Dharma and how to live it within the framework of ordinary life. This book is that blessing. From his decades of devoted practice and study with some of the greatest masters of our time, Sam offers the most profound teachings, fully intact and fully accessible. Both beginners and experienced practitioners will benefit from this view of how to live a life of ordinary magic, right here, right now."

—SUSAN PIVER, author of *Start Here Now: An Open-Hearted Guide to the Path and Practice of Meditation*, *Inexplicable Magic: Meditation for Mystics*, and *The Buddhist Enneagram*

"This book is nothing less than a celebration of Buddhist practice as an art of joyful awakening. I could feel Sam's encouraging and caring presence in the conversational style of the writing. I see this as a reference book, a handbook, and a 'keeper' indeed for all of us who seek a path to fearless loving-kindness."

—DAVID RICHO, author of *By Your Side: How to Find Soulful Allies and Become One to Others*

"An astounding unfolding of wisdom on practice and wakefulness in an authentic Vajrayana lineage, woven with fascinating anecdotes with wit and full dedication."

—KAZUAKI TANAHASHI, author of *Enlightenment Unfolds: The Essential Teachings of Zen Master Dōgen*

"In 1969, a twenty-one-year-old Sam Bercholz offered the world a defining invitation: *He founded Shambhala Publications*. Since then, millions of teachers, students, and practitioners from sacred traditions from across the globe accepted his invitation, offering their curiosity, wisdom, and compassion to a world in need of help. Today, in *Rude Awakenings* Sam shares his wise and noble voice directly with us: fresh, playful, and utterly uncontrived. It was with deep gratitude that I read this book—a gratitude that countless hearts and minds for generations to come will no doubt discover for themselves."

—MICHAEL CARROLL, author of *Awake at Work*

"In my opinion, this is probably the best book written to date about Buddhism. It is said that a teacher is best heard through his or her students. Sam's root teacher was the remarkable Tibetan Buddhist Chögyam Trungpa Rinpoche, an absolutely brilliant import to the West. I knew Trungpa relatively well, at any rate well enough to recognize that Sam is transmitting Trungpa's mind and voice. As a true student of Trungpa Rinpoche's, Sam is stunningly transmitting what Trungpa had taught him.

"That is one of the many reasons I love this book. Sam covers all the main aspects of Buddhism clearly, thoroughly, and brilliantly. Best of all, he offers short exercises where the reader can directly experience what he is explaining. This really is a wonderfully brilliant book—as I said, the single best book about Buddhism now on the market. As a prolific writer on self-help and spirituality, I am often asked what system or spirituality I think works the best or is the most 'life-changing' approach, and I always say 'Buddhism.' So get this book, read it, and have your life changed forever, thanks to the extraordinarily clear mind of Trungpa Rinpoche as wonderfully and brilliantly transmitted through the exquisite voice and understanding of Sam Bercholz."

—KEN WILBER, author of *Finding Radical Wholeness* and *A Brief History of Everything*

Rude Awakenings

An Unconventional Guide to the Buddhist Path

SAMUEL BERCHOLZ

Edited by VINCENT THIBAULT

SHAMBHALA

Shambhala Publications, Inc.
2129 13th Street
Boulder, Colorado 80302
www.shambhala.com

This edition is published simultaneously in hardcover and paperback.

Cover art: Devendra Banhart
Cover design: Daniel Urban-Brown

9 8 7 6 5 4 3 2 1

First Edition
Printed in the United States of America

Shambhala Publications makes every effort to print on
acid-free, recycled paper.
Shambhala Publications is distributed worldwide
by Penguin Random House, Inc., and its subsidiaries.

LIBRARY OF CONGRESS CATALOGING-IN-PUBLICATION DATA
Names: Bercholz, Samuel author
Title: Rude awakenings: an unconventional guide to the Buddhist path / Samuel Bercholz.
Description: First edition. | Boulder, Colorado: Shambhala, [2026] | Includes bibliographical references. |
Identifiers: LCCN 2025040807 | ISBN 9781645473282 trade paperback | ISBN 9781645476344 hardback
Subjects: LCSH: Buddhism
Classification: LCC BQ4022 .B46 2026 | DDC 294.3—dc23/eng/20260209
LC record available at https://lccn.loc.gov/2025040807

The authorized representative in the EU for product safety and compliance is eucomply OÜ, Pärnu mnt 139b-14, 11317 Tallinn, Estonia, hello@eucompliancepartner.com.

This book is dedicated to my grandsons,
Milo Marcel Delcourt and Dashiell Samuel Delcourt—
third-generation American Buddhists.
May it help guide them on their life journey,
and may it also be of benefit to young Buddhists,
and to all who aspire to tread the path,
throughout the world.

Contents

Editor's Introduction · VINCENT THIBAULT ix

PART ONE: FOUNDATIONS 1

1. Embarking on the Path to Liberation 3
2. Living an Artful Life 16
3. Expressing Wakefulness 29

PART TWO: MIND TRAINING AND KINDNESS 39

4. Keys to Mind Training 41
5. Boundlessness and Compassion: The Seven Points of Mind Training, Part 1 55
6. Ceaseless Opportunities: The Seven Points of Mind Training, Part 2 79

PART THREE: WORLDLY WISDOM 95

7. Making Sense Out of Everyday Life 97
8. The Daily Grind 111
9. Sex and the Sacred 126
10. The Energy of Money 138
11. Business Ethics and Meditative Discipline at Work 149

PART FOUR: THE TEACHINGS OF SHAMBHALA 157

12. The Origins of the Shambhala Teachings 159
13. Basic Goodness, Warriorship, and the Great Eastern Sun 180
14. Working with One's World 197
15. The Warrior Slogans 214
16. Authentic Presence, Windhorse, and the Four Dignities 226

PART FIVE: THE INDESTRUCTIBLE VEHICLE 247
17. Secret and Shocking 249
18. The Great Exaltation, Part 1 262
19. The Great Exaltation, Part 2 268

PART SIX: LINEAGE AND TRANSMISSION 285
20. Entering the Student–Teacher Relationship 287
21. The Evolution of the Student–Teacher Relationship 297
22. Lineage and Devotion 312

Conclusion: Across Valleys and Mountains 337
Acknowledgments 341
Appendix 1: A Special Time in History: Reflections on the Teachings of Trungpa Rinpoche 343
Appendix 2: Shambhala Warrior Slogans and Commentary 350
Notes 366

Editor's Introduction

Sam Bercholz, the founder of Shambhala Publications, often found himself at critical junctures in history, meeting the most remarkable spiritual teachers, cultural producers, and thought leaders. In particular, he witnessed pivotal moments in the transmission of Buddhism from the East to the West. His being there all along (notably, but not only, as a book publisher) made him deeply aware of our cultural blind spots and the universal tendency toward spiritual materialism. But he also has firsthand experience of the transformative power of Dharma and a clear understanding of how we can apply it to our lives, regardless of the many challenges we all face.

It wasn't just that Sam happened to be in the right place at the right time. He did not, to paraphrase a warning given to meditators, "just sit there in indifferent stupor." Though he was initially skeptical (and the way he addresses this in the book will speak to many of us), his life story is marked by commitment, devotion, and hard work. This allowed him to mix his mind with the wisdom mind of his teachers. As a result, he's become one of the most fearless and unconditionally cheerful people I know.

Among the countless spiritual teachers he has met, he had a particularly important relationship with two of them, and they became his root teachers. The first was Chögyam Trungpa (1940–1987)—a meditation master, iconoclast teacher, accomplished artist, and prolific writer—who has been one of the most important figures in the dissemination of Buddhism in the West and perhaps one of the most influential figures of the past century, period. Sam speaks of him as "the Guru Rinpoche of the West," evoking Padmasambhava, the enlightened being who was instrumental in establishing the Buddhist teachings in Tibet in the eighth century.

The author's second root guru was Kyabjé Thinley Norbu Rinpoche (1931–2011), the eldest son of Dudjom Rinpoche. Considered an emanation of Longchenpa, the great fourteenth-century enlightened sage who is a central figure in the Nyingma tradition, Thinley Norbu Rinpoche was one of the preeminent Nyingma masters of his time—in fact, a teacher of teachers. Unswerving when it came to maintaining the purity of wisdom lineages, he was also a brilliant and prolific writer.

As we will see through Sam's delightful, moving, and often hilarious stories, Trungpa Rinpoche and Thinley Norbu Rinpoche had two completely different teaching styles. Yet both are indivisibly connected to Guru Rinpoche. And on some level, they were of one mind—the mind of complete wakefulness: wise, unfettered, uncontrived, undeceiving, unfeigned, and boundlessly compassionate.

It was Thinley Norbu Rinpoche who originally planted the seed for this project, asking Sam, "You should write a book on what you've learned from Trungpa Rinpoche." He didn't exactly say "what he taught you" but rather "what you've learned," which is interesting. In any case, Sam found it only natural to also include a few chapters that are aligned with the style of his second root teacher.

The actual writing of this book started many years after Thinley Norbu Rinpoche expressed this wish. More and more of Sam's friends were nagging him, asking him to write such a book, and it became obvious that there was no way out of this! I offered my help, and we started a process that lasted thirty months or so.

The result loosely follows the three-*yana* framework, *yana* being a Sanskrit word to speak of the main spiritual approaches or "vehicles" of Buddhism. In other words, the book starts with foundational and exoteric teachings, and slowly builds up to subtler and more esoteric methods, thus covering a *lot* of ground. That said, there's a naturalness to it. And the book doesn't adhere to any stiff doctrinal distinction between the vehicles. As per the teachings of both Chögyam Trungpa and Thinley Norbu, even the most "basic" methods are imbued with a vast and profound view. The book also acknowledges the spirally nature of spiritual progress and therefore has a great "reread" value: We can always approach the teachings—all teachings—with a fresh mind, so as to deepen our understanding, experience, and realization.

I also find *Rude Awakenings* to be extremely original. For example, in the "Foundations" section, after an opening discussion on habits and addictions, and some key instructions on sitting meditation, Sam launches into an unexpected and fascinating exploration of how to live an "artful life," where we learn that we can imbue every day with a constant invocation of wakefulness.

Likewise, in the middle of the book, after a section on training the mind in compassion and bravery, there are two important sections that veer from the classic so-called three-yana framework to discuss "worldly wisdom" and "the teachings of Shambhala." The penultimate section, on the Vajrayana, is in many ways shocking, mysterious, and paradoxical, but I believe that both beginners and old-timers alike will find it truly useful. It is followed by three chapters on the topics of lineage and transmission, which contain some of the most important pieces of advice we'll ever receive if we're to study Dharma outside of books. Indeed, this section talks of charlatans and self-deceptions, but it also inspiringly discusses how to relate to undeceiving teachers.

Although Sam has been studying Dharma for sixty years, this is not exactly a scholarly book. It is more in the style of personal instruction and counsel from a friend who has "been there," meaning someone who's had a direct experience of skepticism, nihilism, denial, confusion, and pain. In many ways, these instructions are akin to what the Zen tradition calls the "teachings outside of the teachings."

Through his personal touch, Sam makes the most profound Dharma eminently practical and relatable. On that note, his ability to relate to all sorts of people has always made an impression on me. I've wandered with him in Los Angeles, New York, Montreal; wherever we'd go, he would connect with someone there. He would instantly seem to make friends with an old Eastern European clerk, or crack up a young mustachioed barista with the dumbest jokes; we would be eating lunch at a Greek restaurant, and first thing I'd know, he'd be discussing some obscure novelist or swapping film references with the waiter. Tibetans would welcome him as one of their own, and so would Australians; whether rich or poor, formally educated or self-taught, a common denominator would always surface. I often feel like there is no place where he wouldn't belong. Yet he remains so very much himself, just as he is. This, in itself, is a precious teaching: not to use Dharma to become somebody special. Only one thing seems to drive him: He always cares for anyone who has an interest in becoming a genuine person and extracting the essence of their precious human life. That's what matters in the end, and that's what makes this book so helpful.

The author is often bold, if not irreverent. ("Oh," he would often sigh as we were working on some of the sections, "you know that a lot of people will find this controversial, don't you?") But he never turns his back on tradition.

What he points to relentlessly, though never in a cruel or moralizing manner, is our own sense of pride. In this day and age, perhaps especially in the West, we have these misplaced notions of independence and self-sufficiency that insidiously contribute to our painful loss of spiritual bearings. Sam puts the spotlight on this and many other issues, to the point that the book could just as well be titled *Tell It Like It Is*. Yet the whole thing is incredibly uplifting and empowering.

All too often, the teachings of the Buddha are looked at through a folkloric lens, as some kind of artifact that looks exquisitely serene and delightfully exotic, ready to be showcased on a shelf. But as Sam and his predecessors teach, receiving the transmission of Dharma is not like being handed some delicate object to be put in a museum. The process is more akin to learning how to bake fresh bread: Through generations of bakers, the bread is equally fresh and always nourishing. Likewise, this book shows us that Dharma is a living tradition and that each and every one of us can learn to embody it, for the benefit of all beings.

VINCENT THIBAULT
Quebec City
March 20, 2025

PART ONE

FOUNDATIONS

It all has to start somewhere, and that somewhere is whatever our situation is. Just like that, the foundational teachings of Buddhism start in a very realistic manner—for instance, by inviting us to acknowledge our own neuroses. So this is where we'll begin. Chapter 1 explores some tools that will help us slowly see through the veils of our deeply ingrained habits. It also provides meditation instructions. Chapters 2 and 3 discuss how we can start to live an artful life (in the Buddhist sense), through a constant invocation of wakefulness.

I

Embarking on the Path to Liberation

Let's go right to the heart of the matter.

What is it that makes the dawning of wisdom so difficult—or so easy, as the case may be?

It's a tough and important question.

Generally, the dawning of wisdom *is* difficult, because throughout this life we have created all sorts of habits, distractions, and addictions to block out the brilliant rays of the sun that are the enlightened view, enlightened living, and enlightened ways of benefiting all beings.

On some level, though, this is not a problem at all because, as we'll see, wisdom arises from confusion. Therefore, for those of us who are wise and for those of us who are confused, as well as for those of us who have mixed up our confusion with wisdom and our wisdom with confusion, I would like to begin this discussion by looking at the core of it all: habit. Addiction.

I've never been to a Narcotics Anonymous meeting, but I think you say something like, "My name is Sam, and I'm an addict." This is the story of my addiction.

I'm an addict. Since beginningless time, I have fooled myself, constantly, by believing that there is some solid *me* that exists. In this life, just like in all my previous lives—even though it's been pointed out to me numerous times—I'm still totally addicted to this idea of a self that's separate from everything else.

I'm an addict. I'm addicted to duality. I'm addicted to the habit of accepting what I find pleasant and rejecting what I find unpleasant. It doesn't do much good, but I'm still addicted to it.

I'm an addict. I'm continuously fascinated by distractions of all kinds—physical objects, people, screens and all kinds of phenomena appearing on them.

I'm an addict. Even though I have practiced the buddhadharma and know that liberation and enlightenment are my basic nature, I still wander about in delusion.

What am I doing writing on this subject? Well, it may be that it takes an addict to talk with other addicts. I guess that's the idea here. This big-time addict is going to talk to those of you who are big-time addicts, those of you who are small-time addicts, and those of you who are medium addicts. Some of you may be completely liberated; you can then have compassion toward my addictions and those of all the others who have fallen into delusion.

Yet I'm a cheerful addict. Why? Because I know there is something—or nothing, depending on how I look at it—beyond this set of addictions. I'm addicted to my ideas of reality, other people's ideas of reality, science's ideas of reality, certain philosophical systems' ideas of reality, certain political systems' ideas of reality. All of it is called "reality." I'm addicted to this idea that there is a fixed reality, and it's heavy-duty. I can't live without reality, just the same way I can't live without fantasy. But there's a cure to both my addiction to reality and my addiction to fantasy. I believe that buddhadharma provides the best instructions on how to free oneself and how to be of benefit to fellow habitual creatures. Something deep within me knows that just living in habit is powerful but not very beneficial to anyone.

That turns out to be a great basis to work with: the very power of habit. It is said that the Buddha was free from all habits. Therefore, I take refuge in the Buddha. I take refuge in that state of wakefulness that is beyond *any* habit, whether bad or good. If I pay attention to the Buddha's speech, which is preserved in the various sutras and tantras, I find the most fascinating things: actual instructions on how to free oneself from the constraints and bindings of habit.

In almost all cases, what's presented in Buddhist teachings is not exactly an instant fix for going from habit to no habit but rather a path. We are shown a pathway that can take us from our habitual reality to the realm of wakefulness where one has transcended habit altogether. There are a couple of exceptions—especially in some advanced teachings—but for now we're going to keep it simple and discuss the common, or foundational, Buddhist approaches.

As Buddhist practitioners, what we do is we honestly consider each of our bad habits and learn to create good habits using the same power and energy embedded in these habits. This is how we learn to practice buddhadharma, which is a complete gateway to the awakened state. If we use this power to replace our various bad habits with good habits, then that awakened state becomes possible. However, we're not just going dualistically from "bad" to "good." That's not what we're concerned about. We use that process to go beyond the process.

To do that, we have to begin at the beginning. We have the habit of identifying whatever we think we are as being *me*, and we are always self-referential. Here, we are given the good habit of learning how to meditate, and through sitting meditation we start to see that there are breaks in that self-reference. Yes, I am suggesting that we take our addiction and then become addicts of something different. To reiterate, we create good habits with the same passion and power that are usually involved in bad habits.

My teachers taught that sitting meditation is the basis from which all habits can be changed, because through the practice we can begin to see clearly. Likewise, Buddha himself—as well as bodhisattvas and teachers from all the various Buddhist traditions—recommends that we work with our mind, through being observant and learning how to be at rest. Our strongest habits may relate to busy mind, or lazy mind, or overly analytic mind, or any type of deluded mind. Whatever the case may be, the practice of meditation is the remedy.

MEETING THE BUDDHA

I have been a student of Buddhism in this life for more than half a century, and I'm just—*just*—beginning to understand the Dharma in any serious way. It's wonderful, because one can begin anytime. I often find myself with a group of fellow students who are somewhere in the neighborhood of fifty years my junior, and we're learning together, and it's delightful. In fact, some of my most profound experiences have been with these young people, who are sometimes even children, because they revealed to me how amazing it is that Dharma exists at all. They have no preconception. That's true beginner's mind.

Anyone who is holding this book—regardless of their age and background—can make a connection to the Buddha, to the Buddhist teachings, and to the sangha or community that the Buddha has been so kind to manifest. With so much available these days, we take for granted that Buddhism is something we can just casually run into. But it's actually very rare to find the precious teachings of the Buddha and be able to make a connection with them, through receptivity and a qualified teacher or lineage holder.

Supermarkets have spoiled us. We think we need dozens of choices of everything. This mindset is so prevalent that even if we find something that's worthwhile, some of us have a not-stick-to-it-ness. That the Buddha appeared in this age really is quite extraordinary. What's also extraordinary is that we somehow heard about it. Not only have we heard about it but we are also fortunate enough to collect clues, so to speak, or have the intuition that enlightenment is *not* a myth. But then we have to decide: Are we going to do anything about this? Or are we going to just let this life pass like a dream? Are we going to pay lip service to some spiritual system or another? Or are we going to learn from the life, example, and teachings of the Buddha? It's always up to us.

Different Ways to View the Buddha

Many of us are familiar with the life story of the Buddha. I'm not going to repeat it here because there are many wonderful books on the subject. I will, however, point out that there have historically been many ways to consider the Buddha.

The early schools of Buddhism, such as the Theravada, say that Buddha was a man who, just like you and me, was human. He was born into a royal family, had certain experiences, became enlightened, and then taught the truth of Dharma. There are many outstanding stories about how he interacted with his disciples, leading them to liberation, and how he lived his own life. For example, one lesser-known detail that I personally find interesting is that he walked *a lot*. In any event, that is just one way of looking at the Buddha.

The later traditions of the Mahayana offer a different perspective. The historical Buddha is looked at in the same way, but with the understanding that he was an enlightened being who entered this human realm for our benefit and performed many miraculous feats. The Buddha was not just someone who lived at a particular time and place and taught particular subject matters. He exists beyond space and time. He teaches in an ongoing way, without any static time frame. Yes, the physical body of Shakyamuni Buddha has passed, but the wisdom-mind quality manifests continuously, and it is always available to beings. Each of us can connect with that wisdom mind. Each of us can connect with wakefulness.

In the Vajrayana tradition—the extension of the Mahayana tradition—the Buddha manifests in the form of various deities, traveling to various places and presenting what are called the esoteric or tantric teachings of Buddhism. In those cases, the Buddha takes on different forms for the benefit of practitioners so that they can mix their mind and achieve the mind of the Buddha that is beyond conceptualization, beyond birth, beyond death. For instance, from the tantric point of view, the Buddha also manifested in female forms. Wakefulness is in no way limited to a specific gender.

This may be an overly simple way of stating it, but the idea is that the Buddha can be looked at in many ways. He has manifested in countless ways so that we can conveniently relate to him one way or another, and through this, connect with our own wisdom mind.

OVERCOMING HOPE AND FEAR

Though we aspire to connect with buddha mind, or the wakeful mind, our grasping mind tends to try to find some comfort. The stupidity of our own mind is that we seek this comfort in places that are always going to fail us. Always. That is because we don't want to understand the impermanent nature of everything that has been born. Anything that has manifested passes. Even if we hear or say that, we don't believe it. Everything that has been born passes—everything!

Not fully realizing that, we oscillate between hope and fear. We either try to get something or push something away. The place between hope and fear is the stillness of fearlessness—but fearlessness isn't trapped by hope. It isn't just seduced. Ordinarily we're always immersed in hope and fear because we want this and that—or to avoid this or that—so badly. Yet anything we try to avoid will come and chase us. Trying to avoid something is painful and fruitless. It is equally illusory to chase something, because it's all so elusive. In fact, sometimes we get what we were hoping for and it turns out to be bad news!

The point is, we have this fickle mind. We know that nothing is going to save us, and yet we keep looking to be saved. It's a tough situation. However, as the Buddha and the great masters have taught, there is a way through.

HINAYANA: THE FOUNDATIONAL TEACHINGS

But let's not get ahead of ourselves. The answer to the suffering caused by our habits and addictions isn't about some cosmic sleight of hand. There's a path, and—lucky for us—it's been mapped out in detail. My teacher, Chögyam Trungpa Rinpoche, insisted on starting at the beginning, and he wasn't one for shortcuts. He taught the Buddhist journey as a three-yana approach: Hinayana, Mahayana, Vajrayana. Each is a vehicle, a way of traveling through the wild terrain of mind and life. So, before we start dreaming about enlightenment, let's get our feet on the ground and begin with the Hinayana—the foundational teachings that show us how to work with suffering right where we are.

The core teaching of the Buddha is the four noble truths, or the "four truths of the noble ones." These are the Buddha's way of getting right to the point: (1) There is the truth of the suffering of life, which is to be understood; (2) this suffering has a cause, which is to be abandoned; (3) the cessation of suffering is a possibility, which is to be actualized; and (4) there is a path out of suffering, which is to be relied upon. We are thus given detailed answers to these questions: What is suffering? What are its causes? Is there a way out? And if so, how should we proceed?

Trungpa Rinpoche had a way of making these truths hit home. While the traditional teachings often focus on passion or grasping as the root of suffering, Trungpa Rinpoche zeroed in on something we all know too well: Our minds are always on the move, always wanting, always chasing the next thing. He used to say, "Speed kills"—not the kind you get from a car or a pill but the mental speed that keeps us restless and unsatisfied.

In terms of the third and fourth noble truths—that there's a way of dealing with this mess—we are taught that basic sanity already exists. We don't have to go looking for it anywhere. It's more like tuning in to it rather than looking for it. Thus, the Buddha didn't just leave us with a diagnosis—he gave us a treatment plan: the eightfold path. This set of eight practical guidelines for living helps us move from confusion to clarity and leads to the cessation of suffering. (If you're new to this, the eightfold path covers right view, right intention, right speech, right action, right livelihood, right effort, right mindfulness, and right concentration. Think of it as a tool kit for sane living.)

At this stage, Buddhist practice traditionally begins with "taking refuge"—not in a god or higher power but in what's called the Triple Gem: the Buddha, the Dharma (his teachings), and the Sangha (the community of practitioners). Trungpa Rinpoche put his own spin on this: To take refuge, he said, is to give up the familiar ground of our ego—to let go of the constant self-referencing and just be with what's actually happening, even if that includes disappointment or sadness. There is no Pollyanna approach to it. It's totally realistic.

In the Hinayana, the basic meditation practice is called *shamatha*, or "peaceful abiding." It's about sitting still and letting our mind settle. However, in no way should we suppress our thoughts—the practice is to face whatever comes up. Whatever thoughts arise, we just face them and look at them. Trungpa Rinpoche's approach echoes the spirit of the Mahamudra and Ati teachings,[1] where nothing is excluded from awareness. We can deal directly with our thoughts. We don't have to censor anything, and we don't have to sort good thoughts into a little white pile and bad thoughts into a little black pile. We may find this image funny, but that is a technique that some people follow. Yet here there's absolutely no suppression of thoughts. If we observe our mind through practice, it will tire itself out.

Eventually the practice deepens to include what's called *vipashyana* (Sanskrit) or *vipassana* (Pali), which simply means "insight" or "superior seeing." In fact, Trungpa Rinpoche taught shamatha and vipashyana together. While a lot of what's called "vipassana" these days is really about cultivating calm and stillness (shamatha), in reality vipashyana is something deeper. It's about seeing the mind's patterns and neuroses clearly, and opening up to a panoramic awareness that isn't tangled up in self-judgment. In this approach, meditation isn't a special event—it's just life lived with awareness.

But here's the kicker: As inspiring as all this sounds, Trungpa Rinpoche warned against getting too worked up about it. He introduced the idea of "cool boredom"—the kind of boredom that comes up when you're just sitting there, doing nothing, for a long time. At first, it feels pointless, maybe even irritating. But if you stick with it, you realize it's not a problem. In fact, it's a relief. Cool boredom is the antidote to what he called "spiritual materialism"—the tendency to turn spiritual practice into just another thing to achieve or collect.

In this spirit, Trungpa Rinpoche coined the phrase "buddhadharma without credentials." In practicing, we're not concerned about getting to some stage or level and then turning our idea of that stage or level into something that we can feel good about. Just practice and let the rest take care of itself. Interestingly, when we drop the need for credentials, real insight—vipashyana—can dawn, bringing a sense of spaciousness and clarity. If we're still concerned with who cares, there's no possibility of insight because there's no peace.

A natural intelligence, called *prajna*, or wisdom, can then arise. That is actual seeing, and the experience of egolessness: If we pay attention, we find out that nothing is solid. Although there are phenomena of all sorts, there's no need to hold on to anything. That egolessness is the bridge between the Hinayana, or foundational teachings, and the Mahayana, or Great Vehicle, which informs the rest of this book.

All of this is the heart of the Hinayana. All I can do here is finger paint. In any case, the Hinayana approach applies at every level. Even if you're a practitioner of the highest caliber, all this is still true. The truth of suffering never ceases to be true; cool boredom never ceases to be refreshing; and any notion of buddhadharma *with* credentials is never anything but an impasse. Most importantly, the truth of cessation never ceases to be a possibility.

As Trungpa Rinpoche said, "Never forget Hinayana."[2]

MEDITATION IS THE KEY

So, after all this talk on the foundational teachings, you might be wondering: How do we actually embark on the path and loosen the grip of our old habits and addictions? The Buddhist masters have told us that, actually, we can start very simply. Here's the not-so-secret secret: The key to this whole path is meditation. It's the tool that lets us see our patterns in real time, instead of just theorizing about them. No matter how tangled things get, everything begins (and begins again) with simply sitting down and being willing to look at our own minds. So, before we go any further, let's get practical and try some basic sitting meditation together.

BASIC SITTING MEDITATION

Later in this book we will revisit the practice of sitting meditation once more and add some nuance. You will also find that instructions that look alike or seem redundant may unveil their richness over time. For now, I will share very simple instructions so that you can get a taste of basic sitting meditation. We are all beginners, which is a wonderful situation. So let us practice some calm-abiding meditation for a few minutes.

The Approach

Let's stand up for a moment, so we know where we are. We can do meditation practice either by rote or with positive intentionality. Many of us end up doing it by rote: We have the good idea that we'd like to meditate, and then we sit down and go into indifferent stupor. But we can also begin by taking note of where we are. We're standing on this earth. Our feet are on the ground. Our back is straight. When we approach our seat, we do so mindfully.

The Posture

We take our seat, whether it's a chair or cushion. We can leave our hands on our thighs, above our knees. Our back is straight, without too much dependence on the back of the chair, if you happen to be sitting on a chair; in fact, not touching the back at all is good. Our spine is erect but comfortable. Our eyes are open, we're looking out with a soft gaze, ever so slightly down to begin with, so that we're not looking around or busying ourselves.

The Three Mindfulnesses

Like that, with our good posture, we maintain mindfulness of our body. We're mindful of the feeling of the chair or cushion against our bottom, the feeling of our feet on the earth or our weight resting upon the ground, the straightness of our back, the relaxation of our chest. There's a sense of verticality and openness. We're also looking out, softly.

Then, just so that we have something to touch in with, we have the mindfulness of our breath. We don't change our breath in any way. We just have our mind be with our breath. If it's simple and no big deal, we can pay a little bit of extra attention to the outbreath. We are not trying to control or contrive; we simply are a tad more mindful of the breath going out. It then comes in. It goes out... It comes in...

Finally, we have the mindfulness of mind. We're not concerned about whatever happens in our mind. Everything is fine. We are just aware of whatever unfolds within, and we use the breath as an anchor. Our body is there, our mind is doing whatever it does. When we find that we forgot that we're sitting and forgot our breath, we simply make a mental note that we've gone off in our thoughts and we just come back, without making any particular effort to dissipate our thoughts. That mental note can be, quite simply, "Thinking." Then without adding any commentary, we kindly come back to our breath, back to our body, and we sit still, relaxed but fully present.

Let's just do that for a little while.

Mindfulness of our body. Mindfulness of our breath. Mindfulness of our mind.

SINGING AND CHANTING

Sitting meditation is part of a lifelong path and provides the best way to work with our addictions. Another important aspect of the practice—something that almost all Buddhists do—is singing and chanting. Some might react, "What!? But why?" Some people might be uncomfortable at first, especially if they have inherited notions from other religious traditions, so it is worthwhile to look into this.

Buddhists are not theists. Therefore, we're not praying to some deity for them to do something particularly. The singing and chanting constitute a sense of offering to the awakened state of mind. Ultimately it is not that we are *here* while some god is *over there*; rather, it is a way to connect with wakefulness.

There's also something that happens when we engage our mind with our body, and singing is a way to synchronize both body and mind. Dharma artistry—a whole chapter in this book is dedicated to the subject—always has that as part of its modus operandi: Everything points to synchronizing body, speech, and mind. Much of the time, however, rather than synchronization, there's a certain awkwardness and dysfunction. We don't see straight. In fact, we see almost everything the opposite of the way it actually is. Our concept of things is so askew. In particular, we believe that there's a separate self, as a given. That is delusion. Learning to synchronize body, speech, and mind gives us a nudge in the right direction—it is, in fact, a prerequisite to seeing things clearly. When body, speech, and mind are all over the place, it creates a distortion in our perception, as if we were looking through muddy waters. When they are in sync and settled, we can start to see things as they are.

Therefore, meditation is the ground, which mixes with study—that is, slowly finding out about what the Buddha and other great masters actually taught. Along with that, we start using our voice. That's the simplest method, in a sense: You can sit still and use your voice. There's no overt activity needed. It's an easy way to begin a kind of mindfulness practice: You are mindful of what you are singing or chanting.

Using one's voice as a mindfulness practice is an interesting notion. When one chants, there is something to the meaning. For example, when we chant a daily invocation, although we may not know Tibetan or Sanskrit language, we may still know the meaning of the words (through the translation as well as teachings and commentaries), and we can keep that meaning in our mind. There's also something that comes from the melody—from the mindfulness of the right tones and so forth. In this way, there's meaning and constant freshness to our mindfulness practice. Some people may find it a bit odd initially but rapidly find just how natural and powerful it can be.

It is also worthwhile to compare this with the usual way we use our voice. For example, many of us like to sing pop tunes. While there's nothing wrong with that, there's usually no spiritual benefit to it, especially compared to chanting mantras and sacred texts that are charged with meaning and blessings and that help train our mind so as to cultivate wisdom, compassion, humility, and courage. As well, we are constantly involved in discursiveness: One thought leads to another in a never-ending cycle of inner chatter. Orienting our attention toward a particular recitation is a way to make use of the mind's natural tendency to engage with words and sounds. We develop a good habit by exploiting an ingrained mechanism that ordinarily nurtures bad habits. If anything, reciting beautiful texts charged with meaning is a way to uplift ourselves. Usually our self-talk is anesthetizing or purely entertainment. Here, by comparison, we are waking ourselves up and being in the present.

THE PATH IS THE GOAL

We keep coming back to the notion of practice—whether sitting meditation or chanting—as a crucial way to work with our habits and addictions. An important characteristic of Buddhist teachings is that they are path-oriented rather than goal-oriented. In fact, a particularly important lesson is that the actual practices *are* the goal. There's no big carrot out there, no box that you check and then everything's done. That is extremely profound. If there is such a thing as complete enlightenment—and it is clear that there is—it isn't something that you get at the end of some rainbow or yellow brick road. It's all in the path. The whole thing is. It's not that there's someplace you arrive and then, *whoopee*!

Chögyam Trungpa once said, "You've come to the place where you're so confused that you believe that your confusion is the unconfused state." His adamant advice is that there is only one way to break through the confusion, and that is meditation practice. He never, ever varied from that approach, and he endlessly asked his students to "please practice." He ordered, begged, cajoled, and did whatever was required. "Please, please practice." Also, at some of his talks, he said, "There is no reason for you to be here if you don't practice, because then we have nothing in common. Without actual practice, there is no way for us to work together."

That's the bedrock, if you will, for entering the mind of Buddha: meditation. Meditation practice is the only thing that lets us step out of what Trungpa Rinpoche called the bureaucracy of ego, which is all the things in our being that make us believe that we are separate from everything else, that there is something to be gained. We come up with millions of ideas through books, television, discursive thinking, and so on. Nothing breaks through that except meditation practice itself. *Thinking* about practicing, thinking about the deep teachings, no matter what they are, doesn't get us anywhere, really. There is nothing that breaks through it other than meditation practice. There is no exception.

HOPELESSNESS AND FAITH

At the same time that he emphasized meditation practice, Trungpa Rinpoche brought in a unique teaching on what he called "hopelessness." This was the bad-news/good-news part of his Hinayana teachings.

I remember, the first time he used the term, he went through a litany about how everything was hopeless. Anything you thought you could get was hopeless, thinking that he could help you was hopeless, and so on. It wasn't even poetry. There is simply no one to save us! Not only that, but there is also not the slightest chance that there is ever going to be anyone to save us, and we can't even save ourselves! Sounds bleak, right?

The ground of spiritual practice, the ground of meditation, is that hopelessness itself. We have to live, and we have to learn to live with our pain. There is no little gimmick, no special exit to avoid pain. We actually have to be with it. Even if we think that enlightenment is a great idea—and it *is* a great idea—and think that we can pursue it, that's hopeless, too! If we think there's an orderly set of A-B-C steps that we can take, just following the dotted lines, that's deluded.

Interestingly enough, though, out of that hopelessness comes faith. Trungpa

Rinpoche explained that there is no faith until we have faith in ourselves; in other words, until we can begin to trust ourselves. If we can do that, then we can have a relationship with a teacher. But if we can't trust ourselves, there's no way a teacher will do us any good.

That begins with pulling up our socks or our bootstraps. We have to begin with ourselves. Once we make friends with ourselves, then *natural discipline* can arise. From that, we can actually enter the Buddhist path.

2

Living an Artful Life

We have seen that embarking on the path to true freedom requires a reality check, that turning a blind eye to our suffering and confusion only gets us so far. Nevertheless, Buddhism is not bleak in the least. For one thing, it says that no matter who we are, we can learn to live in an artful manner. This is a fresh, uplifting take on life, which has provided me with great comfort again and again. Chögyam Trungpa talked about this notion a great deal, referring to this approach to life as Dharma art. So, let's take a closer look at what it actually means to live artfully—because while the foundational teachings give us the ground to stand on, Trungpa Rinpoche's take on Dharma art invites us to bring those teachings off the cushion and into the thick of daily life. And don't worry, this isn't just for painters or poets; it's about how any of us can express wakefulness right in the middle of whatever we're doing. Right off the bat, we should clarify that Dharma art is not a claim to fame. *Dharma artist* means "Buddhist." It's something very simple in this context. A Dharma artist is someone who lives and expresses their life in a dharmic manner, in a truthful manner. "Truthful" refers specifically to the truth of the Buddha, the Awakened One. It is the truth of wakefulness.

In this chapter, we're not going to talk about art as separated in any way from our ordinary life. Nor are we interested in any technique or endeavor to develop some special kind of ego—the artist's ego or the musician's ego or the filmmaker's ego or the poet's ego (oh, that one's big!)... We're not going to discuss these matters or try to pump up our artistic persona.

Of course, some of us identify as artists and believe that it is our vocation. There's no problem whatsoever with that. We're not talking about staking our claim to artistry. Dharma art is how we live our life, how we express our relationship to mindfulness and *isness*—that is, the way things are.

Maybe the best way to begin this is for me to tell you how a Dharma artist is trained. Of course, that depends on the tradition, on the teacher, and on multiple factors. I can only share my own silly experience!

BEING TRAINED AS A DHARMA ARTIST

How is someone or a group of people trained as Dharma artists? For one thing, Buddhist teachers train their students in meditation. The sitting practice of meditation is the key ingredient in becoming a Buddhist. But if we only do sitting meditation, we're like a bump on a log: It doesn't necessarily mean that anything's going to happen at all. Not that anything's supposed to happen! But sitting in a dull stupor for as long as we do it—if that's what we do—is just sitting in a dull stupor. Therefore, when we talk about meditation, we're not talking about sitting in any kind of indifferent stupefaction. And we're not particularly trying to calm ourselves or reduce our blood pressure or anything of the sort.

We practice sitting meditation so that we can learn the nature of our own mind. As well, we combine our meditation practice with study. Studying Buddhism means that we study what the Buddha taught, as well as the teachings of the great masters such as Nagarjuna, Shantideva, Padmasambhava, Yeshe Tsogyal, Longchenpa, and Gampopa, to name a few. We study what our predecessors have learned. We make sense of it and see if it applies to our own meditation.

That's how Trungpa Rinpoche presented meditation practice and all the fundamentals to us. But at some point, he started doing strange things. For example, he introduced "theater workshops." Strange people from a group called "The Living Theater" in New York City asked to be trained in a dharmic way of doing theater. So, we had these odd New York types, and us dumb Dharma-student types, doing theater together. We were walking in and out of closets, giving ridiculous speeches... This wasn't so odd to us at the time, given it was the early 1970s. But there was something unbelievably powerful about it. I found out years later that this form of psychodrama is part of the most profound methods of Buddhism, something usually done in a three-year retreat situation. Yet Trungpa Rinpoche was doing it with us, and he was imparting it without a lot of baggage.

He also wanted us to learn monastic dance—*cham* in Tibetan. He had been in an auto accident, and he was partially paralyzed on his left side. One day he decided to teach us the basic movements. We thought, "Oh, this is gonna be interesting and energetic!" Turns out, the first move was going from one side of an ordinary-sized room to the other—but you had to take a full half hour to do so.

That was our first exercise. It was excruciating to move that slowly! But it was a transformative experience to be able to watch my mind when moving my arm from *here* to *there*. . . .

That was our first and last lesson in monastic dance. Rinpoche apologized for not being able to show us any more because of his disability. But he then developed what he called the "Mudra Theater," so that Dharma students could involve themselves in theater productions. He even wrote a couple of plays while he was in retreat—seven over the course of his life.

In 1972, Trungpa Rinpoche decided he was done teaching us and that everything had been a failure. He had been in the United States for three years, and his mission, so to speak, was to teach what's called Dzogchen, the Great Perfection. I think he was very disappointed that the students didn't get it. His knowledge of English and the Western mind was quite extraordinary, and he was teaching without any of the constraints of technical language. In fact, his basic meditation instructions were as simple as can be: "Sit down. Be quiet. You know what to do." But somehow his students just couldn't sit still.

Once, in retreat, he decided, "Okay, this noble experiment is over." He determined that he would develop a "stages of the path" relationship with his students, all as a group. That meant that everyone would start going through Hinayana-style practice, then Mahayana practice, and then Vajrayana practice. That was the whole nine yards, with *dathüns*, which were one-month sitting periods of shamatha-vipashyana coupled with study. He also created what he called "seminaries," where his students were able to practice and study the whole path for three months at a time. Those who were able to complete that went on to do the so-called preliminary practices, and then the various *sadhana* practices, and so on.[1] Now, what does that have to do with art?

All those things have to do with bringing body, speech, and mind together and synchronizing them, which we discussed in the previous chapter. Trungpa Rinpoche even recommended special disciplines for us, in addition to traditional disciplines. His point of view was straightforward: If you're going to be a Buddhist practitioner, then you are going to be an artist, a scholar, a healer, everything—in other words, a complete human being, not just a meditation specialist. He also made it imperative that his students understood about politics, about how the world worked, and so forth. We were to look at everything and not leave anything out. But it was always from the point of view of what he called the "Great Eastern Sun," as opposed to a "setting-sun" perspective.[2]

The Great Eastern Sun perspective is that wakefulness is inherent and always available. It's a positive point of view of humanity and ourselves, without having to fool ourselves into any "positive thinking" kind of silliness. It is opposed to the setting-sun mentality, which could be explained as a nihilistic, mechanical perspective that is aggressive, heedless of brilliance and color, and nonappreciative of the sacredness of life.

Therefore, we were taught to look at things as continuously dawning, continuously fresh. The Great Eastern Sun is different from *rising* sun, because the minute you say "rising sun," you imply "setting sun," involving a cycle. One of Rinpoche's standing jokes was that whatever time of day or night, it was always "Good morning." It could be the middle of the night, but it was still "Good morning!" This refers to the ever-dawning sun, as opposed to a sun that rises and sets.

That's the view that was imparted, and that's how Trungpa Rinpoche lived his life. In fact, one thing that I find extraordinary about this teacher and all truly amazing teachers is that that's how they live. And their message to their students and anyone who encounters them is always the same: One can live totally in that brilliance and ever-dawning wakefulness. That's the truth of the matter. We have a choice.

Yet Trungpa Rinpoche found that even though we were finally able to maintain our discipline of sitting and studying, there was something missing in our approach. So, he began introducing things that he personally loved and that we learned to love. In particular, he was a Japanophile, or Nipponophile. When he was younger in England, he became a master of ikebana (flower arrangement), chanoyu (tea ceremony), and *shodo* (calligraphy). He loved all the Zen arts, and he thought we should love them, too!

When you begin involving yourself in these arts, they seem so foreign (unless you happen to be Japanese, I suppose). But in our case, they were not imparted as some cultural imperative. It wasn't about being a good housewife or househusband who arranges nice flowers, serves nice tea, and does nice calligraphy. There was something wonderful and fresh about learning these things from a whole other society. In that way, alongside our meditation practice and studying, Trungpa Rinpoche added this other element, which could be any of the Japanese Zen arts, depending on one's ability or desire. This included archery—he brought over a master from Japan so we could learn *kyudo*. All of us learned calligraphy as a contemplative practice, which was an imperative. Honestly, the way he taught me calligraphy wasn't fancy or exclusive—anyone can do it.

But then some of us got little special, strange treatments. (I hope you don't mind me interweaving some personal stories in this informal exposition. I'm trying to set the atmosphere, where everything was so ordinary and extraordinary.)

Since Trungpa Rinpoche came from a culture with a strong connection to horses, and because his wife was a dressage rider, he was very fond of dressage. Sometimes he would complain that he had no one to ride with. Though disabled, he still got on his big white horse, and as disabled as he was, he rode it majestically. So, he asked; and I got it in my head: "I'll learn how to do this."

I started taking dressage lessons, which was a preposterous thing to do for a thirty-five-year-old chubby guy. But I thought, this is really about "heaven, earth, and human" (which we will explore below), synchronizing body and mind, and all the things he was teaching. Also, having someone to ride with would make him happy. So, I religiously worked three dressage lessons a week into my stupidly insane, busy schedule. I would get on these horses, onto the lunge line. I often took a little nip of whiskey—I had one of those tiny bottles in my jacket—just to get my courage up! You do fall off a lot... I learned these things in my own way, and I also had very tough lady instructors. *They* were rough! But at some point, I was good enough that I could ride on my own.

One day, I go through one of the sets of exercises with Rinpoche, before we go out and ride freely. He has friends there, and he asks me to go through the movements with my horse. I hear him, over in the distance, pointing at me riding the horse. He has his students around him, and he jokes about my riding. It was the most unexpected joke. But between student and teacher, there's a lot of leeway! In any case, I'll tell you, it was one of the most wakeful moments of my life. And I tried to ride, really, as well as I could!

This was one of the great lessons of my life. For starters, it made me sit up straight, which is very profound. But I also understood the joke—I think. See, the thing about his jokes is that *years* later, you would get another hit on the punch line! Part of his artistic ability was to pun endlessly, in Tibetan and English. His mastery of English was such that he made James Joyce look like a minor punster. Double, triple, quadruple entendre—spontaneously! In the case of the horse-riding joke, it wasn't that it *meant* anything; it woke me up in the moment. One can read into it anything one wants to read, and there are probably many things to read, but he didn't have a script there; it was just a spontaneous manifestation. Whatever it was, I didn't have to ride horses anymore after that! It simply wasn't necessary.

Like that, throughout his life, Trungpa Rinpoche's students were all trained in various disciplines. All in all, that was some of the best training I've ever had.

After he passed away, and one circumstance led to another, and because of something Trungpa Rinpoche had suggested to me, I made a relationship with another teacher. When I met this teacher, I thought, "I'm now gonna be free from all this!" Because this person was *really* Tibetan. Culturally, he wasn't as eclectic as Trungpa Rinpoche.

So, I went to meet this new teacher, asking for particular teachings, some having to do with esoteric topics that I was fascinated with at the time. I spent time with this teacher, and I learned how to practice with him. There was chanting every day. At the end of the chanting, what did we do? We danced! And what did we dance? The worst possible rock 'n' roll! I didn't know rock 'n' roll could be so bad—we're talking disco mixed in and all. You have to understand, this man was one of the most traditional and accomplished teachers ever, but he loved dance. For years, we would dance at the end of practice, and we'd go to nightclubs with him and dance...

One day everything changed. He said, "Maybe we should try a different kind of dance."

Suddenly we're learning one of Padmasambhava's spiritual treasures, which is liberation through dancing. Suddenly the rock 'n' roll moves away. It was sort of the hors d'oeuvres for us to get tired of, though we all loved it. Suddenly all of us, including an old gimp like me, are learning very difficult monastic moves. This is probably something similar to the kind of embodiment that Trungpa Rinpoche was teaching.

Those were just a few examples. The point is, life has these interesting twists and turns, and art isn't necessarily what we think it is. There are infinite possibilities.

A CONSTANT INVOCATION OF WAKEFULNESS

In traditional Tibetan monasteries and nunneries, any young student is trained in various disciplines that go along with living—for instance, using their voice, their hands, their mind.

Voice is used for mantra, chanting, and supplication. There are many songs and mantras in Tibetan and Sanskrit. Some prayers translate nicely into English so that they can be sung melodically; others, not so much. (As a footnote, it is my hope that in the future, a Buddhist Shakespeare will appear, or somebody will do such good translations or new versions of the many prayers that they can be sung beautifully and have the same power to welcome, invoke, magnetize, pacify, or destroy, whatever the energies might be. Now, for the most part, English Buddhist chanting sounds like a bunch of cows and goats. But it won't always be like that. Someone will come along. Some Dharma artist, with a small ego, will transform the English language to have those qualities.)

Regardless, so much of the sacred Buddhist approach to living comes down to inviting wakefulness into one's life continuously. The singing; the creating of altars, shrines, monasteries, the space in our homes; how we walk across that lawn by the temple—all these things are there for us to learn to invite wakefulness.

In this way, there is a constant invocation and offering. In fact, much of Buddhist art is simply offering. Offering to what? Offering to the awakened mind, which we call buddhas, deities, bodhisattvas—they have names—so that they can appear. How do they appear? Well, we make the offerings, and they appear. Are they separate from the offerings? Well, that's up to us to figure out. Buddhism is not a theistic religion. Therefore, when we talk about deities, we're not talking about something separate from our own intrinsic buddha-nature—that is, the latent possibility for complete enlightenment that is present in all beings. However, just because it is said that we have buddha-nature—and it's very clear in the Mahayana and Vajrayana that every being does—it doesn't mean that this buddha-nature has blossomed. The blossoming comes with practice. This refers to the practice of meditation but also of offerings and praises.

These offerings and praises are ways to invite all positive qualities. And—at least in the tantric tradition—it's all positive qualities, both peaceful and wrathful. It's not all hugs and rainbows. In fact, it's not a Hello Kitty kind of world at all. It's clear, vivid, brilliant.

LIBERATION THROUGH THE SENSES

Many of the Buddhist chants have been recited over and over for hundreds, sometimes thousands, of years. Some have only been done for ten years. Some were written the other day! But they were written by masters. Others were composed hundreds of years ago and have been rediscovered, which is connected to the tradition of *termas*, or "spiritual treasures." One of the most important termas that were composed by Padmasambhava and recorded by his main disciple Yeshe Tsogyal is what we call the Tibetan Book of the Dead, or *Bardo Thödrol Chenmo*, which more literally means "the Great Liberation Through Hearing in the Intermediate State." But there are great liberations through all the other senses, besides hearing. In fact, Padmasambhava imparted wakefulness through meaning, images, and various other means.

Here is an example.

Once, His Holiness Dudjom Rinpoche, who was the supreme head of the Nyingma tradition, gave an empowerment. It was "the great liberation through seeing." I was a very skeptical young man, but I went anyway.

We were all sitting, there was chanting, and so forth. Dudjom Rinpoche was quite ill at the time. We were in Colorado, high up in the mountains, and he had to breathe using an oxygen tank. He said that he could only speak for a few minutes. Well, he spoke for what turned out to be a couple hundred minutes, giving a complete overview of the Buddhist path—what's called the nine yanas. He offered a complete summary, from the four noble truths to the most profound Mahamudra and Mahasandhi, or Dzogchen, teachings. It was extraordinary even though he was speaking in Tibetan, because he had a translator. Then, after the talk, he said, "Please, everyone, come up."

Then he would touch your head and impart a blessing. He had you look into a little box, and inside the little box was a tiny statue. This was an ancient statue of Padmasambhava, with special meaning. It was a specific type of terma called "Liberation upon Sight." If you look at this statue, you see the nature of mind. "Sure!" I thought. Well, I'll tell you something: I can see it right now. It's that powerful. It's not art in the usual sense of what we think of as art. That was more than half a century ago, and yet as I am writing this, I can see it totally clearly, without question. It made such an impression. And the impression is wakefulness and compassion—and then a whole other thing, but to simplify, wakefulness and compassion.

THERE IS A CHOICE

There are people of various kinds reading this book. We started this chapter, which means that somehow, we're interested in Buddhism and we're interested in art. We're all the same. If we are interested in art, we can be Dharma artists, which is being Buddhists. That's a choice we can make. Or at least we can be a dharmic person, even if somehow in our being we don't want to be Buddhist—I am not trying to proselytize. A dharmic person is someone who lives the truth. But the truth is not a truth sent from on high along with a set of stiff rules. It's an enlightened way of living. In fact, it's said that enlightenment is the way we live our life. Various people have all these ideas that enlightenment is gonna fall on their head someday. Some believe that it's impossible, elusive, Eastern, or whatever. The wonder of Dharma is that enlightenment is possible for any sentient being. That includes enlightenment through art, because when we're talking about "art," we're talking about how we sit, how we stand, how we eat, how we shop, how we look, how we see, how we live our life. We can begin from any situation that we find ourselves in. In fact, to become a Dharma artist, we always begin with where we are.

Now, what is keeping us from being an artist—that is, a practitioner? Fear or hope, or a combination of the two. Sometimes we can be trapped by fear, not willing to go beyond what we think we are. Sometimes we're trapped by hope, thinking that we're already there, that it's a done deal; we fool ourselves.

So much of entering the path of Dharma, which is the same as entering into Dharma art, is learning to overcome our hesitation and fear, and to be straightforward and simple. Any work of art that we do involves this simplicity. If it's with a brush, it begins with one dot. If it's a song, it begins with one note. Dance begins with one movement. The confidence comes with the repetition of those things. How do we develop confidence in meditation practice? By practicing meditation. How do we develop confidence in anything, be it cooking or writing? By doing it over and over, but also by paying attention, being mindful as we do it. Yet it's not *only* about mindfulness or attention. You could mindfully watch yourself being a complete idiot! (Which is fine, I suppose. It's a wonderful thing to watch—I've been watching it for decades and perhaps centuries!) But in addition to sheer mindfulness, there's vipashyana, which is being with the "isness" of what it is we're doing. It is a panoramic awareness that is 360 degrees, plus up and down. The true Dharma artist doesn't leave anything out.

THE ARTIST'S EGO

I was giving a talk on this subject in Australia when one of the attendees kindly shared her experience. She said, "I'm a practicing Buddhist and a practicing writer. For me, they both intermingle, and I don't think I learned the discipline of writing until I learned the discipline of sitting on the cushion. But it's a real struggle, because it is like I need some sort of ego to believe in what I'm writing, but I'm also letting go of that, so that I'm not caught up in the whole ego of it. That's where my practice really helps. It feels that there is a continuous process of letting go, both in one's Dharma practice and in one's art—whether it is the art of living, the art of writing, the art of painting..."

Everyone has their own relationship to these things. When I sit down to write, I freeze. I've suffered from terminal writer's block my whole life, which is probably why I chose to be an editor and publisher as a profession. I can help people unfreeze. I'm good at it. But writing something myself is worse than pulling teeth. I learned to live with my handicap, and I don't feel bad that I'm not a writer. I can rely on some friends. And if forced to, I will write, and then I'll find a good editor to fix it.

There is usually so much ego that comes with these situations. Regardless of whether you're writing or not writing, blocked or unblocked, there's always this internal editor, which is different from an actual editor. A part of you is always judging your own work, for better or worse. The only way I can write anything is when there's a deadline—then I can deliver two days late, because I usually start writing on the day that it's due, just like in college! But it doesn't make any difference: At some point, the hesitation is gone. At some point, you actually get into it, and there's really no ego there.

Sometimes you just write or do whatever it is you're supposed to do. Meditation is not about a perfect state; it's about noticing what happens. Real meditation experience takes into account and notices all the pain. It notices the nuances. Cultivating awareness has nothing to do with looking for a flatland. It's seeing all the textures, which include resistance and judging. At some point, whatever it is we do can fall away. But wonderfully enough, through practice it can also come back just as easily as it fell away. The point is, once we find something that we can do, we just do it. There's no contradiction.

THE RELATIONSHIP BETWEEN ART AND MEDITATION

There are great masters in the Buddhist tradition of art. But wonderfully, everybody is a student. No matter how great the master, the master has a master. It keeps things honest and fresh, and the freshness is always rekindled.

There's not just a homemade quality to meditation practice. There's a connection with the mind of a teacher that is direct, to the mind and heart of a student. That continuity is the continuity of the awakened state. This also applies to Dharma art: There is not just a homemade quality to the artistic creation.

It is also said that the grandfather's accomplishment is always improved upon by the grandchildren, so there's a sense that the continuity of the art gets better. Of course, there's always this idea that there was this golden age when all these wonderful things were accomplished. Yet from our point of view, the golden age is always dawning. It's not something that one is nostalgically trying to go back to. There's always newness to it. At the same time, we are given the tools that come from this lineage, and these tools were indeed passed from teacher to student, across the centuries.

Good art also needs good craftsmanship, whether we are discussing the art of living or the art of creating objects, music, dance, or whatever it may be. There are always interesting interplays. Sometimes, if you don't have the craftsperson's ability per se, you can collaborate. So much of what we think of as Buddhist art is collaborative art—it isn't just one person doing it. That said, there's no problem if it's one person, and there's no problem if it's signed either. It is not necessarily egomaniacal! In the Chinese and Japanese traditions, for example, you'll find that every great piece of art has the artist's stamp on it. That's not because of ego but rather for identification purposes. On top of that, the seal itself is beautifully artistic. It just fits in.

Here, interestingly, good art—whether artful living or actual artwork—comes from the Buddhist sense of mindlessness. We are aware, of course, but in a sense, there isn't anybody minding the store. Good art just comes from the wonderful emptiness of a blank mind, a blank canvas, a white piece of paper, the open space, the sky, or whatever you want to call it. It's always there. If we open ourselves to that, to the *isness*, the simplicity of what there is, something happens. There's awareness. There's meditation, which is just *being with the isness*, being totally at one with the actuality of things. Then the postmeditation is the continuity of being with that isness. We don't make it about *me*, and yet we're always being here, fully present and open.

Therefore, from that perspective, there's a fuzzy line between art and meditation. The more we practice, the better the art. The open space reveals itself even more openly. As we begin to truly relax, the open space keeps opening up, constantly. Yet relaxation is a funny notion. It's hard to talk about it because for most of us, the idea of relaxing goes more or less like this: a beach towel, lying in the dirt, the sun shining on us, the smell of that sunscreen, and, you know, the sizzle of the burning skin, what have you! That's basically our cultural idea of relaxation. But the sense of meditative relaxation is very different. "Relaxed" here has to do with perceptions being totally open. In fact, when one is relaxed, one isn't *trying* to be at ease. There is just ease, and in that ease all phenomena simply appear. It is also said that at some point, the world appears as infinite buddha fields. I guess we have to find out later what that means! But even by just opening our eyes—if we are in a state of relaxation from the Buddhist point of view—infinite colors may reveal themselves.

Through our uptightness, the colors we perceive are limited. Their scale is muted. Even what we think of as bright is not so bright. As we make our way into the vastness of space through real relaxation, colors that we've never seen reveal themselves. It's not like they aren't here. They're always here. It's just that we are busy. Likewise, sounds reveal themselves. Smells reveal themselves. Tastes reveal themselves. Part of this Dharma art is that we're dealing with the seen and unseen worlds. We are dealing with the subtleties, the brilliance, the wakeful qualities of life.

The key to this relaxation is nonaggression, which begins most importantly with making friends with ourselves. If we are constantly criticizing ourselves, putting ourselves down, caught in what we believe our parents think of us or this person thinks of us or this drama or that drama . . . I don't have to make a list, do I? Everyone knows what I'm talking about. Oh, the things we busy our minds with! If we don't give it as much fuel, it will subside and open.

In Buddhist meditation, we have nothing against thoughts. We understand that the nature of being human is partly that we are thinking beings. There's no problem with that. We're simply mindful of our mind. Being mindful of our mind, not feeding it unduly, and simply being where we are will allow the discursive chatter to naturally subside. We don't try to kill the chatter. That's aggression. We don't try to kill any part of ourselves, in fact. We can afford to make friends with ourselves enough to just allow the process to happen. And what allows that process is the continuity of practice.

I can't overstate how wonderful it is to create a continuity of practice. If you make friends enough with yourself to allow yourself to actually practice, then something actually happens, and it imbues your life and your art.

By practicing meditation, our way of relating to the world begins to change. The biggest change is that we become more aware of the environment, more aware of others, and ultimately more aware of space and its infiniteness. In terms of artistic perception, it's that interchange of playing with space that creates art. It's what communicates beauty and wakefulness.

We even begin to see in a different way. If you look at a Japanese calligraphy by a master calligrapher, what do you see? The space or the black ink? Both—sometimes. Sometimes we miss one or the other. But there's subtlety because it is playing with space. It's not just about what's there. The whole issue of nonaggression is that space hasn't been removed. You are *in* the space.

Being with that space also allows your buddha-nature to begin to blossom. All beings have buddha-nature. Even lizards and mice. But are you happy just being a lizard or a mouse with buddha-nature? Not quite, as that nature is unblossomed. Through the practice of meditation and postmeditation, which includes artfulness, buddha-nature begins to blossom, and then that blossoming unfolds in your life. And that life, if you live it from that point of view, *is* enlightenment. It is not that you suddenly wake up—*Boom!*—and then it's a done deal. Rather, enlightenment is how you live your life.

Art shouldn't be viewed as any kind of release. It is not meant to be an orgasmic experience. It is just an ordinary part of our existence, something that can have continuity. It doesn't have to build up to anything and then be released.

From the perspective of Dharma art, anything that we create comes from wakefulness. It doesn't come from trying to develop some artistic materialism: "I'm going to create this or that thing." It doesn't come from eagerness either. It comes from wakefulness.

In that regard, we must acknowledge that there are choices we make. One thing I've heard from so many Buddhist masters is they're always surprised by how violent so much of art is, whether it be paintings or music or films. We may be tempted to write all that off as "just cultural." But it's not. If we truly look at it, art that comes from aggression is *not* harmless. It simply isn't.

Art is powerful. It changes people's lives, for better or worse. From the Dharma-art point of view, anything that we create naturally comes from, and presents some, sense of basic sanity. That's the power of nonaggression.

3
Expressing Wakefulness

In the previous chapter, we found that we can all become Dharma artists. Now let's take a closer look at the *how* of it all.

Trungpa Rinpoche taught that Dharma art is really nonaggression. It was like a constant mantra: nonaggression, nonaggression, nonaggression. You're not trying through art or your life to attack something, to one-up something, or to manipulate the situation. You're also not trying to make a statement about yourself. Of course, as in anything in life, there *is* a statement. But here the statement is wakefulness—that's what makes Dharma art. And wakefulness is never about being aggressive, competitive, cunning, or manipulative.

Earlier I mentioned theater. Well, Trungpa Rinpoche created his mandala, his group of students, and it was like one big show. Everyone had their place in the show. Everyone was, and still is, a different character with parts to play. This is the way it is with any teacher. If you have a relationship with a teacher, particularly a Buddhist teacher, you enter into their mandala. You enter into a particular world. There's a particular play that's going on, and your relationship with that teacher is part of it. For some people, it can be very aggressive. They want to suck on that teat so hard, because they want something so badly. Yet part of the teacher's discipline is to learn to deal with idiots. As the saying goes, it takes two to tango. Enlightenment doesn't just go in one direction. In terms of the mandala of student and teacher, enlightenment comes from the play. If it's an aggressive play or a one-up play, you're in the wrong play!

The play of enlightenment always has an interesting back-and-forth, and it is uplifting—everything blossoms together.

Let's not confuse everything, however. In Buddhism, we're happy with hierarchy—at least the kind of hierarchy that doesn't push anything down and that allows everything to rise. It's very different from the usual tactic of climbing the ladder at the expense of others. The rising we're discussing has nothing to do with the nasty, political approach, under any of its various guises and names. Unfortunately, as we know, people will play politics with spiritual things as well. The only worthwhile play is the play that is truly and sanely hierarchical in that everything rises, and rises together.

That's key to nonaggression. Aggression always has to do with one-upping. Sometimes it can be literally killing. But not paying attention to somebody—not even allowing them to enter our space of vision or our space of hearing—is another kind of aggression. We block them out. I'm not talking about a situation where someone is bothering you on the street in an aggressive way. Sometimes it is best to just avoid them and keep walking. But we have to be honest and acknowledge how dreadfully easy it is to turn a blind eye and that it's also a form of aggression. Compassion involves seeing things clearly.

HEAVEN, EARTH, AND HUMAN

Seeing things clearly and not turning a blind eye both start with simple things. For example, we can do some sitting meditation and then go for a walk, slowing down and noticing what's around us—the fauna, the flora, the natural, and the artificial. We can also do specific, creative activities. For example, we can enjoy object arrangement, which is a lovely way to begin to involve ourselves with Dharma art. It was originally presented by one of Trungpa Rinpoche's students, Molly Nudell.

Prior to working on the arrangement per se, there is a simple and fun exercise through which we become "explorers of the phenomenal world." You can just go around your block or to a nearby park to explore and see what's there. This is an exercise that Trungpa Rinpoche used to do sometimes just like this, and sometimes when he was doing flower arrangements or larger arrangements. It can be preceded by a circumambulation—*khorwa* in Tibetan—which is walking around the mandala or doing a respectful clockwise walk around a Dharma center, stupa, or sacred place. This is optional and depends on where you find yourself. Then you start exploring the surrounding area. Pick three objects that aren't going to bother anyone if you take them. (Don't cut down big flowers, for instance.) It can be anything: a fallen branch that somehow caught your eye, an interesting little stone, a twig, a leaf, a piece of wrapping paper. You simply pick up three things and bring them back to wherever you intend to work on your arrangement. You can do this with friends: Each person will bring in three items of their choosing. As you explore, keep chatter to a minimum and pay as much attention as you can.

One important aspect of Dharma art is the relationship between heaven, earth, and human. All forms that are Dharma art have this threefold situation: Heaven is the overriding inspiration, earth is the embodiment, human is what brings them together. Object arrangements, flower arrangements, calligraphy, painting, and pretty much any truly artistic creation have this threefold situation.

First, lay your objects—whatever you found interesting as an explorer—on a table and just look at the array. There may be an item that would have been considered junk, but that's just one way of looking at it. There might be all kinds of amazing findings. Whatever the objects are, their arranging changes things a little bit, but we have to see it to believe it. This is meant to be an experiential exercise, so feel free to give it a try.

The general procedure of making an arrangement is simple. Start on a blank piece of paper. It carries every potential. Then begin with the heaven principle: Heaven is the first item we lay down on the paper. Then we lay down the earth. Then we make their connection. If you are with friends, you can share your findings and choose any three objects you like.

The heaven principle can be somewhat taller, reaching out or perhaps coming down. It can connote fullness, openness, some higher quality. The earth can have an organic feeling or texture, sometimes literally. It can connote long-lastingness and stability. In between heaven and earth, connecting them both, is something that represents us human beings, whether still or active.

Often beginners' arrangements just need little corrections, so it is good if you can learn from a teacher in person. But you can give it a try and have fun. The idea is that anything that involves heaven, earth, and human has a certain harmony. There's a drawing together. However, the drawing together can have a subtleness to it. It doesn't have to be obvious. And everything has its own beauty. The things you can find just around the corner when you open your senses—it's uncanny!

Sometimes the arrangement needs a little more tension. These are things that you will *feel* rather than apprehend with your intellect. It's very simple, and everyone can do it. If you sense that you need to add tension but feel that through your manipulation you end up *removing* tension (or vice versa), take a step back and look at the space. Sometimes it's all pushed too close together, and there is no sense of heaven going out.

Sometimes the magic happens and you discover pure simplicity. When there is harmony, you find that something is holding it together. That "something" is *space*. It all holds together even though it's just three seemingly random items. Sometimes we don't even know what the person had intended to be heaven, and yet there's a sense that the whole thing has a heaven. The viewer is drawn up.

With experience, we discover that even plastic and broken glass can be amazingly beautiful. There can be a simplicity and beauty that is based on ugliness, which is quite extraordinary. But again, that's when there is harmony. Sometimes everything holds together because even though there is a roughness—with things broken and torn—it's all offering up.

We don't need an explanation when it all holds together. The important thing is that there's a connection. There's no aggression, and things are not being pushed down, so to speak.

Sometimes "heaven, earth, and human" can be very literal. Sometimes it's very poetic. Some have more darkness than light in terms of feeling but still provide a sense of uplift and connection through the shapes and shadows. Each arrangement is different.

We're dealing with simple things here. It's just what is. When we sit, when we take what is and move it onto a piece of paper, we don't have to make any big deal. We just let it speak to us.

As simple as they are, these principles have to do with everything in life. It's not just about arranging three objects on a blank piece of paper. We could take these principles and apply them to every aspect of our life. In any situation—at work, with our family, or anywhere else—we can acknowledge the space. We have a higher inspiration, but we also have practicalities. With the right amount of tension and relaxation, we can find natural harmony. We just allow our mind to be broad enough to see what's going on.

Exercises like this also teach us that anything's possible. But we have to deal with what's there rather than fantasies. We have to work with what's accessible to us. Enlightenment comes in *this* body. And it comes at *this* time. What we do is based on what there is. That's wondrous, because it's always changing.

A very important precept of Dharma art goes like this: "First thought, best thought." But "first thought" doesn't necessarily mean our first discursive little fart. It's the first thought that comes from space. If we remain with that freshness, we can find harmony in everything.

DHARMA ART AND THE VIEW OF ENLIGHTENED SOCIETY

Dharma art, as we said, is about nonaggression. It is also about creativity and emptiness.[1]

I have taught the topic of "art in everyday life" in practical workshops where we made messes, some noise; wrote a few poems, a few songs; and created a complete society, or at least the form of a complete society, in our minds and on paper and in different ways, with the view that it wasn't going to be an ordinary society but an enlightened society. This is meant to be experiential training. In book format, there's a risk that it becomes overly abstract. Yet I will try my best to share a few ideas that you are welcome to explore on your own.

One such notion is that of the mandala, which is a Sanskrit term that means "center and fringe." This center-and-fringe is a representation of the enlightened state of mind. It's not just the representation of the enlightened state of mind of one person; it involves seeing enlightenment as all-pervasive rather than "something I can get." Looked at this way, a mandala is the representation of an enlightened society.

In the center is enlightenment. Enlightenment is usually represented as a buddha or buddhā (masculine or feminine). Sometimes both are represented together, but even if they're not, in each situation, the opposite is implied. The short *a* or the long *ā*.

Here, we don't necessarily need to make mandalas in the sense of finely detailed paintings, sand art, architectural manifestations, or even visualizations. In our specific context, we are invited to work with art in everyday life. The idea of art in everyday life is making a connection between the awakened state of mind that we might experience with the awakened state of mind of others that might experience what we manifest.

This has very much to do with nonduality. Every time we say "I," "you" is implied. Ordinarily every thought we have separates us from everything that isn't that thought. But we can learn to see through that veil. That is why the basis of art in everyday life is the practice of meditation. Thus, when we talk about Dharma art, we imply an art that goes beyond duality. It is not about two, it's about not-two. It's not about one either, because, as we said, as soon as we have one, we imply a second. That's why we call it "not-two," or put another way, nonduality.

The Dharma artist is not particularly someone special. It can be any practitioner. It doesn't require a special state of mind. It does require what in Zen is called "beginner's mind." There's a willingness to begin. So much so that at the beginning, we are not all that concerned about what we're going to create. In fact, there may be no idea of creating anything at all.

ALL THE OTHER DOTS

All art begins with one dot. It can be a flute note, the pen touching the paper, or the ink touching the space. It can be turning on the stove when we begin cooking. Whatever it is, it begins with one note, one dot. That one note, that one dot, is where everything progresses from. The same principle applies to the creation of a mandala, and for that matter, to the creation of an enlightened society. It has to start somewhere.

What does enlightenment look like? That's an interesting question. It does have a look. What does enlightenment smell like? Another interesting question. It does have a smell. Likewise, it has a sound, a feel, and a taste.

That's what the Dharma artist is relating with. There are no barriers to the senses. The senses, from the enlightened point of view, are the play of the buddhas. They're buddhas themselves. Enlightened sound is the sound of buddhahood, and so forth.

Becoming a Dharma artist is not about creating things to be put in a gallery or to be precious. There's nothing wrong with those types of ordinary artistic endeavors, but here we are more interested in the way we create our life. Whether it's creating the space we cook in, sit in, sleep in, eat in, or whatever, if we have awareness, we can make those things into a place where a buddha dwells. Like that, creating a mandala is creating the palace in which the buddha or buddhā lives. And it always begins in the same way: with not holding back.

To experience this, you could take a single sheet of blank paper and make a first dot. It should be sudden, without too much thinking. But as you do, pay attention. This time, if you are with other people, everyone should have their own card or sheet of paper and make a dot. Then you can put them all toward the center of the room, very simply. If you are alone, you can imagine other dots being made by other people, perhaps other Dharma artists in your life, and placed near your dot. Whatever your situation, relax and observe.

Not only is wakefulness or enlightenment the center of that first dot, but it is in relationship to all the other first dots. Each dot is center, and each dot is fringe. There's no separation between my dot and your dot. It's an enlightened relationship. So ask yourself, "Which dot is the center of this mandala?"

This may resemble kindergarten, but if we're open, there is something very deep to be learned from that.

When we make art—whether it's the creation of a place to dwell, a place to cook, or a piece of music—it's always in relationship to others. But this relationship between self and other is a nondual relationship. That is inherent to the mandala, the center-and-fringe. The center of all mandalas is buddha, buddhā; the periphery of all mandalas is buddha, buddhā. Everything is implied in any part of any mandala.

There is a view that Dharma art can save the world. This sounds ambitious. But if we actually pay attention and create an enlightened space—even if it's just on a little piece of paper—it's in relationship to all the other enlightened spaces. We shouldn't underestimate the power of how we live and manifest, precisely because of this relationship between ourselves and others.

In Buddhism, we have the Buddha, which is represented in the center of the mandala; we have the Dharma, his teachings, that are given and received in the mandala; and we have the Sangha, those of us who pay attention to the Buddha and the Dharma and create or attempt to create enlightened phenomena. That is, in this life, what is most worthwhile. Therefore, when we talk about making art, we're not talking about compartmentalizing something outside of our life. When we make Dharma art, whatever it might be—taking a photograph, creating a meal for a friend—it can be viewed as an offering to the Triple Gem, that is, the Buddha, the Dharma, and the Sangha. Everything that we do with this mindset is an offering. Everything that we do with that mindfulness and that awareness is in fact Dharma art. The awareness and luminosity that it contains make it extraordinarily gorgeous.

Therefore it always starts with nonaggression; it is the basis. Aggression has to do with inflicting something on somebody, even if that somebody is ourselves. Aggression is the fuel of duality, and our duality habit is such that it cuts our perception. We don't see clearly, we don't hear clearly, we don't smell clearly, we don't taste clearly, and so on. There's a gap between the *ayatanas*, to use the Sanskrit terminology; a gap between the object of seeing (what we see), the organ that sees (our eye), and the process of seeing. It's said that when those are unified, that's buddha vision. Same with hearing, smelling, tasting... When the object of perception, the organ of perception, and the process of perception are unified, that's enlightenment, from a certain point of view. I am mixing my metaphors here between Hinayana, Mahayana, and Dzogchen, but I suppose that a little creativity is allowed when discussing with fellow Dharma artists!

WHAT ARE WE AFRAID OF?

Many of us are afraid. We fear nonduality, and we fear art. Generally speaking, our fear of nonduality, our fear of enlightenment, involves these questions: "Where am I going to go then? What's in it for me?" It's an interesting fear. It's the same as our fear of death. However, we *are* going to die, right? We all know it, yet none of us believe it. It's mysterious. That same fear of death is linked to our fear of art, our fear of Dharma art. Because where are we going to go? Are we going to be carried away? Is someone going to look at our piece and say, "Oh, they're really icky, and they made that icky thing"? Or are we going to lose ourselves in some game of seduction? Falling in love, perhaps, with our own beautiful dot? If that seems like crazy talk, it may very well be because it is!

In any event, there is, in the dharmic approach to things and in Dharma art, a prejudice toward that which is good; a prejudice toward that which is light, brilliant, luminous. It's not to say that we don't use the color black. It's also not to say that we can't have horrific images. For example, in tantric Himalayan Buddhism, as well as in Japanese Mahayana, there are all kinds of buddhas and bodhisattvas that are extremely wrathful. But the wrathfulness is still a quality of wakefulness. It's not about trying to bring ourselves or anybody else down but rather waking up. So, generally speaking, we're talking about brightening the world. Even the ghoulish Mahakala and Mahakali and other terrifying figures can be painted just as well in gold as they can in black. In fact, they are often represented in gold, because it has this luminous quality of wakefulness.

Dharma art arises from the mind that is attentive and playful. We can then create an enlightened world starting with our simple dot. Of course, whatever is in the center of the mandala, we can decide to represent it in a visual way or through any other medium, such as a song or a dance. The possibilities of Dharma art are endless.

If you are interested in exploring these topics further, I recommend Chögyam Trungpa's *True Perception: The Path of Dharma Art*, an enlightening collection of essays and talks on how to live one's life artfully, whether we are an artist or just someone who would like to improve our inner and outer environment. This is better than a purely "green" perspective. Green is wonderful, but green *and* this is even better!

TRANSFORMATION AND OPPORTUNITIES

In traditional depictions of mandalas, we'll often notice that the four directions each have their own specific buddhas or symbols. The four directions along with the center together represent what's called the "five buddha families." Each family is associated with a particular color, a particular element, and so on. Most importantly, each is associated with a particular neurosis (ignorance, anger, desire, pride, or jealousy) as well as a particular type of wisdom. In other words, the five families provide a system to understand the world in both its confused and enlightened aspects. In their enlightened aspects, all our neuroses and afflictive emotions are transformed into buddha qualities. In this way, wakefulness produces all these other positive qualities.

For a Dharma artist, what this means is that in our life and through our experience, being in any of these emotional states represents an opportunity to wake up *within that very state*, within that very part of the mandala. This view is particularly connected to the Vajrayana, which we will discuss in later chapters, but it is nonetheless something that Dharma artists should be aware of. That is, in fact, a key to enlightened living: It's not just the center that has enlightenment. All aspects of the mandala are enlightenment. Center and fringe, it doesn't make any difference, because it's one. The mandala is a unified situation.

Whatever your specific situation is, I invite you to learn to approach it in a nonaggressive way. Regardless of the medium, something happens when we get into the actual process of creating something that goes beyond our conception of what it will be. If we are stuck in a conception, we are stuck—it's as simple as that. But part of Dharma art is to allow the flow to naturally begin. There's the first thought, the first dot, the first note, and everything arises from that.

There are countless ways we can create things, and Trungpa Rinpoche exposed many other principles that apply to Dharma art. Some of these principles will be explored later in this book, though not necessarily in an artistic context. It will then be up to you, dear readers, to see how they apply to your living an artful life.

PART TWO
MIND TRAINING AND KINDNESS

In part one we saw that there is but one place where the spiritual journey can begin, and that place is exactly wherever we find ourselves. We started seeing the extent to which addictions and habits bind us, and that no good can come from turning a blind eye to pain and confusion. In that regard, meditation is the way to "get real." If we are to stop blindly alternating between hope and fear, if we are to cut through the veils of delusion, compulsion, and discursiveness, we need a sitting meditation practice as the foundation. From that place of calm and clarity, each and every one of us can start living an artful life. However, mindfulness is not the only element required on the path to true freedom. We'll also need to train our mind so as to develop courage, loving-kindness, and compassion. Such are the crucial topics explored in the following chapters.

4
Keys to Mind Training

Throughout part two, we will discuss training our minds and developing loving-kindness. These teachings belong to the Mahayana, or the Great Vehicle. What makes this vehicle so great is that there is no idea of purely individual salvation, no notion of liberation or nirvana just for ourselves. Instead, the Mahayana aims for a larger goal: complete enlightenment for all sentient beings. This includes not only humans but beings of all kinds. No one is excluded.

To help us cultivate such great compassion and bravery, the ancient masters have developed a corpus of teachings and methods referred to as *lojong*, or "mind training." Since these teachings and methods are focused on *bodhicitta*, or the "awakened heart," they are very much central to any Mahayanist's practice and way of life.

I have to confess, however, that I feel conflicted about discussing lojong at length. On the one hand, it was an extremely important part of Trungpa Rinpoche's legacy, and these teachings can be life-changing. On the other hand, there are now plenty of wonderful books on this topic available. Therefore, let's opt for a "middle way" approach: I will focus on clarifying some notions that are easily overlooked, then offer a succinct commentary on a selection of lojong aphorisms and techniques that can apply to our daily lives, wherever we happen to be on the path.

Before we dive in, I feel it is worthwhile to provide a bit of context. As you will see, this is not only history for history's sake. There is something truly precious and meaningful about how these teachings came down to us.

HOW THE LOJONG TEACHINGS CAME TO US

The teachings that we will discuss in this section were developed by Atisha Dipamkara Shrijnana, a Bengali Buddhist born into a royal family at the end of the tenth century. Like us, and like the Buddha, he had some dissatisfaction with his life, and he looked for something better. He studied with teachers in Bengal, and then he heard of a wonderful teacher in Sumatra, Indonesia. Atisha thus traveled across the sea, a long and perilous journey at the time, to the island of Sumatra, where he studied the disciplines of bodhicitta and learned the practice of lojong from his teacher, Dharmakirti (Tib. Serlingpa).[1]

Atisha then came back to India and Bengal, and taught there, especially at the Vikramshila University, which was one of the great universities of India. From there, he was invited to Tibet to specifically share these wonderful Mahayana teachings.

The tradition that Atisha brought to Tibet, and of which lojong was an important part, was carried on and it became the Kadam school. That particular school doesn't really exist on its own nowadays, but its influence is omnipresent. More specifically, the Kadam tradition was a precursor that went in two different directions. In one direction, it was transmitted to Gampopa, one of the great Kagyu teachers and the main disciple of Milarepa. Gampopa studied with Kadampa masters as well, and the meditative aspect of the Kadam tradition went through that line. The second aspect of the Kadam tradition was more dialectical and philosophical, and it was preserved by the Gelug school. In this part of the book, we will follow the Kagyu approach, but know that these teachings have spread; they are used extensively in all the schools of Tibetan Buddhism, including the Nyingma and Sakya.

There is a vast literature on lojong. The root text, *The Seven Points of Mind Training*, we are referring to here is just a couple of pages long. It's a pithy text compiled by Chekhawa Yeshe Dorje (twelfth century), one of the disciples in Atisha's lineage. To study these seven points, we refer to the commentaries. Jamgon Kongtrul the Great wrote one of the main commentaries, available in English under the title *The Great Path of Awakening*. Chögyam Trungpa Rinpoche's modern commentary, *Training the Mind and Cultivating Loving-Kindness*, is one of the great treasures that Trungpa Rinpoche left, as far as I'm concerned. He himself considered this little collection, his commentary, to be one of the most important elements of his legacy. Also, in modern times, we have *Enlightened Courage*, a commentary by the great Nyingma teacher His Holiness Dilgo Khyentse Rinpoche. They are all wonderful, and many others have been published since then.

I would like to point out that in a Western context, Pema Chödrön, an American nun who was a student of Trungpa Rinpoche, has greatly contributed to the transmission of these teachings. She was one of the first of his students to take this practice seriously. I truly appreciate her for this. When I and other students of Trungpa Rinpoche first heard these teachings, it was like listening to gobbledygook! We didn't have a clue what he was talking about. Somehow Pema Chödrön listened a little more carefully than the rest of us. It's to her credit that she understood when the rest of us were puzzled. Some of her books talk about lojong: *Start Where You Are* and *The Places That Scare You* come to mind. She's done a wonderful job of presenting it experientially, in a modern way, without watering it down.

Interestingly, when Pema Chödrön started paying attention, I also had to pay attention. I remember when she sent in her manuscript to us at Shambhala Publications. I thought, "Mmm, what's this nun up to?" But I read it, and it was quite good, and it ended up reaching a lot of people. What's powerful about lojong is that it can have a real effect on your life. It is extremely helpful for your own spiritual development, which makes it helpful for those around you as well.

That being said, as popular as these teachings have become, it should be noted that it is highly unusual to present them all at once to a wide audience. Historically, they have always been presented in a graduated way, over time, after one has developed a strong meditation practice; taken refuge in the Buddha, Dharma, and Sangha; and taken the bodhisattva vow, thus dedicating one's life to the benefit of others. They were held as secret and sacred teachings, but somehow various teachers started testing them on people. For example, lojong was taught to lepers. For reasons no one exactly understands, many of them lost their leprosy—instead of their limbs. They became wonderfully helpful people. Thus, what we are about to study was referred to in the early days as "Dharma for lepers." The idea is that these teachings are for people who are afflicted with the particular "leprosy" of ego-centeredness. I suppose that "Dharma for lepers" was a twelfth-century joke! In any case, because of experiences like that, and because of the effect it had, the secret lineage that held these slogans and teachings began to leak out. These days especially, it seems that we are going through extraordinary times, and great Buddhist masters have granted permission that these teachings can be given more freely, because they seem to truly benefit people. But you should know that at one time in history, these lojong teachings were secret and given only after someone had spent many years practicing meditation.

On that note, here is an important historical detail—a lesser-known though truly pivotal moment. When the Chinese Communists were coming into Tibet, there was a particular teacher there by the name of Khenpo Gangshar, who was an extraordinary monk and a holder of Nyingma and Kagyu lineages. By some circumstances, he became diseased and is said to have died; but he revived. And when he came back, he came back with a vengeance, so to speak. He began teaching in a very unusual way.

A *khenpo* was understood as an erudite who generally teaches to monks. However, Khenpo Gangshar began warning people that times were changing most drastically and that the Tibet that they knew—the Tibet that had been preserved for many centuries—would no longer exist. He stressed that it was necessary to put the teachings into practice immediately because these were desperate times.

Khenpo Gangshar did unusual things. This monk married almost immediately, and with his wife he traveled around Tibet and gave teachings that only monastics had received to laymen and monks alike—to anybody who was genuinely willing to practice Dharma. He emphasized three things: the Hinayana teachings of shamatha-vipashyana, or foundational Buddhist meditation practice; the Mahayana teachings of lojong and *tonglen*, including the slogan practice; and Mahamudra and Dzogchen, the higher meditative paths and practices of the Vajrayana. Buddhism is extraordinarily vast, and it offers countless skillful means that help lead a practitioner to enlightenment. Khenpo Gangshar's vision was to make irrelevant the usual separation between those who are heavy-duty practitioners—monks, nuns, extremely educated people, and so forth—and ordinary people. There was no difference, and the teachings were to be made available to everybody because of the dark times.

You will surely agree that we too live in desperate times. Are they any more desperate than they have been in the past? From one point of view, no. People always suffer. But the ecological disasters that we are now facing, mass weaponry, and so on—those things have never existed before. Surely this, for us Westerners and in fact the world at large, is also a pivotal moment. We can be grateful to Khenpo Gangshar, this man who lived in Tibet before the Communist invasion and who was killed by the Communist Chinese troops. It was his vision that brought to the West a lot of what we know about Buddhism. He was one of the main teachers of Trungpa Rinpoche and one of his main inspirations for how he taught in the West, inasmuch as Trungpa Rinpoche also emphasized the sitting practice of meditation, the Mahayana practice of lojong and tonglen, and the tantric traditions of Mahamudra and Dzogchen.

A key takeaway: Although in part two we focus on compassion and Mahayana teachings, there's no way to focus on that if we don't begin at the beginning, which is learning how to tame our mind.

THE MEANING OF LOJONG

Lojong refers to a diverse set of methods to transform the mind by turning it away from self-centeredness and cultivating bodhicitta. It thus provides ways to develop loving-kindness, courage, and wisdom. Lojong has both meditative and postmeditative components: how to meditate and how to be in the world. The main meditative practice, tonglen, involves sending and receiving on the breath. Everything that's worthwhile, good, and pleasurable we mentally share by sending it out on the outbreath. On the inbreath we receive everything that's painful, dark, depressing. A counterintuitive proposition if I ever heard one.

What is this all about, in a nutshell? It is a *habit reverser*.

As we have seen in the first chapter, an essential component of Buddhist teachings is to point out our habitual patterns. We have so many ingrained habits. Our biggest one goes more or less like this: "Me, me, me, more me, only me, I, I want, me likes some of that, me, me, F-U, me, me, me." Does any of this seem familiar?

It is so very odd: We are completely centered on this thing that we can't even find! Sure enough, we have a body. It is born, it starts little, grows, gets big, gets wrinkles and liver spots or something, starts to disintegrate, and dies. That, in itself, is not necessarily problematic. But aren't we under the impression that there's more to "me" than just that, though it does include all of that?

Interestingly, within this *me* there are all kinds of other me's. There is the habit of me doing this, the habit of me doing that, me wanting this, me wanting to shop, me wanting to eat—me wanting, wanting, wanting. We have all these patterns. As far as *you* is concerned, most of the time, the general perspective is, "What have you done for me lately?" *You* is determined by one's relationship to *me*. It's a funny world.

There are, of course, exceptions to the rule. Sometimes, mother and child, father and child, or certain friendships break this me-ness. But somehow, the *me* is ever-present. In fact, one of the most interesting things about this me is that it can make more me's: It's the original cloner. What does that mean? Me can be having this conversation with you, and this other me can be watching this conversation, and there's another me that can be commenting on me watching me doing this. Well, there's another commentator watching all three of us—and so on and so on. Ego-centeredness is quite formidable.

We are so centered on our own existence that it's extremely difficult for us to experience anything other than our own pain, joy, and pleasure. Sometimes it's even difficult for us to see how much pain there is in this world—and this world is unbelievably full of pain. There are so many beings that experience so much pain: physical pain, psychological pain, the pain of all kinds of habits... It's an incredible situation. But it's difficult to see, let alone to act, because so many of us don't have any real compassion since we're so caught up in our own mind. I am not pointing fingers or pretending to be over this; this is just part of the human predicament.

The power of the Mahayana view is to counter these habits.

And the way to counter habits is to replace the bad ones with good ones. Of course, it's best to get rid of habits altogether, but habits are so ingrained in us. In fact, they aren't just the habits of this lifetime; they're forged over numberless lifetimes. Our tendencies in this very life are astonishingly strong, as our little rat maze is being built since beginningless times.

These particular teachings are essential to anyone who is a Mahayana Buddhist, and they are extremely helpful to anyone who is human. I understand that some readers might not feel that they would like to fully become a Buddhist. This is not a problem at all. You can still have compassion and kindness, and Buddhism has a great deal to offer in this area. However, for those of us who are Buddhists, there's more to this. It is, in fact, essential. Why bother to be a Buddhist if we can't develop loving-kindness—if we can't be kind to ourselves and others? It is paramount. It is our human heritage, and it is definitely worthwhile.

The Mahayana view is vast. As mentioned, that vastness includes not only all people but all sentient beings. The compassion we are talking about reaches out to all beings, including birds and worms. In fact, even though we don't believe in these things in our Western context, it even extends to trapped spirits, demons, and ghosts—anything that is sentient, in all the different realms. That sense of compassion is extremely wide.

More than just feeling some compassion, bodhicitta is at the essence of the training of our mind and at the essence of our ability to connect with people.

As we will see, it has relative and absolute aspects. It's hard to have a sense of the absolute bodhicitta because of its vastness—it has no boundary. That's why we have these techniques to connect our little minds to the vast mind, be it through relative means. It is also our birthright, because bodhicitta isn't something we're going to *create*, strictly speaking; it is something that we nourish and allow to fully bloom.

Our guidebook in this area, *The Seven Points of Mind Training*, includes fifty-nine pithy instructions that fit on little cards. Now, what are a bunch of words on cards really going to do for us?

Well, these fifty-nine habit reversers are priceless. It's amazing: If we use them, actually contemplate the fact that me, me, me is not as important as everything else, and start reversing our duality habit, something real happens. Of course, much of it still involves working with some duality, but we begin to reverse the duality habit so that duality can eventually fall away altogether. Instead of fixating on ourselves, we choose kindness to others. If something bad happens to someone, we take it into ourselves. If something good happens to us, we offer it to others.

Think about it. It is a difficult thing to do. And faking it doesn't really do anything, but we have to begin by faking it. Am I allowed to write that? We are so used to our own habit that we begin by pretending to change things. If we can just begin, perhaps with a little bit of visualization, then we slowly get used to the idea and come to a point where we can actually do it. When that happens, it has a profound effect on ourselves and the world.

Can we measure that change? Well, we can evaluate our progress along the path—and one of the seven points concerns precisely that—but we can't measure the effect it has on the world. No one can even notice what we're doing. This is a practice that we do, and it's about changing the way we think, the way we approach things, the way we act. No one knows it is going on except the practitioner. This is not a way to *fix* everything around us in some kind of material sense. It is breaking the iceberg of our self-centeredness, and it is a great relief when it starts cracking.

SITTING MEDITATION AND TWOFOLD BODHICITTA

We have just discussed the basic outlook of lojong. However, to properly learn and apply lojong, we need sitting meditation. There is no mind training without mind taming! Otherwise we're just fooling ourselves with a new philosophy, a new set of words, a new regime that's going to be over soon. If we can give ourselves the opportunity to lighten up through practicing meditation, we can allow bodhicitta to stir in our being.

In fact, the practice of sitting meditation is not only a crucial component of lojong but also the basis of all Buddhist practice. You begin with that, and you continue with that. The highest teachings are the fruition of sitting meditation practice; they are not separate from it.

Even when we get to the instruction on tonglen as the main meditative practice of lojong, we create a "meditation sandwich," with simple sitting meditation before and after. What's in the middle? The Mahayana practice of compassion. And what is that about? The awakened heart, or bodhicitta.

The lojong approach contains practices focused on both relative bodhicitta and absolute bodhicitta. Relative bodhicitta includes having the intention to benefit all beings and actualizing that intention through actions. Absolute bodhicitta, simply put, is the wisdom that realizes emptiness, and in the present context, it is connected to an experience of vastness. But bodhicitta really is not two things. There is an analogy that was most helpful to me when Trungpa Rinpoche presented it. He had a glass of water sitting on the counter, and as per the American habit, it had ice in it. Absolute bodhicitta, he said, is like the water in the glass. It's there, fluid and accommodating. The ice cubes, then, are like relative bodhicitta. The point was that the specific bodhicitta isn't separate from the absolute bodhicitta: It's of the same nature. The relative is our relationship to compassion, our relationship to wakefulness; the absolute is the vastness of it. The ice cube melts into the vastness.

Two weeks later, he gave the analogy again. A glass of water was sitting there. And he talked about it exactly the other way around! The ice cubes were absolute bodhicitta and the water was relative bodhicitta! The message here? Don't get stuck with ice cubes and water! That is, don't get stuck in the analogies. Bodhicitta is about something that is real and that begins so wonderfully, if you just allow it to begin. It is there in our own heart. We may be hardened, but it can fully blossom.

Our minds, though, might be currently very small, and our idea of compassion is quite limited. Why is it so narrow? For one thing, we're so busy. We tend to compartmentalize things, speculate about this and that, look for constant entertainment, and so forth. Thankfully relative bodhicitta allows us an "in" to compassion. It allows us to actually begin to practice compassion so that compassion can reveal itself fully.

The practice of sitting meditation allows us to begin to grow this thing in our being that is the seed of enlightenment.

How do we do that? First of all, by not being hard on ourselves, by allowing ourselves to be at ease. It is awfully difficult because of our habits. But that is still how we begin—as Trungpa Rinpoche said, "by making friends with ourselves." Not blaming ourselves for all the stupid things that we've done—but not blaming anyone else either. This isn't modern, politically correct psychology. It's nothing like that. It's about easing up.

Interestingly, the easing up comes at the same time that we begin discipline. But the kind of discipline that we are talking about here, in terms of regular meditation practice, is not about some regime, because trying to set up a regime is not going to work. All regimes end, and not so well. It's about changing our habit. Daily. We change our harmful habit of busyness by putting in the wholesome habit of sitting meditation, practicing again and again. We take the bad habit of being stupidly hard on ourselves, and we replace it with the good habit of having friendliness toward ourselves.

Therefore, meditation practice and making friends with ourselves go together. Sitting practice is then the ground to which we can always return, and bodhicitta grows from that ground of clarity.

THE SLOGANS APPROACH

As necessary as it is, all this talk of making friends with ourselves and finding some peace may still sound like it is about *me*. In fact, at this point, the "me" problem has not been solved, really, and this is where lojong comes into play. It is there to challenge us constantly.

The fifty-nine pieces of advice contained in *The Seven Points* are often referred to as "the lojong slogans." Each one offers a meditation, a reminder of how to be, a way to change our mind and reorient our attention toward others. In other words, all these aphorisms go against the grain of our ordinary me-ness. Therefore, most of them sound counterintuitive. Pick "Be grateful to everyone," for instance. *Everyone*, even if they provide us with nothing but heartache and pain. We will get back to this, but the idea is to reverse our way of looking at things.

The way we were taught to deal with these slogans was to study them one by one—we'll look at a selection in the two chapters that follow—to memorize as many of them as we could, and to contemplate them. There are many ways to study these things, but there's no way to do it without actually contemplating their meaning. Some Dharma centers may set up a weekly meditation where one slogan is contemplated. Many people also use little cards at home.

When these slogans were first presented to Trungpa Rinpoche's students, we were perplexed. "What is all this? A bunch of Buddhist truisms that are supposed to make us... what, exactly?" It was shocking. But the approach that we were taught was intriguing. Slogans were calligraphed and put all over the place. This was during a three-month seminary, and the cards were placed hanging from trees in the woods, in the kitchen, inside refrigerator doors, in the bathroom... The idea was to have an onslaught of reminders: "Don't wait in ambush." "Don't make gods into demons." "The Mahayana instruction for ejection of consciousness at death is the five strengths; how you conduct yourself is important." Of course, we learned what all the technical terms meant. And when you study the various handbooks, you learn a lot about Buddhism, and especially about Mahayana.

The dharmic point of view is the exact opposite of our ordinary view. These slogans and the practice of sending and receiving (which is included in the slogans) go directly against our usual idea of taking the good and sending out the bad. Instead, we start taking in pain and sending out health; we take in frustration and send out confidence, and this truly changes us. There is simply no way to attain buddhahood if we don't find ways to get out of our usual, dualistic, pathetic, self-referential habits. These practices not only change us; in a subtle way, they change the world, too.

THE BODHISATTVA VOW

If we are to do the practices of a bodhisattva, we have to consider becoming one. A bodhisattva is somebody who is willing to put all others before themselves, with no exception. One is willing to put off one's own liberation, one's own enlightenment—one's own everything—so that everyone else can go before. Wow! Do we really mean that?

The truth is, currently, even if we think we can benefit somebody else, we're fooling ourselves. We're just referring back to *me*, out of the same habit of duality. Yet for the sake of this conversation, we have to use our dualistic language. So, is it a trick? Well, it is and it isn't. Is the bodhisattva vow something I can do all by myself? Not exactly. Can I become a bodhisattva by just saying "I am a bodhisattva" to myself? No and yes. The yes part is that if our mind goes in that direction, then yes, we can do it. But it is also important to do it in the formal way, with witnesses and lineage. "Lineage" here means those who have gone before us.

The bodhisattva vow is something we take after we have taken refuge, which means after we're done with spiritual shopping. Taking refuge means that we have decided that we don't need to shop anymore, that the teachings of the Buddha make sense to us and we are willing to take refuge in the Buddha, the Dharma, and the Sangha. Does that mean that lojong can't be practiced if you're not a Buddhist? Yes and no. I apologize for this; I am not being facetious. As mentioned, we live in extraordinary times. These practices are most effective and transformational if your mind can embrace the Buddhist teachings. But if, for your own reasons, you cannot do that, then there's no notion that it is a sin of any kind. You can take Buddhist principles and apply them in your life. It's not exactly the same; it's also not inferior. But in all honesty, the Buddhist teachings are best done in a Buddhist context, meaning that your faith is complete. Remember, "faith" means, very simply, that once we have found something that is true, we follow it through all the way—in other words, we practice what we have been taught.

So the "kosher" approach, if I may say so, is taking refuge, practicing meditation, and taking the bodhisattva vow. After that—which means that our life is dedicated to the benefit of others, formally and not just tentatively—there's something powerful that can and does happen. If you can't do that but are nonetheless a decent human being (or would like to be one, if you're not), you can take these teachings and make them part of your life. But please don't mix them up; don't change the terminology or concoct your homemade version of any of this. Let it be what it is, as it is. It's most effective that way. Don't adjust these ideas to what you already believe. If you want to study it, just study it in its own framework.

As far as the kindness aspect of it is concerned—its element of heart, gentleness, being kind to oneself, and so forth—that has no copyright whatsoever. It doesn't belong to any creed; it is ours, as human beings. Take that part and make it your own. But please don't create homemade recipes out of spiritual teachings. One of my teachers liked to joke that Coke and Pepsi mixed together tastes awful. The essential, heart aspect of this is yours and that is totally fine; just don't mix your metaphors.

In terms of the tonglen practice, it is worth repeating that there is no tonglen practice nor any exchanging yourself for others without stabilizing your own mind, which is done through sitting meditation. Tonglen is a visual, visceral, and active practice, but it comes from emptiness—from the simplicity of peaceful abiding and panoramic awareness. Otherwise, it is not effective.

As well, there is no idea of holding on to anything. When we do these practices, we do them; and when we are finished, we let go. We let go by going back to sitting meditation, simply abiding in peace, not making any big concepts about what we have done or thinking that whatever we did has helped us or anybody else. We must learn not to make a big deal out of being simply human. Loving-kindness is natural, and so is compassion.

We could discuss philosophical intricacies and all sorts of categories, but they won't make sense if we don't understand the key points. We are not trying to make ourselves superior in any way or form. We're not *adding* anything; we're stripping away. When we strip away, the heart opens wider. When the heart opens wider, we're not more, we're less. It's not that big of a deal. It is so important for us to understand this isn't some big project; we're not particularly going to get anything; there's no big prize at the end. Any effect is subtle, actually measureless. It *is* profound, but it's not for us to speculate about. The power of lojong is that it counteracts habitual patterns, so how could habitual patterns ever estimate it properly?

MIND TRAINING BEYOND NIHILISM AND ETERNALISM

Sitting meditation helps put our mind at peace, and it changes our relationship to our day and our world. This doesn't mean that other people are going to be any nicer or that disease and death and tragedy are not going to come our way. It's not like using a silver bullet that suddenly solves everything. All that exists around us, the way the world is—all that continues, but our relationship to it changes. Our relationship to pain changes as well. It's not about running away, nor is it just about finding entertainment. Our relationship to pleasure changes, too, by the way. We have so many extreme notions, so let us be clear: Enjoyment is not a problem. Really, there is no reason to feel guilty about enjoying this life.

Meditation practice is the dynamic aspect of the Buddhist philosophy of the

Middle Way. It is neither falling into one extreme or the other: the extremes of hope and fear, eternalism and nihilism, too hyped up or too depressed. We can find the middle way in every aspect of our life. That does not mean that the middle way is precisely halfway between the two extremes. We are not trying to create a flatland world or a communist grayness or anything like that. The middle way is where you find it, and it is not a static, geometrical center. People think, "Oh, if I can just not have this and not have that, then there it is." But it's elusive and changing, not formulaic.

Since all these teachings come from a middle way attitude, it is worthwhile to understand what eternalism and nihilism are.

Eternalism is believing that someone or something is going to save us, that everything is going to be all right at the most basic sort of level, and that somehow me or some idea of me is going to live forever. There are many variations on that theme. Likewise, nihilism comes in many shapes and shades: "When I die, that's the end of everything." "Nothing exists." "Everything is shit." "Whatever I do is meaningless, worthless." "Science is the only truth." "Everything is in some state of entropy, and it's all going to stop someday, so who cares?" I'm being extreme, but we are precisely talking about extremes. Nihilism also involves not, trusting that there is any spiritual reality at all—the opposite of the eternalists, who think that's all there is, in a sense.

The Buddhist view is not to fall prey to these extremes.

If we approach these notions in an intelligent manner, we see how we jump this way or that way. We look at our highs and lows. Sure, if we practice meditation, things become more even, but it's not like popping Prozac. We're not talking about tuning things down in such a way that they remain the same, just in a bit of a haze for the time being. There's brightness to the meditative evenness. It has an "up" quality. This is because this evenness is based on *sugatagarbha*, or buddha essence, which comes with the inherent bliss of wakefulness. Wakefulness is not boring or flat, not by any means. It has a blissful quality. But again, it's not our usual idea of entertaining bliss, which inevitably turns into pain.

We can experience an evenness of mind that is expansive. It is quite wonderful to get off the roller coaster. However, our habits are very addictive. We may complain and say that we hate all the drama that happens in this life. But as soon as it stops, we are bored, and we recreate more drama. We know full well that what goes up must come down, and yet we'll do the same stupid thing again. We'll meet a new person and repeat everything we did—as close as possible to the last time! We know exactly how the game works, but we do it anyway. Then somehow even the surprising elements are part of our habitual pattern. "Oh, look, it hurts this way! I didn't know I could get hurt *that* way!" Or whatever it is.

If we take a step back and look at how we spend most of our time... it's pathetic. I hate to say, because then I'm telling the truth about me, too, but it is pathetic. Sure enough, we always think, "Tomorrow, I can fix this. If I just can get it together tomorrow! Or next week, or when the seasons change, or when I go to Wagga Wagga to attend this and that seminar, I'll learn how to do things and then I'll get it right." Or whatever story we tell ourselves.

It is a joke that we pull on ourselves continuously. I want to make sure that everyone pauses and understands: This is our life we're talking about here. Not the neighbor's.

My dear friend, the wondrous Traleg Kyabgon Rinpoche,[2] asked me to share these wonderful lojong teachings with his students; I care, and I couldn't say no. So now I'll share these teachings here with you. Sure enough, we cannot compress a lifetime's worth of study in a chapter or two, but we can get a glimpse; we can spark something. So let us all try to get a glimpse of what happens when we give up the stupid games that we play on ourselves and that drive us so crazy. Let's give up some of our entertainment and see if we can change things. Let's be real—at least a little bit.

5

Boundlessness and Compassion

The Seven Points of Mind Training, Part 1

In the following pages, we will take a closer look at *The Seven Points of Mind Training*. I will present a selection of slogans from the root text.

POINT 1: THE PRELIMINARIES

The first of the seven points of mind training is called "the preliminaries," which are the basis for Dharma practice. Interestingly, this first point contains only one slogan:

» First, train in the preliminaries.

In the Indo-Tibetan Buddhist traditions, we give a lot of importance to four preliminary contemplations, which we revisit again and again. These preliminaries are also called the "four reminders." They remind us how to view our life. Integrating these contemplations into our routine is the best thing we can do to begin to break our habitual patterns of torturing ourselves and repeating everything endlessly and fruitlessly.

The first reminder is the preciousness of this human life. We take this body for granted. "I'm so-and-so, I was born in such and such a town, and here I am..." But there's more to it, isn't there? Let's examine things. What exactly makes this human birth so precious?

Buddhism, Hinduism, and other Asian traditions agree on this: This precious human birth is extremely rare. Although there are billions of us, when compared to the overall number of sentient beings, it's a small number. In fact, compared to cockroaches and mosquitoes, there really aren't that many humans! But this precious human birth is not only rare; it is absolutely precious, because we can practice what's real—the Dharma—in this life, in this very body. What's even more precious is that we've heard the Dharma, and we are living in a land where it is available. We could be stuck with some fuzzy doctrine or some extreme beliefs, or have no freedom to explore other avenues, but here we are: We have the opportunity to actually listen to the Dharma. Beyond just listening to it, the fact that we have our senses working well, our cognitive abilities, and so forth gives us the chance to put the truth of the Dharma into practice. That's part of what makes this life so extraordinarily precious. It's also precious in that we don't have any idea how long it will last.

Thus, part of this training in the preliminaries is realizing this: We are here in a human body that allows us to do magnificent things. The most magnificent thing is to practice Dharma by developing compassion and embodying kindness. Not only that. We have the possibility of becoming completely enlightened and bringing benefit to all beings. The human body is said to be the best form for that. We have landed in the right realm. It is a totally wonderful situation, but we don't know if this good circumstance is going to ever appear again. Thus, we must take advantage of it at this time.

The second of the four preliminaries is to contemplate the reality of death. It comes without warning. We are here today, and one of these tomorrows—and it could be *tomorrow*—gone. They'll say, "But he looked so good this morning! She really loved that pumpkin soup last night! I just saw her!" Make no mistake—they are going to be talking about me and you. We hear things like this all the time. We see the funeral wagon going by. But one day, sooner than any of us really imagine, that will be *our* corpse. Who knows what earthquake can hit where, or what car can hit what, or what cancer, or what heart attack, or what anything...

There is a sense of urgency. We start to feel the need to actually put the teachings into practice. It is truly foolish to postpone our spiritual practice. We shouldn't think, "I'm fifty. The average person in this country lives to be eighty. I have thirty more years left." It doesn't matter how young or old we happen to be. We have no idea when we will meet death or when death will meet us. There's no guarantee, and there's nothing that will save us from that. By the way, even if we do get old, youth feels like it was yesterday. It really does. So, it is important to contemplate that our death can come at any time, and not to be complacent. It could be very sudden, and in any case, it is bound to happen sooner or later. Remaining aware of this is extremely important.

The third reminder has to do with the unalterable principles of karma. There is no way to escape causality. No way—except for complete enlightenment, in which case, one is not bound by cause and effect anymore. But we, my friends, are confused. The level of confusion may vary from one person to the next, but we are confused nonetheless. What we do, what we think, our actions, our impulses all have an effect. Things don't exist in a vacuum, so we should understand karma. Even the way we think has an effect, because everything that we do comes from our mind. If our mind comes up with something, chances are we'll do it. Fortunately we don't do everything our mind comes up with—that would be a mess! But generally speaking, there is some karmic connection between the way we think and the way we act.

In any event, from a Buddhist point of view, karma is a fact, no matter what anyone says or believes. It is so basic: Everything we do, everything we say, everything we think creates something else. Yet ultimately the idea is to go beyond karma altogether, because as long as we are deluded, karma will be tied in one way or another to confusion and suffering. This chain reaction only ends with complete enlightenment.

The fourth reminder is that samsara is an ocean of suffering. This relates to the repetition of habits that we talk about so much in this book. We're caught up, and we're always going to suffer unless we do something about it. We will remain trapped in this mess as long as we're focused on our own self-importance, as long as we're entangled in thinking about how good we are, how bad we are, obsessing about what we want or don't want . . . None of that does anything that doesn't cause more pain. We might get some form of temporary happiness, but these good times are indeed temporary. None of it lasts.

The only comfort we have is that complete enlightenment is real. It is not a fairy tale. Compassion is real. There is comfort in knowing that the ocean of samsara and karma can come to an end in complete enlightenment, when there is no fixated separation between self and other. What causes all these problems is that we're caught in all the various dualisms. The antidote to these is the actual Middle Way. And that, ultimately, is complete enlightenment.

The precious human birth, the reality of death, causality, and suffering—these four themes require repeated contemplations. You can spend time with them as a prelude to your main practice. You can even find a short liturgy that summarizes them. For example, here is one I like to use:

> Joyful to have such a human birth, difficult to find, free and well favored.
> But death is real, comes without warning. This body will be a corpse.

> Unalterable are the laws of karma; cause and effect cannot be escaped.
> Samsara is an ocean of suffering, unendurable, unbearably intense.[1]

These preliminaries provide the basis for which all Dharma practice and all mind training come from. They help establish the basic understanding that we are serious; that this is not just some intellectual pursuit, some little field of study. This is about our life. This is real.

For those who are Buddhists, we add a fifth element to these four contemplations: devotion to one's teacher. We should be thankful that these things have been pointed out, thankful that the path has been shown so that we can liberate ourselves from these constraints and sorrows. If you are entering into the practice of the Mahayana, I highly recommend that you have an actual teacher. I discuss the student–teacher relationship at length in part six of the book. For the time being, know that it can be simple; it doesn't have to be highfalutin. Half a century ago in the West, I would have said, "Good luck!" But we do have good luck, and there are people here and there who can be our spiritual friends. It is extremely worthwhile to make a relationship with someone who's gone before, who has at least *some* understanding and experience. It doesn't have to be a completely enlightened being. (It couldn't hurt, though!)

POINT 2: THE MAIN PRACTICE

The second point of the seven points of mind training is broken into two parts. The first concerns absolute or ultimate bodhicitta. The second concerns relative bodhicitta.

Absolute Bodhicitta

Bodhicitta is the heart essence of the Buddhist teachings. It just exists, but as part of the practice we engender it. In other words, bodhicitta is not something that we create, strictly speaking, but more something that we bring to mind and cultivate. In this lojong tradition, we begin by engendering what's called absolute bodhicitta.

Absolute bodhicitta involves a sense of giving—a sense of absolute generosity. It has no particular object; rather, it is all-pervasive, all-compassionate. That bodhicitta is the birthright of any human being and, in fact, of all living beings. It exists in a dormant form in each and every one of us, and it can be brought out. The first set of slogans that comes after the preliminaries points to this ultimate way of being and looking at things.

Bodhicitta is the essence of being a bodhisattva. A bodhisattva dedicates their life for the benefit of others; they consider that their enlightenment or their freedom is not separate from any other being. This noble quality of the Mahayana path is the key to complete enlightenment. It is the heart of the Buddha. And since bodhisattva activity is sometimes understood as the activity of the Buddha, bodhicitta is also, in a way, the active principle or active quality of the Buddha.

Three Kinds of Generosity

One of the ways to approach the different points of mind training is to relate them to the different paramitas, or aspects of the bodhisattva's practice.[2] Absolute bodhicitta is here connected to the paramita of generosity.

We often speak of three kinds of generosity.

The first kind is to give material things, such as food and clothing, whether it's to someone we know or someone we don't know.

The second is more of a psychological kind of giving: assuaging people's fear or helping them to become fearless. This could be done through our encouragement, for example, or through education or helping people see things clearly. That is extremely worthwhile.

The third kind of giving is considered the most valuable: the gift of Dharma. The gift of meditation practice, of the teachings that were brought forth and embodied by the Buddha and the various Buddhist masters.

Naturally, these kinds of generosity all have an element of compassion.

The reason we can have compassion is that somewhere in us there is something tender. Something soft. No matter how tough we are, there is something that moves us. Sure enough, the Hitlers and Maos and Stalins of this world have it well covered up. But even the most wicked person has in them a tender spot. You can sometimes see it in their love for their child, a pet, a flower—whatever it is. Every being has something that can touch them and potentially open them up. There's something in us that can feel the pain of others because we ourselves have pain. We can know that other people have feelings because we ourselves have feelings. We have this connection.

This is all connected to *tathagatagarbha*, a Sanskrit term that has to do with buddha-nature, or "gone beyond" nature. We're talking about going beyond the shell of our usual ego-centered self. There lies something soft and wonderful.

Although the main theme of point 2 is training in absolute bodhicitta, it is not a mere abstraction. It gives us the opportunity to be compassionate. Because—let's be truthful—we're usually not! But we have the opportunity to change. And the way to change properly is not by making the usual ego campaign out of it: "I'm now going to be compassionate. Look, everyone, I'm joining the Red Cross and ecological activists!" Not that any of those things are bad. They're good. But the mind that creates a new ego of "I'm now going on a compassion kick" is the same *me, me, me* that is so uncompassionate. True compassion has nothing to do with making a nuisance out of ourselves. It doesn't have to be out there declared. It doesn't have to do with creating new garbage or making a mess with our own self-referential concepts.

The Union of Relative and Absolute Bodhicitta

While absolute bodhicitta is this vast, unobscured sense of giving, relative bodhicitta is *specific* and involves actions. In other words, it involves putting into practice this awakened heart. It's about doing something that actually helps someone.

When we combine these two bodhicittas—engendering absolute bodhicitta, which is a sense of total openness, and then actually putting our body, speech, and mind to be of benefit—then we become a bodhisattva. In other words, arousing this twofold bodhicitta is how we enter the bodhisattva path. But it all begins with the actual practice of sitting meditation. This is constantly stressed. There is shamatha, which is the development of peace, and vipashyana, the development of insight—and only then can we develop a true sense of friendliness that goes out to everything and everybody, including ourselves.

On this note, lojong is not about loving others and hating ourselves. The battle is against habit. Ego doesn't really exist, but habits do. *Habit* is the problem. Ego is but an illusion. Habits are not—so to speak, in this analogy. Part of the friendliness and openness to everything is trusting in our basic goodness and in the fact that everybody has that piece of goodness. If we simply rest in that state, we come to see that everybody has it, be it deep within.

We mentioned that absolute bodhicitta is related to the perfection, or paramita, of generosity. We should add that relative bodhicitta is related to the perfection of discipline. Why discipline? Because it has to do with conducting ourselves properly, with changing the way we relate. To actually be of benefit, it takes some effort. But it's not a constraint. In fact, this is about *natural discipline*. It comes from our good heart—from our ability to take simple kindness and turn it into compassion for others. There's an active quality to it, but it remains natural.

Relative bodhicitta has to do with the fact that at any time and in any situation, we can have a tender heart. No one here is asking us to be naïve. There are situations where we must be tough in order to help someone, but that doesn't mean we have to be hard-hearted. We also have to trust ourselves and be able to love ourselves as we love others. This comes from that same tender heart. We should acknowledge that our usual approach to others is through disdain or passion or lust or aggression or indifference or a variation thereof. With relative bodhicitta, we're changing that pattern. It's not about passion, aggression, or disdain; it's about communication.

So, we're changing something odd and self-centered to communication and openness. It is a very difficult thing to do, but it is totally possible. And yes, by the way, it even includes our relationship with our mother! I'm joking, though it does include her. In a Tibetan context, the nicest thing you can say is, "Be kind to your mother," and everyone understands. Somehow in the West, there's always a problem with that, for reasons that are beyond conception. But mother, father, mosquitoes, bedbugs—it is possible to have compassion for all beings.

Back to our slogans. Remember: The second point of the seven points of mind training is broken into two parts, the first of which is focused on absolute bodhicitta. And the first slogan of that part is the following:

» Regard all dharmas as dreams.

We often use the term "Dharma" to refer to the Buddha's teachings, but here "dharma" simply means any specific event. In other words, regard anything—all phenomena—as a dream.

The basic view here comes as an expression of compassion and openness. From the perspective of compassion and openness, nothing truly happens in a concrete sense. Everything is like a dream, like a fantasy.

Take this morning's breakfast: we can remember eating it, but somehow it doesn't really exist. It's like a dream. What we did yesterday? We can vividly recall it, but it is dreamlike. What happened just a few moments ago outside, as vivid as it was: just like a dream. Our life has this strange quality: As colorful as this moment is, it's gone.

We are used to thinking that everything is so real and solid. These days, even our television is reality-oriented: it has "reality" TV shows, which is a joke. By contrast, the instruction here is to see *all* phenomena as dreams. Do not misunderstand, however: It is not saying that everything is literally a dream; rather, the advice is to regard it *like* a dream. Whatever we're experiencing, whether it's pain, pleasure, hot summer's day, cold winter's night, the manifestation of all these interesting people, everything that we see around us, every aspect of our life, we regard as if it's a dream.

In sitting meditation, one begins to see that those things that we think are so real in our life are trumped up. This includes our passions, our hates, our memory of how things happened, our conception of how things will unfold. Everything that arises in our mind isn't as solid as we like to believe.

This slogan teaches us right from the beginning that we should not take it all so seriously. Even though whatever happens to us may be serious business. Sometimes things really are serious. We're told that we have cancer, for example. What are we supposed to do with that? This happens. To us. The word itself is enough to throw you for a big loop. We are not saying that it's anything light. But it's not as solid as we think.

We are going to have *some* illnesses; that's just part of this life. And we are going to die, there's no question about it. And if we live long enough, our hair will turn gray and we'll wrinkle and sag. Plumbing will go bad. How much of a picture should I draw? We all know about this. But it all depends on how one looks at it. The basic approach here is to look at whatever occurs, whatever presents itself, as if it were a dream. We're not belittling anything in life; we're just gaining some perspective.

In due course, this view is to show us the nature of ultimate bodhicitta, the ultimate awakened heart. As mentioned, it is incredibly vast and difficult to fathom. This slogan can give us a nod in the right direction.

» Examine the nature of unborn awareness.

The idea is: Concepts don't work. And here, "examine" just means *look*; it doesn't mean *dissect*.

So, look at your mind.

See if there's something solid, anything to hold on to.
Look, look, look at your mind. It's constantly shifting and changing.
You will find that it has no shape, no color, no substance.
Just look. No judgment, no anything. Just look.

» Self-liberate even the antidote.

Every one of our thoughts comes from nowhere, exists nowhere, and goes nowhere. We make a big deal out of it, don't we—all our thoughts? But if we really pay attention, we'll see. It all comes from nowhere; there it is, then gone.

"Self-liberate even the antidote" comes after the instructions to regard all phenomena as dreams and examine the nature of unborn awareness. At this point, you have learned some kind of meditative technique. Well, this slogan basically means *drop the technique*. Drop any idea of *how*, and just be where you are. Often when we find something that stops the pain, we become a hypochondriac and are only interested in the drug. We become an expert on the medicines, even when we don't need them. Here, we find out that we don't have to fixate on the medicines any longer.

The general idea is to go beyond just being caught by our conceptions, our discursive thought.

As an aside, this particular slogan, in modern context, also makes fun of "Well, cooking is good meditation. I'm just right there and, boy, I'm cooking away at the wok, and my mind and the wok and the vegetables are one. So why would I have to do sitting meditation?" Or, you know, "Hiking in the woods, now *that* is the best meditation. Everything is so beautiful. The flowers and I are singing together. Who needs to do any formal practice?" This slogan is saying, "Don't get involved in that sort of thinking. It doesn't work. There's no reason to cop out." Meditation is sitting meditation, shamatha-vipashyana is shamatha-vipashyana. It's not replaced by cooking school or writing school or hunting school or cricket school or the Zen of baseball.

» Rest in the nature of *alaya*, the essence.

Buddhism often talks of eight types of consciousnesses. The first five are the various sense consciousnesses: seeing, hearing, smelling, tasting, touching. The sixth consciousness is the mind that puts all those things together. The seventh is the "nuisance mind," or that part of us that complains and moans and is totally confused. The eighth is "the all-ground consciousness" (Tib.

kunzhi; Skt. *alaya*). These terms can have different meanings depending on the context, but here we will simply take it as the deep background from which the other seven consciousnesses arise. The eighth consciousness is also spoken of as a "storehouse" of consciousness or a sort of primordial basis from which every thought, every image, every experience arises.[3]

We're familiar with the term *Himalaya*. It connotes a sort of storehouse or range behind everything. Likewise, in our own experience, before everything becomes vivid in this way and that way, there is something from which it arises. The slogan tells us that we can go back to and rest in that basic place, without all the perturbations, without all the persnickety details. We can go back home to that, anytime, right now, right here. It's available to us. It's always present. All it requires is simple awareness. *Rest in the nature of alaya, the essence*: That is our meditation instruction. That's why in meditation we don't have any problem with whatever thoughts occur. They all arise from alaya, and they all go back to alaya. Likewise, any feeling that comes up arises from alaya and goes back into alaya. The recommendation is to just rest in that simple nature itself. We begin there, and it is connected to the notion of mindfulness of mind.

This alaya is not enlightenment. But it's something still quite wonderful, and since we're talking at a beginner's level here, we have no problem. Alaya is that which is basically good. It's before all the senses come into play, before *I* and *that*, and the like. That basic goodness, again, is part of our nature. That's why it's called *basic* goodness. It's that part of our mind that is almost "alpha-pure." The awakened heart comes from that.

Behind alaya, as it were, there is tathagatagarbha, the "essence of having gone beyond." That's complete enlightenment, which is the goal. But we begin very simply. Through our meditation practice, we simplify things enough so that there is some peace. We simplify enough so that we can see our basic nature, our basic goodness. From there, all opportunities of compassion and kindness can arise, and in fact do arise. Thus, here, resting in the nature of alaya is just resting in that basic goodness, without getting caught up in any of the sense perceptions or the nuisance mind or the usual discursiveness.

Traleg Rinpoche and other masters pointed out that it's not good enough just to rest there, but we *begin* there. We learn to transcend the seven types of consciousness and just become simple. It really is about simplifying. This is our resting place. We agree to begin as beginners. Why wouldn't we? There's actually some place where we can begin that isn't complicated.

This uncomplicated alaya has no particular bias and no particular distinctions. It only has basic goodness. It's simple that way. There's a sense of wakefulness in it, in and of itself. However, this slogan comes with a warning: Don't make this the end-all. But we can use this. We don't have to believe in it as something all that wonderful, but we can use it, and we can cultivate resting in alaya as a stepping stone toward actual enlightenment. It's a resting place only in the sense that we as beginners can actually find a place to begin. We can begin *right there*—there is an opening. But we don't get caught there. We rest, and then we can go on from there.

» In postmeditation, be a child of illusion.

I find this one to be particularly helpful. It's about not being caught up in our experience. It's cutting through all our preconceptions about how things should be, and just being simple.

This is basically an instruction on how to continue that resting in alaya off the cushion—that is, in postmeditation practice. During sitting practice, we come to that place—there we are. Then when we stand up, we do so as a child of illusion. The analogy that Trungpa Rinpoche gives is that when you come out of meditation, you go out and you swim rather than float. There is a sense of actually going through life instead of just being carried away by it. It has an active quality rather than a passive quality.

To be a child of illusion means that if our perception of the world becomes heavy or solid once we have finished our sitting meditation, we don't get caught up by the illusion. We can be simple about it. We can be fully present and realize that whatever situation presents itself in the world is workable, in the same way that whatever thoughts that arise in our mind are workable.

This slogan thus provides the basic instruction for meditation in action—how to be in this world. There's no need to be claustrophobic, because there is lots of room. There's open space. It depends on our view. But again, this comes from meditation. There's no postmeditation without meditation, is there? In fact, they are one. This is not the power of positive thinking or creating some mental framework; it's the direct result of what happens in sitting meditation. This view easily arises from that.

Interestingly, the saying "First thought, best thought," mentioned in the chapter on expressing wakefulness, comes from this slogan. Here the angle is a tad different, though complementary: Whatever appears, we don't have to rethink it, check again, check again, check again. Whatever comes up, that's *it*. We don't have to regurgitate the situation endlessly, trying to change things again and again.

RELATIVE BODHICITTA

A Warning: Don't Isolate the Practice of Tonglen

The following slogans, which are still part of the second point of the seven points of mind training, have to do with relative bodhicitta. This section includes the actual practice of tonglen.

As mentioned in the previous chapter, presenting these teachings in this way and sharing them publicly is fairly new. When Trungpa Rinpoche first presented tonglen in America, it was for people who had taken the bodhisattva vow and had hundreds of hours of meditation experience. Over time, it's been introduced to practitioners at all levels because it seems to be so helpful. But I have to warn you that it's extremely important, in practicing tonglen, that you do ordinary meditation practice before and after. Trungpa Rinpoche, who was one of the first to present this practice outside of a monastic context, made that clear—almost a requirement, as far as practicing it and teaching it were concerned. Once you learn this practice, it is yours; but please proceed properly by doing some simple sitting meditation beforehand and having some simple meditation experience afterward, without mixing everything up. The practice is like the center of a sandwich: It doesn't quite work without the bread, does it? We are not talking about a soup.

You'll pardon the repetitive preamble, but I do feel my teacher at my neck, so I cannot stress this enough. This practice is simply not meant to be isolated. These teachings are presented to us because we live in a particularly dark time, where things aren't always done in the right order. But really, we should have years of practicing meditation before we do this. All the same, it is a difficult and desperate time. This echoes the story of Khenpo Gangshar mentioned in the last chapter and told by Trungpa Rinpoche in his autobiography, *Born in Tibet*. Of course, our situation is different, but some of the things that are happening in this world are unprecedented and quite difficult. I don't know how to formulate this without sounding too trippy, but somehow there is *less* time. I am not just saying that because I am now old.

Tulku Thondup Rinpoche, one of the great Nyingma masters, who lived in Cambridge, Massachusetts, said that what he noticed since he started using computers is that they eat time. At first he thought it was just his mind—but it seems that time sort of changed for us, too. Whatever the case may be, certain things, including these very teachings, become more and more important. This is how I felt twenty years ago, and it is still very much how I feel today.

These teachings are powerful, and we have to trust people to do them properly so that they can be of benefit. It's not about proceeding haphazardly, and it is not just for our self-aggrandizement.

All these caveats for such a simple practice! But what can I say? Let's now look more deeply at tonglen, beginning with the following slogan.

» Sending and taking should be practiced alternately. These two should ride the breath.

This is the pith instruction of how to exchange ourselves with others, and the way to put the Mahayana and the bodhisattva view into practice in our life.

This slogan presents the actual meditation of tonglen, which has to do with giving away all happiness, pleasure, and everything good with the outbreath, and taking in everything that is causing resentment, pain, and worry with the inbreath. As we do that, we don't hold on to our usual idea of ourselves—this is why we practice shamatha-vipashyana beforehand. There's not some big, solid "me" taking it in, nor is there some big, solid "me" sending it out.

In fact, this particular practice comes naturally from the previous ones. It arises naturally because once we have done the previous practices—once our view has opened—what do we see? That it's not just about ourselves. Tonglen is a way of working with that fact.

What we begin to discover as we practice meditation is that any solid sense of a self doesn't exist. Our idea of a self is really empty. If we actually look, there's nothing solid there. That doesn't mean we disappear. But if we really ask ourselves—if we really try to find out "Who am I?" and investigate and inquire—we come to a shocking discovery. This is a discovery we have to make for ourselves. (While a joker like me might say all these things, it is quite different when you find out for yourself.) But the way it is described is that, in fact, there is no self. What that means is that there is nothing inherently solid. And just to add to the wondrousness of things, if we actually look at any outer phenomenon—whether it's other people, other beings, the material world—there's nothing solid there either. Of course everything exists, somehow; but it's not as solid as we like to think.

Tonglen is based on an aspiration to take on the suffering of others. This goes completely against our ordinary logic. We don't try to secure ourselves in any way. Instead, we extend ourselves out. But we do this step by step. We begin with our parents and friends, we work up to our enemies, and we open our heart more and more, working up to ecological crises, pollution, war, and so on. And we take this practice quite seriously. It's not a form of entertainment or self-help. It's serious business in a way. It is extremely powerful when done properly, though it is hard to imagine the effect that it has, as much as we like to materialize everything. This, you can't materialize. You do it, and you let it go. It has nothing to do with your ego or seeing results in an ordinary way. You have to be real, literal; there's no faking. If you don't want to be real, don't bother! It is not going to do you or anyone else any good. This practice is also not about credentials of any kind.

The basic approach is that we always start with *this*, and then we go out to *that*. And once we've finished the practice, we drop it, not looking for any results.

Now, the actual practice is quite simple.

The "sending" is giving out everything good and positive to all beings, all individuals, with the outbreath. The "taking" comes with the inbreath: We absorb all resentment, pain, and negativity. They're done alternately: giving, taking, giving, taking. In the beginning, we may have to concentrate a little bit more on one at a time, but it's so that we can get to the place where on the outbreath we give and on the inbreath we receive.

We are advised to "ride the breath," but sending and receiving is not done exclusively in and out of your nose. Every pore of your body gets involved, so to speak. Of course, we literally use the breath, but we're not fixating on just the air that comes in and out of our nostrils, nor on any part of the body, for that matter. In other words, rather than a purely nasal phenomenon, there's also a sense of going out and coming back.

As well, it is said that we could see our "selves" as a little emptier than usual—that is, not made of flesh and bones but almost like a balloon. The idea is that when we're taking in, things don't stick; and when we're sending out, we're not sending out something that comes from our usual corporeal self. This isn't about smoking meat with bad things, and sending out good from the unsmoked part, or whatever. It's not your usual meat-oriented activity!

The Stages of Tonglen

There are four stages to the practice of tonglen.

The **first** step is to flash a sense of openness. In our mind, we kindly touch base with a sense of boundlessness, which is akin to absolute bodhicitta. In a way, it's as simple as opening our hand: We're just opening up and being simplicity itself for a moment.

The **second** stage is to work with our breath and the textures, so to speak. With the taking in, we feel the heaviness and ruggedness of what it is we're taking in. Then when we're sending out, we feel the freshness or soothing quality of what's going out. This is sometimes described as sending out light and taking in black smoke—but remember, we're not smoking meat! Different commentaries provide different metaphors: The imagery is not solid, but using images like that is fine. Also, unlike ordinary shamatha-vipashyana practice, we *can* manipulate our breath a little, and we can accentuate the out and the in rather than just keeping the light touch of basic sitting meditation. As we pay attention to our breath, we're very much there with the going out, sending out the freshness, the brightness, the clarity; and taking in the claustrophobia, the resentment, the pain.

The **third** part has to do with working with a specific person or situation. The traditional literature says that you can begin with your mother whom you love dearly. If you have a problem with that, please don't worry. It can be anybody—anybody who is in pain, anybody whom you love, anybody whom you hate, even—it has to be *somebody*, right? It can even be you or your idea of you that's in pain. Whomever we choose, we make it specific rather than abstract. We bring that person to mind, and on the inbreath we take in any of their pain, discomfort, frustration, illness, or negative qualities that they may have. Then we send out to that person everything that is positive—our health, our goodness, our competency if they're incompetent, our cheerfulness if they're sad. Then we proceed with the inbreath again.

After we've been practicing that for a while, we move on to the **fourth** stage, which is to open it further. We extend the practice to others, expanding it as far as we can. If we begin with our mother, we can extend it to family and friends. Eventually we want to be able to embrace as vast a world as we can. We can think of anyone, anywhere. People in hospitals, people who are suffering because of a tsunami, people who are suffering because of ethnic cleansing in Sudan or elsewhere, people who are suffering from psychological problems, pollution, and the like. We can extend it out to all the animals—in fact, to any type of being—that are hurt and hungry. We send out our goodness to specific persons and then to as many beings as possible; and we take in as much as possible. That's the basic idea. We are still riding with the breath, but we work toward a universal, all-encompassing practice.

Many people find it easy for a second or two, then fall asleep. Or they become paranoid. Or they start thinking about anything but that. In my experience? It is not easy, and that really is okay. If it were easy, I don't think it would have the same power of transformation. So please don't feel bad if you can't pay attention. The nice thing is, anytime we're practicing and we catch ourselves being lost, we simply start again. If you forget or fall asleep or whatever, you wake up and come back. No one's watching but you. You don't practice this to impress anybody else—not even to impress yourself.

Sure enough, there are various barriers to taking things in and sending them out. For example, falling into a blankness is one of our most common ways of dealing with what we find difficult or unpleasant. But the wonderful thing about this practice—and any meditation practice—is that we can begin at any time. There is no special place to begin our practice from except exactly where we are.

It may also be that your mind jumps around, especially if you are not used to this kind of practice. If that is the case, be a little patient and know that stability will develop over time. In fact, tonglen isn't about concentration particularly; it's about being compassionate. However, if you're really having a problem with either agitation or torpor, you can let it go and just practice simple shamatha-vipashyana. If you would like to establish a daily practice, a good framework would be to start with fifteen to twenty minutes of basic sitting meditation, followed by fifteen to twenty minutes of tonglen, followed by another fifteen to twenty minutes of shamatha-vipashyana or formless meditation. This is what Pema Chödrön calls "cushion tonglen." There's also a "tonglen on the spot," which we will discuss later.

Remember, let's all just be simple and human. Let's not make a big deal out of it. Once we receive these instructions, the practice is ours. Then we should use it, but not abuse it. So, rather than trying to become somebody special because we do this, let's just be simple.

TONGLEN (GUIDED MEDITATION)

Begin with basic sitting meditation. During this part, it's preferable to keep your eyes open; when you get to the tonglen part, they can be open or closed, whichever helps you.

Remember your good posture.

Be mindful of your body.

Be mindful of your breath.

Be mindful of your mind.

Stay with basic shamatha-vipashyana meditation for a few minutes.

Now, flash a sense of openness, a sense of boundless giving and of being right here at this moment—just completely open and fresh.

Then start to feel the textures as you breathe in and out. As the breath goes out: goodness, freshness, aliveness go out. On the inbreath, pain, resentfulness, claustrophobia come in. Just feel the textures. Light out. Soot in. Health out. Sickness in. Joy out. Sadness in. Clean, soothing coolness out; hot, disturbed painfulness in.

Now think of someone specific, some individual who might need help, perhaps someone who is frustrated or in pain. It could be your mother, someone who is ill, someone you hate, or even yourself. Breathe out everything that's good and send it to them. Your health and well-being, your goodness, your love just goes out to that person.

On the inbreath, take in all their pain and suffering. Let that darkness and heaviness come in.

Just clearly have that person in your mind. It is direct, simple, vivid. Breathe out the positive, breathe in what's negative.

Don't leave anything out when you take in. Take all of it.

Likewise, don't hold anything back on the outbreath: Send out all that is good, all of it, wholeheartedly.

Continue.

Out: everything good. In: everything negative.

Remain alert and fresh. Occasionally—*right now*—just wake up right on the spot. Your body is awake, alive, with your spine straight. You inhale, you exhale.

If your eyes are closed, open them. If they are open, close them. Give it a try.

If you forgot the person, remember them again. Be with that person or with the dog or the fly and with the texture. Send... receive...

You can just concentrate on one person, or if you like, see if you can open your heart a little more. See if you can extend out and accept more—the pain and discomfort of others. Whether you know them or not doesn't make any difference. It could be someone up the street or in the hospital. Someone who's suffering from a huge earthquake. Someone who's mentally distraught. Or all the people who might be in a state of confusion because they've just died. Take it all—the confusion, the pain, the suffering. Send out love and everything that is strong and good and cheerful.

Just let it ride back and forth on the breath.

Send out to as many beings as you can: the goodness of your life, freshness, vitality, bravery; everything that's sane and enjoyable. Then take as much pain as there is.

Don't hold on to anything. Just let your heart be open. You have your good posture to allow your heart to be open and allow anything to come inside you.

Whatever images that come to mind that might be difficult, just take them in with your breath. And send out positive images on the outbreath. Send them out as far as the expanse of suffering exists. Don't feel you're not good enough to do this. Each of us is good enough to do this. Just take it in and send out all that is good. Don't worry, you do have so much—*so much.* Just offer it wholeheartedly.

Now let all of that go and just do shamatha practice again. Simple mindfulness of body. Simple mindfulness of breath. Simple mindfulness of mind. Or just relax in formless meditation.

Informal or Postmeditation Tonglen

We have just seen the formal practice that involves sending and receiving while sitting in a meditative environment. There's also an informal tonglen, which you could call "postmeditation tonglen." If we ever find ourselves in a situation where someone is in pain, or we encounter a difficult situation, we can try tonglen and see what happens. We could mentally take in whatever negativity arises in the situation or whatever pain there is. For example, if you're with somebody who is extremely ill, someone who is dying or under great emotional stress, you can take in their pain and send out loving-kindness. You run into a beggar in the street and they're really bugging you? Try tonglen right on the spot and see what happens.

Here is the important thing about tonglen, whether you're sitting in formal practice or doing it in a more informal, in-the-world way: Don't expect any result. Whatever your idea of helping somebody is, just forget about it. It's not about *me* achieving or causing something. There is a power to tonglen, but it's not about feeling gratified. Whatever it is, we do it, then we let go. We do it again. We let go. We shouldn't fixate on what we've done or what we're doing. There is no need to contrive; we're just being natural. We practice and let go. We practice and let go.

About the Motions to Protect Ourselves

Some people are afraid of catching something bad on the inbreath. We have countless habits that have to do with protecting ourselves, and lojong tackles these very habits. If you realize that they make you tense to the point that they deter you from practicing, it helps to stop regarding your body as flesh. It's rather like empty reeds where the breath comes in and the reeds move inward, and as the breath goes out, so do the reeds. It's just an image, but don't think of the liver, the kidneys, and all the messy, bloody stuff.

That being said, I did hear an interesting story. Once, someone told Kalu Rinpoche, "I've been doing tonglen and I think I'm getting sick." And Kalu Rinpoche, even though he was a serious man, joked back, "Oh! It's starting to work!" Now that I think of it, maybe it was a joke, maybe it wasn't!

Regardless, the idea is: Don't have a body fixation. There's no harm here. There's nothing but goodness. It's not like some kind of reiki. It is also not about *me*. I keep repeating this because it's really not about that at all. Even if it does provide help to someone else, it doesn't necessarily help them physically; there's something else that helps their mind. For example, there is no way, ultimately, to keep anyone from dying. Anybody who is born will die. Sickness is also part of life. But then there is all the trauma, mental pain, fear, and distress that come along with that. The practice mainly helps with that part; any physical side effect is a side effect. The main thing is helping to release the clinging and to assuage the suffering of mind, which is often worse than the physical pain.

Allow me to share a personal story. Once, I was in a particularly excruciating pain from nerve damage. It was so agonizing that the myth of morphine didn't work. You always hear, "If worse comes to worst, they'll give you morphine and everything's going to be all right." Yeah, sure! For ten minutes, it felt great, but then the effects dissipated. So, I started going to a doctor who had an alternative therapy that was covered by insurance. He used a particular anesthetic on the end of a needle that he inserted up my nose—it's all empty back there, so it didn't hurt. The anesthetic goes to the ganglia, nerves, and so forth. It helped a little, physically. But what I found most interesting was that the doctor had an open clinic. You didn't do this by yourself. You were there with other people in pain. It was a strange experience... As horrible as my pain was, compared to the next person, it was nothing! I had this horrible nerve damage, sure, but the next person had cancer, the next one had brain ticks that were painful beyond conception. We were all together in this, with these ridiculous things sticking out of our noses. I started noticing these people that I wouldn't otherwise notice, fixated as I was on my own pain, focused on getting someone to help me.

That is an acute situation. But in lojong, we learn to look at the pain of others. Whatever pain that we ourselves feel now or will feel, we can rest assured that many other beings endure something similar. There's so much pain in this world. However, we don't really notice when everything is hunky-dory, do we? And it is comforting to know that even if we're in pain ourselves, we can be of help to others. Some say that tonglen is actually good for our health, but that is not really the point. We just do it, without thinking of our own well-being.

In this personal medical example, I remember being there, debilitated by pain. I tried tonglen instead of suicide! Those are the two choices, right? It's a grim joke, but when you are in tremendous physical pain, at some point it gets really tough. I remember going to the doctor and finding out that my body couldn't produce endorphins anymore. There were none left—it was just raw. This can also happen with emotional states and all kinds of situations. But what you can realize when you're in pain yourself is how much you're connected with other beings who are also in pain. You look at people differently. You see them differently. For the most part, we pay extremely little attention to each other, unless we have an ulterior motive. It's pathetic. We pay even less attention to nonhuman sentient beings, unless we're hungry or irritated. The practice of relative bodhicitta is to open up and help create sanity in all this pain.

It is said that we don't experience the pain of the world *fully* until complete enlightenment. The Buddha's first teachings made it clear that life is painful, unsatisfactory; that is *duhkha*. It is a realization that comes from complete enlightenment. But it's good news, not bad news. It is good news because there is in fact a way to deal with it. And part of this is cultivating bodhicitta, learning lojong, and practicing tonglen. We are not just succumbing to pain as the lowest common denominator, quite the contrary. It is wonderful.

It is also important to remember that tonglen is not just about pain. It is about pleasure, too. It's about everything. There is no need to get fixated on one side, and we don't exclusively practice when we notice pain. If pleasure arises, we give it out to others; we don't just absorb it into ourselves.

Tonglen and Social Issues

The other day, my partner Amy reminded me of something Trungpa Rinpoche mentioned in his mind-training teachings. He said that we can be happy about the opportunity we have to take it all in. For example, with all the pollution there is in the world, we can be grateful—as practitioners—to be able to breathe that in, as counterintuitive as this may sound. We can take on all the blackness and pollution into ourselves and breathe out clean air and light. In fact, that's the only way, because if we don't take it in, we see it as someone else's problem.

I think that Trungpa Rinpoche was talking about the fact that the larger problems of this world relate to the same problems of me-ness, institutionalized. The institutions have the same problems that we have. They do, of course. They're *us*, even though we like to say, "Oh no, that is so not me!" But they are us. It's *our* institutionalized, funny idea that everything is supposed to protect me, and forget about the other people. In this respect, tonglen is also wonderful socially. But there's no social tonglen unless there are individuals practicing it. One comes from the other; the social habit comes from the individual habit. If we change the individual habit, there is some possibility of changing the social habit, but not by making a nuisance of ourselves and being proselytizing and self-righteous—we would then be right back to the same old game.

Additional Bits of Advice on Tonglen

Over the years, friends and Dharma students have raised many interesting questions, and I would like to briefly address some of them before we move on to the next selection of slogans.

Spacing Out

We tend to do tonglen for a few minutes and then space out. That's because it's not easy to do, not easy to pay attention. But we can always come back. Tonglen practice has an element of mindfulness. The receiving and sending is in itself the object of mindfulness. If it helps, consider how the "three mindfulnesses" of basic sitting meditation still apply. For starters, we still have our good posture. Then the mindfulness of breath has to do with riding on the breath as we bring in those pains and sorrows from those who suffer and as we offer all the goodness that comes from within our being. The mindfulness of mind is being there with it. We're not labeling anything. We're not making any value judgments. We're just there.

Becoming Overly Emotional During Tonglen

If this happens to you, just be with it, without adding too much commentary. Emotions coming our way is not a problem. We're human. Let's just be simple about this. Also, remember the sandwich approach: We begin and end with shamatha-vipashyana. When we go back to basic meditation, we drop the practice and don't look back. Whatever arises in our mind is fine; it is just thinking. We don't own whatever happened during tonglen. We don't own what we have sent out to others. We simply let that pass. That is extremely important. We begin from that sense of emptiness, then we have the main practice, which is quite active, and then we let it go back into emptiness.

The Space in Between

A perceptive person wondered about the space between the taking in and the sending out. This is the openness of what we call "the gap," and that's the place of actual awakened mind. It doesn't need to be messed with. It just is.

Having a Hard Time Applying Tonglen to Ourselves

For some people, tonglen is hardest to do on themselves. I would say that even though one of the other slogans says, "Begin the practice of taking with yourself," there is no reason to fixate too much on ourselves. If it poses problems, just deepen the practice with others; you'll be taken care of in the process. It is also one of the reasons why we should have at least some training in basic sitting meditation before learning tonglen. It helps us to become friends with ourselves.

The Heaviness of Transitioning Back to Shamatha

For some, moving away from tonglen and back to shamatha is uneasy. A person who attended a talk described this as feeling on a high tide during tonglen, then finding the transition abrupt, heavy.

To begin the practice of tonglen—and to continue it—is not the easiest thing in the world. It is a difficult and rather advanced practice. Usually we practice calm abiding beforehand, until our mind is settled. The exact sequence of it all, and how much time we spend on each part, will change over time, and so will our experience of it. But the sense of that tide comes with the territory. There's a visceral, textural quality to tonglen that is unlike shamatha-vipashyana, and we may occasionally experience some heaviness after the tonglen part of our session. But it's not a problem. That heaviness, we call it "thinking." It's just like any other thought or feeling that we have in our practice.

Reducing the Effect of *Me*

Someone once told me, "During tonglen, I breathe in all this stuff about, say, detention centers or the bad behavior people may have in our society; and when I breathe out, I try to send out goodness and kindness. The thing is, it's still *me* that is doing the exercise. Is there any way I can reduce the effect of *me*?"

The practice is not about disappearing into some kind of nihilistic void. But I understand where the question is coming from. My friend wanted to make sure she didn't make the practice about herself, which would be anathema to lojong. Practicing Dharma, after all, is about reducing ego and its power. In short, my answer is this: If we practice shamatha-vipashyana, engender absolute and relative bodhicitta, and exchange ourselves for others, the effect of this self-centered *me* will indeed diminish. And something much better than *me* will come out of it. There is no question about this.

The Fear of Not Having Enough to Share

Just like you should not worry about catching anything on the inbreath, never worry about not having enough on the outbreath. You have an infinite storehouse of goodness. Of course, sometimes you might feel exhausted by this practice. It's okay. But the transformative power that exists within compassion is quite extraordinary.

6

Ceaseless Opportunities

The Seven Points of Mind Training, Part 2

Let us continue our exploration of lojong by examining another set of aphorisms taken from *The Seven Points of Mind Training*. In fact, one of the slogans of the second point encourages us to do so:

» In all activities, train with slogans.

Training in the slogans is a wonderful technique. With familiarity you find that these slogans arise all the time. You could also trick yourself with little cards, design a screensaver, put some in your wallet, use lipstick on the bathroom mirror if you feel so inspired—whatever gimmick you want, just to remind you.

As mentioned, lojong is basically a habit reverser. The idea here is to catch the first thought, which reverses our ordinary habit of mind. We just catch it *right there* and remember and apply any slogan that fits the bill.

Here is a verse connected to the lojong slogans that really helps, even though it is absolutely not how we're used to dealing with the world:

> May I receive all evils and pains,
> And may all virtues go to others.

"Everything that is unpleasant is mine; everything that is pleasant is yours—you're welcome." Let's just begin to think that way. Now that's a counterintuitive proposition if I ever heard one! However, let us be clear: We're not talking about going out in the middle of the street and getting run over. We're also not talking about becoming some kind of martyr. We are talking about dealing with our own mind. We are so deep in our "me, myself, and I" view that it takes a big shift to mess with it. So, we do something radical and make a 180-degree turn: "May I accept all evils and share all virtues." Wherever you go in your life, try to think that way. It's all right. It works. It's not what it seems, but it's not self-help either, I'll tell you. It's about changing our habitual point of view. It's really that simple.

POINT 3: TRANSFORMING BAD CIRCUMSTANCES INTO THE PATH OF ENLIGHTENMENT

The third point of the seven points of mind training is the transformation of bad circumstances into the path of awakening. It shows us how to carry on with absolute and relative bodhicitta and make it our life path. Whatever happens, no matter how we label it—good or bad, happy or sad—doesn't make any difference; it could and should be included as part of our spiritual journey. In fact, our spiritual journey is nothing different from our life. This is all about not having two realities, with our ordinary self and reality on one side, and our spiritual practice or reality on the other. It's not separating our life into outer and inner, or breaking it into any other dichotomy.

The third point is connected with the perfection of patience. This involves being patient with ourselves as well as with others. Wakefulness simply isn't possible if we're impatient. I'm a very impatient person. I'm willing to react impulsively—as instantaneously as many of the rest of you are. But lojong is changing that.

When we talk about "perfections," such as the perfection of patience, we are referring to the qualities of a bodhisattva. This is what a bodhisattva works on, so to speak. It doesn't mean that it's perfect right from the beginning. It is something we practice.

The obstacle to patience is aggression. It is a common reaction: When somehow we feel that *me* is attacked, me-ness turns to meanness. When that happens, it is preferable to stay still. Being patient is being dignified. The way of the bodhisattva truly is a dignified way. A person who has dignity is willing to look at what comes their way. We don't have to be so easily disturbed by the world's aggression. There is always bad news. In fact, in our society, "news" means "bad." The very idea of "good news" is considered unnewsworthy, isn't it? Therefore there is a constant flux of bad news, and there will always be bad news. It is up to us how we react to that. There is so much unfairness in this world, so much that is wrong. It doesn't do any good for us to get aggressive about it because it's just adding to the mess.

Again, these particular practices, slogans, and ways of dealing with situations offer a reversal of our normal logic, a reversal of the bad habits that we have been creating since beginningless time and that we dwell in—habits that we even perversely end up taking pleasure in! Now, by some good stroke of fortune, we have the opportunity to change that and to actually make this life worthwhile. For instance, aggression can change into true patience, which is much more powerful than aggression.

» When the world is filled with evil, transform all mishaps into the path of bodhi.

One little footnote to this slogan: It's "When the world is full of evil or *good*." The world also includes goodness; it just happens that evil is more difficult to deal with.

Lojong encourages us not to blame society, politics, the economy, our environment, and the like, for all of our problems. Of course, some things are plainly wrong. But we can't just angrily blame our problems on outer circumstances and leave it at that.

This is certainly not easy to accept, but at some point, we must reverse our karma and our bad habits. We want to blame our parents—that's very fashionable this last century. We want to blame our so-called friends or so-called former friends. Nowadays people even want to blame their teachers: If they're Buddhists, they want to blame their Buddhist teachers; if they're Hindus, they want to blame their Hindu teachers. Everyone wants to blame everybody for all their ridiculous problems and all their serious problems, too. This doesn't do anyone any good. There's no valuable result from finger-pointing. Again, this is not about being stupid. We are not, in any way, condoning abuse or saying that criminals shouldn't be held responsible for their actions. We are talking about our daily life and how we can show up and start to make a positive change in our subjective view and experience.

Actual wakefulness results from the practice of meditation—calmness and insight—and the twofold bodhicitta. The latter includes absolute bodhicitta, which is the larger, nonreferential sense of compassion and giving, and relative bodhicitta, which involves specific ways of putting compassion into action. That's where wakefulness comes from; it doesn't come from blaming others, nor from trying to fix outer conditions.

In this world, obstacles of all kinds—to our practice and to our life—will always occur. It could be illness, the passing of someone close to us, a lawsuit, food poisoning, an auto accident... There is no perfect, fully Jell-O-ized state where everything is smooth and delightfully bouncy and we're floating forever in the tangerine sweetness. Let's face it, people: There isn't enough Jell-O in the world for that. Obstacles will always arise. That's just the samsaric predicament, a fact of our existence as sentient beings. But we can do something about it.

We can take any mishaps or obstacles that come our way and transform them into the path of wakefulness by accepting them into our life, into our being, rather than rejecting them and blaming others. Anything, no matter how wonderful or horrific, can benefit our wakefulness and our ability to be compassionate to ourselves and others. We always have that opportunity.

One thing that Trungpa Rinpoche always emphasized was for us not to have what he called a poverty mentality. Of course, many of us were hippieish when we first met him in the late 1960s and early 1970s. Regardless, he wasn't particularly talking about money. He was talking about a feeling of not being worthy, not having what it takes to become a dignified person, not having the right stuff to develop bodhicitta and tread the bodhisattva path.

The wonderful thing about being human is that there is an amazing richness that comes with this precious human birth. It is true, no matter what the circumstance is. We could be born in a nomadic tent, in a state-of-the-art hospital, or in a refugee camp; with a perfect body or with a heart murmur or some birth defect; with a genetic predisposition to diabetes or cancer, or whatever the case may be. It doesn't make any difference: There is an unbelievably rich storehouse of goodness that comes with all that other stuff. It's part and parcel of having a human life.

That richness is always available to us. It applies even to the most wretched monsters in this world, and you will agree that there are many wretched monsters—we could name a few famous ones, a few infamous ones, and perhaps a few not-so-famous ones in our own lives. And I suppose some people could name us as one of those! Regardless, buddha-nature is everyone's birthright. We all have that noble awakened heart—at the very least as a seed. It has to be nurtured so it can blossom, but it's undeniably there. So, there's no need to be poverty-stricken, ever.

Through lojong we can build up confidence and joy in this richness. This comes from the reversal of havoc-wreaking habits, and for that, patience is one of our greatest allies.

As we become familiar with tonglen, we come to see that regardless of how difficult our physical situation is, regardless of how broke or sick we are, there is always the opportunity to give. You may have met people like that, either your parents or someone else: No matter how much pain they were in, they were willing to give you something. People like this actually exist, and they are people just like you and me. We can be like that, and it is worthwhile. Our love and compassion can extend beyond a few friends and family members to include all beings. Not being poverty-stricken has nothing to do with how much money we have in the bank. Sometimes our karma is such that we have a lot of money. Sometimes we are unbelievably broke and in debt. Other times it's just all right. Some people have one extreme or the other, with not much variation. Despite all that, even if we only have one slice of bread, we can always give something, whether it's something material, a way to alleviate someone's fear, or the gift of Dharma, which is the best. There's always something we can give, no matter how desperate our own situation is.

» Drive all blames into one.

This is a tricky one, but it is crucially important.

This slogan implies that *ultimately* our problems are not other people's fault. Of course, none of this is about being stupid or easily exploited. It is an attitude of real intelligence, while stupidity is always blaming the other, as if the other were separate from ourselves.

It all comes under the general category of friendliness toward ourselves and compassion toward others—friendliness and compassion being at the heart of the bodhisattva path and what it means to be a Buddhist. Understood correctly, driving the blame into ourselves is a way of loving ourselves. This sounds paradoxical, but the anger that comes from lashing out only hurts us. If we can accept whatever comes to us, we can begin to ease up.

This world would be so much more harmonious if everyone didn't try to blame someone else for their problems. We should acknowledge problems, sure, but then we should do what we can to help solve them. Otherwise who will? Rather than a blaming process, it's about owning the situation and using our intelligence in doing so.

Sometimes there are extraordinary and extreme situations where someone else should be held accountable. Most of the time, however, we are not in the room with Hitler. Yet we are in the room with the polluters—we are the polluters. We are in the room with the aggressive—we are the aggressive. We are in the room with the greedy—we are the greedy. This is a way of changing our point of view. Now, what effect does this have on society? We don't know. It's not about being calculating toward society. But there is the possibility to change things without it being about *me*, and that really is the point.

Often when people get involved in politics, they forget why they're doing it because they get so involved in *them* being involved. The same thing can happen with charitable situations, where you may start to fixate on "I'm being helpful." You have to get yourself out of the way. We follow this training so that we can actually be helpful rather than create more confusion and chaos by adding another *me* to the mix. We are so caught up in this funny self-preservation of something that can't be preserved. It was born, it lives, it will die. But really, it's so much better to open our lives rather than to close them.

A friend confided that she was struggling with this slogan. She asked me how to avoid the dichotomy of blaming others and then thinking, "I'm not supposed to blame them, so it must be my fault." Say, "My children are fighting, it must be *my* fault."

I kindly suggested that she stay there for a while and see what happens.

She is not the only one who has a problem with this. This is extremely difficult. There's no way to just happily dive into it eyes closed. We need to investigate a little.

Who is this self we're driving all blames into? If we look closely, this self is a construction that we have made. Not only that, this construction changes. Let's say your name is Alex. How many Alexes are there? Is the Alex of today the same one as the Alex of yesterday? *Sort of*, right? But not really. However, when we're talking about driving all blames into one, it's whatever there is at that moment. It's not about the Alex that people see.

If you find this confusing, you can look at it from another angle. Say this person is badgering you right at this moment. You could consider that you have put yourself in this situation or that something in you wants to be badgered. This is a thorny subject that can be easily misunderstood, so let's take our time to explore the actual meaning. Every teaching and practice has a context. Here we are not saying that victims of violence, abuse, or catastrophe were somehow "asking for it." That would be horribly uncompassionate. We're saying that we have a responsibility in how we react to outer circumstances. Let's say we go to work and find ourselves constantly disgruntled. We then lack insight and believe that the very source of our irritation is external—that bad driver on the road, that stupid coworker, that darned Xerox machine. But the main factor in our experience of suffering is our own state of mind; the main troublemakers are our own habits of perception. Our deluded ego—our sense of a solid self along with its defense mechanisms—acts as a target or a problem magnet.

Yet this idea of a self is but an idea. So, ultimately, from this point of view, there is nothing to be hurt. Pain is pain, yes. But who experiences the pain? That part is questionable. "Drive all blames into one" doesn't really say *into oneself*. It says "into one," because our idea of self is ultimately groundless. Still, it would certainly be better to drive all blames into that so-called self than to drive all blames into our mother or our daughter or anybody else for that matter.

A complementary take is to consider that "the one" here refers to our attachment to self. In other words, this is about clearly identifying the true culprit. There's no problem with a functioning self—having a name, an integrated personality, and so forth. The self *as a solid entity* being just a mental construct, it is empty. The actual culprit is our self-importance and, more fundamentally, our *clinging* to the notion of a fixed identity. That's the one we're to blame. If we release that clinging, our experience of the world is very different.

So, we're not saying, "Oh, everything is *my* fault." It's a very mature approach to things: "I have this life, I have these habits." Adopting that larger perspective gives us an amazing amount of confidence. It is counterintuitive, but there's unbelievable strength that comes from accepting responsibility for our life.

» Be grateful to everyone.

Here is another counterintuitive slogan. Be grateful to everyone—grateful for what, you may ask? For being so irritating and causing us so many problems! By doing so, they are reminding us to wake up. That mosquito? That idiot who almost runs us over? Can we really be grateful to them? Yes, we can.

Admittedly, it is a funny view. If there's no irritation, there's no chance for enlightenment. The way of the bodhisattva is not about being stuck in some dream of ourselves. What others offer us by being who they are and by behaving as they do is the opportunity to wake up. "Thank you, each of you. Thank you for being so wonderfully the way you are." That's the attitude we are looking for. There would be no world, no journey, no enlightenment if we had our perfect little universe of just ourselves. Thankfully life doesn't work that way. There's everybody else, so let us be grateful to them.

This slogan also refers to physical pains and sicknesses. Perhaps we're hoping for the complete absence of aches and pains—no discomfort whatsoever—but where would that lead us? During meditation, we could just sit there perfectly, with no thoughts, no feelings in our body, as the best possible zombies that ever existed. But then, so what? We are more interested in the process of waking up. If there are no aches and pains, there's no mindfulness. There's nothing to be mindful about.

In any case, the traditional view here, if one is following the bodhisattva path, is this: "Profit and victory to everybody, loss and defeat to myself." We're not talking about sports or money but rather our point of view, which we are trying to change. This isn't a guilt trip. The point is not to feel embarrassed about ourselves.

Wishing happiness for others and accepting loss and suffering is one of the most difficult things to do. Our usual way of thinking is that we want to be the winner, and we want everyone else to be the loser. Here we are doing the old switcheroo. There's no reason to be afraid of becoming less of a positive person or anything of the sort. We want to hold on so tight to something that doesn't really exist, and this brings up so much confusion. There is also a modern self-esteem problem. But remember that this lojong attitude comes from strength, not from weakness. It comes from a sense of compassion, not from a sense of being poverty-stricken. We are willing to take failure and defeat because we have compassion for others, not because we are losers. From the point of view of strength, we can *afford* to take failure because we inherently possess infinite riches. We are not at all corroding ourselves.

Thus this slogan and the previous one do not involve any guilt trip. This doesn't come from the Christian tradition of feeling guilty because we've done bad things, or the Jewish tradition of "Oy vey!" There's real dignity in taking responsibility for ourselves. Trungpa Rinpoche uses an interesting analogy: You don't need a lawyer to attain enlightenment. You don't need someone to go to explain your situation with your teacher or with yourself, or with the Buddha or with your idea of some God. You're on your own cognizance here. You don't need any intermediary to explain your special circumstances.

A famous example of this gratitude toward everyone is provided by Atisha, who developed this system of mind training. When he was invited to Tibet, he had heard that the Tibetans were the most wonderful people. Meanwhile, there was one of his students that really bugged him. The guy couldn't do anything right. He'd go to make tea and take forever. When he would finally bring the tea, "Oopsie, sir, I forgot the sugar." He'd go back to fetch the sugar, and by then the tea would get cold. I suppose the cups were also dirty, and Atisha was a neat guy! You get the picture—continuous irritation. All the same, when he went to Tibet, the great master brought this Bengali guy as his attendant because he thought, "Oh, I hear these good people in Tibet love Dharma so much that I won't have any opportunity to train my mind." As the story goes, once he got there, he found out, "I didn't need the servant! I could be grateful to every one of them!"

My Tibetan friends love that joke.

POINT 4: APPLYING THE PRACTICE THROUGHOUT ONE'S WHOLE LIFE

The lojong teachings then tackle the perfection of exertion, or being free from laziness.

If we lack mindfulness, none of this makes any sense. With mindfulness, however, all these practices, including tonglen and the various slogans, begin to come together. In other words, we need to put our mind to it. If we put our mind to something, we're not lazy. Interesting, isn't it? Something positive happens. And it's not about a big struggle; it's just about putting our mind to it.

Procrastinators and speedy people and anyone in between can benefit from mindfulness, and from cultivating attention and diligence. Even the worst of us procrastinators know that some time or another, we must do it. How do we do it? We just do it! There is simply no way to do anything without just doing it. Nothing else works, right? I am being facetious, but there is actually some lightness to the exertion we're talking about. As we procrastinators know, if you try to be too heavy, you can't do anything; but you have to do *something*. This putting our attention out is the beginning of doing something. And it works. Choosing to be mindful of something positive causes positive activity.

Strangely enough, being mindful also makes us happy. There is a joy that comes out of discipline and being able to exert ourselves. When we allow our mind to mix with the Dharma, these teachings, and meditation practice, laziness begins to fade. It is in fact the antidote to laziness and letting our life slip through our fingers.

Exertion, however, isn't one big push. In Spanish we would say *poco a poco*, "little by little." You proceed step by step, knowing that you have to begin with something. But then from that little comes another little, and everything comes from that. If you try to do the whole thing all at once, you're just going to get frustrated and miss the point.

Therefore, please take heart, dear friends, as you study and apply the slogans. It is all extremely worthwhile.

POINT 5: EVALUATING ONE'S TRAINING

Trungpa Rinpoche connects the fifth point of mind training with the paramita of meditation. At this point, we catch what he calls "prajna fever"—the fever of actually beginning to *know* and having confidence in what we know. There's a progression. The usual sense of awareness and mindfulness that we might have had previously begins to open. We can see things, including our own thoughts, with more clarity. There is still a constraining factor, but somehow, at some point, it is almost like a whole new world opens up for us. Yet it is not any place different. There is just a sudden vastness, and that is the blooming of meditation practice. It brings up joy, because all the perceptions widen, but the "nuisance mind" doesn't.[1] In fact, the seventh consciousness starts becoming irrelevant. The nuisance factor goes away, and that is part of what allows everything to open up so much.

As Trungpa Rinpoche says, this fever "protects us from the lethal fangs of wild animals." What are these wild animals? They are the emotions that attack us, the various *kleshas*, as we call them in Sanskrit, which affect us in so many ways: aggressiveness, passion, ignorance, jealousy, pride... The practice of meditation—the ability to hold our seat and be where we are—begins to protect us from the fangs and claws of these metaphorical beasts that come to get us. Naturally, these feral animals are nothing but our own mind. All the same, we have all experienced our mind as something fierce and unworkable at one time or another. Thankfully, prajna fever begins to provide protection against that. *The Seven Points of Mind Training* contains a series of slogans that help us evaluate the degree to which we've made progress in that regard.

» All dharma agrees at one point.

All the teachings of Buddhism have to do with one thing and one thing only: subjugating, or eliminating, the deluded sense of a separate "I" or ego. There is nothing in the teachings of Hinayana, Mahayana, or Vajrayana that doesn't deal with that. The way of evaluating that is very simple. The more ego we have, the heavier we are. The more of a sad sack we are, the more screwed up we are, and the busier our mind is—busy, busy, busy. The less ego, the lighter the load. When ego is fully subjugated, there is no sense of heaviness at all. There's a lightness and even—although there is nothing giddy about it—a unique kind of bliss.

» Of the two witnesses, hold the principal one.

This is an important teaching. The two witnesses are how others view you and how you view yourself. Someone tells you, "You're a wonderful human being." Well, that may be true, but don't just trust the other person! Each one of us knows everything there is to know about ourselves. We really don't have any secrets from ourselves, even though we'd like to compartmentalize and cover things up so that we are blind to them. At some point, we must begin to trust our own point of view.

However, the other notion that goes along with this slogan is this: That view of yours, keep it to yourself. Don't leak out your view of how things are going to other people because then they'll leak *their* view back to you, and you will get confused. It is important to be able to trust yourself about yourself.

Even if our teacher tells us something, it doesn't mean much if we don't believe them. Being very kind, our teacher will normally tell us the truth. However, how we hear it is always subject to our interpretation. Thus, we must be open to hearing—even from our teacher—and we must trust our own point of view. There is one important caveat, however: We're not talking about our neurotic point of view but rather the view that comes from actual meditation practice. We are not relying on the usual idea of *me*, which comes with tons of blind spots.

Years ago, I was giving a talk on these very slogans in Australia, and a participant asked, "Given that we are deluded beings, how can we differentiate between delusion and clear perception?"

This is one of my favorite questions in the world! I used to ask my teacher this in every possible way. And he wasn't being tricky, but the answer was always something along those lines: "You know." At some point in our life and in our spiritual practice, we must take responsibility. The teacher, the guru, whatever we call him or her, isn't just someone "over there." We have our own wisdom mind. When we find that wisdom mind, we know. This is what is alluded to here, and we have to trust that. It exists in every one of us. Every one of us has a wisdom mind. Every one of us has buddha-nature, which can blossom. We cannot always depend on something out there. But that's as elaborate as I can get. If my teacher were here, I would ask again!

» Always maintain only a joyful mind.

Whatever comes our way, it's good. If we know how to practice, everything is fertile ground. Whatever mishap comes our way, it's all right. Other people's mishaps: They're all right, too. We can use them. We take it and apply a joyful mind to it. There's no need to feel guilty about anything, nor to go on some sort of bad ego trip.

Also, in our own life, let's not be surprised by any wretchedness that comes up or any bad feelings that arise in our being. Whatever comes up, we can uplift ourselves from it. Things will happen, there's no question; but through practice, we can transform and uplift—suddenly, right in the moment. If we can't do it at this moment, okay—then we do it suddenly *this* moment, because that other moment already passed. No problem! The point is that it is always possible.

We're able to do something because of compassion, which is extremely powerful. This understanding is also based on the view that buddha-nature exists in each being and is only dormant. By definition, *dormant* means that it can be awakened.

Once, Trungpa Rinpoche was asked how he felt. I think he was quite ill and sitting among a lot of people, and he looked a little odd. He answered, "Cheerful, but strange." This is a very interesting attitude. All kinds of things can affect us and make us feel this way and that way, strange or else, but it is possible to be cheerful throughout whatever it is.

Look at the life stories of various Buddhist teachers, whether they be Milarepa and others from a distant past, or more recent teachers such as Trungpa Rinpoche and Dilgo Khyentse Rinpoche, and whether they be Indian, or Tibetan, or the various Zen masters, or the hundreds and millions of unnamed people who have lived their lives happily . . . We can be like them. They are just like us—except that they turned to a joyful life. We can do the same.

This ability to maintain a joyful mind is one of the ways to evaluate our mind training.

» If you can practice even when distracted, you are well trained.

Practice isn't just for the quiet days when the sun is shining and nothing is threatening us. If we are distracted by pain, emotional upset, or anything else, we can still practice; we can still meditate, and we can still do postmeditation practice. This is truly important.

The question is: How do we get well trained? We practice. It is self-fulfilling, won't you say? Well trained means that you train; well practiced means that you practice. As the slogan says, if you practice even when distracted, then you are well trained. If you've ever learned to ride a horse, you understand. You're riding along, at canter. Then the horse hits a rock and it almost slips, and you almost slip with it. But as soon as the horse slips, it's right back together again. The slipping actually makes it correct itself. In much the same way, we can correct ourselves: If we slip, the slipping allows us to correct ourselves right in the moment, and there we are.

Of course, this is all so ideal—easier said than done. But millions of people have done this. It has been so effective for them. We can do it, too.

POINT 6: THE DISCIPLINES OF MIND TRAINING

The second-to-last point of mind training is related to the perfection of prajna, or the perfection of real intelligence. Prajna is sometimes called "wisdom," but it is akin to a good intellect that allows us to actually see things. It is a sharp intelligence; however, it is more than our usual street smarts or academic smarts. This is the kind of intelligence that transcends usual smartness.

The development of prajna comes with a larger sense of life. Here, too, there is an opening. It's the unfolding of an intelligence that truly allows us to see and feel things in a more profound way, not constrained by our usual modes of thinking. It's almost like a new way of thinking, but strictly speaking, nothing is replaced; it is just widened. With the disciplines of mind training, whatever occurs is governed by this greater intellect. Prajna cuts our habitual neuroses, as well as our habitual techniques to deal with problems and people. This, by the way, includes the things we get mad at ourselves about—it cuts through those as well. Since our usual *I, I, I* is cut, it is much easier to relate to the rest of the world. The sense of *I* has been reduced greatly—not yet to the point of complete enlightenment, but to a large extent nonetheless.

This section contains numerous slogans, many of which speak for themselves. We will simply look at a few of them.

» Work with the greatest defilements first.

If you have a problem with anger, there is no reason to waste your time on learning how to be efficient. Because if you're efficiently angry, it's not going to do you any good at all. Work with the anger first!

Whatever is in the foreground, that's the starting point. We don't have to make anything up. We don't have to go look for anything. We just begin right here with whatever is going on with us.

» Abandon any hope of fruition.

This has been said all along. Lojong isn't exactly a self-help regime, where in the end you live forever.

As Trungpa Rinpoche puts it when he's talking about complete enlightenment, you can't be there for your own funeral. We can't have it both ways! So, better abandon any hope of fruition from our practice. Fruition is real and possible, but expecting it isn't going to do us any good at all.

» Abandon poisonous food.

"Poisonous food" refers to the things that mess with our mind: gossiping, particularly saying bad things about others; putting ourselves down; and all kinds of mental activities that cause us problems. Another example is that some of us have a problem watching television and seeing violent images that affect us. Well, we don't have to do those things. We don't have to take in all kinds of negativity. It's easy enough to stop. We have our own inner gossip, and then there's television gossip and newspaper gossip and movie gossip and so on. We don't have to eat it all just because the poison tastes sweet at first! Of course, we can stay informed, but we can choose healthy food over poisonous food.

» Don't wait in ambush.

We may have this tendency—with friends, family members, or other people—to sit around and wait for them to make a mistake so we can grab them and say, "Look, you idiot!"

Don't do it! Just don't.

» Don't bring things to a painful point.

This is a good one because it refers to another tendency that we have: to let things build up and then blow them up. It causes all kinds of negativity in our being and with others. This is not necessary. Sure enough, a lot of these slogans are common sense. This one almost sounds like, "Grandma said, 'Don't do this' because she's watched what you do and knows that it can cause you pain." I think that Atisha even described this as "Grandmother's instructions."

» Don't act with a twist.

This is about not taking these ideas and making something weird out of them. We could take all these slogans, we could take up meditation practice and collect teachings—and then make some sort of bad meal out of all this and lay it on somebody else. Let's avoid this.

» Don't seek others' pain as the limbs of your own happiness.

In comedy routines, if someone else falls and gets hurt, it's time to laugh. But this is different. We shouldn't make life into slapstick humor, using other people's pain for our jollies.

To be clear, we have no problem with humor. In fact, we can even make light of a lot of this. In a sense, it is important to take our neurotic patterns with a grain of salt, precisely because they control us so intently. These slogans are actually aimed at lightening up these patterns. As serious as Atisha was, and as serious as all these masters were, I am confident that every one of them had a sense of humor. This is not a heavy-handed approach; or if it is heavy-handed, it's heavy-handed with some humor in it. You know, part of what's humorous is how heavy the hand is!

POINT 7: THE GUIDELINES OF MIND TRAINING

The last section of *The Seven Points of Mind Training* contains twenty-two precepts or guidelines that show us how to approach our everyday life. They give us advice on how we can conduct ourselves properly in our relationships and general postmeditation practice. I will just give two related examples that encapsulate the basic idea:

» All activities should be done with one intention.

That intention is to actually be of benefit to others and not to cause pain and suffering.

» Correct all wrongs with one intention.

That one intention is the determination to lessen ego and the willingness to be compassionate.

There are many more of these slogans, which give us little pointers on how to live our life. But let us remember the most important thing...

A very close friend of mine, who was one of the main disciples of Trungpa Rinpoche, was receiving what is called the pith instructions from His Holiness Dilgo Khyentse Rinpoche, a wonderful Nyingma teacher. Khyentse Rinpoche gave him and a group of people these extremely profound teachings. At some point, Khyentse Rinpoche asked my friend to come up near him; he was going to give him the ear-whispered, secret instructions—the most important advice. Khyentse Rinpoche didn't speak English, but he gave these particular instructions in English. Here is what he whispered into his ear: "Be kind to everyone."

That is the most important secret, the most profound and valuable instruction that any of us can receive. "Be kind to everyone," including ourselves. We don't leave anybody out.

This was an informal introduction to lojong. I invite you to study the commentaries, especially since I didn't present all the slogans from *The Seven Points of Mind Training*. In any event, I pray that this is something that you can incorporate into your life. If you don't remember any of it, please remember the secret instruction that was just mentioned. If possible, please practice meditation, please practice tonglen, and see what happens. If we actually put these teachings into practice, there is no question that there will be thousands of buddhas and bodhisattvas on our continent.

PART THREE

WORLDLY WISDOM

So far, we have covered some foundational teachings of Buddhism, such as the importance of basic sitting meditation. We also went through a series of Mahayana practices to train the mind and develop the courage and compassion of a bodhisattva. But pretending to be a bodhisattva, or aspiring to become one, makes little sense if we take spirituality as a way to extricate ourselves from this world. Fully entering the human stream will help us not only put our practice to the test but also deepen it. In fact, it will prove essential if we are to truly communicate with others in a sane and beneficial way.

Regardless of our own situation, we have to recognize that most of our days and nights are spent off the cushion, and that topics such as work, sex, and money occupy a lot of our time and mental space. We might as well get to the bottom of it all. There is a way to work with these aspects of our life that isn't neurotic but fresh, inspiring, and powerful.

The next several chapters are deeply informed by Trungpa Rinpoche's *Work, Sex, Money*, a book that has shaped much of my own thinking on these matters. I follow some of the paths he charted and share a few detours of my own, hoping to continue the dialogue he began.

7
Making Sense Out of Everyday Life

Work. Sex. Money.

This may sound mundane. Troublesome, perhaps. But it is where we live. It all relates to who we are, what we identify with, and what causes us pain and pleasure.

I remember Trungpa Rinpoche warning his students that we have to *know* what we're talking about if we're going to relate with people, especially regarding work, sex, and money. We should not do it unless we feel confident, because these are sensitive topics.

If we tend to feel disdain for these themes, it is worthwhile to ask ourselves, "Why do I bother to consider Buddhism as a path? Why do I bother to learn meditation?" We might believe that it is somehow going to make our life easier or produce some sort of bliss outside of our ordinary, everyday activity. We may make plans for retreats, hoping that they will provide insight and that maybe, if we're lucky, that insight will allow us to extricate ourselves from our ordinary lives. In other words, we believe that being in the world is being in a trap and that we need to find a way out. This is a common approach to spirituality, but I think it's a cop-out.

Even if we fully tread the path of meditative discipline—even if we practice the sutras, the tantras, and the most esoteric and powerful teachings—we still live in this world. There's really no place to go. If we look at the history of great practitioners, many of them—even the ones that went on retreat for years and years—ended up back in the ordinary world, relating with ordinary people, doing ordinary activities. And that's not a bad thing.

There's nothing wrong with wanting to meet our mind in a retreat situation. There's nothing wrong with wanting to experience something beyond the mundane—as long as it's not wishful thinking and as long as it doesn't cut off others. The path of meditation and the various Buddhist practices that go with it are about fully entering into the human stream, into the human potential—not running away from it. If we try to accomplish something that takes us away from this life—something that makes us better than our neighbors, better than our friends, better than our parents or anybody else—we are missing the point.

Many great masters have talked about the relationship between the practitioner and the world and society. The *enlightened* relationship with society and with other people is to view everybody as a buddha—or at least a potential buddha—and to view society as a mandala, that is, a vibrant and sacred place, full of vibrant and sacred beings. However, this is not about cultivating a naïve attitude. Looking at things in a sacred way means that we're able to see things clearly. And "clearly" means that we see the vicissitudes of people's pain, anger, desires, and all the various foibles that beings have, because we have these in common. Society and what goes on in society aren't separate from us. They are reflections—a mirror.

We're used to separating ourselves from what we observe and from what we relate with. Entering the stream of enlightened mind means changing our view and seeing the sacred in everything, or at least the potential of the sacred in everything. It also involves understanding what we do and how we influence our world. But it's not just about ourselves. We're used to that, already: this constant reference to me, mine, my family, my little groups, my tribe, my country... We have this habit of always referring to some central operating headquarters that is one up from everything else—and sometimes it's so upped that it views itself as downtrodden. But one up or one down, it's still self-referential.

How do we see the world as sacred? Why would we even want to do that? Do we have to make something up? If we do, then it's fake; and so much of what we do is fake—just filling time. We fill time by having a job and fulfilling it. We fill time by thinking about sex—that is, mainly *thinking* about it, because doing it usually doesn't take all that much time! This is not a joke: Take into consideration the time we spend thinking about it and planning it and all the various things that go along with it, complaining about it, having the relationship, texting, talking on the telephone late at night, children, arguing about everything or nothing... Not much of it has anything to do with the physical act itself, but sex does take an amazing amount of energy. Likewise, our work takes an incredible amount of time and energy. Same for money: thinking about money, earning money, spending money, counting money, counting lack of money, never having enough money, and so forth. We have to admit, these topics totally fill our life.

But in and of themselves, there's nothing wrong with work, sex, and money. It's our relationship to them—our desires, our attachment—that creates so many problems for ourselves and society as a whole.

There is a way to work with these aspects of our life that isn't neurotic; that isn't just compulsive or time-filling. It is truly up to us. Whether we're eighteen years old, thirty years old, fifty years old, seventy-two years old—we haven't just been wasting and filling time in this one life; it is said in the Buddhist teachings that we have been doing this since beginningless time. If we fritter away our lives doing busywork, having busy relationships, worrying about money, and so forth, all we get is more of *that*. Really: The net result is precisely more of *that*.

But there is a way to help create an enlightened society. The starting point is mindfulness, which begins with mindfulness of small, simple things. We pay attention to how we act and to how our mind reacts. We become aware of the little waves that occur if we do one thing or another, or if we do nothing. As we develop mindfulness-awareness, it's extraordinary if we can see others as friends, as fellow travelers—in spite of themselves and in spite of us.

If we want to traverse a real, genuine spiritual path, that path must tie into this world and have an effect on this world. It can't just be some little private heaven that we're trying to establish for ourselves. All too often there's this misunderstanding of why we take on a spiritual pursuit.

Now, we have choices. We can become a monk or a nun and enter a society of monks and nuns. In the West, this is rather impractical, because who is going to support that society of monks and nuns? We may have romantic ideas about wearing a robe and dedicating our life to practice. However, if we look at what most monks and nuns actually do, we find that they cook and clean and administer and think about sex and have to relate with supporting the community, and so forth. The life of a nun or monk isn't some idealized existence. It's a subsociety of society at large, with the aspiration to be of benefit to all of society. It is a choice we can make, and it is absolutely beautiful. If you feel inspired and can find a way to do it, more power to you! But from my observation, it is fairly impractical in a Western context because there aren't enough people who believe that supporting monks and nuns is a worthwhile way to spend money (while in Buddhist countries, there's the notion that one gains merit by supporting a monastic community).

There is also the possibility of becoming a non-monastic yogi. A "yogi" is someone who is on the path of achieving union. Union with what, you may ask? Well, I'll have to answer that by referring to a corny joke. His Holiness the Dalai Lama is in New York; he goes up to a hot dog stand and asks, "Make me one with everything!"

Our approach as practitioners, in this context, is that we don't have to make a big deal out of ourselves. We don't have to change our outfit. No need to make any big announcement about our intention. We can just quietly practice the teachings. And while practicing the teachings, we can see clearly and be in harmony with our environment, instead of *opposed* to it. That's the best. You may be doing the most esoteric practices ever developed by humankind, methods perfected in the sacred caves of Tibet, Bhutan, Nepal, China, Japan, or wherever; but your own cave can be your little condo on whatever street you happen to live on. It works just as well. And you can still relate to the grocer and the barista on the corner. You don't have to run away.

Sometimes retreat is a good thing. It provides a concentrated immersion so that we can learn meditation techniques. There is a problem with being a retreat junkie, however: We learn and immerse ourselves, then we come out and three days later it's like nothing happened. Really: You forget everything. Some people are lucky—it lasts a week. Then there are the really lucky ones for whom it lasts ten days. After which, habits reassert themselves and realizations are little jokes, forgotten. True retreat is to be a practitioner in this life. It is establishing a meditation practice that is regular, ordinary. Not ordinary in the sense that you aren't doing a lot of esoteric things; as I said, you could very well be doing the most esoteric practices. But you can do them at home. That's okay. There's even a name for that: *householder yogi*. It's the complete catastrophe! You could have a partner, kids, a job, all kinds of responsibilities, and still be a true practitioner.

I find it fascinating that in my life experience with my Buddhist teachers, there is one thing that both of them agreed on continuously, and it is that there were two really good things to do: (1) practice meditation, and (2) work hard. And there's absolutely no contradiction. But it is up to us (a) to not just pretend we're practicing, and (b) to not just pretend we're working! It's a full situation.

Now, how much are we supposed to work? This is connected to the money issue. If we're going to be a practitioner-yogi, we have to make enough so that we have time to practice. Working all the time is ridiculous because then we're working so we can feed ourselves to work. That's a no-go, except occasionally, or at a particular stage of our life when circumstances demand it and we have to adapt. But truth be told, many of us find ourselves in a very different situation—that is, a situation where we do have *some* control. This applies whether we're young or old, by the way. It's about how we use our energies. Even though we may work hard, if we work hard and there's mindfulness in our work, we don't get as tired. It's an interesting phenomenon. In fact, sometimes the easiest way to practice is to have a very full schedule, because our life is then schedulable. Those who find themselves with no work or very little work often have a hard time practicing because there's no schedule. We may think, "Oh, if I just had more time, I'd be a really good practitioner." That is a myth. It depends on how we approach our life and what habits we choose to cultivate.

PROPER LIVELIHOOD

To have a "right livelihood" is one of the instructions that the Buddha gave on how to untie the knot of samsara. Most people think it means having a job where you don't cause any harm, a beneficial job. But "livelihood," I believe, doesn't just have to do with our job. It's about how we live. In this sense, right livelihood is the key to all of this. As the following story shows, it involves rejoicing in what we have.

Many of my friends came from Tibet. They were refugees. In their Tibetan context, they were great teachers, part of the monastic system, with important roles and considerable responsibilities. Yet somehow they ended up in India where they were just refugees. In the early days of the diaspora, if you were a Tibetan refugee, the main jobs you would get were in road building, because no one likes to bang rocks and move them around.

Many of those people made their way to the West. One particular person, who is one of the most cheerful people I've ever met in my life, was told by his teacher that he should go to America and establish a Dharma center. He ended up in Whitehorse, Yukon—a cold and remote place.

Once my friend got to Whitehorse, he had to support himself, and there was only one job he could get: packing salmon into cans. From an ordinary Buddhist point of view, this is the worst possible thing you can do. Not because it smells but because you're dealing with these beings that have been killed, and you're slicing them and dicing them and sticking them into narrow metal containers... And he did this for several years—very happily. Twelve hours a day! And on the weekends, he was teaching people how to practice meditation. He would pay for the place for them to learn meditation. But there was this ridiculous situation where people didn't like to come to the classes all that much because it smelled so fishy!

Why am I telling this story? Because sometimes we find ourselves in ridiculous situations. In this person's case, even though being involved in the dead-animal business would be considered, from an orthodox point of view, wrong livelihood, here it was a right livelihood. In fact, it was absolutely choiceless. He had faith in his teacher, his teacher sent him to Whitehorse, and there was only one job available in town. That's it.

Life gets so much easier when we see the humor in it. We don't have to be serious all the time when discussing the issues of work, sex, and money. They deal with the basic functions of our life, which have to do with our desires and their results, and what we want to acquire and what we want to push away. That's where we live. Most of the things we want or want to avoid we can associate with either work, sex, or money, in one way or another. They are so basic in life, we might as well befriend them.

Thus one of the premises of this whole section of the book is this: Let's look at desire. Let's look at what we want and the results of what we want. Let's look at what we don't want and the results of pushing things away. It's more than just interesting; it is enlightening to look clearly at those topics. They tend to be the issues that move our world or rock our world or sometimes dull our world.

AWARENESS OF OUR PLACE IN SOCIETY

In our work situation, often we're not really attached to the money per se. It may be that we're attached to a job that is boring, unchallenging. Regardless of how much we may complain, we often develop an attachment to how boring our job is! We must ask ourselves, "Is this right livelihood?"

I'm beginning with this situation because in this world, there is no free ride. Whether we're a monk, nun, yogi, whatever, somehow there's a balance of payment based on labor, effort, and interdependence. I know that in modern times we like to borrow money—whole countries do it—and pretend that nobody has to work, except the people in China! We believe it is all going to come out in the wash. That's wishful thinking. If we're living in *this* society, American society, Australian society, or whatever the case may be, we must make choices that have to do with living in this world. It all comes down to having our eyes open and awareness of what we do, awareness of where we live, awareness of other people, and awareness of political issues.

Strangely, my Buddhist teachers and people such as Traleg Kyabgon Rinpoche were astutely aware of politics and very interested in it. There were two reasons for that: (a) It makes for great entertainment, because it's so funny; and (b) it affects our society. As a side note, I also find it interesting that most Asian Buddhist teachers tend to be more conservative than their Western students. The latter are often quite progressive in their social values and political choices. The teachers—although some of them are shy to talk about it—tend to be quite conservative in their views and interests. For example, they can't understand how someone could be anti–one's own country; it's a mystery to them. They can't understand how, if you're a Buddhist practitioner, you can equate meditation with left-wing liberalism. They look at us and wonder what this is all about. Maybe we should take a closer look, too. Not that we have to change our politics or anything; I simply find it interesting that there's this dichotomy between traditional Buddhist teachers and their students in the West. I think this is partly because those who come from the Tibetan tradition, and some of the other Eastern traditions, have seen the havoc that socialism wreaks on societies—not the ideal of socialism but the distorted political socialism.

In any case, it is up to us to have an awareness of our place in society and to have a relationship with society. What's the use of practicing if our practice doesn't go out? Is meditation and Buddhism just a self-help course? Is spirituality just some pop psychology to make us feel good about ourselves? We have to ask ourselves those questions. Are we just trying to feel better? This is not a rhetorical question. Why are we even reading this book? What draws us to things spiritual?

OTHERS ARE NOT UNLIKE OURSELVES

Genuine spirituality has to do with opening. Part of that has to do with opening to other beings, other people, and society as a whole. It's not about closing and disappearing from it. (Although, again, retreat is sometimes advisable.)

The sign of a good community is that it has engagement as part of its mission, at least at the neighborhood level. It doesn't have to be some big cause.

It's about not being foreign, even though there may be foreign elements inside it. In other words, it's all about good-neighbor policy. Not viewing others as the enemy—even if they might view you as the enemy, which is a whole different thing. The Buddhist approach, when it comes to relating with the world, is nonproselytizing. We're not trying to convince anybody of anything, not even ourselves. Often, we proselytize to ourselves: We try to convince ourselves about how good things are going to be. For example, we may think, "If only I could get the transmission for this and that practice, and if I really do it right, I'll be somebody," or "I'm going to go on a three-year retreat, and when I come back I get to be called *lama*!"

Trungpa Rinpoche described this as *spiritual materialism*. If we try to materialize spirituality or use it to solidify our sense of self, we're making a big mistake and missing the point altogether. This includes all sorts of variations on trying to gain advantage over others. "I'm more aware, I use eco paper bags. In fact I don't even use paper bags anymore. I have my little canvas bag, and I take it with me wherever I go, and I'm living the enlightened life, looking down on all the people with the plastic and paper bags that I used to carry around like crazy. I look down on them because they're not as enlightened as I am or as eco-conscious as I am." I'm not saying that there's anything good about plastic! But there's nothing good about separating ourselves from the rest of humanity.

The right way to relate with people is to look at them, see ourselves in them, and then view them as spiritual friends. Even if they're jerks! Even if they're insane. Even if they're egomaniacal. There's something to be learned from everybody. We don't have to like everybody. And we can make fun of people, too, but not just to be mean. We simply must remember that, at a most fundamental level, whatever we see is not unlike ourselves.

We can make a further and further solid me. But real spirituality is never about making anything solid like that. It's about making life fluid. In a sacred society, a mandala, things are fluid. Everyone shares the mind of wakefulness. There may be different roles in the mandala, different roles in society; but the unifying situation is the aspiration for positive, worthwhile, beneficial phenomena. Our relationship with society is, in a simple way, to encourage that. If you are aiming for an enlightened self without an enlightened society, good luck with that! Without that relationship, the mess of this world is just going to go on and on and on.

This isn't a utopic vision. It's a simple practicality. We can view the world as sacred because it is. Most of the problems that happen in the material, social, profane world have to do with the *loss* of the sense of sacredness; with taking things for granted. For example, if we eat meat, we go to the supermarket, and we go to the meat section. There's this neat little plastic package, with the white stuff that collects the red stuff—I guess that's blood, huh? There's no relationship with the fact that a being died and that we're going to eat it, because it's all so neatly packaged.

We've become spoiled. Spoiled about work, spoiled about what we eat, spoiled in so many ways. As a result, we don't have any real relationship with whatever we rely on. If we're eating a being, we should acknowledge the fact that we're eating a being, and we should be thankful for the fact that that being's life is nurturing us. If we're in the hospital with a nurse taking care of us, that's not just because the nurse is being paid; there's something else going on there, too. We can't just take that care for granted. The same is true for our parents. It is amazing what our parents did for us, even if we have many complaints about them. We tend to mainly deal with the complaints (because of Freud, I suppose), but there is more at play.

So much of being mindful and aware has to do with being thankful. It's extraordinary what others have done for us so that we can have the life that we have. It's not all a given. It doesn't have to be like this.

SACREDNESS, APPRECIATION, AND HUMOR

The fact that nothing can be taken for granted is very much linked to sacredness. This planet is sacred; likewise, societies of people are sacred. That sacredness invokes a sense of appreciation. A sense of exaltation, even: Things are wondrous.

It's easy to take everything for granted while this whole life is miraculous. It is all the more extraordinary because of the fact that enlightenment is possible. It is latent in each being. This is what makes everything sacred. If I look at this group of beings—my readers—as a mandala, I know that each person has buddha-nature, which is not only latent but one's *nature*. Each is individually wondrous, with beautiful differences. It's not like some kind of socialist grayness; the possibility of wakefulness is absolutely unique. Likewise, look at the natural world and at the constructs that humans have made—they are extraordinary. Unfortunately, because of jadedness and a lack of mindfulness, we take everything for granted. We can't even see, hear, and feel properly.

The sense of sacredness comes from seeing clearly, hearing clearly, and so forth. That's why meditation practice is so important. Mindfulness practice is crucial because it allows us to see the ordinary magic of this world. This ordinary world that is so incredible! The magic is: reader A is a buddha, reader B is a buddha, reader C is a buddha, and so on—as screwed up as these buddhas may be or as we think they may be. Sometimes things are not as they appear!

There is, indeed, some humor in that. Not only is there some humor in our deluded life but there is some special humor in the very magic of it all. On some level, there's nothing funnier than the way things are. See, there's an ordinary kind of humor that you can drum up, but really, there's nothing more humorous than the human condition and our own attachment to it. How we cling so tightly to empty concepts! It's a drama and a comedy at the same time. Often the humor comes from seeing the preposterousness of the human predicament and our own preposterousness. What makes certain situations so funny is that we can totally identify with them. That's why this special sense of humor is connected to a sweet kind of tenderness.

Sometimes it is even simpler than that. I remember an odd thing that happened when Trungpa Rinpoche and his teacher Khyentse Rinpoche met in America. Trungpa Rinpoche had invited him to come visit. They both sat outside, and Trungpa Rinpoche pointed at a tree and said in English, "This is what they call a tree." They both just cracked up and laughed for minutes. I couldn't see what was so funny! On top of that, Khyentse Rinpoche didn't even speak English very well, so I don't know if he really understood what Trungpa Rinpoche had said. But somehow it was outrageously funny. And it was also funny for those of us who heard it because, you know, "This is what *they* call a tree." I guess you had to be there. But then again, maybe you didn't!

There is so much delightful stuff in this world, and humor is just being open to it. If we're open, we can't help but laugh. It really is that simple.

FLUID VERSUS SOLID

What gets some people attached to work, sex, and money is a desire to make things solid—as opposed to seeing the fluidity of it all—along with a fear that has to do with security versus insecurity.

We tend to consider that our thoughts are concrete. However, one thing we learn through the practice of mindfulness is that there is no continuity of thoughts. Every thought has a beginning, a middle, and an end, and then there's a gap before another thought arises—this we see when we actually look.

The sense of self is exactly the same. It's something we're constantly reconstructing. Our sense of self is the so-called solidity of all the things we think are solid as they relate back to us, but even that is full of holes. It's not solid in the least, but there is the *illusion* of solidity. The only way to find out that it's an illusion is to really look at the nature of our own mind.

The wonderful skillful means of Buddhist practice provide a way to look and see. It provides clues, but we have to find out for ourselves. We're so attached to our idea of ourselves. But it's questionable whether this idea has anything to attach itself to, other than itself! Is that a clue? I'll let you decide. But clues are important.

Life itself is a good teacher, but if we have an actual teacher, a true spiritual friend, that special friend is always poking holes into that sense of solidity. That is part of the job of a spiritual teacher. To be more accurate, they're not really poking holes into any sense of solidity; they're just feeling around the space of what we think is so solid. Really, there are countless skillful means that help us see the actuality of things. One of the ways to look at this notion of skillful means, by the way, is to understand it as the advice of sublime beings. It is their advice on how to live properly based on their experience and realization. Then it is up to us to find out what's workable for us. In this way, skillful means can be regarded as something that's passed on, like a tool or a toolbox from sublime beings, in the Buddhist sense. Many of these tools are meant to help us find out how things truly are. When we do find out, our sense of solidity can drop away. It then reestablishes itself, but it can drop away again.

If we closely look at it, it's reconstructing itself constantly. We can't maintain it; even when we go to sleep at night, at some point that sense of self goes, and then at some point we're awake and the sense of self isn't there, until suddenly we have to pee. Or, you know, "I want a cup of coffee." *I* has to do something, or *I* wants something. There's a desire, or perhaps a "Damn my boyfriend," or a "Damn somebody"—some kind of reaction. Or perhaps there's simply a sort of censoring of what is. "Let's get dull. It's just too much!" We have different ways of creating this idea of ourselves. Yet it's just an idea, and what it relates to is always in flux rather than solid. Seeing and familiarizing ourselves with this is very liberating.

SIMPLY BEING, BEYOND HOPE AND FEAR

Someone asked what happens to those who manage to become familiar with the fact that it's all an illusion. "Where do they live?" is how she phrased her question. Of course I teased her: "What, you want a list of addresses?" She kindly asked again: "How do you function in the world knowing that it is all illusory? How do you live in that space without getting depressed?"

You can live anywhere. People who have an awareness of the truth of nonself are generally sweet and cheerful. There's a choice, you see? What the person who asked the question might have been thinking of was a nihilistic sense of nonself. The problem with our language is that when we say "nonself," it's freakish—as if you were not here at all somehow. But the Buddhist sense of nonself is not nihilistic. It's simpler than that.

In essence, our friend wanted to know, "How do you just be?" But I think a more potent question would be, "How do you just *not* be?" Why do we have to constantly fill up our space, other than out of sheer habit?

"Because it's too intense if you don't," our friend said.

"How do you know?" I asked.

"I've tried. Or at least I think I've tried," she replied.

That was a beautiful, honest answer. I suggested that maybe she needed to try a different way. It is important to develop a way of looking at things properly, which in the Buddhist context is called "right view." It is part of the eightfold path that we alluded to earlier when we discussed "right livelihood." In other words, right view is one of the antidotes to the unsatisfactoriness, pain, and suffering of life. At its most basic level, it's about not being duped by hope and not running away because of fear. For the time being, that roller coaster of hope and fear is what fills most of our life. We constantly dupe ourselves, scare ourselves, and so on and so forth. Awareness practice, and the numberless skillful means presented by the Buddha and by his spiritual sons and daughters who've gone after him, allow us to *not* fool ourselves. Being constantly chasing rainbows just doesn't work. Being afraid of our own shadow doesn't work either. There's another way to live, and it's truly workable.

Part of the practice of meditation is the development of courage and bravery. We can have in the posture of our body, in the posture of our mind, and in the posture of our being the strength to encounter anything—that is, without being taken away by it or controlled by fear. Through the practice of meditation we can meet anything head-on: life, death, and everything in between. We find that we don't have to sugarcoat anything. In fact, that's ultimately what we're looking at: not putting a sugar coating on everything, nor putting a vinegar coating on anything either.

For some people, meditation can bring up all kinds of dross. For others, it brings up giggles and laughter. However, if we learn to maintain a good posture in our body and mind, then come what may, we don't have to accept or reject; we can just be with it.

A PERSONAL EXAMPLE

Someone asked me to give some examples of how my life has changed in relation to these topics.

It's a bit unfair because I'm now of a particular age, and part of the change in my life has to do with the change in my circumstances. But the biggest change in my life, over the decades, is that I like meditation practice. I used to run away from it. Now I only run away from it every once in a while.

Why would we want to run away from it? Because it's so real. The intensity of just being with what's real and genuine ... it's quite something. Of course, it is another matter of habits. Our habit of lifetimes is to fight that rawness, that vividness. That is our personal habit as well as the habit of society. Practicing skillful means is the warrior's way, the brave way. Running away from it is the coward's way. I happen to be a coward. But the way I choose to be brave is that I put myself in situations where I can't be a coward. As a skillful means, that works for me.

That's what is different now: I put myself in situations where there's no escape, and that's good. My children are convinced of the truth of Dharma, so they practice meditation. My wife is convinced of the truth of Dharma, so she practices meditation. I'm also convinced of the truth of Dharma, but I'm lazier than they are. However, since we spend so much time together, we have to do it all together. There's the trap! But then again, I suppose that's the best possible outcome of sex!

In a sense, the biggest change is social. The way to change things and make them worthwhile is by making your own situation worthwhile. If you have a family, you make your family situation worthwhile, and it extends from there. If you can't have an enlightened life in your family, you're not going to have an enlightened life anywhere. It's really an interesting issue. Everything's connected.

I like to say that I do the best I can to relate with my friends and family in this way. That's a lie. *Sometimes* I do the best I can—you know, when I'm not too lazy. There's constant struggle, but I think that the struggle is part of the sacred, because it's that irritation with self that cuts its power. It's like having a thorn, without which I could just snore away. But the inner and outer irritation is a good thing. We're interested in wakefulness, not the big snooze.

8
The Daily Grind

I would like to discuss how we mix the mind of meditation with our ordinary, worldly experience. More specifically, how we put the principles that we learn in the practice of meditation into our work, whatever our situation might be. The whole question of spirituality, wakefulness, mindfulness, and all the positive qualities described by various teachers over the ages isn't about something outside of our ordinary life. We're not trying to create anything that's all that different from our daily life. It just becomes a question of making this very existence worthwhile.

In this regard, the principles of Mahayana Buddhism provide a particularly helpful guide. Those principles begin with the fact that we can view ourselves as having buddha-nature in our heart, and we can view others in the same way.

As we know, buddha-nature is the latent possibility of complete, full-blown enlightenment. However, it is currently like a seed that doesn't do anything if it isn't watered and fertilized. For buddha-nature to blossom, we have to create the right environment, and we have to put some effort into its development.

One might ask, "What's the water, then? What's the fertilizer?" The first step, naturally, is learning how to practice meditation. But it's crucial that the practice of meditation isn't viewed as some sort of project—something that's going to produce a concrete, substantial result. The thing with watering is that it's regular—that's also why it's called *practice*. It's not about that one time.

What helps us develop is being with ourselves, by ourselves, and not being judgmental. The "not being judgmental" part is key. We would like to have some ideal situation, some ideal state of mind, something that's different from the way we are. That's a refrain of the human condition: "I want to be somebody else. You want to be somebody else. There's got to be something better than *this*," whatever our version of *this* is. But through the practice of meditation, if we begin to see that thoughts and emotions aren't the ogres that we've made them out to be, then they cease to have this overwhelming power that we usually grant them.

There are so many conflicting elements in our life. We get advice from our parents, from our teachers, from the health department. We get advice of all sorts, including advertising advice about what's gonna make us happy. We end up with the Rolling Stones—that is to say, "I can't get no satisfaction!"

There is something marvelous about accepting who or what we are because whatever it is, it includes buddha-nature. It is undeniably there, within. The bad news, shall we say, is that we are who we are. The good news is that who we are contains the seed of wakefulness. This combination of good news and bad news is one whole wonderful package.

Our experience is the fertilizer that allows our buddha-nature to develop. We may think that we've had a lot of bad experiences or a lot of good experiences. We have a whole collection of experiences, and we may hold on to some of them and try to forget some others. It's an interesting journey. We even change our memories to adjust one way or another—sometimes to cope or sugarcoat; other times, because we are angry at someone. For example, because of one little thing, the positive experience we've had with someone becomes totally negative—that bastard! We put all kinds of filters on our experiences. But all our experiences do not just amount to a useless pile of crap. There is a use for crap. Manure, dung, whatever we want to call it—we know what we're talking about—can enrich our approach to allowing buddha-nature to blossom.

That's our basic situation. We are whatever this collection of stuff is. But if we practice meditation, we see that whatever it is, it's just that: a collection rather than some kind of monolithic block. In this way, we can make friends with our life. We can relax a little bit into our being. Buddha-nature cannot blossom if we hate ourselves.

What I mean by "ourselves" is not our usual idea of some kind of fixed identity or ego. We're just talking about what we are when we wake up in the morning, what we are when we're sitting here, wherever it is, *right now*. And right now, whenever that is, we can view our stockpile of judgments, emotions, and concepts as just a collection—a transitory collection made of parts with plenty of little gaps.

The practice of meditation helps us cultivate this insight. But like a coin, it has two sides. The other side is meditation in action. In other words, there is meditation—being with ourselves, by ourselves, making friends with ourselves—and then there's the rest of our life, which is being with society, making a living, having relationships . . . or a lack of relationship, as the case may be!

The Mahayana approach to being in the world is quite simple. It is based on buddha-nature and on seeing buddha-nature in others. Thus, for someone who follows the path of the bodhisattva, being in this world is doing things not just for their own benefit but also for the benefit of others. Importantly, this doesn't mean self-referencing that "I am doing something for your benefit." If we are compassionate, generous, or patient because *we* think that it's "our thing," that we're some sort of superior being, then we're getting it all wrong. The Mahayana ideal of benefiting others is about not expecting any return, nor any self-edification of any kind. We can give without having the problem of thinking that we must receive. There's no problem in receiving, but it should not be viewed as a quid pro quo, "a favor for a favor" kind of situation.

If we study the conduct of the Mahayana, we find that the activities of someone who takes the bodhisattva vow involves a waiting process, a waiting game, if you will. We vow to the Buddha and all beings that before entering into complete enlightenment, we will help all others go before us. There is no enlightenment that is separate and individual.

It's not just a trick. But we must understand that the Mahayana ideal also views the self as being empty. So, who is this being vowing? Who are these beings that we vow to bring to enlightenment? We have to put a big question mark on all that, but it doesn't change the activity: We still practice generosity, patience, diligence, and so forth. The basic approach is still that everything is done to benefit all sentient beings.

So, there's the ideal, and then there's our life. The big question: How does the ideal fit into our life? In this chapter I am particularly interested in how it fits into our work situation. In the next chapter, we will talk about sex, and in the one after that, we'll discuss money.

SHOWING UP AND CLEANING UP AFTER OURSELVES

Work is something that isn't frowned upon in any way in the Buddhist teachings. If you look at the early sutras, or suttas, an argument is made that work is indeed positive. For example, when you read descriptions of the Buddha and his disciples, you find out that along with meditating and begging for food, there was constant cleaning. It is one of the most interesting forms of work.

My late teacher Thinley Norbu Rinpoche was a fanatic about cleaning. I would think that along with meditation practice, there's nothing that he loved more than vacuuming rugs, mopping floors, dusting shelves and tchotchkes. It was never possible for anything to be clean enough, because as he pointed out, there is always dust. So, once you have vacuumed, dusted, washed, cleaned... it is time to do it again, because everything has gotten dusty again.

Another thing that I found peculiar and fascinating about his approach was that he often gave detailed instructions on how to defecate properly and on the whole cleanup process after defecation. He would make fun of other Tibetans, even very high lamas, who would come to visit him and who smelled bad because they hadn't showered during a long journey. He would make jokes about dirty bottoms! He was totally outrageous about issues like that. It was quite wonderful because everyone always has to laugh when you talk about poop, right? That's the nature of poop! But one thing I learned from him over the years is that there is always poop, and if you try to pretend that shit doesn't exist at any level, you create problems for yourself. We even have planetary problems concerning what to do with all the shit we produce, all the garbage we generate. We have got to take it into account. This is extremely important.

When we enter the spiritual path, we may think that poop is no longer going to be an issue. But poop is *always* an issue. It's an integral part of life: We can't do without it. As it turns out, I found Thinley Norbu Rinpoche's teachings about poop to be astonishingly profound! They're very direct: We have to clean up after ourselves. That's really what it all refers to. No one is going to do it for us. Even if they do it for us for a little while, it is—as we say in modern parlance—unsustainable. Whatever we do in our life, we have to take into account that it has an effect, a result. Treading the bodhisattva path involves taking responsibility for what we produce. This is paramount.

ORYOKI

In Zen, which is a Mahayana tradition, the *Platform Sutra*, alternatively called the *Sutra of Hui-Neng*, is a formative text. It's a Chinese sutra that relates the enlightenment of Hui-Neng, a monk whose job was woodcutting. He attained enlightenment through chopping and delivering wood and hearing the *Diamond Sutra*, or *Vajracchedika Sutra*, at the same time. There are also similar stories with sweeping and cleaning, instead of woodcutting.

As it turns out, much of Zen training—if you go to a Zen monastery and become a monk or a nun—involves meditation and cleaning.

In addition, the whole process of eating is considered part of one's practice and mindful living. There is the Zen tradition of *oryoki*, which is the way you eat your meal and clean up thereafter, with everyone proceeding likewise. Each monk or nun is issued a set of bowls, a spoon, chopsticks, a cleaning utensil, a napkin, and a larger cloth that holds all the above. When it's mealtime, food is served in the meditation hall. The cooks and the attendants from the kitchen bring in and offer the meal—it is offered to the buddhas, bodhisattvas, and all sentient beings—and then each person is served. There is a ritual opening of the large cloth, placing of the bowls, placing of the chopsticks, placing of the spoon, placing of the cleaning utensil. As the food is coming down the line, you hold each of your bowls, in which rice and whatever else is placed, and you eat mindfully. At the end of the meal, the servers put hot water into your main bowl, which you then clean with the stick. You also use the hot water to wash the smaller bowls. You offer the little gruel that's left to beings, and you drink the cleaning water. Then you fold back your set.

This is a complete paradigm of how to deal with our situation. Everything is taken care of within the confines of that larger cloth. Of course, in the kitchen, someone has to clean the pans and appliances. That's part of it. But each person takes responsibility for their own situation, and then the community takes responsibility for the larger situation, which is the kitchen.

It all comes down to taking notice and bringing awareness to our situation rather than just allowing things to stream out and assume that it's going to be taken care of. That's a key aspect of the Mahayana approach to how to be in the world, how to have an enlightened attitude toward life: noticing, and taking care. You are not expecting others to take care of it. Rather, it truly begins with *your* awareness and *your* taking care of the situation.

OBSTACLES TO WORK

As we have seen, some of the key points, shall we wish to embody wakefulness in the world, are to take responsibility and clean up after ourselves, and generally speaking, to notice and take care. These core principles are straightforward. Yet as simple as they are, obstacles arise, and it is worthwhile to learn about them.

In this whole section I draw heavily from Trungpa Rinpoche's *Work, Sex, Money*. In that book, he deals so directly with these ordinary issues of life, which are the ground, the manure, and the watering process of enlightenment. At some point in the book, he invites us to overcome several obstacles to work, which he describes one by one.[1] These are obstacles to working in the world in an enlightened manner, and the ways to overcome them are based on Mahayana principles.

Frivolity

The first obstacle to overcome is frivolity. That is, as opposed to a sense of humor. Frivolity is taking everything lightly in a happy-go-lucky but slightly cynical way. It creates a half-assed approach to how we work in the world, how we work on a project, what we do at home, and so forth. A frivolous attitude means that we don't have respect for the sacred world.

Part of what makes our society and our world sacred is our relationship to them, our awareness of it. If we view the world as sacred, it in fact is sacred. In other words, it is sacred *through* our awareness. Things become a mess when there's no awareness, no mindfulness. Sacredness, mindfulness, and awareness—it all goes together. As the *Lankavatara Sutra* teaches, as the thing is viewed, so it appears.

Thus we have this relationship with our work and with the world. Things are sacred because we are there with them. In any situation, our true nature can be expressed. From the bodhisattva's point of view, what we do and how we are—wherever we happen to find ourselves in the world—can be the expression of our true nature. Frivolity, on the other hand, is a kind of nervousness that takes us away from our true nature, away from sacredness.

Frivolity is different from a sense of humor, which is wonderful to have. If we actually see the humor in situations, that's confidence, while frivolity precisely comes from a lack of confidence.

One thing we learn as meditators is that we can't put a lid on anything. So, we're not saying we should attempt to put a lid on frivolity but rather that we should notice when we're frivolous. We should take account of the frivolousness; we don't have to suppress it. Look at it; it's something that arises. It's okay, there's no need to be embarrassed. We have our basic dignity, and that basic dignity of wakefulness naturally cuts at the frivolity. Frivolity arises, then awareness comes into that situation, and then there's a double take: We see the fault, and its power vanishes.

There is a paradox in there. If we learn to take things seriously, it leads to the ultimate sense of humor: being able to see that things are as ridiculous as they actually are! That is not frivolity. I have seen sublime beings laughing together, and there was nothing frivolous about them.

All the same, frivolity can transform into something else altogether through sheer awareness. This involves a certain seriousness, but seriousness from this perspective is being with the situation, and not trying to escape. Or at least, if we see that we're trying to escape, actually noticing that we're trying to escape. Often frivolity is the nervousness that comes with being in a situation, feeling insufficient, and thus wanting to get out of it.

We have built so many mechanisms to escape from the intensity of simple awareness. We've created all kinds of complex habits to frazzle ourselves, tire ourselves, fill our minds, fill our time . . . anything so that we don't have to face what is. These days, the word *conspiracy* is loaded, but I will use it anyway: It's a vast conspiracy that we have created for ourselves, and we even have a social contract with everyone else based on these very habits. "I know you're really stressed, but screw it, so am I!" Then we can social-network about how screwed up and stressed out we are. But so much of what we call stress and overwork has to do with the fact that we avoid the ever-present situations. We're so busy trying to avoid our life.

I find it fascinating that many people beatify Steve Jobs, the inventor and cofounder of Apple. Jobs, strangely enough, was interested in Buddhism and practiced Zen. He learned meditation from a genuine master—his teacher, Kōbun Chino Roshi, was a friend of mine—and developed an aesthetic based on Zen. The irony is that he was involved in creating the most time-eating machines ever to be invented. The greatest distractions on earth—so much so that they have changed our perception of time forever! Our lives are so much shorter because of these gadgets that do everything, and do it all the time. It's very hard to maintain mindfulness if we're constantly distracted. This is all connected to frivolity and our creating ways to dull ourselves. There is something frivolous about the 24/7 communication, 24/7 everything. It dulls the mind, and it messes with the sacred. It's up to us to have discipline over these machines. In and of themselves, they are empty—little objects that are full of zeros and ones. The ultimate yin-yang devices, if you will. But they exert a fascination over us, and I know this firsthand, as do most of us.

Interestingly, Thinley Norbu Rinpoche, a very traditional person in many ways, loved these machines—but not for what they were made for. He found ways for his students to use them for dharmic purposes rather than for frivolous distractions. Sure enough, there was the occasional entertainment, which was the news and *The Colbert Report*. But the main use of all these machines for his students was for Dharma—for collecting practice texts and work, storing visual Dharma, audio Dharma, and the like.

It all depends on our habits and what we become addicted to. The empty machine is like a mirror: We stick our projections into the machine, then it gives us feedback. But all it provides us are the zeros and ones of our discursive mind. Our discursiveness comes back in the form of messages, images, and sounds. In this age of materialism, it makes our fickle mind seem even more solid because we believe we can access it objectively.

Speed

The second obstacle to work that Trungpa Rinpoche talks about is speediness, which comes from a sense of insecurity about ourselves. It's a little cover-up. We do things in a speedy way to compensate for our feelings of inadequacy. However, if we're speeding in our work or in our way of dealing with the world, we don't actually have a relationship with the present moment. We don't truly connect with what we're doing. We are going through it by rote.

Very little is accomplished by speed. This is worth emphasizing, as accomplishment is sometimes confused with speed. Accomplishment comes from being *with* something and following it through. Speed is just going through the motions. Let us not mistake the two. Speediness always causes inefficiency because all kinds of mistakes are then made. Speediness doesn't see situations in a whole way, and things are missed.

We create a sense of speed in our life: "I'm very busy, leave me alone. I've got to finish this thing!" Whatever our relationship to speed, speediness is about territoriality and a constant sense of self-reference.

The antidote to speediness is mindfulness. If we actually are *with* something and follow through, it tends to be completed in less time because we make fewer mistakes and lessen confusion. This is true even on a worldly level.

The effect on ourselves and others doesn't have that sense of jaggedness and defensiveness that we might otherwise create.

Daydreams

The third obstacle is described as daydreaming. What we mean by "daydream" here goes like this: If there's something we need or want to do, we think about it and somehow confuse ourselves into almost believing that by thinking about it, it's done. We create this illusion of things being *done*.

As we have seen in the chapter on expressing wakefulness, so much of Mahayana training is about being in the moment and beginning. If we're writing something, it begins with pen to paper and the first dot. If we're cleaning the floor, it begins with picking up the broom and making the first stroke. From the first movement, whatever it might be, then things are accomplished. Overthinking them just creates dullness and confusion. It's extraordinary what can happen if we begin with the first thought, in any situation. Nothing is possible without that first movement. We can think our lives away—it's frighteningly easy to do. But accomplishment comes from being realistic and from relating with the earth instead of just relating with our own mind.

Thinking too much and daydreaming is a little bit like being a pothead—without the pot. It is much better if we can overcome that dullness. The way to do that is by that first thought, then we see what comes from there. Sometimes things don't pan out. No big deal; it just didn't work out. Sometimes we begin and everything works out wonderfully. Regardless, without that earthiness, without the realness of it, there's no accomplishment or genuine mindfulness. *Mindfulness* doesn't mean "stuck in your mind." Mindfulness is about the relationship we have with phenomena, the relationship that we have with the earth, and so forth. The relationship—that's what's important.

Interpersonal Conflicts

Another obstacle to work is interpersonal conflicts. This is an interesting notion, because we could have interpersonal conflicts with our different ideas of ourselves. We can have a fight with nobody there! So here we're talking about that as well as conflicts with others. The minute you're in a situation with a partner at home, or with people at work, or even with yourself, there's going to be more than one view of how things should be done. It's inevitable.

We must learn how to meet different views and inhabit a space where there are conflicting opinions. For example, I live with a truly wonderful person, but we have very different views about neatness and messiness. My wife is the queen of cleaning; when she cleans something, it's absolute perfection. But the way she lives has a bit of a tornado effect, so there is this constant dance, with some areas having to be tidied up again and again. It used to drive me crazy! But I had to learn how to accept things as they are, and she had to learn to live with my flaws and quirks—and she's been remarkably sweet about it.

The way to overcome interpersonal conflicts is to be frank. These issues breed if we try to go around them. It's much more effective to be simple and direct, in a way that respects the situation. If your partner isn't so great with the dishes, you can learn to work with it. Wouldn't it be stupid to leave someone over pots and pans? It is much better to learn how to overcome conflicts and make peace with others. That requires being simple and open to the fact that different people do things in different ways. It really comes down to that. There is no point in trying to shove your view down someone else's throat. There must be a meeting of minds. If you do shove something down someone else's throat, at some point they're going to vomit, and that's not a good situation.

Viewing Problems as Universal

The fifth obstacle to work is something that Trungpa Rinpoche called "viewing problems as universal." In situations where we have some personal issue, and even in a group situation where an issue comes up, we may view it as a universal problem rather than as *our* problem. When we do that, things take on a monumentality and become unworkable.

This is something we do in our mind, whether it's at home, the workplace, or elsewhere. The bodhisattva's way of dealing with problems is to remember that someone has to make the first move. Who is that someone? Not someone *else*! If there's a logjam or if things are frozen, it's up to us to begin to create *some* motion that breaks the logjam, some heat that melts the ice.

So here, "universal" means making it bigger than it is. Basically we have a problem but see it as everybody's problem. We can also use it to conveniently push issues into abstraction or sheer generalization.

Sometimes it can be about planetary issues, such as climate change. We could wonder, "What can anyone do about that?" and withdraw. But often it is simply a situation at home with our partner. For example, our spouse does something that bothers us, and our sole reaction is to say that all men or all women are like that. We are then universalizing the problem instead of taking the situation into account. This can also happen at work when things are really stuck. We frame the issue as everybody's problem, and instead of asking what we can do, we just see it as too big—then it becomes all the more frozen. In that way, this can happen at any level: one person, a couple, a village, a country, the planet...

The bodhisattva's way to overcome this is to remember that it's up to us. No one else is going to do anything. But that in itself is not a problem. The thing is, we can't just wait. And being a bodhisattva, we have to be willing to make mistakes. We have to be willing to be a fool, be made fun of, or whatever. That just comes along with the territory. For there to be any resolution in a frozen situation, it has to begin with us making the first move rather than just being paralyzed or overwhelmed by the drummed-up monumentalness. The first step toward change must be made by somebody, and that somebody is us. We don't act from ego's point of view but with the understanding that if we don't do anything, we could very well wait forever.

Conceptualizing Good and Bad

Here is another obstacle to doing things properly. Once we have begun to study the buddhadharma, the bodhisattva's way of life, and we find ourselves in our ordinary working or domestic situation, it's easy to get hung up on "What would Buddha say?" or "What would my teacher think of this?" or "What's the right way to be patient and compassionate?" Trungpa Rinpoche called this "referring to the Teaching with a capital *T*." Believing that there is only one right way—this way or the highway—causes tremendous self-consciousness and another kind of freezing.

"I'm in this difficult situation," a practitioner might say. "Rats have infested my house, but I'm not supposed to use poison!" There are situations like that at work when we must act but get frozen because we just don't know how: "Am I supposed to be patient now?" When that happens, we're usually stuck in concepts of good and bad.

If we can break the barriers of self-consciousness and let go of this referring to the Teaching as if there's a big *T*, then it is said that we can act like Buddha. We can act in a way that's natural and as situations call for. We can take things into account. We don't always have to frame everything in the context of our own doctrinal interpretations. It's about seeing things clearly, acting in a clear way, and taking responsibility for our actions.

We have to give up some big idea of these big-*T* Teachings and become ordinary. What I find so wonderful about great teachers is how ordinary they are—in some ways—and how they deal with very ordinary situations. It's so extraordinary how ordinary! Things are much more matter-of-fact. They're serious when it's time to be serious, funny when it's time to be funny, and it doesn't require a lot of thinking. They show that we can deal with things as they are called for.

ACKNOWLEDGING THINGS AS THEY ARE

We can be straightforward about situations that arise, without putting any kind of veneer over them. If we can acknowledge things as they are, they become workable. When we have cancer, or when someone else does, we acknowledge it. It doesn't do anybody any good to *not* acknowledge it. That's an extreme situation, but if we live to an older age, the chances of us getting either cancer, diabetes, or heart disease are nearly 100 percent. We always try to play down the fact that we're going to die, and there are many ways to do it, but it doesn't do any good.

Working around situations only takes us so far. It's very rare that avoidance creates a better situation than actually acknowledging things. Yet there's no need to make someone feel bad or to make ourselves feel superior in any way. We can acknowledge things as they are with sensitivity.

Trungpa Rinpoche retells the story of Lekpe Karma, one of the disciples of the Buddha. He served the Buddha as his attendant for twenty-four years, and that filled him with pride. After the twenty-four years, he thought, "What's the big deal about the Buddha? I can do what he does. Really, what's the big whoop here? There's no big difference between him and me."

As the story goes, on one occasion the Buddha told him, "Lekpe Karma, you're going to die in seven days." Not as a direct result, mind you; that was just the situation. The guy thought, "Nah. No way." So, Lekpe Karma fasted and did all kinds of things that were viewed as ways to cleanse oneself so that there wasn't any way he could catch anything and die. Intent on disproving the prophecy, he stayed focused for a whole week, at the end of which he was ecstatic. He was going to see the Buddha, fantasizing about how he would tell him, "Look—I'm still alive. I proved you wrong!" On the way, he got a little thirsty, so he picked up and drank some water that turned out to be poisonous. He died before he could go tell the Buddha that he proved him wrong.

Unfortunately, this disciple's arrogance had him on a trajectory, and even the Buddha couldn't help him. When relating to situations, we have to remain honest and rely on our own cognizance. For instance, all of us know we're going to die, but we live our life exactly the opposite. Even though we *know* we're going to die, we think somehow that it has to do with other people—not me, you. We tend to live as though life will last forever.

That's an extreme example, but there are countless situations like that. We must acknowledge things as they are, not with conceptions and misconceptions.

Sometimes, not acknowledging things manifests in how we leave things unsaid. For instance, there are family situations in which assumptions are made, and relatives start to live in wholly different realities because of a lack of communication. Sometimes it is better to say things. But it's not about heavy-handed communication, either. Working with things as they are, from the bodhisattva's point of view, is not about softening anything particularly but it still takes into account other people's situations.

Family issues are very complex, as we know. Or at least they can be. Sometimes they're not! Likewise for work situations. Either way, a gentle version of the truth is generally the best approach. To live in a mutually defined world of lies has never done anyone any good. However, it's not about "*I* tell the truth, and you don't. You're no good, while I'm the truth teller!" Rather, we're allowing open communication and taking the other person into account first.

RESISTANCE AND THE POSSIBILITY TO BEGIN ANEW

Bodhisattvas can approach all situations as opportunities to train in the paramitas. However, at work and elsewhere, there are obstacles to those paramitas. For example, the main obstacle to generosity is always expecting a return. Likewise, there are also obstacles to discipline with which it is worthwhile to familiarize ourselves. We will explore them in more detail in the chapter on business ethics, but I wanted to close this chapter by discussing resistance and discipline. This is the daily challenge, in fact. We create a set of habits, and it's very difficult to buck them.

Strangely, this is where faith comes in. Generally, across the three yanas, we know from studying the teachings that our habitual patterns aren't necessarily in accord with the way things are. Some act of faith is required to break the barrier. Faith implies that we can still do the right thing, so to speak, *regardless of the resistance*. It is difficult, there's no question about it. The good habits that are faith-based are currently outnumbered by our bad habits.

But there is an unknown factor. Ready? Here we are: The good habits of Dharma are powerful beyond what we can comprehend in any ordinary way.

If we are practitioners and something happens, we have access to an arsenal of skillful means. But having access to the arsenal is not enough. When it's needed, we have to take it and use it. There's no way to quench our thirst without taking the drink, no way to *think* our way into resolving situations, no way to just cogitate ourselves into enlightenment. There is a reason why we speak of meditation in action.

Here's the thing: There is no magic bullet. You simply do what you can. You've got the arsenal, right? It is there, and it is vast. Think about all that you have been given so far. At least muster up the courage to take the one step that you *can* take—adding a little bit of meditation to your schedule, for example—and go for it. Then everything comes from that. It is how discipline slowly becomes natural, which is what you want. No discipline lasts that's artificial.

Some days are easier than others. Some are more complicated than others. The worst thing is to just get depressed. There is a notion that if we've taken the bodhisattva vow but then wallow in any sort of reference back to ourselves, it's not a good thing. It's really that simple. In Vajrayana, a form of Mahayana that we will explore later in the book, we actually make vows to ourselves and to our teacher that we won't go there. And the only way not to go there is not to go there. That's both huge and straightforward.

That being said, there's always the confession, see? Every practice that has a binding factor includes a confession. We can then begin anew. However, please understand that confession in Buddhism is very different from confession in Catholicism or other religious traditions. We confess openly to the buddhas and bodhisattvas, and to ourselves. There doesn't have to be a priest there or anybody else; there's just a sense of acknowledging that our view has been clouded. It's very simple. In almost all Mahayana and Vajrayana practices, there's a section for such a confession. It's always good to clean house. Even if we don't know we made a mistake, just in case, we acknowledge that we are a mistake maker, which is not at all the same thing as being inherently flawed or inherently sinful. And it's wonderful that everything begins clean, anew.

9
Sex and the Sacred

In this chapter we will discuss sex, friendship, and union. Even within Buddhism, there are many different views about sexuality and human relationships. I'm not an expert on any of this, but I am also not squeamish, and I believe that these subjects can be discussed openly.

A PROMINENT FORCE IN OUR LIFE

Naturally, sexuality is part of being human, part of being an animal. It's a driving force in people's lives. Depending on the person, this force could reach different levels of intensity; some people also complain about lack of intensity. We have so many preconceptions about what sex is or should be. Indeed, so much of our relationship with sex, as well as with people, is based on preconceived notions of how things should be. Unfortunately society doesn't help much, because there are so many mixed messages. In our modern world, products are sold using sex, sexual images pop up all around, and we're supposed to both feel good and bad about sex, all at the same time. It's very confusing!

There is this basic impulse, which is physical, psychological, mental, and spiritual—a sense of passion and wanting that arises in us and comes up with so many notions. At its most basic level, sexuality is an energy of desire. It may be about wanting something or wanting to give something or wanting to possess something, but fundamentally it's all about desire. Since desire is such a prominent force in our life, it is worthwhile to take an honest look at it.

DIFFERENT VIEWS ON THE MATTER

Buddhism has developed a full range of approaches to desire. At the most basic Hinayana level, the best way to deal with sexuality is fairly simple: *Don't*. The idea is that if you don't give it credence, it's not going to cause you any harm. You can harness sexuality—you could become a monk or a nun, for example, or what's known as a *brahmacharya*. *Brahmacharya* refers to being complete: You don't have to rely on someone else to find contentment, nor even on any kind of carnal pleasure to feel whole. Thus, in that context, sexuality ceases to be a source of conflict with others. Or, if you want to start a family, you can have simple sexual relations between two people for procreation.

In the Mahayana, there's still the idea that one of the best ways of dealing with sexuality is to harness it rather than just letting desire run rampant. But people will be people, and that includes monks and nuns. All kinds of things happen, and sexuality is something that has its natural result. So how can we deal with that, especially if we are not the abstinent type?

If we really look at sexuality, it has to do with the essence of human communication: being open, totally open with another being. That communication is dependent on a physical body. In lieu of being a brahmacharya, there's the notion of *abrahmacharya*, which connotes incompleteness. One way to remedy this sense of incompleteness involves a relationship and communication with another person through sexuality. That's not meant to be a bad thing. Sexuality can thus be viewed in many different ways. But the basic idea is that the only sexuality that is destructive is frivolous sexuality.

This comes back to the same issues that we discussed along with work in the previous chapter. Somehow, frivolousness is what doesn't allow things to be whole. If we're just frivolous in our emotions, frivolous in our sexuality, frivolous in our friendships even, then the essence of communication cannot be complete. Even if we're a solitary, celibate brahmacharya, if we're frivolous about sex in our own mind, that also creates problems for us.

From this point of view, sex is viewed as a serious endeavor. However, much like work, by looking at sexuality in a serious way—by being nonfrivolous—a sense of humor comes into play.

There are many skillful means related to sexuality and being human and using the passions in a way that benefits the practitioner or in a way that benefits others. The problem with sexuality is when it's used or abused through frivolousness, which causes pain for others and all sorts of unwanted situations.

CULTURAL AND PERSONAL PHENOMENA

Of course, our attitudes toward sexuality are shaped by not only spiritual teachings but also the cultures we live in and our personal histories. This interplay can make things even more complex. An interesting example is that of monogamy. Monogamy and the cultural ideas around it are tricky, and there's no set of rules that universally apply. Really, it's about trust and what it implies for one person to have a relationship with another. It may depend on many factors, and it can all be quite confusing. But one thing is sure: If things are done in a frivolous way, it always causes harm. The nature of frivolous sexuality doesn't do anyone any good.

Generally speaking, monogamy is undeniably better than promiscuity. Yet the ethics and morality of it are extremely personal. For example, we can be monogamous—strictly speaking—and still be deceitful, which depends on our intention. I'm not advocating for any particular lifestyle here. I suppose it all comes down to whether we're being frivolous, or self-centered, or holding on to certain expectations, or just looking for some kind of entertainment. This dictates whether it causes pain within and without.

Another interesting example of the interplay between cultural and personal phenomena is provided by our sense of guilt.

Some people come from a fairly conservative background and have long had to deal with guilt. It is a common thread in their lives: guilt in relation to sex, how it can lead to all sorts of blockages, and how it plays out in their relationships.

We can work with these issues by allowing fresh air to come into situations. Guilt isn't just a religious thing, by the way; it's a human thing. But we have to understand that these issues are merely concepts. And really, the only way to overcome guilt is to look at our own mind and to see what's genuine and what's imposed. No one can do that for us. If it were only so easy!

Overcoming guilt is about openness and awareness; it's about being mindful and finding out for ourself. There are other views than the one we may be stuck on. As far as Buddhism is concerned, it is not big on guilt. It acknowledges that we do stupid things all the time. But how do we deal with the stupid things we do? We try to change them. It doesn't do any good to just cry about it. We make efforts to replace bad habits with good habits.

But it's always up to us. It's really about looking at the nature of the guilt and investigating it. We can look at certain aspects of our mind and see how solid they are. That's part of vipashyana practice. We should look at the nature of our mind and our conceptions and see how solid it all is. Find out. How solid, really? Give yourself the time to really look at it. Otherwise, you need a special kind of priest to absolve you. But even then, they won't necessarily, because they would be out of a job!

INTIMACY AND THE BINDU

We can also think about intimacy through looking at the traditional description of four stages of meditative absorption, or *dhyana*.[1] Their progression can mirror that of sexual communication for a spiritual practitioner, where the progression goes from gross to more subtle. I have heard the Indian philosopher Jiddu Krishnamurti describing his experience in the exact same way.

At the first stage, sexual communication with our partner comes from sexual intercourse. At the second stage, it is achieved through holding hands. At the third stage, it comes from smiling at each other. At the fourth stage, it is done through simply gazing at each other. Thus, there's a sense of progression in the relationship, from a meditative point of view: profound communication through intercourse, through physical contact, through gesture, and then simply through seeing.

Years ago, I was giving a talk on this subject in Australia, and a gentleman pointed out that in our ordinary, secular life, we typically start with the gaze and the smile, then hold hands, then conclude with sex. He wanted to know more about the spiritual progression alluded to in the dhyana stages, where it seemingly goes in reverse. The most important thing to understand is that it's really about the development of nonattachment. The problem with sexuality comes with being attached to it, attached to other people, and then wanting to hold on to something. That is when we really get into trouble. We're with somebody and we want them, or we want what they offer to us—we always want this and that and the other, and it is all based on "I want." By comparison, the progression that is described in the dhyana stages is not about wanting but rather simple communication. Its development is akin to a blossoming flower. It begins in an earthy way, and then it rises and goes out. Real passion involves a progression. It's not just based on a one-minute orgasm. Most people only care about that bit. But from a spiritual point of view, what we're looking at is a long-term issue, not just a sense of release—and that is regardless of our gender or identity.

Another aspect of the Buddhist yogic approach—which is sometimes associated with its Indian roots in what later came to be known as Hindu yoga—is that there is a basic energy within us, which is our essence. In Sanskrit, that essence is called *bindu*,[2] which can be translated as "drop." It is at the core of our being, developed through the practice of meditation, and mixed with the simple actuality of being alive. There is this idea that essence is spilled during the act of sexual intercourse, whether one is a man or a woman, and that spilling it should be avoided or at least reserved to produce offspring. But there is also the notion that the bindu has the nature of bliss. There are in fact various yogic practices that involve being with a fellow practitioner and experiencing that sort of bliss together.

As you can see, there is this whole spectrum of views that go from total abstinence to being in a state of bliss with someone you care for. We can talk about these things in a clinical or juicy way, but in essence it is about larger issues. It is about communicating caring and love.

THE SO-CALLED TANTRIC SEX

The tantric tradition, which we will look at in more detail in later chapters, is really quite amazing in that it takes everything about life and meets it head-on. The emotions are just the flip side of the buddhas. Everything is transmutable, and all aspects of life are aspects of enlightenment, depending on whether the perception is pure or impure.

Our tendency to view beings dualistically as male and female—and all the various yins and yangs of this world—is part of living as a human being. But these teachings show that this perceived duality is the play of deities and buddhas. In fact, from the tantric point of view, all deities and buddhas contain male and female in union. Male and female are in *complete* union because it is the actual state of things: There is no duality. The union of male and female buddhas is symbolic of that.

The brilliance of the tantric perspective is that all sense of duality is viewed as an illusion, and that the dance of the buddhas, the dance of dakas and dakinis,[3] is in union. Even when you just see a male in that tradition, female is always implied—be it by a symbol of the union, perhaps an implement—and vice versa. The teachings keep pointing back to that.

In terms of the Vajrayana practices, it's said that the ideal situation is that everything is within the yogin himself, or within the yogini herself—that is, without relying on a partner. But it acknowledges the fact that it's also literal, so that this relationship of nonduality can exist between two practitioners. In particular, practices called Karmamudra, "symbol of action," refer to the union of the masculine and feminine.

To be clear, this is not an advertisement. Some modern cultures are fascinated with "tantric sex." For example, there are those so-called tantric sex gurus from around the world selling things that are not based on the genuine Buddhist principles. They may be based on some Hindu principles, but even that is questionable.

If you look at the history of the development of tantra in India and later in Tibet, it contains a mixture of internal and external yoga. It's literal and figurative. There are accounts of yogic traditions where even Hindu and Buddhist yogis met in Orissa and other places in India and had "tantric sex." But you know, it's not like going to a club in NYC or Melbourne, where everyone is just doing each other! That is based on frivolity. The meetings that are alluded to in some historical accounts involved an irrefutable sense of the sacred. It was about experiencing the true essence of what is. It also involved a sense of secrecy. In fact, traditionally, those meetings were held in charnel grounds. Imagine a place where bodies are burned, with little pieces of fingers and noses and different things around, jackals biting away at the leftovers... That weeded out the pleasure-seekers, I suppose! It was a different approach to the whole thing.

In any case, there is no idea that there's anything wrong with pleasure. In fact, from the tantric point of view, *sukha* (bliss) is good. Only we are told not to be satisfied with the compulsive and trivial. Unfortunately this very tendency can be even seen in the way people practice meditation. They practice for a little while, have a little realization, and consider that it's enough. We are more concerned with the long term, and not just with sukha but with *mahasukha*, the ultimate great bliss, which is enlightenment itself. That's what we are working toward. It is tricky to discuss this because it sounds like it's some ego thing, which it is not. It's about wakefulness, not just a little temporary bliss—and especially not just the *release* part of it.

On that note, there is some idea that the essence, or bindu, should be controlled. But in some situations, I've heard, it's an all-or-nothing: You hold it all, or it's all expended, and somehow in-betweens don't work well. I have also heard that it's different at different times, and for different people. The skillful means that the teachings contain are extremely vast. What matters, really, is the progression that leads us to be able to do things in a nonfrivolous way. Teachings such as those related to Karmamudra are considered top secret. The reason is that we can easily misconstrue and misunderstand them as frivolousness and promiscuity. And really, ultimately, that never made anybody happy. So, to reiterate, the Buddhist view is not caught in some small idea of bliss; it is about sugatagarbha, "the essence of going beyond to (ultimate) bliss."

THE EXAMPLE OF TRUNGPA RINPOCHE

Someone asked me about Trungpa Rinpoche's personal relationship to sex. People hear stories and wonder. That particular person asked how Trungpa Rinpoche used sexuality to teach people, or as a means of communication. I could only reply that I don't know because I never had sex with him! So, my understanding of this aspect of his life is purely secondhand. But I had discussions with him about these issues. I was twenty-something at the time. I am now in my seventies, and some things are different. The level of naivety, notably.

His basic view was that frivolous sex is frivolous sex and has no value. It just causes trouble. Also, despite his reputation, he was very much against promiscuity. He really disliked it, and it was not what he presented in his teachings. He openly had relations with female friends, and he didn't view it as a big deal because he wasn't a monk any longer. Of course, I don't know what went on exactly, but I believe that it was just a sense of openness between him and whomever he was with. It was pretty straightforward and simple, from what I could tell. And unlike many people, he didn't choose to keep it a dark secret. He didn't view sexuality as evil or bad. But he did view frivolousness and promiscuity as problematic—very much so. If he found that any of his students were acting in a frivolous or promiscuous way, he would in fact let them know that he was extremely displeased. In that community, at the time, there were no rules against having sex, as we weren't monks and nuns. The basic rule was: Don't be frivolous and don't hurt anybody. It wasn't all that loaded, and these were not politically correct times either. It was the 1970s. Everything has its context, and this was part of American culture at the time. What we view as American culture and the sexual revolution was pretty damn frivolous. However, I am convinced that what Trungpa Rinpoche and his friends did together was far from frivolous.

HAVING APPRECIATION FOR THE BODY AND ITS ESSENCE

Traditionally, the way to increase the essence, or life energy, and to work with it is through the body, using yogic methods. For example, sitting meditation, dance, or physical postures combined with visualizations. There are so many different skillful means, many of which have nothing to do with sexuality.

Part of the problem we have in our society is that we don't view it in a sacred way. We don't view our body in a sacred way. We don't view our relationships in a sacred way. Everything is expendable, disposable. The bindu is thus squandered, not just through sexuality. It is, in fact, discarded through lack of connection to the sacredness of all life.

Part of what genuine Buddhism has to offer is a complete way of working with the sacredness of being in the world. It does create a very different situation. But then people will be people. Stuff happens. Some people still become criminals; some have drug or sex addiction problems. People have problems—it comes along with being human. But if the sense of the sacred is provided from the beginning, then people have something that they know they can come back to.

Unfortunately, people often experience a great despair that comes from the nihilistic, scientistic point of view: "So what if I get my act together? What does that mean? Getting a nice job working for McDonald's?" Or whatever depressive ideas one can come up with. There's no sense of engagement with the sacred world. This is very much connected to the question of essence, since essence comes from a relationship with the sacred. The relationship with sacredness comes with seeing the interplay of the mandala that we call society, the interplay of those in the mandala that we call people but who are in fact buddhas and bodhisattvas. Not only that: Our own body is also a complete mandala made of buddhas and bodhisattvas. And not only that: There are also innumerable buddha fields—utterly pure and enlightened realms—vaster than our five senses can ever apprehend. In this way, the teachings are inspiring a larger perspective on the sacredness of life. It is available to us. We can practice, and we can be with other people in that way, whether they are aware of it or not.

On that note, I always find it interesting that it's easier to get along with someone who blindly and cheerfully believes in God and is not trying to lay their trip on you than with someone who is a complete atheist and is trying to tell you how stupid you are to believe in anything. I'd rather go for the more pleasant being. I think that the person with faith is so much better off. As I like to remind my friends, in the game of eternalism and nihilism, it's much better to err toward the eternalist view. Of course, the best situation is not to fall prey to either!

There is a fascinating interplay at work here, and the view is developed from that interplay—from finding that which goes to neither extreme.

THE EXPERIENCE OF LUMINOSITY

I would like to briefly mention another reason why sexuality isn't considered taboo in the Vajrayana.

In the tantric teachings, we find a description of four situations where one can have what's called an experience of *ösel*, the "luminosity of the clear light." This could be understood differently depending on the context, but to put it simply, the idea is that there are four situations outside of meditation per se where we can get a glimpse of the nature of mind.

This can happen when we are frightened. For example, you step off the sidewalk; a yellow cab comes and almost kills you. In that very frightening moment, you might be in a state where you don't really exist and there's a sense of clear-light bliss. Likewise, it is said that that experience is possible at death. More commonly, this can happen when we are falling asleep. There's this particular point when we aren't exactly awake nor exactly asleep, with this in-between state where the clear-light luminosity appears. Finally, it is said that's also the case during intense orgasm.

All of us probably have had an experience of luminosity in one of those scenarios. We may not have put words on it—in fact, it has an element of non-conceptuality, so trying to describe it with ordinary references and categories would be beside the point. Regardless, that experience is considered extremely positive. In fact, it is said that these scenarios represent powerful opportunities for Dharma practitioners, who can also develop that sense of luminosity through their practice, not just on those very specific occasions. The point is not to find some kind of "special place" to get "blissed out" or anything of the sort. It is a natural process, the point of which is to slowly familiarize ourselves with the simplicity and purity of our own mind, to further allow buddha-nature to blossom so as to be of true benefit for ourselves and others.

FRIENDSHIP FIRST

Regardless of our level of practice, if we're going to have a relationship with somebody and it's just based on sex, it's going to fall apart. It's very rare that it lasts, for various reasons—or that the intensity of it lasts, or that the fantasy of it lasts. If we want to have some continuity in a relationship, the most important factor is friendship. More specifically, from the Buddhist point of view, it's about spiritual friends who are together because they share the view that enlightenment is not a myth. That's really what it comes down to.

If you can't be friends, why be together? Just for the thirty-minute buzz? Oh, it may be a couple of hours, or perhaps even all day at the very beginning. But generally speaking, that kind of intensity diminishes, and often it diminishes right down to zero. However, if we have a real friendship, then that is not the issue. The continuity of that friendship is so much more important than the temporary pleasure.

The marriage ceremonies that Trungpa Rinpoche gave were really simple. It was about these two friends. What do these two friends do? They practice the paramitas. The reason you're together is to work together, to learn to become real-life bodhisattvas. That's what it's about. If the sex is great, that's wonderful. But that's not what makes a good relationship.

Also, it's strange: Sometimes the "best sex" is with the worst person for us to be with. Everything is wrong about that relationship except that! If we're really stupid, we get attached to that and we mess up our whole lives because of our attachment to this situation.

In that way, there are all kinds of issues to consider. But the most important aspect is the spiritual friendship. That's the key. The Mahayana view is wonderful and doable. It's about viewing people—teacher, mate, fellow practitioners—as spiritual friends and relating to them in that way. Now *that* is a good society. Of course, sex fits into that because it's part of human life and tied to human emotions, but it is not the end-all.

What makes the energy of the bindu so extraordinary is that you can't bottle it. The communication is so of the moment. The minute you start to try to bottle and possess it, the essence begins to dwindle. That's just the nature of the beast.

THE SENSE OF OFFERING

When it comes to the sacredness of sexuality, so much of it has to do with opening. It's less about desire and the fulfillment of desire, and much more about opening to somebody else and to the immediacy of a situation. Even more so, opening to one's own being.

That sense of opening is also connected to a sense of offering—offering out. It is quite literal in that way. Generally speaking, in Buddhism, offering is a way to acknowledge the basic goodness within ourselves, and it allows us to develop positive habits. Here, "offering" includes our relationship with our mate, the world—everything.

If there's an expectation, if it's just based on wanting, which is frivolous, then there's a disrespect that comes in relating to our mate or our life situation. Then sexuality just becomes something that is self-conscious and physical: We get off, or however you want to describe it, and it's a done deal. By contrast, if we experience real orgasm, so to speak, then we don't exist any longer. This is not a fast-food approach. "Real" in the sense of really being in the moment. There's a complete sense of nonduality.

Offerings are often connected to the idea of merit.[4] Merit opens the world's sacredness to us. Creating a "field of merit" and offering to that field further acknowledges the basic goodness within ourselves. In other words, merit comes from basic goodness and in some sense leads us right back to it, with no sense of duality. If we have the view that there's no separation between the offerer, the offering, and the object of the offering, it is wonderful. That, in fact, is the view.

DISSOLVING DUALITY AND TAKING THE RIDE

Ultimately sexuality has to do with the sense of union. The reason we talk so much about union is that we currently believe the lie of duality. The lie of being an entity—me—separate from the rest. This habit of duality involves constant self-referencing. We function from that habit. What the buddhadharma points out, from the most basic teachings all the way to Ati, is that our duality habit is at the basis of our confusion and our whole life—this ceaseless circling of birth and rebirth; being constantly caught by ignorance, passion, aggression. Not only that: This duality habit also makes us look at samsara and nirvana as being a duality as well! We should aim at transcending that duality. We're not particularly looking to end samsara and find nirvana. It's about transcending samsara and nirvana altogether. This is called complete enlightenment: We are then a *samyaksambuddha*, a *sugata*.

By comparison, all too commonly we oscillate between wishful thinking and despair. That which is about union—a relationship with somebody else, which can be wonderful emotionally and sexually—will inevitably turn to anger and aggression if it's purely based on desire and passion. That's the nature of samsaric existence.

Part of what we can do is develop a sense of humor and understand that if we have passion, there's going to be aggression at some point. A relationship with another person is not just all love and light. That's why it is important to view our relationship in terms of a spiritual friendship and take into account how emotions function, how the human predicament unfolds, how samsara works. The person we love one day can be the person we despise the next. Then it is up to us if we solidify our love or our despising. But if we have a real, deep relationship, we can do better than just going from passion to aggression, from lust to lashing out.

The union we are talking about includes all the emotions. This comes back to the sacred view. The obverse side of passion is compassion. The obverse side of anger is clear seeing. From the enlightened perspective, the ignorance that creates grasping, desire, and aggression can be viewed as space. It is up to us if we are just going to be pushed around by samsara or if we'll develop a sense of being a true bodhisattva warrior that doesn't allow samsara to win by playing its tricks on us constantly.

How does sexuality work with this? It's an interesting and funny issue. There's this electricity, which is really dangerous because it sparks and it doesn't have good insulation around it. But we can take the ride anyway, because there's great potential in it. The "taking the ride" is about not being frivolous. Indeed, the potential that lies in that great spark shouldn't be taken lightly. This involves a sense of union, of joining in. But it also involves understanding that it's dangerous, having respect for it, and acknowledging its sacredness.

Frivolousness always has to do with referring back to an ego, while bodhisattva activity always has to do with nonreference back to an ego. Briefly stated, that is the situation. Ego always contains ignorance. It's always trying to possess; it always wants. We now have the opportunity to see that this ego is a mere construct. It doesn't really have any life of its own other than the life that it's given. Sacred outlook, in any aspect of life—sexuality or else—undoes the trap of ego. In the end, that's really what it's about.

10

The Energy of Money

It is worthwhile to get a perspective on the energy of money, the karma of it, and how to deal with it in a sane way. Many people have serious issues about money. It may be that they don't have any or that they have some but never enough. Some people die rich, some people die poor, and that also involves all kinds of issues.

Money in and of itself has no substance. These days, most of it consists of digits on a computer screen! What, then, if there's a mistake in the digits? We can even look at an actual bill, which seems more concrete: There's a little picture, a slogan of sorts, a number, but then you can see right through it, which really says it all. These bills are made of paper, plastic, and cotton, and maybe there's a little bit of metal stuck in there. It's a pretty worthless piece of linen with some scribbles on it, if you ask me. Yet something happens when you see it, touch it, feel it. You either get excited or you're bored. However, in our minds, money is something else.

The reality of having to take care of ourselves, take care of our family, take care of our environment, isn't as symbolic as the piece of paper. It's much more real. The money is the symbol of it all because we must have an easy means of exchange. There are practicalities in our life, and money is a big part of it.

VALUE, PERCEPTION, AND KARMA

Years ago, I went into a coin shop in Melbourne's central business district because I wanted to see the Perth Mint's Year of the Dragon gold bullion coin. Picture a hunk of yellow, heavy metal with a rich feeling and a dragon striped on it. It was particularly attractive. But then there was also this *big* one—weighing like a kilo of gold. That was even more impressive. Its size made it look like it shouldn't weigh that much, yet it really was heavy. And though it had the same dragon, it looked so much better when big, somehow. Now the funny thing is that it said something ridiculous on it, like "500 dollars." But if you wanted to *buy* it, it was $65,000, or a suchlike figure with a lot of zeros. Apparently they can add a large percentage because it makes people happy to see dragons. But really, it's a symbol on a symbol. That's double good fortune, which is meant to be quite good! Yet these big hunks, you can't eat them; you can't do much with them. Because they're worth so much, you can't even keep them out because you're going to be worried that they're going to be stolen, unless you have a situation where you trust everyone in your house and you don't think anyone could break in. In which case, you could have these big, expensive paperweights on your desk to hold down your important papers that also have numbers on them. In that way, you can have a symbol on a symbol holding down the symbols. That's even better!

Here is the thing: Gold has no mind. It is neutral; just something that comes from the earth. But we project meaning onto these things, and then we value them. Much of it is a combination of psychology and something objective, because we can *get* something—which we can then trade for something else, such as a pretty sports car, on a bunch of digits that will show up on a screen.

Money is all very relative, and the whole thing has a dreamlike quality, except this dream is our life. All the same, a relationship with money is necessary if we are to live in this world. We need to have a relationship with the flow of money coming in and going out, and so much of that relationship has to do with how we view it and how attached we are to it.

So, our relationship with money really has to do with how we live our life and what we can be comfortable with and not neurotic about. From the Buddhist point of view, money is not viewed as a bad thing in the least, because it is a symbol of energy. It symbolizes that something has been expanded, thanks to which one will receive something. Money is really about karma.

Of course, some people have easy times with money, understandably or inexplicably. Some people have difficult times with money. Circumstantially, over the years, it can vary. But regardless, it's something that we all have to deal with. It's an interesting, rarely acknowledged situation: On *some* level, enlightenment doesn't even work if you don't have money! How are you going to practice and sustain meditation if you can't feed yourself? How are you going to travel to receive teachings if you can't even take the train, or enjoy retreat if you can't pay your electricity bills? Money is not separate from spiritual pursuit, and we don't have to view it as a problem.

The key to not viewing it as a problem is not falling prey to poverty mentality.

POVERTY MENTALITY

Economics talks about scarcity. What makes money valuable is that there are only so many notes, and the bank will only give you so many digits. It's not exactly infinite—unless you're the Elon Musk or Jeff Bezos kind, I suppose. But even then, all those numbers are never big enough, and it doesn't seem to make these people all that happy. It makes the lawsuits even worse, and it brings up a lot of problems. Regardless, what we are interested in here is not so much the scarcity of money but our mentality.

Poverty mentality does not correlate with bank statements. It is feeling poverty-stricken, whether one has money or not. It's not a poverty-stricken mind that's only related to dollars and cents but to all kinds of other phenomena as well, including self-worth and relationships. This mentality is something that we can easily fall into—the "woe is me" approach; the "why me" syndrome, if you will, which can also surface if we get ill or hurt.

As in everything that has to do with developing the enlightened point of view, we have to begin by easing up on ourselves. The antidote to poverty mentality begins with being comfortable with ourselves, seeing that our situation is the way it is, and having some comfort about that.

There's the saying "I've been rich, and I've been poor. Rich is better!"[1] In Buddhism, the view is that richness is not based on our bank account. It's a sense of richness that is inherent to our comfort of just being. If we have confidence, then wherever we land in this world, and whatever the situation is, we can make do. If we trust ourselves and don't freak ourselves out, the money part becomes workable one way or another. The symbolic part, such as the actual number of dollar bills we have access to, might be difficult at times. Yet fundamentally, the energy exchange remains possible if we don't freeze the situation. If we fall prey to poverty mentality, there's an unworkability, even if we have suitcases full of pieces of paper with numbers on it. Conversely, if we have a calm and clear mind, everything becomes workable.

MONEY AND THE EARLY DAYS OF BUDDHISM

In the history of Buddhism throughout the world, we find countless examples of how to deal with our situation.

For instance, at first sight, much of the life of the Buddha may seem very different from ours. He was a prince born into a royal family surrounded by every possible comfort. The hunks of gold in his neighborhood were big and plentiful, in addition to rubies and diamonds. I'm sure he was also surrounded by what we would call—in unprincely language—babes! But as we know from the history of the Buddha, he understood that it was all just temporary glitter; it wasn't really going to do anything when confronted with the harsh realities of life and death. The prince ultimately renounced it all and left the palace.

So, Buddha lived the life of a wandering ascetic, and he tried various things, without cash, without gold, without diamonds, without babes, and even without his nice clothes. It seems that he tried all kinds of brutal practices with a group of wandering yogis. They would hang weights from their tongues and go through such ordeals to test out their bodies, improve their concentration, and so forth. But Buddha found that *that* life didn't work either. Thus, it seemed that neither 100 percent nor 0 percent provided a workable situation, if the percentage makes any sense. It was all about finding a middle way.

In this context, the extreme of eternalism can be associated with some notion of total security—God and richness coming in and lasting forever—while nihilism involves despair and nothingness. It is worthwhile to understand that these principles of eternalism and nihilism, which are so basic to establishing the general Buddhist view, also apply to our relationship with money. It doesn't work to think "always rich," and it doesn't work to think "always poor," nor do the extremes of giving away everything or the extreme of having everything. It's all about finding someplace that is between those extremes and understanding that it's not a static center point. It's a play.

In some of the sutras it says that the first teachings of the Buddha were given to traveling merchants. The interpretations vary, but it seems that traveling merchants let people all over India know about the Buddhist teachings of the four noble truths. Not only was there no problem giving these teachings to merchants, but if you look at the history of Buddhism, it seems to have traveled along the merchant paths, because these guys traveled to India, China, Southeast Asia, and so on. Consequently a large part of the history of Buddhism has to do with commerce. Therefore, there's no notion that commerce, business, or money is evil in any way. Money is only evil if our intentionality is evil. Money in and of itself, gold in and of itself, has complete neutrality. Whether it's a saint or a dictator who has the stack of golden dragon kilos from the Perth Mint, it doesn't make any difference for the dragons! It's how those hunks of metal are used—the intention behind them—that matters.

WHEN MARPA MET NAROPA

Other examples of how some genuine practitioners related to money can be found in the Kagyu lineage of Tibetan Buddhism, which goes back to its early figures: the great Vajradhara, Tilopa, Naropa, Marpa, Milarepa, Gampopa... In the transition of this lineage from India to Tibet, there is one story that always sticks out to me: that of Marpa's first meeting with Naropa.

In those times, if one was to receive teachings from a master, one had to make an offering to the master; teachings weren't given freely in any way. Thus, before Marpa, who was a Tibetan farmer and a *lotsawa*—a venerable Dharma translator—wandered to India to further his studies, he worked extremely hard to get a big stack of money so that he could receive teachings from the masters that he imagined he would meet there. In some versions of the story, it was a big sack of gold dust; in other tellings, it was a big sack of gold coins in the shape of knots of eternity. It doesn't make any difference—it was a lot of gold! It was a lot because in Marpa's mind, he expected to receive the gold of the teachings in return. The important thing was that he earned every coin, every speck of gold dust. It's not like his daddy gave it to him and said, "Go." Everything was earned. The gold was symbolic of his intention.

As the story goes, he met Naropa and made an offering to him. Picture Marpa getting out his sack, taking out several pieces of gold, wrapping them nicely, and kindly presenting them to Naropa. But the master replied, "No way. You're holding back on me! Is that all the gold you got?" Marpa being the very practical person that he was, thought to himself, "How does he know that I've got more stashed away?" He pondered about it for a while, went to get the rest of his gold, and offered it to Naropa. Again, Naropa asked him, "Is that all you have?" This time Marpa said, "That's everything." Naropa then pounded the floor, saying, "I have so much more gold than you!" The whole world around manifested as pure gold. After that, Naropa began to present the profound teachings of Mahamudra to Marpa.

There is a lot to learn from this. In particular, it shows that the energy we put into things is totally worthwhile.

PERSONAL ANECDOTES

I have another story. It is personal and thus contemporary, but quite odd. Some will not get it. And in these politically correct times, it could easily be misconstrued. But I suppose that we can think in a simpler way, enjoy the humorous anecdote, and see if there's anything we can glean from it. I'm going to tell it as my story, and it is subjective, but there's something more to it. Somehow, rather than just me, it has something to do with *us*.

As we said, in the Kagyu lineage there is the Great Vajradhara, Tilopa, Naropa, Marpa, Milarepa, and Lord of Dharma Gampopa. One of the main disciples of Gampopa was Düsum Khyenpa, the First Karmapa. That was in the twelfth century; today we have the Seventeenth Karmapa. The following story happens at the time of the previous lineage holder.

Somehow the Sixteenth Karmapa is invited to the United States by Trungpa Rinpoche, and he magically appears. A few days after he arrives, he's going to give a teaching and an *abhisheka*, or empowerment, connected to Karma Pakshi, a previous Karmapa. The event is held in Berkeley Hills, Northern California, in a beautiful, old former nunnery that became a school, with plenty of exquisite dark wood. There's a small throne where His Holiness the Karmapa is going to be giving the empowerment. Trungpa Rinpoche is with him as his translator, and there are all the various students who were living in California at that time. It's the time of day when the sun comes in through the windows, at the top of which is delightful stained glass. The Sixteenth Karmapa is this amazing being who himself is sort of luminous and glowing. But on this special occasion, it was all particularly beautiful, with this light coming in... I can see the whole display very clearly. There's this sense of expectation. It's a truly wonderful scene. And it's quiet.

People are making various kinds of offerings to His Holiness. Those are hippies, mind you, so it's a mixture of all kinds of strange offerings, including a few envelopes with twenty-dollar bills in them, miscellaneous junk jewelry or good jewelry, and other stuff. The offerings are up there, with people unsure what to offer but willing to make an offering, and there's this tenseness.

Now, I'm sitting in the front row. Right as His Holiness is about to give the abhisheka, he gestures toward me. It is unexpected, but I immediately think, "Oh, something really special is about to happen because His Holiness is calling me up." And just like that, my mind fills with egotistical bullshit of every possible kind. Very subtly His Holiness makes a sign again, and I think, "Yes, he *does* mean me!" and I go up.

He's just beaming and smiling. And I think, "This is gonna be great!" Someone brings over the little sack with all the offerings people have made, and a translator comes over. And His Holiness says to me in Tibetan something that was translated as, "How much do you think we can get for this?"

It was the most amazing pop-the-bubble! This was my introduction to the mind of the Karmapa. It was absolutely fantastic to have preconceptions drop away.

I want to share a second story. It is not really about money, but it *is* about money.

A few months later, we're in Boulder, Colorado, and His Holiness wants to watch a movie with some of his monks. I think we rent the Marx brothers and *The Three Stooges*. The Karmapa and the monks are watching this stuff, and they just love it because it's so physical and funny. There's quite a lot of laughter.

After the movies, His Holiness says, "Come over here. Show me your watch." I say, "Excuse me?" He repeats in English, with his authoritative voice, "*Show me your watch.*" What can I do? I show him my watch! His Holiness sits there, looks at my watch, and wants me to take it off. He tells me, "Timex. No good. *No good!*" He then pulls up his sleeve, points to his own watch, and says, "*Rolex.*"

Shortly thereafter, His Holiness goes back to Sikkim. A few years pass. One day I'm told he is coming back to America. I remember the story about the watch and go down to the jewelry store. I ask them, "How much is a Rolex watch?" They say, "$600." That doesn't sound like a lot of money, but it is 1976 and let me tell you, $600 is an impossible number. I retort, "You've gotta be joking!" The seller replies, "We can make an arrangement where you pay twenty dollars a month for thirty months." To which I reply, "Done deal!"

So, I get my Rolex. The very one I'm wearing today, by the way. And I am *so* ready! None of this Timex nonsense for me, right?

A few days go by, and I find myself in a situation where I'm serving His Holiness. He asks me to sit down, and it finally happens. He says, "Show me your watch."

I'm so happy! Turns out, His Holiness looks at my watch and says, "Rolex. Rolex... *No good!*" He pulls up his robe and he's got what looks like a white platinum watch. He says, "*Piaget.* Very good. Very good!"

To this day, I love having this watch because it reminds me of His Holiness the Sixteenth Karmapa. And I view this as a profound teaching. It sounds ridiculous—it's a Rolex-Piaget teaching, which is silly because "Rolex" and "Piaget" mean nothing. But it is symbolic language.

As an aside, there was a lot about watches because His Holiness really loved watches. He loved birds and watches. Go figure! Once, Trungpa Rinpoche was with His Holiness. The latter was wearing this gold watch and he was showing it to Trungpa Rinpoche. The watch had a gold bezel on it. Trungpa Rinpoche said to His Holiness, "I don't know if it's such a good idea for you to wear a gold watch with a gold bezel. It looks so Third World." His Holiness looked at Trungpa Rinpoche and said (as was translated to me), "If you don't like my gold watch, I'll get gold shoes, too!"

You may wonder what this has to do with poverty mentality and our current predicament, but my point is that there's a sense of humor that comes along with all these issues.

By the way, when Trungpa Rinpoche got his own Rolex, he got one with a blue bezel so he wouldn't look "Third World." Right! And he complained about my watch because it was also gold!

TAKING RESPONSIBILITY AND APPRECIATING THE FLOW

Relationship to richness and money isn't in any way separated from spirituality or the path. There's no necessity to have a Rolex or Piaget. As it turns out, Timex would have been just fine. It's not about competing or anything; it's about our concepts. Materialism in the most basic, ordinary sense of just handling and using material things, is not viewed as a problem. The question is whether we're *attached* to the objects of our life or whether we enjoy them. We naturally have to make certain choices. It's fine to own quality items, and to live in a decent environment.

Also, there is obviously no problem having money that supports good things. Part of the non-poverty mentality is generosity, and the willingness and ability to make offerings. It turns out that offerings have to do with the level of relative wealth that we have. Sure, someone who has very little can make a beautiful and meaningful offering based on their effort and on whatever is available to them. But one can have the notion that if there's more wealth, the offerings can be even richer. It is difficult to be charitable toward others and institutions that are working for the greater good if we are poor. This understanding is very much present in Buddhism.

Traditionally monks and nuns in ancient India or Tibet, or even in modern Thailand and elsewhere, go begging for food. They usually don't have to go very far because part of the mentality of being a Buddhist is to help support practitioners. But it is not like the modern idea of being on the dole. In fact, monks and nuns are meant to be paid for, in some sense: Either their parents or some kind of sponsor have to pay for them. There has to be something. Even at the time of the Buddha, it wasn't just that you went off and Buddha covered all your bills! There's still a sense of responsibility for your situation, a sense of effort, and a sense of being a useful part of a larger community.

Also, as mentioned, there is the notion of offering to the field of merit. In traditional societies, that field of merit can be the ordained sangha of monks and nuns. If Buddhist monks were wandering around begging in North America, Australia, Europe, or other suchlike places, it would be difficult for them because the social milieu is not one where they're viewed as part of the field of merit. That kind of relationship simply isn't prevalent in the West.

Part of the way we want to relate with money involves a sense of offering and the development of generosity, which have to do with an enlightened point of view, instead of trying to keep everything for ourselves or for our family. For example, practitioners often make ritual offerings to buddhas and bodhisattvas, and sometimes these material offerings are rather elaborate. Some could think that we're throwing away hundreds of dollars' worth of flowers and fruits and so on, a thinking that would be in line with a poverty mentality. But it can also be genuine and wonderful. If we're involved in a practice center, for example, we can be cheap about it, or we can be generous, depending on our mentality. The traditional view is that it's better to be generous because then the sense of wealth increases. There's nothing wrong with the sense of wealth increasing when we are not attached to it. Wealth is a flow rather than stasis. Prosperity is when the energy of the goldenness is moving, not when it's frozen.

Although this is yet to be understood in the West, we can see that in various societies, there's always the idea of making offerings to the field of merit. For example, in the Chinese milieu, making such offerings is believed to bring in more richness. Chinese people generally are quite practical: If it doesn't increase, they find a different field of merit to make offerings to! But culturally, over thousands of years, they have seen proof that if you make offerings, wealth generally tends to increase. There's a bit of fickleness in it, however, and it is okay to be a little bit cynical about it.

Sometimes I feel very Chinese because I also believe in offering to the field of merit! It is something that enriches, though not in a quid pro quo way. It's the same with work, sex, and money. There's more to generosity than just getting something immediately back. There's something about the energy of giving that is quite profound and changes one's life for the positive.

That said, we must be careful, and not stupid. If we give away everything and find ourselves stuck, then we made a mistake. There must be prudence even in generosity. That just means being reasonable with yourself and others—except when you're in a Marpa-Naropa situation. Sometimes, indeed, there's no way to hold back. But who knows when that is? You must determine that yourself. In the case of Marpa, if he had *not* given everything, if he had kept some little package for himself, he wouldn't have received what was most worthwhile to him. And he would have been lying, in a way. Thus, there are subtleties in this.

Giving also engenders connections. Receiving in particular has a sense of heaviness, much like the heaviness of gold. In other words, giving and receiving have some karmic implications. This is sometimes called "karmic debt." Therefore, occasionally, it's not good to accept something even though it is, say, a beautiful horse (which may or may not be a Trojan horse!). One must be discerning.

I will end this chapter with another funny story.

Several years ago, the late great Nyingma teacher Thinley Norbu Rinpoche was invited by the prime minister of Bhutan to be the guest of the Bhutanese government and to perform empowerments for the people of Bhutan. Over there, Rinpoche was considered perhaps the greatest saint of the country. He had a very special relationship with the area. Because of his bad health, he declined and declined, but finally the prime minister came over to America with his cabinet secretary and a letter from the king, and requested, "On behalf of the Bhutanese people, *please* come to Bhutan."

Rinpoche accepted and said, "Yes, but I have to bring a group of my students with me." He created a list of the twenty-five or thirty people that would go with him, and that list was sent to Bhutan, where they made all sorts of arrangements for Rinpoche's accommodation and so forth. But he added, "I want to pay every hotel keeper, every food waiter, everything—I don't want to have any karmic debt to anybody in Bhutan, including the government. I'll go because I feel that it's beneficial, not because this is a junket for myself or for my students." So, we paid for every place, and sometimes we paid double!

Sometimes you have to approach things in a different way.

11

Business Ethics and Meditative Discipline at Work

Interestingly, Trungpa Rinpoche often encouraged his Buddhist students to develop businesses, even if that just meant working for yourself as a consultant, a health-care professional, or any kind of independent professional. One of the reasons was that in those situations, you had control of when you could practice. It was an engaging and important point. If you were in control of your own economic destiny, when the three-month retreats came up, you could attend. You could likewise adjust to all sorts of events that came up. Even people who didn't have a business and who had a regular job working for a boss were able to figure out ways to do it, but it was easier if you were "in business" for yourself.

There was also encouragement to set up mandalas within the mandala. In that context, his group of students could be seen as the larger mandala. Within that larger situation, everyone was invited to actively participate in the enlightened perspective. The idea is that for enlightenment to exist as a whole, it has to exist in each individual part. So we were encouraged to create an enlightened family situation, as best as we could. This also involved creating businesses, societies, and all kinds of subgroups, such as groups with particular interests in the arts. Then this could be a place to foster dharmic relationships—a testing ground, if you will. This was early on, when Buddhism was just coming to the West.

In this context, basic principles were laid out so that we could learn how to be in a business. These principles also apply if you want to help the situation as you work for someone else, the government, or for any given company. The idea was not just being a worker bee but bringing our good intention—the same good intention that we have when practicing meditation—into the workplace. In other words, this is about bringing the bodhisattvic point of view in every situation, whether we're running the place or just working there.

OBSTACLES TO BUSINESS ETHICS

We spend a lot of our time and energy at the workplace. Many of us work more than half of the day, if you take sleeping into account. Therefore, it is worthwhile to reconsider our relationship to our work situation.

Here, the workplace is viewed as a space where meditation in action can happen, just like our home. The basic Buddhist perspective that has been presented over time is, Don't be two or three different people. We can learn to be at ease with ourselves enough that we don't have to create a fake work persona. If we truly trust ourselves, we know that we can be the same person, no matter what the situation is. It may sound pie-in-the-sky, but it really does work out that way.

Sometimes at work or in some odd situations, we feel that we have to create this other person. It may be fun to do that occasionally! But the problem is that we might believe the fake person that we make up. If we create lies that we tell ourselves and others, it can create many issues.

In any event, there are many obstacles to maintaining proper business ethics and discipline at work. Here are some that Trungpa Rinpoche pointed out.

Habitual Patterns

Part and parcel of being a Buddhist practitioner is maintaining ethics. A crucial part of it is that we should be aware of our habitual patterns and make every effort to not fall prey to those that cause distress to ourselves and others. These patterns are obstacles to maintaining meditative openness and discipline. They unfortunately run on autopilot: Once we create a set of patterns—a mindset that we repeat—it takes on an energy of its own.

How do we relate to habitual patterns in the sitting practice of meditation? Through awareness and observation. For example, we place our mindfulness on an object, we see what arises, and we neither accept nor reject; we just see it for what it is. We can deal with our habitual patterns in the workplace exactly in the same way: by paying attention. Yes, our patterns will run themselves, but they don't have the same power if we're mindful and aware of them. There's an amazing amount of power that comes from simply *seeing* a pattern unfold—the little abrupt waking up in the middle of it and seeing it for what it is.

The antidote to this kind of habitual pattern is developing another pattern that Trungpa Rinpoche called basic sanity. We come back to the simple approach of not making a big deal out of anything. It's a basically sane approach! And it's up to us. I talk endlessly about the replacement of negative patterns with positive patterns until there are no patterns. What I find incredible about enlightened people, or at least my perception of people who I think are enlightened, is that you don't know what they're ever going to do or say. You might think, "Oh, A + B always equals C," but no way! There are D's and E's and F's and G's, and there are letters you've never even seen or heard of! So, the predictable isn't necessarily the best thing. From basic sanity, everything is possible.

Slander

The second obstacle to ethics and discipline in the workplace is slander. We're all familiar with slander in our family, neighborhood, or religious community; and we have to acknowledge that it is also frequent in our work situation. Us bad-mouthing them, them bad-mouthing us. We have an issue, and we say, "Don't tell, this is just between you and me." Which, by the way, is called the *broadcasting system*. The best of them all!

Slander comes from a lack of loyalty to the situation, the organization, or whatever it is, and from a lack of loyalty to our own integrity as well. When we slander, we have lost our sense of dignity. It's essential to have good intentions, and good intentions never include slander.

I started Shambhala Publications when I was twenty-one years old, and I have been the boss for decades, all the way until my retirement a little more than a decade ago. In the early days, I had another job: I was working for Trungpa Rinpoche's organization, Vajradhatu. I had certain responsibilities as a director of that organization. I found it interesting having two jobs: one where I was the boss, and one where I was just some guy. I had to learn to go back and forth between being the ultimate authority and being a minor authority, and this required good discipline. But somehow, in the minor authority position, which was within a much larger situation, there was a lot of gossip and nonsense. At some point, we realized that we were being awful to each other. We then created a gesture—sticking out our tongue and symbolically cutting it with two fingers as if with scissors—to remind each other that we didn't have to do that. Whatever works! It's best to catch our mind before venom comes from the tongue. That's real Vinaya.[1] But if venom does come, you can cut it and make amends. This is about being loyal to a situation. Not slandering is an important aspect of that. You don't *have* to slander just because you perceive someone as being an idiot.

Lying

Lying is another obstacle that can come up for us in the work environment. The issue of lying can be tricky in interpersonal dynamics. There are people who unreservedly tell the truth and end up hurting everybody because they're so unskillful. Here, we're not advised to go to the extreme of being a thoughtless, hypercritical "truth teller."

The basic idea is that you don't lie to yourself, and if you don't lie to yourself, you don't believe your own lies, and so you don't have to perpetuate them with others. As well, in any business, it is not necessary to aggrandize our own situation, our own importance, our own numbers, or anything else, for that matter. But if we do—and ego has its way of aggrandizing things—it's important not to believe what we said. That's where lying, even if it's accidental, begins messing with our mind and with the relationship, for then we'll always end up having to support the lie. That is a very neurotic situation, won't you agree? Of course, it is best to avoid lying altogether, because then we don't need to create elaborate strategies to keep it going. But if we have lied—if it slips out, for some reason—the important thing is to not repeat the lie to ourselves and to try not to repeat the lie to others. This involves working with our mind.

In any life situation, we can return to our own sanity rather than create some other version of ourselves. If we find that we have created an alternate version of ourselves, we can let go of it anytime. It's not necessary to continue that version. No one really cares, you know! Really, no one truly does. People may have heard one version of you that's a total lie, but you can return to your sanity and decide that you don't have to keep up that storyline.

I find this extremely helpful in any situation, not just in a business environment.

Laziness

Trungpa Rinpoche listed laziness as the fourth obstacle to discipline in the workplace. It has to do with forgetting what's important. It also has to do with simple things like being on time and being *with*. For example, if you're in a managerial position, you don't have a double standard about when your gang gets there and when *you* get there. We must be as vital as the people we work with, otherwise we create a dichotomy that really doesn't pan out. Very little respect comes out of that style of leadership.

In any case, it is important to fight laziness. How do you fight laziness? You don't be lazy! I like that because it's both a joke and a truth. Really, there's no other way! It's about changing the lazy habit into something that's a lot different and actually working with situations.

Each of these obstacles is workable as long as we are aware of their existence.

MEDITATIVE DISCIPLINE IN THE WORKPLACE

As meditators, we should understand that the way we deal with our mind is not just for that time when we're sitting on a cushion or we've created some special place. Being a true Mahayanist involves being the same when we're in any situation. This naturally includes our workplace, where we can indeed practice meditative discipline, which has three attributes.

Being Free from Aggression

First, it's important to look at our level of aggression. Just because we're in a work situation doesn't mean that we have to change and become an aggressive human being. The same applies when we're doing sitting meditation. If we aggress ourselves, at some point we're going to rebel. An aggressive attitude toward ourselves as practitioners will simply never produce anything of value. True discipline is natural and gentle.

Whether we're doing basic sitting meditation, lojong, or tantric practice, it's all about gentleness. There's a light touch. Then when we are in the world, that absence of aggression is also the key. We can't be one person on the cushion and another person at the desk.

There is, however, a major difference between being gentle and being a pushover. Gentleness, from the meditative point of view, comes from confidence. If someone comes on like gangbusters to us, we don't have to just bite back. There's a different power, and that is the power of gentle confidence. Sometimes, though, we have to react. But even if there is anger, it can come from a place of gentleness. Whether the anger is screwed up depends on whether it's a clean or dirty cut. A clean cut is when something goes out, it's presented, it's important—*done*. A dirty cut is when something goes out, it's presented, and we keep on biting—we identify with the object, and we keep going. In a gentle perspective, if it's time to make a cut, we make a cut. But then we don't hold on to the cut.

It really has to do with our identification with emotions and concepts. They often carry us away. But we are changing our patterns. Gentleness still allows us to accept when it's necessary to accept and reject when it's necessary to reject. We just don't have to cling to the notion that this is *my* decision, *my* view.

Being Free from Hypocrisy

We saw that the first positive attribute that comes from the application of meditative discipline in the workplace is freedom from aggression. The second is what Trungpa Rinpoche called being free from hypocrisy. We can't say one thing and then do something else. This sows nothing but disdain.

Hypocrisy contaminates everything in life. If you're a meditation teacher and you don't have faith in meditation, what are you doing? If you're teaching something—Buddhist practice, yoga, or whatever it is—just because it's cool or because you're being paid, and you don't have faith in it, where's the power there? What are you teaching, really? It's amazing what people teach—and what drivel most of it is. If we're real practitioners, we shouldn't be teaching anything that we don't personally have faith in.

I'm a broken record on the topic of Buddhist faith. But very simply, if you hear Dharma and the teaching rings true to you, faith is putting it into practice. Otherwise you're just a parrot and a hypocrite to yourself.

Being Free from Competition

The third positive attribute that comes from the application of meditative discipline in the workplace is being free from competition.

Whether in the workplace, a social situation, or even a spiritual setting, it is easy to fall into some sort of competition with somebody else. For example, in the context of a spiritual setting, say someone is doing a given Buddhist practice and you start to think, "Why can *they* do that?" But things aren't like that. In the Buddhist tradition, all practices are contained in every practice. Strangely, there is no hierarchy. Of course, there are the nine yanas, the "stages" or *bhumis*, and all those categories that evoke a notion of progress on the path. But it's not exactly a ladder. Things happen in a more organic way. What may be the most advanced teaching for us is the beginning teaching for somebody else. That doesn't mean that our practice of it is any less or more profound because everything is included in it. We don't have to be competitive in a dharmic situation. In the same vein, there's no need to compete with others at work either. That's just ego's game.

Of course, it's good to have jobs that pay more, and so forth. But it's the *attitude* of one-upmanship that is unnecessary. We don't have to compete with our idea of who we should be, either!

WORK ON YOUR OWN OBSTACLES

Sometimes we seemingly have personality clashes with others we encounter in our lives, in work or elsewhere out in the world. I met a Canadian woman who was working with Americans in Australia. She mentioned that Americans tend to claim what they do, while Australians and Canadians often do the opposite, with the result that what they have to say about themselves often comes out in funny ways. She wanted to know how to say what we do without self-aggrandizing.

There are plenty of cultural manifestations like this. For example, Trungpa Rinpoche once described Canada, the United States, and Mexico as the land of ignorance, the land of aggression, and the land of passion, respectively. There are different characteristics to national ways of acting and thinking. I find Australia to be a mixed bag because it's so aggressively, stupidly passionate! They've got everything going at the same time! (I'm being naughty to make my Aussie friends laugh. I love Australia.)

Regardless, everybody's human. Everyone has passion, aggression, and ignorance in them. Sometimes one characteristic manifests more than another, and we have more of an affinity to one or another. There are countless variations. That's not the issue.

The issue is that you can do something about you. The only way you can do something about anything other than you is through your own example. You can't expect anything, but at least you can be at peace with yourself.

Much of what we think other people are doing is just that: thoughts and concepts. It's what *we* think other people's intention is. We project so much onto others. The truth of the matter is that all phenomena are subjective. It's always what *we* are experiencing. And unless we're the Buddha, it's hard to say what this or that person is thinking or being. We may have *some* idea, but whether it's true or not remains to be seen, and rarely do people really tell us. Therefore, the real impact we can have is through changing our own habits. That is where the power lies.

For example, it is said that if we take on the bodhisattva ideal and live according to it, it has an effect. We don't know what the effect is, however, because our subjective world changes, and it affects others in their own subjective way. We don't have to worry about that. The important factor is changing our sense of self.

A GOLDEN LIFE

To summarize, there are real obstacles to discipline and business ethics: habitual patterns, slander, lying, and laziness. There are also positive attributes that develop through integrating meditative discipline in the workplace: gentleness, freedom from hypocrisy, freedom from competition. They all have to do with finding ways so that natural discipline takes over from some idea of a forced discipline.

I want to thank each of you for reading this somewhat unusual section of the book and for being open to these simple but profound ways of looking at our life. They have been given by great masters for us to use. We shouldn't underestimate the power of developing these kinds of views and putting them into practice. It does make a huge difference in our lives. We can live a rather amazing, golden life. It's up to us. It always begins with being gentle with ourselves—that's the key—and then allowing natural discipline to dawn from that.

I have been steeped in these teachings my whole life, and I've been skeptical about them my whole life, and I've been accepting them my whole life, but the truth of it is so amazing. As they say, the proof is in the pudding.

You got the recipe. Check out the pudding.

PART FOUR

THE TEACHINGS OF SHAMBHALA

Although the deepest spiritual truths are timeless and unaffected by temporary circumstances, the way humanity relates to spiritual paths and systems changes over time—for better or worse. Occasionally, new sets of teachings and practices are thus required and discovered or rediscovered by accomplished masters so as to provide us with fresh means to reconnect with our basic sanity.

The Shambhala teachings, as unveiled by Chögyam Trungpa Rinpoche, offer a complement to the Buddhist teachings. They give us an inspiring glimpse of what an enlightened society could be. More specifically, they provide instructions on how to embody bravery, human goodness, and gentle warriorship in the world.

12 The Origins of the Shambhala Teachings

I am pleased at the opportunity to present the Shambhala teachings. I will try my best to highlight their relevancy for us today. As you will see, those teachings are unique, but they are also applicable to this time. In fact, they were formed in ancient times but are made for our current, dark times. In this first chapter of the section, we will explore the myth these teachings are based on and provide some historical context. But first let's look at the current state of affairs and at what Trungpa Rinpoche called "the three lords of materialism."

BUSY MIND AND THE THREE LORDS OF MATERIALISM

The Shambhala teachings are based on a myth. But "myth" doesn't mean a lie. "Myth," in this case, means a story that is true but not necessarily true in its factuality according to our day-to-day ordinary senses of seeing, hearing, smelling, tasting, and touching. This is partly because even though we have those senses, we use an infinitesimal fraction of their capabilities, since our minds are extremely busy. I don't know if any of my readers can identify with the notion of busy mind... In this day and age, it's hard not to! We have created a whole array of technologies, excuses, psychologies, and entertainments to keep us constantly as distracted as possible. "I don't have anything to do? Oh, well, let's look at this for the 10,237th time," or whatever it may be. Sound familiar?

It is said that after the time of the Buddha, his teachings would take effect and many people would attain enlightenment—in fact, thousands and millions of people would. But over time, there would be a dark age, and it would become difficult for people to attain complete wakefulness. It is said that what would prompt that dark age is that the banks of materialism would flow over, as the constant habit of wanting to materialize everything would come into effect. More specifically, as Trungpa Rinpoche put it, we would fall prey to "the three lords of materialism."

Physical Materialism

The first—physical materialism—is easy to understand. It is the ordinary kind of materialism, which is wanting more and more material goods. If we're poor, we want more stuff in terms of basics. If we have a little bit of money, we want another appliance or a better TV. If we're a little wealthier, we want to make sure that that closet is chic and full. If we're a little bit wealthier, we want to make sure that it says Porsche or Mercedes-Benz on our car. Ad nauseam... We spend much of our life looking for these objects.

There is no problem with the objects themselves. The material world is neutral. It has no thought, no mind, no desire—it just is. Besides, we all need food, clothing, and shelter; and it's certainly better if we have good food, good clothing, and good shelter. So, there's no problem with the material world. The problem is the constant desire for stuffing it with more. Every one of us, except for the minimalists, is familiar with this. It's a habit of always desiring more, as if when we're going up the hill in our life, we don't realize that we're going to be on the hill, and then over the hill—and then buried by the hill. I don't think there's a single one of us that doesn't know that this body will die. Yet we act as if that's a fiction. In modern parlance, we would call that *denial*.

However, that's just one form of materialism, and in fact, probably the least problematic, because the material world is just stuff. You can stuff more and more stuff into all kinds of spaces until you run out, or you can buy more space to put new stuff in there! Sure enough, we have a constant desire for material possessions, and we have created a culture that is based on wanting more—and here we're not even discussing the environmental and social issues associated with this. Some counterculture types have said they didn't want to buy into that when they were young, only to find themselves wanting more than ever as they got older. The irony of baby boomers: The anti-materialists probably ended up being the most materialistic generation ever to be seen on this planet, in any culture. That is pretty amazing! In any event, there is that simple form of materialism.

Psychological Materialism

Then we have psychological materialism: As it turns out, we also have problems with our mind, which have to do with concepts, philosophies, and intellectualization. We want to be better and healthier, whatever that means. Fundamentally there's no problem with that, and when discussing psychological materialism, we are not at all trying to put down psychology. However, we want to feel good about ourselves, and the way we approach this tends to be neurotic. We have self-esteem issues, and we rely on all kinds of tricks as we want to solidify our identity.

The problem is that we're trying to materialize things that aren't material. We want to *possess* sanity, health, and so forth. We also want them to not have anything to do with the seasons of our life. We're young, we want to be more mature; we're old, we want to pretend we're young. We play all these mental tricks on ourselves trying to create an image of ourselves that we view as real. Whatever our name is—Charles, Lynn, Dechen—and whatever goes with it, we want that to be something solid. We want to be able to hold on to it and transport it whole, so to speak. The truth is, nothing is solid. Our being is totally in flux, always. There's no solid *me*, no matter what the shrinks try to tell us! Of course, we have experiences, and we have our body, but this idea of a solid self doesn't exist in the way we like to think it does, and it causes us nothing but heartache and trouble.

As it fills our mind, the constant struggle to materialize our identity keeps us from the moment. It keeps us from experiencing even our simple five senses because our busy mind is always referring to a self that needs to be hated or pampered, depending on the mood. We create a whole machination to consolidate this idea of *me*—*me* and my relationship with my sister, *me* and my relationship with my parents, *me* and my relationship with my lover, *me* and my relationship with my dog, *me* and my relationship with my university, *me* and my relationship with my job, *me* and my relationship to my age...

We have so many stories that we repeat. And here is the twist, a fascinating effect of psychological materialism: If we repeat something long enough, we believe it's the truth. So, the stories we tell ourselves become our reality—at least in our view and experience of the world. We know full well at the beginning, when we're telling a lie, but somehow when we tell a lie constantly, it becomes our truth.

But why am I telling the bad news first? The Shambhala teachings say, "Tell the good news first." It seems that I am doing this backward! Please put this on account of age, and bear with me for a moment. We are, in fact, getting to a particularly important matter.

Spiritual Materialism

The most difficult of the three lords of materialism is what Trungpa Rinpoche termed *spiritual materialism.*

Generally speaking, the spiritual has to do with that which we do not and cannot see. It has to do with the most sublime and subtle aspects of our being, whether we're Buddhist, Christian, Daoist, whatever. It also has to do with the subtle dimension of this world. We have a problem in the spiritual realm when we try to materialize it. In other words, spiritual materialism has to do with our trying to materialize our spiritual life as well—somehow we solidify that which transcends! We attach ourselves to credos. We say we are a Buddhist, Christian, Jew, or Hindu, or whatever it is, and we attach our identity fully to that label. It also goes beyond that, as we materialize everything about our spiritual beliefs. Even if we follow Buddhism, which says that the underlying nature of everything is *shunyata* (emptiness), we want to concretize this emptiness into something solid. We want to materialize every little insight that we have into a monument.

That materializing is about becoming *somebody*, an important person. It's about blowing ourselves up because we have a certain belief system. Or blowing ourselves up because we feel that we have spiritual realization. Then we go out, make disciples, and sell books! I am being facetious and obviously don't have any problem with books. But there is a serious issue: Most of what has to do with religion and spirituality has become unbelievably materialized, and mixed with ordinary psychological materialism as well as physical materialism. That which is most sublime, sacred, and subtle becomes a commodity. Yet spirituality has nothing to do with commodity—that's why it's spiritual. It is, well, inner. There's no need for that to be materialized. It just turns out that the human condition is such that people make a big deal out of themselves because they have this or that belief. However, all the great religious and spiritual traditions have nothing to do with being big shots but rather the subtlety and sacredness of the inner world.

These are the gross aspects of materialism. There are also the subtle material, psychological, and spiritual materialisms that underlie the rest: the constant chatter of our mind, which accepts and rejects, accepts and rejects, wants more, hates itself, then tries to make peace with itself, then hates itself even worse... There are all these various mechanisms just to avoid being able to relax and be present in this moment.

We've created every possible excuse to be busy. We even make a project out of relaxing. We need big plans, don't we? We're gonna relax at this place at this time, and we materialize in our mind how it's going to be, depending on our particular inclinations. We may picture palm trees, or a TV, or whatever it is. We each have our own variations on these strategies. If we don't, it may be that we are saints!

Now, the prevalence of three lords of materialism is the bad news, I suppose. But the bad news is also good news. It is good news if we can identify that this is really no way to live and a horrible way to die. If we're busy up to our last breath—well, that's rough.

THE ACTUAL GOOD NEWS: BASIC GOODNESS

Underlying all this business is something much more powerful than that. It is the ground of all being, which in the Shambhala teachings is described as *basic goodness*. There's a goodness underlying everything. All these material issues that we have just discussed, or any variations that come from that, are just ripples added upon that goodness. The goodness is accessible at any time, like the sun on a clear day. The ripples are adventitious, conditional, just like the clouds: They will pass. This situation is also akin to the night, which depends on longitude and latitude, while the sun always shines.

In the Shambhala teachings, that sun is referred to as the Great Eastern Sun. We will get back to this in the next chapter, but the idea is that the Great Eastern Sun is continuously dawning; there's no sense of setting at all. There's not even the notion of a midday sun: It's the *dawning* sun. It is something that we can go back to at any time—the warmth of that sun is the basic goodness inherent in life itself. Even the most depraved murderer has just gone astray—in a big way, sure, but just gone astray—from that basic goodness that underlies everything.

For those of us who are interested in befriending that basic goodness and making our lives worthwhile, we are given the Shambhala teachings.

But before we dive deeper into these teachings, let us explore where they come from.

THE MYTHO-HISTORICAL CONTEXT OF SHAMBHALA

The Shambhala teachings distill the way of civilized living that has arisen from the matrix of Asia, then spread across the world. It is not that England, Hungary, or South Africa are uncivilized or anything of the sort; simply that these particular teachings arose from and became part of Asian culture. Where specifically they saw the day is hard to say—you can't necessarily pinpoint a birthplace—but according to the mythology, they arose in the kingdom of Shambhala.

According to the *Kalachakra Tantra*, which is one of the key texts of tantric Buddhism, Shambhala was a kingdom north of Tibet. Various people have tried to figure out where it physically existed, based on its description in that particular text and many others. Some people have guessed that it was somewhere in Russia or Persia. Different scholars have come up with different places where it might have existed. The most commonly assumed place is Zhangzhung, a historical kingdom northwest of Tibet, in Central Asia, with its own language. That's complicated because there's more than one Zhangzhung—there's an outer Zhangzhung, an inner Zhangzhung... Also, that part of Central Asia went through some tremendous changes because a lot of it is desert, and the ecology has changed. In the end, no one really knows.

This is what we could call a "mytho-historical" context, as there are millions of people who believe this myth, including most Tibetans and many other Central Asian peoples. The cultures of Mongolia, Japan, China, Korea, and Vietnam all refer to some Central Asian cultural matrix, which one can only assume is this. For example, it is said that the court dance and court music of Japan didn't come from Japan; it didn't even come from China; it came from Central Asia. So, there is this notion of a cultural matrix somewhere. Does the exact place make a difference? Maybe it does, maybe it doesn't.

Regardless, in the eighteenth century, the Sixth Panchen Lama wrote a famous text on how to find Shambhala. He describes his journey to Shambhala; he said he actually got there, and his narrative is very detailed. If his book were available today, it would be classified as travel/religion/mythology/I-don't-know-what-else. But it's very interesting because he says things like,

"You go into this valley, and you follow this river to its source; then you go to that cave and recite this mantra 1,800,000 times. After reciting the mantra, you go to this other place, and you do this particular practice, and then you'll be able to see this trail that goes behind that mountain, up and over," and so on. It's this mixture of geography and spiritual practice. Strangely, this is fairly well known because various filmmakers have borrowed the plot lines of this mytho-geography, for lack of a better term.

According to the *Kalachakra Tantra*, there's a genealogy of the various kings of Shambhala. It is said that one of these rulers, King Suchandra (Tib. Dawa Sangpo), requested of the Buddha to teach the imperial teachings. The king asked, "I would like, for the benefit of all my subjects, to attain enlightenment and have every subject in my kingdom attain enlightenment, too. However, I don't want to give up this kingdom; I want it to still exist, I want my queens and ministers and the people to still exist and there to be a totally functioning society. Would Lord Buddha be so kind as to give these teachings?"

According to the tantra, Lord Buddha agreed and taught the *Kalachakra Tantra*. Everyone became enlightened, as the king had hoped, and thus an enlightened society was formed. *Kalachakra*, by the way, is often translated as the "Wheel of Time." Some of you may be familiar with the term because His Holiness the Dalai Lama and other Tibetan masters give teachings and empowerments connected to this tantra at various times. For example, in 2006, when I was in Australia giving a talk that would later be drawn upon for this very chapter, I believe that His Holiness the Dalai Lama was giving those teachings on that same day in India, to tens of thousands of people. For reasons unknown, wherever the *Kalachakra* is taught, people come out of the woodwork—people you wouldn't even expect to be interested in the subject! Somehow it has this attracting power. Why?

It says itself why: These are special teachings for this age of decline. They're also special teachings that have to do with how to be in this world as an ordinary human being—not necessarily a monk, nun, or mendicant—and yet live this life in an enlightened manner. It is not about separating ourselves from the social fabric or disconnecting ourselves from whatever situation we find ourselves in. It's about being in the world, being true to basic goodness, and allowing that to manifest through ourselves. That's the key to the Shambhala teachings. In addition, there have been masters, particularly in Tibet and other areas of Central Asia, who have kept the tradition of Shambhala alive since the time of the Buddha.

If you read the *Kalachakra Tantra*, it says that from the time of the Buddha, six kings thereafter, the kingdom of Shambhala would disappear from worldly existence. That's why we can't find it: For the time being, it is hidden. There have been expeditions in Central Asia to look for this place. A particularly famous one was when the last tsarist government of Russia sent out the archaeologist and artist Nicholas Roerich. Who knows what secret political schemes motivated this whole endeavor? This was during the Great Game, a period of rivalry between the British and Russian empires over influence in Central Asia. The Shambhala legend gave them all kinds of excuses to nose around and craft their own imperialistic narratives. Regardless, it seems that Roerich believed in Shambhala, and the Russian government sent him out, as part of his geographic expedition, to find the kingdom. There are many intriguing elements that have led to speculation, but in the end we're not sure whether he found it. Regardless, the basic theory is that if the kingdom existed, it most probably existed in the desert, and the sands have since covered it.

Some European mystical types talked about it as well. You may be familiar with the philosopher and mystic George Ivanovich Gurdjieff. I always think it is funny that in his book *Meetings with Remarkable Men*, he describes how they went to the Central Asian desert, most possibly looking for the city of Kalapa (which happens to have been the capital of Shambhala), and that they went on stilts. I suppose that one reason was to be above the sandstorms. But another reason might be because it says in the tantra that the mythical kingdom had *risen*! According to the text, by the sixth century, apparently everyone in the kingdom had become enlightened, and because of the levity of the situation, it rose into a celestial realm. Interesting, isn't it?

The *Kalachakra* then gives a history of Shambhala rulers, which were known as the Rigden Kings. The approximation is that each king's reign is about a hundred years, with some time for a regent in between two monarchs. But the Kalachakra is a self-contained astrological calendar system, and it's hard to compare it with anything else. We don't know exactly how to convert Kalachakra times to Gregorian times. Interestingly, it is said that Shambhala exists as long as the teachings of Lord Buddha Shakyamuni exist.

It is said that at the time of the twenty-fifth Rigden—Rudrachakrin, the last Rigden King—all sorts of problems will affect the world, such as famines and various blights having to do with physical materialism, psychological materialism, and especially spiritual materialism. It discusses a point in time when the river of materialism bursts its banks—when the materialistic outlook becomes the main perspective and overruns the world. When the dark age has completely taken over and materialism is so rampant that it is the predominant force, it is said, it's necessary for Shambhala to fully reappear. It is also said that it's necessary for there to be a war—it's one of those warmongering tantras—and that war would be between the warriors of basic goodness and the three lords of materialism. The text proceeds to describe the various weaponry of the three lords of materialism, which are not unlike weaponry we are familiar with (prophetic depictions include tanklike machines and flying devices that shoot). It also describes the strange weaponry of the warriors of Shambhala, which are things like guns that don't kill but just stun. So, there's benevolent weaponry and horrible weaponry.

There is also a mention of a particular river where the final battle is to take place. According to the narrative, of course, the good guys win. Then, after that war, comes the time of Maitreya, the next buddha. But just to complicate the issue, it says that a false buddha claiming to be the real deal will come and that stupid people who want to materialize again will claw onto that. The prophecy adds that after that, a true buddha will come and that those who don't want to materialize can have the same realization as that buddha. Then it says something strange to the effect that the ones who believed in the deceiver will become the matter of the enlightenment of the others—whatever that means.

This is just to give you a mythic perspective. There are various notions and commentaries that go with it. Make of that what you will. Somehow, both Westerners and Easterners believed that this place might exist. What does that have to do with the Shambhala vision? In some ways, not much. Those are legends and myths. The Shambhala vision, which is the inspiration for these teachings, comes from the fact that King Suchandra of Shambhala requested a teaching on how to have complete enlightenment as well as a completely enlightened society. That was requested from the Buddha, who in his kindness and wisdom gave those teachings. Those teachings were practiced, and the result was good. The point of the legend is that everyone in that society—from the sweeper to the maid, from the minister to the soldier—was able to attain complete enlightenment, which resulted in an enlightened society.

The description of how the society manifested as an enlightened one is simple but quite telling. The king was the king, the queen was the queen, the general was the general, the cook was the cook, but they were all of one caste—the same as the king. Everyone fulfilled their particular role but within a one-caste system. This was a truly radical idea because in India, there was no such notion that everyone could have the king's view; only the king had the king's view. Politically speaking, it's groundbreaking that this view, these teachings, and these levels of realization were made accessible to every subject in the kingdom.

I find that quite inspiring. Whether it's myth or fact—and in some ways it doesn't make any difference—it says that it is possible to have not just an individual spiritual enlightenment but also a secular enlightenment that fully works in society.

ON FATALISM, PREDESTINATION, AND PROPAGANDA

Before we continue exploring how the teachings of Shambhala made it into our time and place, there are a few potential misunderstandings that I would like to address. Some of the topics we have discussed—such as prophecies concerning the bursting of the banks of materialism; the mythology surrounding the notion of a war—might lead some to believe that this is a fatalistic system. Also, generally speaking, there has been a Western perception that Buddhism as a whole was fatalistic. However, I think that this perception is changing.

Historically, Buddhism as fatalistic may have come from the early Western scholars of Buddhism who talked about nirvana as a "blowing out," a separation from the world. That understanding didn't take into account worldly life and instead looked at a small part of Buddhism. As the Buddhist teachings are translated, integrated into a way of studying and practicing that comes not from people *outside* of the society explaining them but people who come *from* Buddhism, it is changing. In any event, Buddhism and the Shambhala teachings are far from being fatalistic.

There is also a misunderstanding of karma. The idea of karma, to some, is also a kind of fatalism. But in Buddhism there's good karma, bad karma, and neutral karma. You can create any of them, but the best thing you can do is to stop karma—that's enlightenment. The Shambhala teachings even take it one step further: They say that enlightenment *includes* this world; that you don't have to leave it just to the Christians or the Shintoists to take care of society!

Another interesting question was raised by an attendee at one of my lectures, after I had presented the myth of Shambhala. Someone wondered about the idea that "people who materialized would become the matter of the enlightenment of the others," a notion that we alluded to when we discussed the time of the last Rigden. That person asked me, "Is there any predestination when it comes to people being in one group and some being in the other?"

I told them, "Yes. You'll be in the one group, and your spouse will be in the other!"

That's a joke, of course! It's *nothing* like that. The important thing about these teachings is that basic goodness is open to everybody; it's our basic nature. Now, what do we do with it? We can become fearless, or we can become cowardly. If we become cowardly, we go against people. If we're fearless, we help people. Because we have nothing to fear, we're not just holding on to our own idea of ourselves. Cowardice is getting stuck in ourselves. It's up to each and every one of us if we are a fearless warrior or a coward. There's no predestination. It's what we do with that basic goodness, what we do with that soft spot in our heart. Do we let it open, or do we let it close? Do we believe our lies by repeating them, or do we add some insight and humor into the mix? Sometimes it's very hard, after repeating a lie, to *remember* what the truth is. But there's always that choice.

This happens on an individual basis and, in a wider sense, on a social basis, in a complete society. Propaganda on a mass scale is no different from the inner propaganda of our own mind. We say something, we say it again, we say it again, we say it again... then we believe it: "Oh, it must be true. I've heard it a million times!"

If we allow ourselves to be genuine, there's no question about the various repetitions that we say to ourselves, or the various repetitions that are on the television or the radio or said among our friends. There's always a choice and there's no predestination: Everything is a decision. How we live our life is our decision. Many things happen that we can't control. One day we may not be able to walk by ourselves. One day we will draw our last breath. But how we meet that day is up to how we live each and every day. We can be busy our whole life and meet things with that busyness. Or we can change that busyness to something a little more profound and meet situations with that vast, nonaggressive, fearless mind. We have that choice.

In a way, there *is* predestination: the predestined basic goodness and the predestined fact that we might lose connection with that basic goodness by building messy things on top of it. But just because we built on top of it doesn't mean that we have to be controlled by whatever we have built. There is always a choice, and the choice is simple because the basic goodness is *basic*. There is no basic badness. It's an aberration; it's not basic.

EPICS, WARRIORS, AND KOOKS

Let's get back to a bit of storytelling. There is another mythology connected to this, which comes from the Kham area of eastern Tibet. It is the great epic of Tibet, *The Epic of Gesar of Ling*. Gesar is the quintessential warrior-king, sort of the national hero of the Tibetan people. My vajra brother Robin Kornman, who passed in 2007, published a translation of the first chapters of *The Epic of Gesar of Ling*, and my friends Sangye Khandro and Lama Chönam translated fantastic material related to this epic. We thus have the opportunity to read about it in English. What's wonderful is that there are storytellers who tell this epic in Tibet, and it's added to constantly. In fact, there are now hundreds of volumes. Each generation memorizes and adds. There are yearly Gesar festivals during which the tales are told. "Epic parties," as younger folks would say!

This is connected to our discussion of the Rigden Kings of Shambhala. These celebrations and chapters from *The Epic of Gesar of Ling* extend to the time of the twenty-fifth Rigden. Also, according to Tibetan tradition, Gesar is an emanation of Padmasambhava, the main person who was invited to Tibet from Greater India to teach Buddhism. Gesar is considered to be an emanation of this great master, and they are both connected to the Rigden Kings in one way or another. Therefore, in Tibet, these notions are all interwoven.

So what does this have to do with Australian, American, or British culture? Probably the same thing it has to do with Japanese, Chinese, or Korean culture. There is something in these teachings of basic goodness, of how to live our life properly, how to have a proper society, that is applicable to any human being in any society. What the Shambhala teachings say, quite simply, is that even though this world is far from perfect, we can, in this world, create a just and sane society. But it will not create itself. There is no divine providence that will do it for us. It begins by *you* creating a sane environment in yourself, in your own home, in your own relationships with family and friends, and with your own small community. It is based on caring, compassion, and fearlessness.

This lack of fear is called warriorship. It's interesting that the term *war* is used. But it is used in a special way. The Shambhala teachings say that the ultimate warriorship is victory over war—it is *all-victorious*. It's not about being *at* war; it's victory *over* war—in our own being, in our family life, in the social fabric, altogether. It's an enlightened vision based on fearlessness and non-ego. It is based on the fact that it is possible to live this life without always fixating on ourselves as the end-all. It comes from the understanding and realization that *me* and *mine* are not necessarily (and in fact, not at all) the most important things. There's something bigger than *me* and *mine*, which actually benefits me and mine, strangely enough. In fact, what is most beneficial to me? Precisely that which doesn't fixate on me. This is a paradox that I have a difficult time understanding because I'm so fixated on myself. But it is a core principle of the Shambhala vision.

Over time, the Shambhala teachings, notably of Chögyam Trungpa Rinpoche and of those who have come after him, will unfold and develop further. Like *The Epic of Gesar of Ling*, it's a work in progress. As mentioned, in terms of the mythological perspective, there are still some Rigden Kings to go before the twenty-fifth appears. I'm sure a lot of people will put out many fake teachings, but there will be real ones as well. It's interesting because the Shambhala vision is claimed by so many kooks. We find references to Shambhala in various Western occult literature, such as in the works of the mystic Helena Petrovna Blavatsky, the occult writer Alice Bailey, and others. I think they're well-meaning. Even in Colorado, there's a town called Shamballah-Ashrama; if you take a detailed map of the Douglas County area, you'll see it there. It was a utopic community created in the late nineteenth century by some people who had heard the name and tried to create something. There are also cults that have nothing to do with the teachings we're discussing that use similar names. There was even a best-selling novel with the name "Shambhala" in the title, packed with weird and occult ideas. We don't have to fall for that.

But there are also the main holders of this tradition, those who have carried it through since the time of the Buddha, or at least since the time of Padmasambhava. That's the genuine tradition. Yet even there, there are usurpers. Anything powerful is just like our mind—there's a tricky side to it. If there's something pure, there's always the criminal mind to have a different version of it, especially if you can make money, gain power, have sex, or whatever the attraction is to busy our mind. Remember, that is how we began this chapter—our busy mind.

By contrast, the true teachings of Shambhala always begin, continue, and end with basic goodness, gentleness, caring. Anything else is BS! This may be a shocking way to put it, but I feel allowed to give this warning, and I believe that it is extremely important.

CHÖGYAM TRUNGPA AND HOW THE SHAMBHALA VISION CAME INTO THIS TIME

The modern teachings of Shambhala came through the revelations of Trungpa Rinpoche, one of the first Tibetan teachers to come to the West. He and his lineage were holders of the Shambhala teachings. Chögyam Trungpa was the eleventh Trungpa Tulku, and the Trungpas were among the holders of these teachings in eastern Tibet. I want to share a little bit about him and how he was instrumental in the dissemination of the Shambhala teachings. These are not teachings on the *Kalachakra Tantra* per se; they are based on his own revelations.

We mentioned Kham earlier, the area where much of *The Epic of Gesar of Ling* came from. It is the most far-eastern part of Tibet, close to Sichuan Province in China. In around 1940, a boy was born there and was recognized (at the age of two, I believe) as the incarnation of the Trungpa Tulku, the leader of a nearby group of monasteries called Surmang.

The young Trungpa Tulku was enthroned as the abbot of the Surmang Dutsi-til monastery and was trained traditionally in the Kagyu and Nyingma schools of Tibetan Buddhism. There came a time when the Chinese Communists stormed in and routed the monasteries, at which point the young tulku and those that could go with him escaped and made their way into India. This was an arduous journey described in his autobiography, *Born in Tibet*. I think that only about 10 percent of the group that left made it from Tibet to India. It took them ten months, and at the end they were eating their own shoe leather to stay alive.

The Trungpa Tulku, who led this group, was particularly accomplished as a meditation master and as a writer of Buddhist philosophical works, even at a young age. A lesser-known fact is that from a very young age he had visions of the Shambhala kingdom. During his escape from Tibet to India, when he and his people weren't hiding from the Chinese troops and making their way across rivers, he had a particular vision, which he wrote down. In English, the title of this text would be *The Annals of the Empire of Shambhala*. It is a history of the Shambhala world that came to him spontaneously. I believe that the text was a collection of Tibetan lore along with his own insight into Shambhala.

I'm now going to try to explain something that I don't understand myself.

Around the time that Trungpa Rinpoche and other Tibetan refugees made their way into India, the Canadian high commissioner to India was His Excellency James George. He and his wife were very moved by the plight of the Tibetan refugees. By a set of circumstances, His Excellency befriended this young man, Chögyam Trungpa, and often the latter would visit him and stayed at the home of the Canadian high commissioner to India.

Now, Trungpa Rinpoche had an oracular talent. In the Tibetan tradition, when you're trained as a lama, you're trained in various arts, including medicine, philosophy, astrology, and other oracular arts, in addition to your general training in Buddhism. Somehow, Trungpa Rinpoche, from a young age, became well known for his ability to make predictions based on *prasena*, which involves seeing things in a mirror. It's a very old form of divination that you'll find documented in ancient China, Tibet, and Mongolia. It turns out that Trungpa Rinpoche was a master of that form of divination.

Mr. George was interested in the legend of Shambhala. He had read about it in various places, in particular, in the works of the Theosophical Society, founded by the mystic Helena Petrovna Blavatsky. In her works she says she was inspired by Shambhala. And actually, a lot of the Western ideas of Shambhala come from her writings and her meanderings in Asia—though sometimes people question her writings because there was quite a lot of hashish involved! I think she was a bit of a Victorian-age hippie. But she was also extraordinary, and I'm sure that at least some of what she had to teach and transmit was legitimate.

Mr. George was aware of these things. He had also been a student of P. D. Ouspensky and Gurdjieff, these Western mystics who lived in London and Paris at the time, and he was familiar with the legend of Shambhala. One day he asked Trungpa Rinpoche about it. According to James George's writings, Trungpa Rinpoche took out of his robe a small hand mirror. The practitioner of the divination doesn't look directly into the mirror; they view it with their peripheral vision rather than with concentrated vision. In any case, Mr. George said they were just sitting there and Trungpa Rinpoche gave a complete description of how the main city looked, along with a thorough description of the palace, as if he was right there. He took Mr. George on a tour of Kalapa, the capital of Shambhala, the various mountains around it, and so on. Obviously Mr. George was fascinated by this, to the point that he wrote about it later. Historically, this is a special event, for reasons we will understand later. It wasn't just a little aside.

But let us get back to the life of Trungpa Rinpoche. He had been a very promising young lama in India. The Dalai Lama had created this homeschool for young lamas, and he made the young Trungpa Tulku the head of this school to train young lamas from all the various sects. The young Trungpa excelled at that. Yet somehow he had a fascination with the West—even when he was still in Tibet—and he had seen places like New York and London in his prasenas.

By sets of circumstances, he received a Spalding Trust scholarship to study at Oxford University. So, he and his bursar, Akong Tulku, ended up on a boat to England, then on a train to Oxford. Trungpa Rinpoche improved his English and learned to speak what we could call the Queen's English, with an Oxonian accent at that. He established a Buddhist center in Scotland—Samye Ling, south of Glasgow. However, by another set of circumstances—fortunate or unfortunate, depending on how you look at history—he had a falling out with his friend of years, Akong Tulku, due to differing views on how to teach Tibetan Buddhism and especially on Westerners' receptivity, and he left Scotland for North America. He arrived in Canada, because the Americans wouldn't let him in. He had just married, and what a huge scandal that had been! The front page of all the tabloids ran headlines such as "Monk Runs Away with 16-Year-Old!" It turns out, that week, Scotland had reduced the age of marriage without parents' consent to sixteen, and Trungpa and his young student Diana Mukpo eloped to Glasgow and got married. They sort of got out of the United Kingdom quickly because it was a huge scandal. Trungpa Rinpoche's students in Great Britain were extremely upset. I think a lot of them were jealous, and others were upset for various reasons. But it wasn't just a salacious story or anything of the sort. Many events converged around those years in Trungpa Rinpoche's life and contributed to refining his vision. In particular, he had been in an automobile accident that left him partially paralyzed, and he saw this as "an accident of giving up self-deception." This, along with his falling-out with his friend Akong Tulku, coincided with his decision to fully give up any kind of distance from Westerners. In that context, his marriage symbolized his becoming part of the world he was now living in. He also credited Diana Mukpo with saving his life. In any event, he ended up in Montreal, where he would wait for a visa to the United States.

After that, for seventeen years, he taught Buddhism. Some say—and I definitely do—that he was the driving force, the main progenitor of Buddhism into North America and the West. Before that, there were very few Buddhist centers, and few Buddhist works of any significance in English. Through his language and skill as a meditation master, he presented the complete Buddhist teachings—the early teachings, the Mahayana teachings, and the Vajrayana teachings—in a way that was accessible, understandable, and practicable by Westerners desiring to enter that path. He established dozens of meditation centers—in fact, nearly a hundred; Naropa University; a Japanese Tea Ceremony society, a photography society, and groups for various arts. He was himself a flower arranger, calligrapher, and poet, among other things. He published many books: His public collected works total over five thousand pages. One would think that would be enough.

This Shambhala vision, though . . . He was busy planting the seed of Buddhism in North America, but somehow he could not get the Shambhala vision out of his being. Remember the anecdote about his writing *The Annals of the Empire of Shambhala* as he was crossing the Himalayas into India? In the last week of this lengthy journey, Chinese troops were still chasing his group, and the text was lost in the last stream that he and his friends crossed before making their way into India. However, his vision of Shambhala stayed with him.

To understand the rest of the story, we need to understand another aspect of Trungpa Rinpoche. In addition to his ability as meditation master, Dharma educator, artist, oracle, he was also a *tertön*, a term that translates as "treasure revealer." There is this tradition that various male and female lamas have visions through which they discover *termas*, or teachings that were mostly hidden by Padmasambhava, the founder of Tibetan Buddhism, and Yeshe Tsogyal, his closest disciple.[1] Yeshe Tsogyal wrote down these teachings of Padmasambhava and buried them in caves all over Tibet, as well as in Bhutan and parts of Nepal. It is said that these are special teachings for the future that are often written in a special language: "*dakini* script." The term *dakini* often refers to an enlightened feminine figure[2] but literally means "sky dancer" or "sky walker." We're not talking about Luke here!

In the tradition, and especially in the Nyingma school of Tibetan Buddhism, some of the most profound teachings are these discovered works, or terma. They come out in different ways. Physically, there are texts buried into stone, for example. It is said that others are buried, as we would say in English, into the subconscious—in other words, they're somehow hidden in the collective mind, and they can be unearthed from there. There are other kinds, and it is a profound and subtle subject, but here it suffices to say that the tertöns are accomplished practitioners who have a profound connection with the wisdom mind of Padmasambhava and Yeshe Tsogyal. Trungpa Rinpoche, from a very young age, was a treasure revealer. He discovered various texts left by Padmasambhava around the Kham area of Tibet.

Back to our main story: Trungpa Rinpoche was now living in the United States. At one point, he went down to an area in Mexico, in the mountains near Guadalajara, on retreat with a couple of his students. One of his students had bought a small, funky house in Pátzcuaro, which is a town by a sacred mountain. As Trungpa Rinpoche described it, he was there when his interest in Shambhala was fully reignited; the *Annals* themselves were coming back to his mind, and he felt compelled to do something about that. Yet he was so engrossed in teaching Buddhism and establishing Buddhist practice in America, he thought it would be impossible to add this to his plate. At which point, by circumstance, one of his students brought him a letter, which was on Her Majesty's service.

It turns out that Her Majesty was also the Queen of Canada—Queen Elizabeth! You may remember Mr. George, Canadian high commissioner in India; the letter was from him. He was in Tehran, Iran, at that time, and he wrote to Trungpa Rinpoche. The letter said something to the effect of, "I couldn't get out of my mind the times that you spent with me in New Delhi, and especially your descriptions of the kingdom of Shambhala. Can I have your permission to publish my account of this in a book that's going to be published in New York? And will you please look at the essay and correct my errors, if there are any?" The letter arrived on the day Trungpa Rinpoche had decided that he was going to forget about all this Shambhala stuff, that there was no time to do that and start a whole new set of teachings. He hadn't really set his mind, but he felt there was no way he could do that in addition to everything else he was trying to accomplish.

I believe that this letter had quite an impact on him, from the moment he looked at the envelope. You see, Trungpa Rinpoche was proud to be the first

Tibetan subject of Queen Elizabeth. Wherever he lived, there was always a portrait of the queen or the royal couple on a wall. It's hard to understand. Sort of old-fashioned, isn't it? Regardless, he loved being a subject of Her Majesty. So, since this envelope was on Her Majesty's service, he had to perk up! High commissioner letters are very official-looking, with special stamping. Trungpa Rinpoche described it as like it had weight. In other words, it was something he had to pay attention to—not just a letter. He opened the letter, read it... and the rest of us are very lucky that he did. Because somehow, for him, that moment was what he called the auspicious coincidence that told him he had to do something about the Shambhala vision.

Shortly thereafter, something else that is hard to describe happened. Trungpa Rinpoche received termas—spiritual treasures, as discussed earlier. For example, a text came to him spontaneously while he was sitting at this house in Pátzcuaro, which was gifted to him by Mr. and Mrs. George. The house was rustic, but the area was beautiful. It was in rural Mexico. Rinpoche and some of his students were sitting out on the patio, and somehow Rinpoche was transformed. Suddenly he dictated this text, which he said had just come to him. It's a beautiful text, which, along with others that he received later, became the outline of the Shambhala vision.

In the terma tradition, some of these texts are very pithy. Unbelievably logical and profound, but succinct, they contain a lot in a very few words. An example would be *The Golden Sun of the Great East*, which is only, perhaps, the equivalent of a dozen book pages. Some parts of it are reproduced in *Shambhala: The Sacred Path of the Warrior*. A short time after his utterance of that pithy text, he wrote an auto-commentary, which is a common Tibetan thing where the text comments on itself, if you will.

In any case, Trungpa Rinpoche eventually came back to Boulder, Colorado, where he and many of his students were living at that time. I believe there were about a thousand of us living in the area. He gathered a small group of perhaps fifty students, and over a period of several weeks, twice a week, the Shambhala vision unfolded. After that, a few more termas magically appeared. And over a period of three or four years, he gave perhaps two hundred to three hundred teachings on this subject. Therefore, it's a rather complete vision, a spiritual and social vision that he was simultaneously teaching us.

This was merely a rambling history. Yet it is something that I cherish. By auspicious coincidence, the shared name between these teachings and the publishing company that I started with Michael Fagan in 1969 is a curiosity of history—Shambhala Publications actually had the name before Trungpa Rinpoche had even come to America. We were amazed by this coincidence! The publishing company is also not affiliated with the organization Shambhala International and its network of centers. After the passing of Trungpa Rinpoche in 1987, the organization took a turn that I found disappointing.

PARALLELS WITH OTHER CULTURES

If we look at other cultures throughout the history of Asia, there have been times when such a view of human dignity and enlightened society has been part and parcel of civilization. For example, I think that the basic impulse of Confucianism, and then the later impulse of neo-Confucianism (which is a Confucianism that included some Buddhist ideas), were based on that sort of premise that you could have a society that was based on goodness, and on a broad social vision of this one-caste understanding. Certain emperors also had this view. In India, after Ashoka killed a lot of people and put together his kingdom of Greater India, he realized that he was an evil fellow and something changed in his being. Instead of just rejoicing that he had this immense kingdom, he felt deep remorse for the pain and suffering that he had caused. He became a Buddhist, changed his view, and was the first person historically that we know of to create free public education and public hospitals, in addition to a moral code of conduct for the kingdom. Today, in India, you can still see the sandstone pillars of Ashoka, which include inscriptions of his edicts. That is an example of how the same type of vision made its way into India from the same type of matrix. Likewise, Prince Shotoku changed the face of Japan; he ushered in a golden age also based on this sort of view. In China, there is the example of Emperor Yong Le—though he is sometimes historically held in ill repute, possibly by those who took over his kingdom.

Many aspects of Western cultures also resonate with Shambhala. One can think of King Arthur and Camelot, chivalry, and the sense of warriorship that goes with it. In the Bible, the story of King David is akin to this. Various Indigenous cultures—Native American, Australian Aboriginal, and so on—also have a similar view of human dignity.

Interestingly, the person who presented these teachings to the West, Trungpa Rinpoche, overtly stated that not only was he Tibetan but he was also a Britophile and a Japanophile. In presenting the Shambhala teachings to the West, he added the best of Britain and Japan to it, unabashedly. From his point of view, these elements embody the Shambhala spirit, which doesn't have a particular border. His whole approach is that this teaching is not just for Tibetans but for a world—*this* world—in decline.

Thus, Trungpa Rinpoche—I'm proud to be his student—added the best of Britain, which he adored. We mentioned his always having a photograph of Her Majesty and Prince Philip at his house. Along with that, he had a tokonoma, a Japanese-style alcove, with a hanging scroll. This is a Tibetan gentleman, mind you, who came from the roughest part of Tibet. (Interestingly, the Trungpa Tulku was not only the head of his monastery but also the regional ruler of that part of Tibet. Tibet was in fact divided into many kingdoms, and those kingdoms were further divided . . . the feudal system at work!)

In any case, these teachings allude to elements from other cultures, but Rinpoche doesn't mix his metaphors. When you talk about the Arthurian legend, you talk about the Arthurian legend; when you talk about Prince Shotoku, you talk about Prince Shotoku. You don't get the analogies mixed up, but you say that there's a spirit in common between this and that.

No particular culture owns or has the copyright on the Shambhala teachings. There is simply something in the human spirit that clicks with the dignity of being human, isn't just out to get everybody else, without any morality that needs to be imposed or enforced from outside. In the Shambhala vision, as mentioned, we call that underlying ground "basic goodness." That is the most basic thing to being human. Underlying everything is this basic goodness that is an integral part of our being, accessible to everyone, and in fact where everyone came from. Regardless of all the legends and stories we have discussed in this chapter, that basic goodness is *not* a mythology. That, in fact, is our birthright. We are born with it; whatever else happens in our lives is the dirtying up of that. Each of us come from that, and that basic goodness is in fact the underlying ground of what we are, regardless of what we think. Our thoughts, concepts, and ideas are just stuff we add on top of it.

The Shambhala teachings offer us methods to unveil that basic goodness and relate with it so as to relate with the world in a gentle, fearless, and fundamentally sane way.

13
Basic Goodness, Warriorship, and the Great Eastern Sun

Trying to put a complete worldview onto a postage stamp is no easy task. Be that as it may, I want to offer an introduction to some of the fundamental teachings of Shambhala, as presented by Trungpa Rinpoche.

The heart of the Shambhala teachings is something that we all share. But let's begin in a very simple way. To do that, we have to look at our own situation. We are human, and here we are in this society. Most of us have been around for a little while. Even if we happen to be young and look innocent, each of us has collected quite a load of baggage. What I mean by "baggage" isn't just *stuff*. We've collected a load of ideas about ourselves based on, I suppose, our own fears, self-criticism, and feelings of inadequacy. We have all kinds of psychological hang-ups.

I have often asked groups of people who attended talks what they were looking for. I am genuinely curious, and it may be worthwhile to ask yourself the same questions: "What do I want at this point? Why am I even reading this?"

Once, a man answered, "I'm not quite sure." I thought it was almost honest—almost. He knew a little bit, didn't he? So, I asked him, "What's the little bit that you're sure about?"

"Well," he said, "I want to be happy."

Happiness. Nothing wrong with that.

And, of course, other people have different answers—we want insight or love or fulfillment or whatever it is. Right there, we are being human. But the interesting thing is that most answers are quite different from ordinary self-centered desires. They are more than just something for *moi*. When people really ask themselves those questions, each of the aspirations that are expressed takes into account a larger picture. That fact is not insignificant.

This brings us back to the notion of basic goodness. We should really take a look and see what that is and that it actually exists within our own being.

When we talk about Shambhala, we can discuss how some people think it's real and some people think it's a myth. However, basic goodness itself has nothing to do with mythology, and it has nothing to do with *maybe*. It's one of those things that just are. But how can I make such a sweeping statement?

Well, as difficult as this world is, as painful as so many situations are, as sad as any of us can get, or as happy as any of us can be, we share something that allows us to reach out to another, even if it's challenging; to gently touch another, or even to make love if that's appropriate; to appreciate the greenery, the sunshine, the birds, whatever it is that presents itself. We have the ability to look at another being and just see them and be happy with that, or see them and be scared by that, but see and *be with* them before we have all kinds of opinions about them. I can look at you, you can look at me, we can look at each other, and there's a moment where our minds and hearts meet, before we start to make judgments or commentary about the situation—that is, whether the commentary is positive or negative. "Oh, right, that person is so-and-so," or "Oh, she's so pretty," or "He's such a handsome man," or whatever. We're talking about something that's there even before all that.

Isn't it quite unique that we're discussing this in a chapter that is also about warriorship? *Warriorship* is a funny word, especially when talking about qualities such as tenderness. But here's the twist: This warriorship is really about being *above* war.

It sure has to do with bravery, but the bravery begins with ourselves. Just think of it: You wake up in the morning, you look in the mirror—there you are. Actually, that's not you but a reflection of you. There it is—your face, eyes, teeth, hair, just like that. Before the makeup or the shaving. Whatever it is, it's just like it is. But then, as Trungpa Rinpoche explained, you can look at that and be comfortable with that—which we all can be, even if you're like me, that is, over-the-hill. Those of you on the hill can be comfortable. Same for those of you under the hill, you just starting the climb, you seeing the hill from afar, and the rest of us—we know who we are. It doesn't make any difference: If we just look and if we can be simple with that, then that is seeing our basic goodness. Looking and freaking out is something else altogether. (Although sometimes you look and you *have* to freak out—but that's different; that's if you had a rough night!)

BUDDHA-NATURE IS ALWAYS AVAILABLE

The Shambhala teachings are about establishing ourselves, our mind, our body into a real sanity, a *basic* kind of sanity. We shouldn't think about bravery, goodness, or even enlightenment as some sort of myth concerning somebody else. Within our very being, we have buddha-nature, the awakened quality within our heart, as part of our birthright. And though it can be clouded and we can suffer from confusion, depression, anxiety, anger, or fear, that awakened quality is always available to us. Even dogs—and I love dogs—have buddha-nature. Same for mosquitoes and all other beings.

For buddha-nature to blossom, for basic goodness to shine forth, we need to be genuine and real. We can't always go looking for stories and distractions. Of course, we're always looking for stories and distractions; I don't mean we absolutely *can't*. That's what we do most of the time. Yet to allow the goodness that is buddha-nature in our being to blossom fully, we need to look at our own mind, at our own life, and see it for what it is—the good, the bad, and the ugly. Just look at it straight in the face. We don't have to make up something different. If we're trying to make up something different, we're cowards. To allow buddha-nature to shine is to acknowledge who we are, inclusive of everything that we experience, everything that we think—the whole beautiful mess. If we're going to be fully human, we must acknowledge our vulnerability; we must open to our own being and to the world around us. If we can be fully vulnerable, then we have absolutely nothing to lose, and we thus can't be defeated. That's the dawn of fearlessness.

FEAR, WARRIORSHIP, AND BEING OUT OF SYNC

What's fear? It is connected to feelings of insufficiency about ourselves, jumpiness about difficulties, bouts with fluctuating emotions. It has to do with wanting to avoid pain or intimacy—wanting to *avoid* in any way. As humans, we create fields of avoidance, fields of distractions.

To be fearless is to be a warrior, but not in the sense of someone with a gun or sword trying to kill an enemy. Rather, "fearless" and "warrior," in the language we're using here, refer to being willing to face all and everything. It's about the willingness to be openhearted enough and to be with what is actually going on with ourselves and in the world. This sense of warriorship involves the ability to be still in the middle of all this storminess and turmoil. Warriorship really is about being still—not fake stillness; actual stillness. It's about good head and shoulders. It's about being able to open enough to look out, see, and experience fear directly. There is no way to become fearless without seeing fear. Franklin D. Roosevelt and others have said that there is nothing to fear but fear itself.[1] It's a little bit like that.

The key to becoming a warrior in this sense is the practice of meditation. It is the weapon of the warrior. It is the armor of the warrior. It allows us to be vulnerable and totally strong at the same time. The practice of meditation is about good posture and allowing everything that arises to just arise.

Becoming a warrior, a meditation practitioner, means facing ourselves. It's like looking in the mirror and not getting scared, wondering, "Who's that?" It's about looking without judgment, exploring, and simply practicing wakefulness.

We might ask ourselves, "Where does fear come from?" The nature of fear comes from a discontinuity of our body and mind. We're so much out of sync so much of the time, and it produces a discomfort. That discomfort is where the anxieties come from. We may think one way, and then our body does something totally different. This is not about how focused we can be when we play rugby or attempt an athletic prowess. By "out of sync" I also don't mean the occasional "jet lag out of sync" or anything of the sort. I mean *basically* out of sync. Yet even that is not truly *basic*—unlike basic goodness. In other words, we are not doomed to remain out of sync with our body, our mind, our world.

THE SETTING-SUN POINT OF VIEW

Being out of sync is described as being caught in the setting-sun point of view. We are trying to escape from the brightness and brilliance of the wakefulness of the world. The setting-sun approach is about receding into darkness and just trying to absorb ourselves with distraction. These days, the biggest absorptions are things such as the internet. We get absorbed by screens of any size, just so that we don't have to deal with anything. "Just take me away..." The setting-sun view is avoidance, avoidance, avoidance—anything to keep us from being real and in the present moment.

In the setting-sun world, we are attracted to dungeons. You know, downtown, you'll see these places with dimmed lights and loud music. We have nothing against music, and nothing against dancing. But sometimes what we are attracted to is not the beauty of music or the people. We just want to be absorbed in drink and sound and smoke or whatever. That's one form of avoidance. Or, even though it's really bright, it may be that our idea of being really "with it" is going to lie on the beach and bake. Again, there's nothing wrong with the beach. There's nothing wrong with any of it. It's the mentality. It's all about the mentality of escapism—escaping from our life.

We make up so many distractions. And then we get cancer. Or we have a heart attack. Then we get distracted by the details of the cancer, the details of the medical phenomena, and what have you. We even distract ourselves from the reality of the rawness of dying. Actually, we can even distract ourselves when we're dying. "Everything's going to be all... *right*." The avoidance is so strong. The setting-sun point of view is about avoiding not only life but also the truth and brilliance of life. It's also about avoiding the truth of death.

I'm not trying to be morbid here, because there is an alternative to this avoidance mentality.

THE ALTERNATIVE: THE GREAT EASTERN SUN

The alternative to the setting-sun point of view, the distraction point of view, is the Great Eastern Sun, which is the sun of wakefulness and human dignity. It is about non-avoidance; being present, uplifted, open, gentle. It is about acknowledging our birthright of basic goodness, the buddha-nature in our being—the fact that we too can be like Buddha. *Buddha* means "awakened." We too can be present, genuine, real.

In "Great Eastern Sun," "Great" has to do with the sense of upliftedness, openness, gentleness. The "East" part has to do with dawn: Even before the sun rises, there's a sense of light that comes from the East and dawns. It is the smile we have when we wake up. And "Sun" is the totally wakeful quality.

The avoidance point of view is not inherent in our being; it is a habit. Our habits, as we know, are fairly strong. We even go out of our way to find distractions in spiritual searching. It may be in how we do yoga to improve ourselves. Again, I have nothing against yoga; it is one of the greatest inventions of India. I'm just pointing out how we do things sometimes. We'll go to yoga to get away from our life, to do something different. Or we'll go to the café. Again, don't get me wrong: I love coffee shops. What we won't do for one little cup of water squeezed through a bean with some milk steamed into it—and what we won't pay either! The whole thing's amazing. The level of distraction involved in something so simple... We can be obsessed with that little cup of liquid, whether it's flat white, espresso, or cortado. I'm a coffee lover. Thankfully coffee is not the issue; distraction is.

But those distractions are minor. The distractions of trying to create a better version of ourselves and pretending that it can exist outside of this world, outside of this body—that there is something spiritual that we can attain somewhere *else*—is more problematic. So is the idea that we can be saved by somebody or something. Again, I'm not putting down religions. I'm a religious fanatic. But the idea that we can be saved and not have to do any work on ourselves, that we can be saved and then appear magically in some other realm where all's good—such ideas are real problems. They boil down to the spiritual materialism we discussed in the previous chapter. We try to create the distraction of a better *me*, another *me* that has nothing to do with *my* problems, *my* pain, *my* thoughts. All that is just fooling ourselves. It has to do with that basic desynchronization of body and mind. Being spiritual is not something separate from our life, separate from our body.

We want so desperately to have something to hold on to. The warrior's point of view is about letting go. It is acknowledging the vulnerability that in fact there is nothing to hold on to and that is perfectly wonderful.

We can do this in stages. That's not a problem. In fact, there's no wakefulness that is guaranteed. Wakefulness is of the moment. It is how we live our life. The blossoming of the buddha-nature is something that happens day to day with our spouse, our children, by ourselves, at work—anywhere.

Yet the key to opening the warrior's way is sitting meditation. The practice of meditation is to bring our attention to the wakeful quality within ourselves so that we become accustomed to it. The practice then carries into the rest of our life. It is not a panacea to make us feel good. It includes the whole gamut of human feelings, emotions, and thoughts. Yet here with the Great Eastern Sun, there's a view of a sun at full brilliance—a ten o'clock sun—that can radiate in our life. We are not talking about the literal sun; we're talking about the sun of wakefulness.

When we meditate, we are present, and we're carried away. We're present, and we're carried away... just like everyday life. But the practice of meditation makes us become accustomed to the wakeful quality; to being able to simply experience whatever arises without distraction, judgment, fear; without being caught up by either elation or depression. However, even if we do meditate, if we don't have the view—in this case the Great Eastern Sun view—meditation isn't going to do us any good. If we're just meditating because we think it's going to be good for us, it's not. The practice of meditation is based on the wakefulness that is already inherent in our being. It's not about looking for something somewhere. It's about allowing that wakefulness to arise and becoming accustomed to it.

I'm an old man now. I was taught this as a young man. I found it unparalleled. This isn't a sales pitch. I'm just telling you that I have now lived for a long time, and I've seen so many things—spiritual, material; all sorts of phenomena . . . Here I'm talking about the most worthwhile thing that I have found. I was trained this way, and I'm a happy camper. It is real. And it's something that's been passed from one human to another human over thousands of years. It is totally worthwhile. We just have to give ourselves enough of a break to allow it to come into our being. It's never too late—really.

MEDITATION IN THE SHAMBHALA TRADITION

So what does sitting meditation mean in the context of the Shambhala teachings? Simply this: mindfulness of body, mindfulness of breath, and mindfulness of mind. This threefold mindfulness was introduced in the first chapter, but now is a good time to revisit these instructions. Since the spiritual development is not exactly linear, it is often worthwhile to review and deepen so-called basic instructions. We may also notice that the view here is ever so slightly different: The emphasis is not just on calming the mind but on slowly familiarizing ourselves with basic goodness.

First, there's **mindfulness of body**. Meditation has to do with establishing a good posture—making a relationship with our body and the earth. Whether we're sitting on the floor, on a cushion, or in a chair, there's the sense of being present; feeling the ground, our body, the space around us. This exercise comes from an eyes-open tradition: We begin with our gaze slightly down, just so we're not distracted, yet with an awareness of everything. We're not looking for distraction, but we're not trying to avoid anything either.

In this way, we have our good posture. There's openness in our shoulders and our heart. Our spine is erect and our head comfortable. We're just right here. We are mindful of our body, we feel the earth below and the space around us, and we are cognizant of our environment.

Then we have **mindfulness of breath**. We don't try to control our breath in any way, but we use it as a touchstone to wakefulness because the breath is always there. Now, there are some specifics to this aspect of the practice. We pay attention to just breathing without forcing it in any way. We essentially ride the *outbreath* with our mind—in other words, we're just conscious of the outbreath, but then we don't pay any particular attention to the inbreath. The inbreath happens, but we don't make any big deal about it. We have outbreath; there's a gap; the inbreath comes in by itself; there's a gap; we follow the breath out again. We're just there with it. If this is a new approach for you, we'll look more closely at this in the guided meditation below.

The third part is **mindfulness of mind**. Here we're not trying to control or censor our thoughts, or even to differentiate them as good or bad. We're human. We're simply observant of whatever comes up in our mind. That's entirely nonjudgmental; we're just with whatever comes up. Thoughts *will* carry us, whatever they might be—Mom, apple pie, who we love, who we hate, that bad driver—but as soon as we notice that we've been carried away, we just come back to our breath. Thoughts are not viewed as a problem. Emotions are also not viewed as a problem—they're just a form of thought. If they become a problem, we just notice that we have the thoughts or emotions and that they're becoming a problem. Whatever arises, it's just there.

In that way we simply sit with our good posture, mindful of our body, mindful of our breath, and mindful of our mind, which is just being with whatever arises. That's what we mean by sitting meditation in this context. We have more to say on this subject, but first let's give it a try.

GUIDED MEDITATION

It is best if we can establish regular practice. Regular cleaning of the armor—that open heart and solid back—provides for a cheerful warrior! That's what allows us to be brave, so that we can accept what comes our way and accept it solidly. Such practice is truly worthwhile, and we can be thankful to have that opportunity.

Meditation begins with taking our seat. As you choose and approach your seat, pay attention to the fact that you're actually going to sit down.

Once you're seated, take a dignified posture. This begins with a straight back. Open your chest, allow your heart to be just right here. Your head rests comfortably on your shoulders. Your hands can be folded or resting on your thighs or knees. Whatever the case, be comfortable. Your eyes are open, with your gaze out and slightly down.

Take a moment to feel the earth below you. Even if you're on a chair, you're connected to the earth. Feel your body—your whole bodily experience, especially your seat.

Then begin paying attention to your breath. Simply follow the outbreath, gently riding it all the way to the end, and then let the inbreath just naturally come in. Don't change or force your breathing in any way; just gently touch your mind to the outbreath, then let go. Outbreath, let go. Outbreath, let go. Likewise with the natural gap between the breaths. There's no need to contrive anything.

Remember what you're doing: You're allowing the basic goodness in your being to shine through. Just be there with it.

Whatever appears is just thinking. Don't try to censor it. Don't try to make it go away. Whatever it is, it's just there.

When you notice you have been carried away, simply label the thinking as "thinking," and gently come back to your breath.

At the same time, feel the solidity of your straight back. Your heart is open, vulnerable, yet you are perfectly strong and still.

Again, if you notice you are thinking, just mentally note, "thinking," and return to your breath.

Occasionally, to refresh, feel the space all around you.

Then go back to the outbreath, and let go. Outbreath. Gap. Outbreath. Gap.

Thoughts will return. Label this as "thinking" and gently come back to your breath.

Feel the solidity of your back. Feel the earth below you. Feel your tender heart, wide open. There's no need to avoid anything. Just let whatever is here be here.

"Thinking," then back with the breath.

Again, just be aware of the space around you. Feel your body sitting straight. Feel your breath. Feel the solidity of the earth below. A good, simple, dignified person just simply sitting straight.

Take your time before moving on.

THE COSMIC MIRROR AND GARBAGE COLLECTORS

The underlying basic goodness makes it totally possible for us to be unconfused, healthy, and for real. Yet for the time being, who *isn't* confused, really? Where does the confusion come from? Usually from some idea about ourselves. Perhaps we blame the confusion on somebody else, but this has to do with some idea of ourselves anyway. That's what we call dualism.

The teachings show us the way to go beyond that. However, there's no reason to take anyone's word for it. We have to look into our own being and see what's there, warts and all. If we can do that in a simple way, without making a lot of noise, we have a beginning. That's where fearlessness starts. If we can feel our heart, not dependent on anyone else's approval, we have a really wonderful beginning. From that, all the things that people aspire to, deep down, become possible. When the chatter of *me* and *mine* quiets down, and we can feel the tenderness of our heart, there's an opening. That's what basic goodness refers to. Everyone can find it. That's why it is *basic*. And it is *good*, as it doesn't particularly have any complaints. It also doesn't have to be compared to anything else, which is extremely important.

To find some inspiration and deepen our understanding, let us read the beginning of *The Letter of the Black Ashe*, which Trungpa Rinpoche received in Boulder, Colorado.

From the great cosmic mirror
Without beginning and without end,
Human society became manifest.
At that time, liberation and confusion arose.
When fear and doubt occurred
Toward the confidence which is primordially free,
Countless multitudes of cowards arose.

> When the confidence which is primordially free
> Was followed and delighted in,
> Countless multitudes of warriors arose.[2]

The text talks about the view of the Great Eastern Sun. We have warriors and cowards—simultaneously. But before that, the text speaks of this "cosmic mirror." It is that which reflects everything that is. A mirror doesn't make any commentaries, does it? When we get up in the morning and look in the mirror, there it simply is, without the blah-blah-blah that we may project onto it. Likewise, the cosmic mirror is just the reflection of what is in this world.

The text speaks of a cosmic mirror "without beginning and without end." Generally speaking, we have the big bang theory, the evolution theory, as well as all kinds of religious theories of how we all got here. As far as I can tell, whether or not we believe in them has never brought anyone closer to enlightenment. We find ourselves in this world, in this body, with this mind, and with other people, not to mention animals. And not to mention institutions, responsibilities—oh, where did those come from?—and so forth. It doesn't really matter where we arose from: Here we are. From here there are essentially two ways to go: We can be a coward, or a warrior. This is the basic dualism. The warrior is willing and open; the coward avoids. This may sound harsh, but we're not alone in this; we all avoid. Yet fundamentally we all have dignity, and we can all move toward bravery. The choice is ours.

The mirror doesn't make the choice. It just presents what is. You don't like what you see? You can get mad at it, I suppose. Perhaps you can try to murder it. This world is lovely, in fact. It has a lot of odd and horrible things, but the very basis of our life is on the lovely side. That is wondrous. I'm not going to do much philosophy here, and this isn't touchy-feely either. This isn't honeyed New Age—we have enough of that in California. This is actually our life we're talking about. Whether we're young or old doesn't make any difference. If we can just touch into that tender place in our heart and look at the world from there, that is truly wonderful.

But we are afraid, aren't we? Why are we afraid to do that—afraid to touch into that tender place and look at the world from there? Did we get bashed when we did that before? What is the fear of just being simple? Do *you* have any fear? Heaps, I'm sure. But why? We have fears, we could say, based on our experiences, on comparisons, and so forth. Whatever the case, to understand how to go from fearful to fearless and how it all relates to basic goodness, we must talk laundry.

Tenderness, the warm and openhearted way of relating to the world, is not a one-shot deal. However, if our outlook gets dirty, dirtied, or pooped upon—whatever happens—that doesn't mean we have to get stuck with the dirt. We can get Mr. Clean, or whichever brand is most popular in our country, and we can clean and begin again.

When we begin again and can thus reconnect with our basic goodness, things become clear, vivid. Even as you are reading this, if you can be just simple for a moment, things appear vividly. When we don't get too caught up in our thoughts, life is fairly simple and pleasant.

How do we live our life that way? Not by philosophy. First, we must have the view, and that view is touching into our heart. As soon as we touch into our heart and look out, we can feel the basic goodness. But we need something in our life to provide us with a touchstone to that. In both the Shambhala vision specifically and in Buddhism in general, that touchstone is the practice of sitting meditation.

The practice of sitting meditation gives us the opportunity to punctuate our usual habits that constitute the dirtying in our life and do a cleanup. The Shambhala vision is about learning to be good garbage collectors. Seriously. We learn how to take out the garbage and properly dispose of it. That is, our garbage and other people's garbage as well. By that I don't mean that we start to judge other people's garbage or try to control them, only that we do what we can and kindly take responsibility for our place in larger situations.

The first thing we've got to clean is our own messy mind and sense of inadequacy. Whatever sense of inadequacy we hold on to is a lie. Inadequate in comparison to what? And if we truly look at it, who cares? That's easy to say, but it is true. Who really cares? And if someone really cares, so what? It doesn't affect the fact of our own basic dignity.

The basic goodness is the dignity of being human. Cleaning, the process of cleaning, is the ongoing continuity of that dignity. No matter how dirty we get, we can always get clean. If the Jif doesn't work, we get the Mr. Clean "Clean Freak" edition.

In terms of our own lives, our own existence, the best way to clean is to give ourselves the time to be simple with our own mind.

DEEPENING OUR UNDERSTANDING OF MEDITATION

As we have seen, we put great emphasis on the practice of sitting meditation. However, no matter what people say, it's not enough to just sit there. It's also important to understand *why* we're sitting there and what's going on. From the Shambhala point of view, we practice meditation as a way to key into the most basic part of our being, which is the basic goodness, and to cut our habitual tendency, which has sullied or dirtied our basic goodness, if you will. Yet we don't view dirt as a problem. We don't view our emotions as a problem. This is about being brave, so we welcome the whole mess. When we sit down to meditate, we are not trying to escape or forget our problems. There is no place to go. We're not trying to make our thoughts disappear, and we're not doing mental gymnastics either. It is about opening—first to ourselves, which is difficult. The biggest dirt that basic goodness collects is this strange self-hate. I have no idea where it comes from, but I experience it. All of us experience it, for reasons unknown. But it's not inherent; it's just a conditioned habit.

In the previous section, we quoted a text that talks about cowards and warriors. We're born into this world—every day. We wake up, and uh-oh, there's a choice. It may not seem like it, but every day we do have a choice. And the warrior's way, the way of bravery, implies that we choose to cheer up.

Cheering up basically goes like this: You open yourself to the vision of the Great Eastern Sun; you maintain good head and shoulders, a simple sense of dignity; and you meditate, which provides the cleansing mechanism. However, cheering up is not a methodology; it's just an attitude to be nurtured. But there are some specifics to the meditation part, and it is good to deepen our understanding of them.

The kind of meditation we practice in the context of the Shambhala tradition is exactly the same as the usual Buddhist meditation. It's shamatha (the development of peace) and vipashyana (insight, deep seeing). As we saw earlier, this is also connected to the three mindfulnesses.

When we take a good posture, our situation is immediately changed. If we slump, we have a slumped feeling. If we sit up straight, we have a sit-up-straight feeling. It's dignified, and we feel we're really alive.

It is important to understand that good posture connects us with our tender heart. In meditation, no matter what pain we've experienced in the past—and I understand that many of us have experienced a lot of pain, and pains of different kinds—we still allow everything to be open. We expand our chest and allow our heart to beat wide open. At the same time, our spine is erect, and that is our strength. In the language of Shambhala, we say, "Hard back, soft heart." It goes together, and it's the best combination.

Inevitably we have thoughts—no problem. Thoughts are part of being human. However, during the process of meditation, when we get lost in thought—when the thought carries us away from our breath and body, when we can't even hear the sounds around us—we simply say, "Thinking." We don't censor what's going on. As soon as we say "Thinking," the thoughts haven't carried us away anymore. We have noticed. We come back to our breath, back to our body, and we simply are here.

What does this do? If we can punctuate our life with the sitting practice of meditation, it allows that openness of our being and unveils our tender heart so that we can start anew and see the world anew. We can begin our day with a certain openness. Of course, all kinds of things are going to happen. However, whatever thought arises, whatever emotion arises, we view it as equally the same, whether it's mindless chatter, a feeling of love, a thought about harming somebody, or any strong emotions or desires. In sitting meditation we view it all as equally the same: *thinking*.

Bravery and strength comes from viewing anything that comes our way with equanimity. We are used to categorizing and hierarchizing everything. From the meditative perspective, it doesn't make any difference what arises in our being, whether it's scary or funny. We view everything equally. If we can begin to do that, we can become absolutely fearless.

Remember, fear comes from our sense of insecurity. We are not saying that if a car comes careening in, you just sit there and let it squash you. Of course you don't. You move out of the way. The kind of fear we're talking about here is the fear that comes from inside, which is the basis of all fear. That's a fear of our own mind, strangely enough, and of what our mind can produce or what our mind does with what presents itself.

Therefore, the process of meditation is very simple. We view everything that appears equally, without judgment. If it takes over and takes us away from our breath, away from our body, we label it as "thinking." No matter what it is, whether it's an emotion or a thought, we give it all the same name.

FEARLESSNESS IN A TROUBLED WORLD

At this point, if we have a meditation practice, we may start to recognize basic goodness within ourselves. We may also understand, at least intellectually, how fear can, in most cases, be based on fixating on our own sense of self. We may see how fearlessness can go hand in hand with insight and openness. But we may be struggling to find that fearlessness when there is so much happening beyond our control—horrific, inconceivable events happening to good people every day. This is scary and heart-wrenching. What should we do then, especially if we don't believe in a higher power that takes care of everything?

This goes to the heart of the matter. I think it is one of the most important questions, and with no easy answer. I wish I could just say, "Do this and do that and everything's going to be all right." It takes more than that. However, one thing is sure: If we run away from fear, if we have aversion to it, we can never become fearless. The only way to become fearless is to experience fear and not run away from it. Fearlessness comes from a direct experience of fear.

The Shambhala and Buddhist teachings give a method to develop that fearlessness: the practice of sitting meditation. As explained, through the practice of meditation, everything that presents itself to our mind, we simply allow it. By being with it, we develop confidence in our own mind. That's key. By allowing anything that enters just to be there, not giving it any particular significance, everything is viewed equally as just thinking. What happens if we practice that? In our ordinary life, as things present themselves, they don't have the same power. I don't mean that a gun doesn't have the same power. A gun is a gun. But if you see a gun, your mind can look at it differently and react differently. There's a different way to react to situations. Again, this is not to say that if we meditate, all the horrible things of the world will go away. Not at all. But we will see them clearly. The development of peace that leads to the development of insight means that everything becomes clearer. Our perceptions become clearer; our senses become clearer, and we can see what is good and what is bad without being *judgmental*. From that clear seeing, being with fear, we can conquer that fear. Confrontation is not as automatic or frightening.

Again, that's not to say that a terrorist won't blow up the place this afternoon. We're not talking about changing that over which we have no control. We're talking about learning to deal with our own mind. This means that if we see something, we can act clearly because our mind is not clouded by all the baggage that comes along with our mental busyness. Clarity of mind means we can see clearly; seeing clearly means we can act clearly. Then what we do is on our cognizance as a warrior. How we relate to society, how we relate to the problems of this world, depends on our understanding of the situation, but it is based on clarity, not our neurotic fears.

So much of what we fear is fear itself. For instance, many people can be in pain when they go to the hospital, but then they also make up all kinds of scenarios that create further problems—with what they've read on WebMD, what they've heard here and there, or out of sheer hypochondria. However, we can help ourselves and we can help others if we have insight. How do we develop insight? We *practice* insight. That's why the teachings on fearlessness are inseparable from the practice of meditation. Without the practice of meditation, these teachings are worthless. They're just thoughts, lovely ideas to put in a book, something nice to talk about, or perhaps a drag to talk about, but just talk in any event. However, there is the practice of sitting meditation, and then there are further practices, if we get into these things. We enter further and further into it, and the instructions on fearlessness become more and more to the point.

In Asia, these teachings are sometimes related to the martial arts, strangely enough. A lot of people don't know that, but many martial arts emanated from Buddhist temples and were developed by monks. It's a way of practicing meditation in action. These pacifists are the toughest guys! A certain awareness and fearlessness come from that because there's no clinging to so many ideas of self and so many ideas altogether. There's just clarity.

What's at the heart of these teachings: You have the view, which is the view of warriorship—seeing the Great Eastern Sun, taking responsibility for your actions, and being willing to cultivate kindness to others rather than self-centeredness—and you put that view of warriorship into practice, which is the practice of meditation. In addition to that, the Shambhala teachings suggest many other practices, such as the various martial arts, flower arranging, tea ceremony, or horsemanship—something where we put our mind and body on the line. It's not just a mental discipline. There are disciplines that teach us to be fearless that relate to the synchronicity of mind and body.

But we begin at the beginning: We listen to the view, and we develop a sense of peace in shamatha meditation. From that, vipashyana meditation arises and we develop insight and discernment. From there, the real warrior training begins. For example, when you've learned to thoroughly synchronize body and mind, you can synchronize yourself and society. But if you put the cart before the horse, you're gonna be a mess. Before you can help anybody, before you can befriend anybody, you have to help yourself and make friends with yourself. Otherwise, it's a sham. If we can't take care of things at home, how can we take care of things in society? Our society is a wreck because we have people who barely take care of themselves and their families taking care of countries. It's a joke. But the joke is a reflection of us. The joke's on us, not on them! Most politicians and heads of countries are there because people like us put them there, one way or another, by caring or not caring.

If you want to develop fearlessness, look at the face of fear very closely. See what it looks like. Be with it. Be afraid. Meet it head-on. It's not what you think it is. The only way you can rise above pain is to lean into it totally. If you are experiencing a lot of pain and you try to run away from it, the pain will run with you. Likewise, the only way to deal with fear is to lean into the fear. It won't just go away. The world is not all rosy, but we can deal with what comes up in the best way that we can: from a mind of clarity that isn't constantly busy. That was the starting point of this whole conversation: our busy mind.

Thus, we have these teachings, and then we have the practice. And as much as I like the teachings, the practice is better. Am I afraid of the practice? Yes. Why? Because then I'm responsible for myself. I can't blame anybody else.

If we really mean it when we pretend that we would like to alleviate the suffering of the world, then we take responsibility. We actually practice. We meet things in our life straightforwardly. That is the warrior's way. We have to let go of frivolity and habitual laziness. That's rough but definitely doable. Good luck!

14
Working with One's World

Trungpa Rinpoche's books on the teachings of Shambhala[1] are powerful yet simple. That element of simpleness is deceptive because it's not about simple-mindedness but rather the simple truth of how to rouse our being. The books don't exactly provide do-it-yourself kits but subtle clues on how to adjust our view. It's very important—one of the most important things in meditation practice, in fact, and in life in general—to develop a view that we can live from. It's a sad affair when we develop a view that is nonsense or that doesn't deliver.

The Great Eastern Sun point of view has subtlety and it delivers. As we have seen, it is contrasted to the setting-sun perspective, which is based on distraction and avoidance: We are always escaping the rawness of pain, the vividness of life, the brightness of wakefulness. Even joy, in the setting-sun world, is either dimmed or drummed up and totally artificial—it takes us away from an actual appreciation of our life and a genuine, natural cheerfulness. The setting-sun point of view is also connected to a poverty mentality, and to nihilistic and materialistic tendencies. Our world feels dark and limited. By comparison, the Great Eastern Sun is the sun of wakefulness and human dignity. It is ever-dawning. While in the setting-sun approach, we insidiously feel downtrodden by our own self-referential habits. In the Great Eastern Sun approach, we constantly feel uplifted, and our upliftedness is connected to openness and gentleness. The view here is acknowledging our birthright of basic goodness and remembering that we can be fully present and genuine.

If we make a connection with that view, we can live it. The Great Eastern Sun view involves tuning in to something that exists in our own being and has just been covered up. This has nothing to do with the so-called power of positive thinking.

We can't expect fear to just disappear in one moment by reading something or by practicing meditation. There's no instant remedy. Fear can and does arise over and over. Even when we become accustomed to a fearless way of looking at things, there are always challenges. So, we're not looking for any quick fix. We're talking about how we live our life and our willingness to look fear in the face.

In fact, the instructions on how to deal with fear are quite specific: You jump right into it. Think of when you go to the beach and the water is cold. You can take the approach of tippy-toeing: getting your feet wet, then your ankles wet, inching your way in. Or you can just jump right in. Here, we jump right in. We be with the fear. We be with the indecision. We don't separate ourselves from it. By not avoiding it, it becomes workable. But the only way to find out what this means is through our own life experience.

The warrior's path is not just a one-time situation. It's about developing that stance or view in life. Here, "warrior" means a gentle warrior. So, this stance is based on gentleness, goodness, and being above fighting.

However, just living in this world invites conflict. It's the nature of existence. We face all kinds of circumstances. We might love someone, we're totally infatuated, then one day, "I hate you." Or worse. Things happen, you know. It's challenging because situations can turn so strangely—sometimes gradually, sometimes suddenly. Also we have a body that is bound to decay and have diseases. It is going to be cast aside one day. So, there's no quick fix that "I'm a fearless human being and nothing can harm me." That would be absolute nonsense. However, true fearlessness is based on being able to face whatever presents itself—not only being able to face it but also rejoicing in it regardless of the intensity. Rejoicing, not by being fake about it, but by being genuine in how we face situations.

The essential result of developing an enlightened point of view is living out that view. If we can develop an enlightened point of view and follow it, then we have an enlightened life. We're not talking about some kind of highfalutin lifestyle here. It's about becoming genuinely human.

But what does it mean to be genuine, really? And how does it relate to our place in the world?

FICTIONS WE CREATE

Because of fear—and fear is sometimes strangely mixed with boredom, for reasons I don't particularly understand but have experienced—we make up all kinds of stupid things. We even create identities because we're bored or we're afraid that if we tell someone the truth about ourselves, they may think we're really boring. We create fictions, caricatures of ourselves, and then we live out caricatures. That's just part of being human, I suppose. Viewing it as a theater is one thing. The problem is when we believe it. Being the sometimes-stupid animals that we are, we tend to believe things if we repeat them long enough: "It must be true because it's been repeated so many times!" We believe the nonsense that we create in our mind and discuss with ourselves over and over.

From the Buddhist perspective, all ideas about ourselves are fictions. The *me* that we've created is a fiction. But the Great Eastern Sun view is not based on *me*. It's not necessary to always self-reference back to something solid. That may seem scary, but believe me, living a lie is scarier. Ultimately the time of death comes, and if everything's been a lie . . . how pathetic that would be! We can afford to uplift ourselves and take the view of our basic dignity; we can afford to allow that basic goodness that is inherent in our being to be our emphasis rather than all the little wretched fictions that we like to rehash. We don't have to be in a constant struggle with some idea of who we are.

I just want to make sure everyone understands, though: There's no one-time trick, no magic wand to wave. It requires some discipline. And that discipline involves understanding what to accept and what to reject. This is not based on any exterior rule book. But basically what we need to reject is the setting-sun world and the setting-sun view—the view that is always taking us away from being genuine.

We each have our own version of the setting-sun world. In some cases, it's more extreme than others. No judgment here. But we can reject being caught up in that. It doesn't mean that we have to become a goody-goody. It's not about showing off. In fact, others can't really know what's going on within us and whether we truly cultivate warriorship. This is all deeply personal.

So, generally speaking, we want to reject succumbing to the setting-sun world. However, it turns out that the setting-sun world is very much part of this world. So, what shall a warrior do?

There is no easy answer, but it does remind me of an amusing story. His Holiness the Sixteenth Karmapa, a great Tibetan saint mentioned earlier, came to visit America. This was way back in the 1970s or early 1980s. He was the living embodiment of the Great Eastern Sun. Really, a brilliant person in the literal sense. It's rare to see people that actually glow; this was a glowing being. Funnily enough, one of the things he really wanted to do was to go to Disneyland! I mean, he came to America to teach, but he wanted to take monks and everyone to Disneyland. Now, in some way, you can view that kind of entertainment as a distraction. But as even Trungpa Rinpoche pointed out, because of the Karmapa's fascination with Mickey Mouse, Goofy, Donald Duck, and all the others, even though it's trying to distract you, still you can see the goodness in that. There's something even worthwhile in that. It doesn't have to be a distraction; it can be a celebration.

The point is that there's no guidebook. For example, entertainment as such is not a problem; it's how our mind relates to it. It's all about developing an enlightened view and interacting with our world in a fundamentally sane way.

HUMILITY AND EVENNESS

In understanding what to accept and what to reject, the rejection part is the easiest because each of us knows what it is that takes us away. Individually we all know what we do when we're uncomfortable, when we feel insufficient, or whatever it is, to get away from our mind. We try to fill it with something or other, and we're all too familiar with it.

The Great Eastern Sun view is allowing ourselves to tune in to an infinite bank of basic goodness, tenderness, and appreciation. It's also allowing ourselves to be humble in the sense that we really don't know. But we can be simple. Likewise, we're allowing sadness to be there, without becoming sentimental. We can even have a sense of broken-heartedness with the result as a strange, wonderful cheerfulness. We don't get depressed. Yet the view involves that we're not attached to elation either. Because if we become attached to it, all elation, at some point, becomes depression. It's just the nature of the beast. Here we are cultivating a sense of evenness. Not a bland one—we're just not getting overexcited or overly depressed, and we don't have to fake anything.

We have our habit of accentuating things to create a sense of excitement for ourselves. Through habitual patterns, we can become addicted to elation. In the same way, we can become addicted to depression. We don't even listen to the message that if you hammer yourself on the head, it feels *so* good when you stop. Out of sheer habit, we keep hammering!

If this sounds too serious, it may be that we need a spark of magic. We will get to that. But in order to ignite that magic, first we need another aspect of the warrior's method.

ACTUAL APPRENTICESHIP: WHERE THE SHAMBHALA TEACHINGS AND BUDDHISM MEET

In the previous chapter, we started to explore the methodology involved in becoming a warrior. As we have seen, sitting meditation is an important part of it. But there's another aspect to the tradition of warriorship: apprenticing ourselves to a master warrior. We will discuss the relationship with a teacher at length in the section on lineage and transmission, but it is worthwhile to take a moment to look at it from the Shambhala warrior's perspective.

All of us have some kind of internal BS detector. Yet it helps to have an external BS detector as well, because we have become so used to our own habits that it's sometimes hard to separate the B from the S.

This is where apprenticing ourselves to a master warrior comes into play. That, by the way, is one way of saying things. In a general Buddhist context, we'll often speak of finding a genuine teacher or a spiritual friend. In any case, the methodology is simple. However, we still have to use our BS detector because it's easy to find charlatans in this world. There are people willing to tell you all kinds of things in order to get power, money, or sex—those are the usual three, but there are variations on the themes. We must have discernment in making a relationship with the master warrior. It's like a courting process; trying to go too fast is risky.

Do we really need a teacher? Some might say that the Buddha, for example, didn't have a teacher. But if we look at the life of the Buddha, he had many teachers. It is his enlightenment that wasn't based on any of his teachers. He had various yoga teachers who taught him all kinds of ascetic yogic practices. He found that, in his situation, those teachings weren't what he was looking for; but at least he made the effort.

In the 2,500-year tradition, since the time of Buddha, there has been a transmission of the truth that Buddha discovered, the awakened state of being. It has been transmitted thousands, tens of thousands, millions, perhaps billions of times very effectively—and completely. The best combination is to practice the teachings and to have a spiritual friendship with someone who's been there—a relationship based not on being naïve but on our own genuineness and working with someone genuine.

This is very much aligned with the practice of sitting meditation. To begin with, we must face ourselves honestly and without condemning ourselves. We don't have to analyze, reanalyze, regurgitate, re-regurgitate every day, like an animal that eats its own vomit. It's okay to stop the crazy self-talk. We can be cheerful even though we can see the whole wretched mess. Seriously, I'm a wretched mess, but you know, I'm smiling. The whole thing is workable. As the saying goes, from darkness comes light. Things aren't just bright; there has to be something for it to be bright in contrast to. Everything isn't just black and white. From the darkness there's light, and all kinds of variations. Darkness in fact inspires light.

Dharma is a term used a lot in Buddhism, though it literally means something like "the truth of what is." It is not necessarily a doctrine but rather the simple truth of what is. We can connect this idea to the Shambhala teachings, too. When we meet something genuine in that way, the best thing we can do is acknowledge it. But we don't just acknowledge it because someone calls it "the truth." We must use our intelligence and investigate. If we are interested, we should see if what's called the Dharma is in fact the truth. If we get a glimpse of that, a glimpse of the brightness of the Great Eastern Sun, and if we're truly a warrior, we acknowledge that. It's good to be questioning and investigating, but when we find something to be real, it's then time to make a change, and sooner is better than later.

Once they've heard the Dharma, many people think they can put off practice for a long time or that they have a long time to accomplish it. But as we said, death is real and comes without warning.

There's also pride. Part of being human—especially in modern culture—is a sense of individuality. In America we talk of "rugged individualism." It makes it very difficult for us to acknowledge that there might be someone else who has wisdom, more than our own, and that we can learn from them—especially when it comes to spiritual matters.

The thing is, it's not good enough to read a book, go to a lecture, or think about these topics. The best we can do is find a genuine teacher and form a relationship with them. It really is the most expeditious methodology. When we are willing to make friends with ourselves, then we can open enough to make another friendship with a wisdom teacher. Our relationship with the spiritual friend or wisdom teacher is based on the fact that we understand that it's beneficial.

However, such apprenticing is not a one-way relationship. It may sometimes seem like it, but every teacher is somebody's student. Not only that: Students learn from their teachers, and teachers learn from their students.

It's a nondual situation. There's a meeting of minds. If our heart is open, it is said, the teacher will be there. But we must make sure that the relationship is not based on naivety.

Our relationship with our teacher is even more intimate than the one we might have with our husband, wife, boyfriend, or girlfriend—not intimate in the physical sense but in the meeting of minds that takes place. If you apprentice with a master warrior, you're asking that person to mind your business a bit. And you're going to find out about their business, too! If they are a genuine teacher, it will be raw inasmuch as it will be real and not just a joyride.

What a spiritual teacher can do for you is awaken the heart of enlightenment in you. A spiritual teacher, like a medical professional that has a defibrillator, is someone who will zap your heart awake! There's a catalytic power that happens when we are willing to meet somebody not just halfway, not 75 percent, but the whole way. It's a profound approach not suited for dabbling, which is why I so often repeat this: You must make sure that your teacher is genuine. If you make a mistake, run. Quickly! Don't be polite. Run, run for your life!

There is a long and unbelievably successful tradition of passing these teachings from one human being to another. It's not made up. It's not about India or Tibet, Europe, the United States, or any country. It crosses cultures and genders. It's about being fully and totally human, and awakening buddha-nature in our being. That is totally not cultural.

The Dharma has migrated around the world, interestingly, without proselytizing. Its power is not based on trying to convert anybody. Of course, there are those who use "Buddhism" and "Shambhala" for all kinds of stupid reasons—people will use anything for the usual agendas. But there are genuine teachers, genuine students, and it's up to us to discern what's genuine if we have an attraction to these teachings.

At first, of course, it may seem foreign. Yet maybe these days it's less foreign. When I was in my teens and told people I was a Buddhist, they looked at me really strangely. When I was in my twenties, it became slightly less strange. Now I'm in my seventies and no one even blinks anymore. They ask which kind of Buddhist! There's a funny cultural shift.

Do you have to be a Buddhist to practice meditation? You don't. It's not about being card-carrying. It just happens that the best teachers that I have run across with these kinds of teachings are Buddhist teachers—and I've looked to see if there are others. There is a pure transmission in Buddhism that is accessible to us. If you find some other situation, no problem. I simply believe it is easier, so to speak, to find a genuine Buddhist lineage holder because the transmission has been going on unbrokenly and so successfully.

I'm not advertising for anybody, by the way. Genuine teachers are sometimes known, sometimes unknown. It doesn't have to be somebody with a title. It doesn't have to be someone of a particular race or gender. It's all about the genuineness of their wisdom and their ability to impart it to you and not want anything in return from you.

THE MOON AND THE SUN

Back to that defibrillator analogy: The teacher activates your buddha-nature. Time to wake up! There are other interesting analogies that illustrate how the teacher awakens your knowledge and experience of basic goodness. For example, the great fourteenth-century Tibetan meditation master Longchenpa said that from one flame another flame appears. The flame is wakefulness, and there is a process of illuminating. The Shambhala teachings, for their part, describe the process of activating your buddha-nature as "transplanting the moon into your heart." It may seem foreign and odd at first, but ultimately it is already part of us.

Just a warning, though: Once we have a taste of the truth, it's hard to go back to the lies. So maybe it's better not to find the truth, if we don't want it. Better not to be a baby warrior if we don't want to be a full-blown warrior. Better not to be born if we don't want to die. It's like that.

It's also like getting pregnant. Buddha-nature is there, and it's growing. But unlike being pregnant, there's not a growing-up process that goes from pee-pee and diapers all the way up . . . When the full moon of buddha-nature is pregnant in our being, it's fully mature. Full-tilt boogie. There's the shock of it. Our ego is going to feel . . . deflowered. I'm sorry, but it *is* a bit of a shock to the system. Our toughness, self-aggrandizement, aggression toward ourselves, aggression toward others has been overcome. We can finally be a real person. Or at least we catch a glimpse that it is indeed a possibility.

"Real" doesn't mean we can't make mistakes. We can make lots of mistakes. "Real" also doesn't mean we don't lie; we just know when we're lying that we are lying. We don't necessarily have to apologize every single time, but we take notice. We're not fooling ourselves anymore.

Yet once the moon has entered our heart, there's still a sense of loneliness. Even though the moon is full—never waning, always waxing—there's still something missing. There is a longing, a feeling of incompleteness.

In other philosophical systems, the moon is talked about as feminine, but here it symbolizes the masculine energy. It's a sense of steadiness and loyalty. It is wonderful. Yet even though there's an awakened quality to it, it's not complete. What's missing is magic.

Magic has to do with the feminine principle. The unexpected, the changing. The symbols include a flame and the crack of a whip. Along with the masculine principle and the moon that has been planted into our heart, we talk about the feminine principle as "allowing the sun into our head," or brain. It is that sense of magic and openness to transforming our world. It includes an openness to the truth of birth and death. We are willing to transform and experience the phenomenal world totally. We can take our normal experiences of passion, aggression, and ignorance, and transmogrify those things into positive qualities—wisdoms, not just that which fetters us.

Allowing the sun into our brain is welcoming the power to transform. It is welcoming the power to organize, beautify, elegantize. It is also connected to the fact that there is a natural wakefulness that's always accessible. We've gone beyond fear so that we don't need to pretend. There's no need to try to manufacture any idea of fearlessness, any idea of gentleness. We can be with that and acknowledge it.

When discussing magic in this context, we're not meaning magic *tricks*. But it does connote joy, a spark, and what we call *auspicious coincidence*, as opposed to inauspicious coincidence. The magic that the warrior experiences, with the metaphorical sun in their brain, is toward the good. Yes, the warrior's view is generally equanimous, but it is not *absolutely* neutral inasmuch as it favors that which is good. The type of magic we're discussing here comes out of that view of favoring that which is good, genuine, real. In this sense, it's not so much about rejecting the setting-sun world but rather accepting the radiance of the Great Eastern Sun. Rather than focusing on fear, we let fearlessness bloom. The quality of magic has to do with acceptance rather than rejection. It's a process of opening up to what is rather than trying to manufacture something that did not previously exist. That's an important distinction.

INVITING WAKEFULNESS

As we know, the view is the key. There's no reason to meditate without a proper view. It doesn't make any difference if we put our butt on a cushion and just go into a dull state for an hour. We would be fooling ourselves, and there would be no result. I'm even going to be controversial and take this a step further: There is no reason to meditate or do anything without the view. It's a waste of time.

We develop the view by inviting wakefulness through several means. For example, when we sit down, we pay attention to why we're sitting down, and we pay attention to our posture. The posture relates to the view because it is the posture of wakefulness. That means we don't want to just go into a dull, sleeplike state. The posture of wakefulness is the posture of non-avoidance.

We also discussed magic. When the view comes together with meditation, there's a spark. Even if we're just pretending, something happens. The posture and intention of wakefulness somehow invites wakefulness. That's true magic. Wakefulness has to be invited. It's not going to just dawn on us, though it does.

Of course, if you're crossing the street and suddenly a car almost runs you over, as soon as you notice, you're having a wakeful moment. But games of chicken aren't the best way to develop wakefulness! There are better ways to do that. The best way is to establish the view and mix it with the meditation. In our ordinary life—life outside of formal meditation—it's exactly the same. The view is the same: It is the view of decency, dignity, and not falling prey to our wretchedness and tendency to be so hard on ourselves.

THE EARTH AND THE SKY

The view of wakefulness starts to imbue every aspect of our life. As it does, we open to the bigger picture. Consequently, once we have embarked on the warrior's path, we may start to wonder about our place in the world. There are different ways to look at this, one of which has to do with the earth and the sky.

If we open up to this new day, to our current circumstances—whatever they happen to be today—we find that here we are, sitting on the earth. We walk on this earth, we do everything on this earth, and it totally accepts us. It accepts everything that we do, as ridiculous as many of these things are. Sometimes it moans and groans, but it accepts everything. Likewise, at all times, the sky is above. There's the basis of earth, accessible and accepting;

there's the principle of sky or heaven, vast and beckoning in its vastness; and here we are in the middle. It's unchanging. No matter what, earth is always earth, sky is always sky. There is no variation on that theme. That is a wonderful thing, and something we can depend on. There might be earthquakes and turbulences—I live in California part of the year, and the earth shakes every once in a while—yet there's still a solidity in that shaking.

In the same way that the earth is there to support us and the sky remains above, the basic goodness that is our inherent quality remains present. It's something that we can depend on in the immediacy of any moment. It does not go away. It is the ground itself.

Think of how the day or seasons—winter, spring, summer, autumn—follow a pattern. In the same way, we can learn to live in this world properly by paying attention to the natural flow of how things are. Heaven, sky. Day, night. The flow of the seasons. They exist in a natural form. The trees, the greenery, the weather—they're not for or against us, they just are. Whatever presents itself, that's what we have to work with. There's nothing that's against us or trying to do us in. Except confused beings, I suppose, but that's a different issue.

As part of awakening our heart—allowing our heart to be as it is, to be open, to be connected to earth and heaven—we have the opportunity to appreciate what is. We can appreciate the elements—earth, water, fire, wind, space. We can appreciate the colors—white, blue, red, orange, purple, green. We don't need to block anything out. If we're too busy trying to avoid, we miss the wonder of all that simply is. If we can open our mind, we can look beyond the surface. This wondrous world has amazing depth. It is not a one- or two-dimensional world. There's depth not only in the natural world but in our own being. We're not just tiny surface critters. We can look and see precisely, if we give ourselves that opportunity.

How do we do that? By not having a little discussion in our mind about everything we look at. As soon as we have the little discussion, we take ourselves away from the immediacy of birdsong, the color palette, the beautiful dance between light and shadow. In the same way, just in working with our own being, it is possible to see who, what, and where we are in a simple yet profound way. As Trungpa Rinpoche tells us in *Smile at Fear*,

> You discover a further commitment to working with yourself on the warrior's path and a further feeling of connection in your life. At that point, you

are actually witnessing the joining together of heaven and earth. Heaven means sanity, or a good and direct understanding. Earth is practicality. Joining them together means that practicality and sanity, or wisdom, are put together so that we can actually transmit that sanity to others.

Another way of seeing this is that heaven is oneself and the other is earth. The joining of heaven and earth is oneself and other joining together in sanity. In the past, you may have felt as though there were some kind of missing link with the universe. Sometimes there was no earth; sometimes you had no heaven. Sometimes the two didn't come together properly. Now, finally, experience feels full and completely joined together. You rediscover the sense of healthiness, a strong, healthy state of both mind and body. Your attitude towards yourself and others begins to brighten up. Only then can you actually hold the universe in your hand.[2]

THE MANDALA PRINCIPLE

In addition to the notion of heaven and earth, another way to look at our place in the world is provided by the mandala principle.

As explained in chapter 3, *mandala* means "center and fringe." In their artistic form, mandalas are representations of palaces, whether of a king, queen, or buddha. In Buddhist art, mandalas tend to have a masculine or feminine deity, or deities in union, in the middle of the palace. Therefore, there are wisdom palaces, and there are secular palaces, which—if they're considered as mandalas—are imbued with wisdom.

The basic setup of a mandala is always the same. The figure in the center is looking east. This doesn't have to be literal. Of course, if you're creating an actual palace based on these architectural notions, then, yes, it should face east where the sun rises. But it's also symbolic in the sense that in any mandala, the central figure faces east. The idea is that the Great Eastern Sun is in front of you and shining upon you. So, as part of the Great Eastern Sun point of view, when we practice meditation, for example, we are at the center of a mandala of wakefulness, and the sun is in front of us and above us, shining directly into our being.

The mandala principle also has to do with our household. The idea is that our mate, whether male or female, shares the center. In other words, it's not just about *me*. There's a sense that the king has a queen, and vice versa. If you live by yourself, you can be the king and queen. That's okay. These things are symbolic rather than literal. As well, all aspects of a household are included and equally shined upon by the Great Eastern Sun in that mandala.

Then there are wider perspectives. There's our family. The mandala principle can also apply to social structures, cities, countries... Basically, regardless of the scale, it's always informed by the enlightened point of view, which faces east. That's the basic principle, and though symbolic, it is strangely practical.

This palace of wakefulness includes other people in our life. At the center is the enlightened being, but the enlightened being is not separate from any other part of the palace. Earlier we discussed the one-caste view, and this very much applies here: All beings within the mandala are of the same nature; they share the same caste. If it's Buddhist symbolism, all beings within the mandala are of the nature of all buddhas.

Yet it's not that everyone is equal per se. It's not a democracy. The king's the king, the queen's the queen, the minister's the minister, and so on. But it is so that things will work. In terms of the view, the fundamental richness is shared by everybody, but responsibilities might differ. It's very practical. In a society, somebody has to make sure that the water mains are working. One person can't do everything.

The mandala principle comes with a vast view. Part of this vision is that it's not just about our individual basic goodness. It is about seeing the basic goodness in others, too—developing a sacred outlook; seeing people as enlightened beings rather than as idiots, or at least as potential buddhas rather than as oafs. It's about seeing the potential in people. We can actually see beings differently. I'm convinced that enlightened beings see stupid people like us very differently than we see each other!

All of this is not about *me*. That's crucial. It is so that we can truly be of benefit. Through the practice of meditation and the Great Eastern Sun view, we begin to understand that *me* is a fiction. Then we can have a sense of compassion for all the others who believe their idea of a *me*, which is also a fiction. We then understand why people are so confused and act in so many ways. Compassion arises spontaneously from that. That doesn't mean we let people take advantage of us just because they don't understand that their *me* is a fallacy. There are pragmatics to it. We have to hone our intelligence at the same time as sacred view dawns. It goes together. Sacred view is not based on being naïve. It is seeing things clearly.

Again, no view, no result. We always begin with that, and we always come back to that.

If we want to go deeper, we should understand that part of the sacred view is that there's not just necessarily one mandala. There are buddha realms that intersect infinitely. In contrast to this sacred outlook, our ordinary perception is based on the conditioning of our mind through egotistic attachment and habits. But from the Buddhist perspective, especially Mahayana and Vajrayana, reality isn't described the way most of us see. It is described as these infinite buddha fields that exist outside and through space and time. Although the Shambhala teachings don't have the same emphasis and terminology as Mahayana and Vajrayana Buddhism, both visions agree that the ideas that we have about space and time are constricted by our view.

The interesting thing about all these buddha fields is that each one is contained in every other one. There's not a hierarchy of buddha fields. Likewise, each buddha contains all other buddhas. So, there's a sense of intersection, though not in the usual way we think of in terms of dimensionality. If we have that view and are applying it, we can actually begin to see that way. The training is just like everything else we're talking about here: First you have your conception of what things are supposed to look like, then your conception drops away and you see how things actually are.

So within the mandala situation, how important are all the other aspects of the mandala?

To answer that, we must understand that it is based on non-ego—that is, the absence of any fixed, permanent identity that we cling to. From non-ego's point of view, everything is important except for any idea of a separate *me*. That's the twist! So, in a sense, all that matters is the periphery. If we get our ego tied up in the center, then it is not at all an enlightened mandala, not at all a wisdom palace. The center of the mandala is always based on non-ego. That's why it's the center.

NOT GRASPING AT EXPERIENCE

When we learn how to be meditators and warriors, we practice without grasping, without trying to hold on to any experience. The minute we try to maintain something that comes our way, it's gone. Therefore, it's very important in the practice of meditation not to try to hold on to positive experiences, which we're not even deliberately trying to create. We can simply practice without grasping, which is always tied to some idea of a self.

Real meditation experience is a combination of all aspects of being human. Fear, joy, depression, and so forth. There's not just one thing that is considered meditation experience. Meditation experience is what happens during meditation. Sure, the result of meditation is a settling of our mind, which we could ultimately describe as bliss. But it's not something that we can hold on to. It's just what's there. Why do we call it bliss? In Buddhism, especially in the Mahayana and Vajrayana, the buddhas are spoken of as *sugatas*, or "those gone beyond to bliss." Like the Great Eastern Sun of the Shambhala teachings, it is totally radiant. And it is blissful, although not in the sense of our ideas of bliss, where it goes up, reaches an apex, and comes down. It's beyond undulating.

If we practice meditation, things will happen—we will have positive and negative experiences, but we don't hold on to either. Some people blame meditation for their problems: "I've been meditating for twenty-two years and I'm still fucked up!" Or whatever the storyline is. It is much better to take into account the larger situation. If we become a Shambhala warrior, it is not just for our own benefit. Much like in the Buddhist approach to mind training, or lojong, if we meditate from the Great Eastern Sun point of view, we meditate from the point of view of practicing to benefit other beings, and there's not going to be any complaint. It's not a self-help course. We're not just trying to make ourselves feel better. If you just want to feel better, go to the jacuzzi! I know, sometimes meditation is sold like that—as a commodity. But we're talking about something genuine, not something to be bartered or sold in that way.

Communicating the view to others can never be done with a sense of proselytizing or trying to convert them. When we understand that we practice not just for our own benefit but also for the benefit of others, we don't have to go tell everybody, "I'm practicing because I want to help you out!" Or, you know, "You should do it like this." Rather, communicating sanity to others becomes natural. We can communicate as situations arise. Besides, our actions, the way we are in the world, is often so much more potent than what we say.

DISCIPLINE AND CONFIDENCE

Warriorship involves discipline and confidence. How do they relate to the view?

First, we should understand that the way we look at ourselves—our attitudes and opinions about ourselves—is extremely important. When we're always denigrating ourselves, it creates a bad state of mind. Likewise, trying to jack ourselves up too much also creates a bad state of mind. It's much more worthwhile to allow ourselves to tune in to the richness of our goodness, that positive quality within, and not to make a big deal about all our wretchedness, thinking, "I am inadequate, I can't do this, I'm not good enough." This kind of chatter sows negativity in our life. Whenever that negative conditioning arises in our being, we could look toward the Great Eastern Sun and let that luminous view spark. This echoes the mandala principle: We look east. Rather than navel-gazing and focusing on our own sense of inadequacy, we look out at the Great Eastern Sun. That's extremely powerful.

If we can do that, we tune in to what's called *unconditional confidence*. Unconditional confidence is not based on any specific situation or method. It comes from being able to be real—totally genuine. It's pragmatic. It also derives from not being too hard on ourselves or others; from a sense of tenderness and gentleness. In *Smile at Fear*, Trungpa Rinpoche describes the development of this confidence as like watching a sunrise. If you're up before dawn, you go and first there's light; you don't even see the sun yet. Then there's this sort of feeble little fire that comes up, and it's very tentative. And then as the sun rises, it becomes brilliant and lights up all of space. The development of confidence is like that. Let it rise in your being in that way. You don't have to invent it. It's part of your being. If we are genuine, if we are not trying to be somebody else, then we have that sense of indestructibility in our being, which is the ground of true, unconditional confidence.

WORKING WITH OUR WORLD IN A DIGNIFIED WAY

From this perspective, we are willing to work with our world. "Our world" is wherever we live, including our bedroom, kitchen, bathroom... Wherever we live, we're willing to clean up messes. We are willing to reside in a court, in a palace. It may be a humble palace, but it's our palace. We're willing to be the sovereign of our world and treat others with love, compassion, and whatever is necessary. Sometimes love and compassion manifest as a hug, sometimes as a bark. We're not all lovey-dovey. But we care for our world and for all beings within it.

Whatever our situation is, we are allowing it and ourselves to be dignified. We're not talking about old David Niven movies or Emily Post's *Etiquette*—for those who are old enough to get the references. We're not talking about being proper British people, let's just put it that way. The sense of being dignified involves having proper manners, but it's not necessarily about all these ideas of what's polite or impolite. Basically, we are dignified by respecting other people's sensibilities. Dignity comes from being conscious of other people. That's not to say that we adjust to try to be some fake person. We acknowledge other people's dignity by being dignified ourselves. Caring is what it comes down to. And it applies to whoever "enters our realm," whoever is our guest, including dogs, cats, and spiders.

We can be both dignified and honest in our environment without having to be fake in any way. Fakeness is interesting, since most human beings are used to creating fictions. We might be uncomfortable about ourselves, so we create a version of ourselves. Sometimes we create a version of ourselves that is our idea of somebody else that we might want to be like. Sometimes we have some ideal; we respect someone, so we mimic them. But anytime we try to do that, we run into that fake territory.

We can't be Shakyamuni Buddha. That's a particular person who awakened. We can't be the Dalai Lama. We can't be Mahatma Gandhi, Mother Teresa, or Nelson Mandela. It would be fake. But we can be who we are. If we allow the moon to fully enter our heart, allowing our buddha-nature to blossom; and if we allow the sun into our head, accepting the unexpectedness of magic and brightness, what we are is darn good. Not just good enough: It is as good as it gets. Solid gold! It is totally worthwhile, totally extraordinary, totally delightful, and totally accessible. But no one can do it for us.

15
The Warrior Slogans

By now it should be clear that the actual practice of sitting meditation is part and parcel of the warrior's path and lifestyle. We should make this practice ours. We are going to forget much of the rest. However, Trungpa Rinpoche has provided us with many tools and trainings to help us stay on track. In particular, he synthesized the pith teachings of this tradition into what he called the "Shambhala warrior slogans," a large selection of which we will cover in this chapter and chapter 16.

As we see again and again, we have to remember basic goodness. It is the underlying foundation of the warrior's way—that on which everything else is built. Even the slogans we are about to study emanate from basic goodness. It is always there. We always refer to it. It is always gentle and caring, and there is never any aberration from it on the warrior's path. That path includes the practice of meditation, but don't knock yourself over the head to practice. Rather, let the exertion come of its own. You need to be able to at least move your butt to the place where you're going to sit and meditate, and then just be there. It's as simple as can be, yet getting your bottom onto the cushion or seat is 99 percent of the battle. Once you're there, you really don't have to do much, but you will experience resistance. We are creatures of habit after all. So, overcome it as best as you can, but don't be too hard on yourself when you don't do it. The nice thing about this approach is that you can begin anytime. If you lapse, you lapse; then you begin again. There's no reason to feel bad about what you haven't done; you can do it now—you don't need any special occasion. If you're waiting for some ideal situation, it'll never come. But there are things we can do to help us summon the courage to get to the cushion, remember the key points of the view once we're on the cushion, and navigate the world in between sessions according to the warrior's way. One of these is to study the following slogans.

The warrior slogans work just like the lojong slogans discussed in the chapters on mind training. Using such aphorisms was part of Trungpa Rinpoche's training in his early years in Tibet, and this is something he introduced to the West. We can find all sorts of ways to memorize these slogans, perhaps using little cards. If we truly familiarize ourselves with them, they tend to resurface in our mind when we need them most. The difference is that while the seven points of mind training were written down in the twelfth century to encapsulate the Mahayana teachings of Atisha, the Shambhala warrior slogans were offered by Trungpa Rinpoche in the twentieth century to remember the key points of the Shambhala warrior's path and view. To be more precise, he composed some of these slogans in the 1970s for a secular audience, and some others in the early 1980s for advanced students. Then, after his passing, his disciple Carolyn Rose Gimian crafted additional slogans, drawing them from Rinpoche's book, *Shambhala: The Sacred Path of the Warrior*.[1] These slogans were developed as a way of touching into the teachings in a very direct way. Each one opens something up, and Trungpa Rinpoche has commentary associated with each one as well. Let's take a look at some of them in detail, taking cues from his commentary.*

Here is the first one:

» Don't be afraid of who you are.

There is no way to be a warrior in this world if we want to be somebody else. We have to begin with who we are and what we are, and that is perfectly fine. There is no other ideal situation or time.

You can examine your experience to see what it contains and how you can be of help to yourself and others. Warriorship is the opposite of selfishness. You can be who you are without having to always refer to *me*, *me*, *me*. The thing is, we're only selfish when we're afraid of ourselves or the threat that the world presents to us. If we open, and if we just simply are who we are, we don't have those problems. We don't have to build a little nest or cocoon that's just ours, something to shield us. We can be braver than that. We can live beyond those self-made confines. Even if we have big problems—and if we don't have them today, they will come someday, whether they be personal, social, or something

*Note to the reader: This chapter and the following one discuss a selection of the warrior slogans connected to the Shambhala tradition. As is common in the Tibetan teaching style, Sam's comments on the slogans are interwoven with Chögyam Trungpa's own commentary on the slogans. The complete set of slogans, as well as Trungpa Rinpoche's complete commentary, is included as an appendix.—Ed.

else—we can be heroic and kind at the same time. To help us do that, we can remember that slogan, which is easy to memorize: "Don't be afraid of who you are." It goes along with a sense of gentleness. We don't need a big commentary on who we are. Big commentaries involve the tendency to go back and forth about how wonderful we are and how horrible we are, which is tiring and fruitless. We can just be who we are, and we can begin there, anytime, anyplace.

» Goodness is the ground of all.

I find it interesting that this is listed as the second slogan. I personally would have put it first, which may be why I felt compelled to mention basic goodness at the very beginning of this chapter! In any case, that basic goodness is the underlying reality, and it is unconditional. It's there already, in just the same way that heaven and earth are here. It's as simple as this: When we sit down to practice meditation, there we are, sitting on the ground, sitting in our chair, with the earth below and heaven above—*that* is the basic goodness itself. There's nothing to reject, nothing to accept. It's just exactly the way it is. Simple.

» Goodness dawns like the sun.

Trungpa Rinpoche says that this notion of goodness isn't just an arbitrary idea, but that we can experience it as real.[2] Being human, we have the potential for intelligence and dignity at any time. We can be attuned to the world—this world that has the brilliance of the blue sky, the freshness of the leafy trees, the heaviness of the mountains. We have a connection to this world; we are not separate from it. The connection to this reality can wake us up and make us feel good. If we separate ourselves too much from the natural world—stuck in our little apartment or whatever our cocoon is—we can get figuratively constipated, backed up into this idea that things are very small and that our mind is very small. The world is much bigger and richer than that. Goodness can happen to us. In fact, it's happening already. It's all around us. We're connected to it. It dawns like the sun, if we can open up to it.

» Never give up on anyone or anything.

My teacher, the master warrior Trungpa Rinpoche, gave us instructions on how to be teachers. One thing he said is that he never gave up on anyone, no matter how pathetic they may have acted or seemed. This is important.

Interestingly, he added that he never gave up on anyone or anything—unless they gave up on him. But even then, I don't think that he *actually* gave up on them; that's the twist. No matter how stupid people may act or seem, it doesn't make any difference: Everyone's potential for warriorship is in fact equal. Everyone's potential for buddhahood is likewise equal. How they present themselves doesn't alter that fact. No one is a lost cause.

In modern parlance, we often hear of so-called losers. That may be a modern idiom, but I'm afraid that the idea behind it has been going on for a long, long time. However, it is just a construct. We always have the opportunity to flower. Knowing this, we don't give up on anyone or anything, including ourselves.

Once, a student asked me for some clarifications about this slogan. Coming from a Christian background, he observed a kind of missionary approach to helping others, and he was wrestling with the idea of "doing good" that came to his mind when he heard this slogan.

To tell you the truth, it also bothered me when I was younger. For example, when I was in San Francisco and I wanted to be of help, I went to community meal programs, like those of the Salvation Army. There, if the people were going to eat, they had to accept a particular view or pretend that they did, and as far as I could tell, most were pretending. In the end, I couldn't help in those places because I couldn't eat what they were putting out, and I don't mean the food. Therefore, it's better if you can find a place where you can be genuine. But the student who originally asked that question was struggling with a certain attachment to doing good, and this is a slightly different issue.

It's simple: We can do good. There's no question about it. But as soon as we do good, we should disown it. The good isn't about our ego or ourselves. It comes from basic goodness rather than me-ness. We run into problems when we start thinking *we* are good; when we start pumping ourselves up because we did something great. Egomania is a real problem. As soon as it arises, we stop doing any good.

It is possible to do good in so many ways. If you can heal someone, feed someone, or alleviate someone's pain, be it just a little, that is wonderful. But then forget about it, as if it never happened. That's truly ideal. You do it and you disown it. It's not yours anyway. It's basic—it has to do with your humanity. It's not *that* good. It's normal actually! It's the given, not the added. The added is, "Hey, check me out. Look what I did."

On another note, this idea of not giving up on anyone or anything, including ourselves, also implies that we are loyal to situations. In fact, we must have a loyalty to our own wakeful quality, our own seed of basic goodness that is in us, and to the fact that it can blossom. If we allow it to, it *will* blossom.

» To overcome uncertainty is utterly good.

How do we develop confidence? There's only one way: We have to be confident. I'm afraid there is a bit of a catch-22! These teachings can be both subtle and simple, but don't let that simpleness deter you.

In this slogan, "uncertainty" refers to doubting ourselves or the existence of basic goodness. If you don't condemn yourself when you relax, and when you appreciate your body and mind, you begin to contact basic goodness in yourself. We can all do that through the process of sitting in meditation and letting go of all the little things that we do to try to entertain ourselves and keep ourselves busy: watching TV, reading a magazine while surfing on the internet at the same time, or whatever our version of that might be. It's extremely important to give ourselves the time to be with ourselves openly and see what happens, with no agenda.

The way you are with yourself, by yourself, is as important as, if not more important than, the way you are with people. You're not fooling anybody when you're with yourself. There you are; make it the best that it can be. Just because no one's watching doesn't mean anything. Allow yourself to open. Be willing. You can uplift your human experience even when you're on your own.

Because we have this mind and body, we can comprehend this world fully. We take what we call "existence" for granted, but it is a wonderful and precious treasure, and it runs out very quickly. We don't know how long we're going to live. We don't have a clue! While we're in this life, we might as well make use of it. And that applies even if we're young. Some of my readers are very young, and for all we know, they may die before the old readers. For those of us oldsters, we know we're going to die fairly soon because most of our life has passed. We can still make the best of it. Constantly make the best of it and appreciate that.

We always have the opportunity to overcome uncertainty, and that's utterly good.

» Don't assume the posture of a wilted flower.

This slogan is about how to be in the world with our body. It means don't slouch—literally. Dignity comes in having a good posture, or at least the best posture we can have. Even when we're all alone. When you slouch or slump, you're trying to hide your heart. You can sit upright but relaxed: your heart naked and open to the world, your entire being exposed to yourself and others.

It's important to have that mindfulness of body, especially in the practice of meditation. If we sit like a wilted flower, it simply doesn't work. It's a yogic practice, and the posture is part of it. Good head and shoulders are part of it. The erect back is part of it, as well as the relaxed neck, the gaze, everything. It's also all about connecting with the world, letting ourselves be as we are. When we sit in an erect way, straight and confident, willing to face whatever comes our way, we're sitting in the way of the warrior. The way of the warrior involves sitting, standing, and doing any other activity as a full human being.

» Hope and fear cannot alter the seasons.

The four seasons come and go, having nothing to do with our emotions, problems, fears, hopes, thoughts, demands, political preferences . . . They just happen. The natural way of the world is neither for us nor against us; it is just the way it is. The world is there. Our hopes about how it could be, and our fears of how things might be—they are meaningless. That is not to say that aspirations or joyful efforts toward the greater good are meaningless. What's meaningless are the discursiveness, speculations, and fixations. Oppression, social justice, climate change—it is okay to feel moved to do our part. It is also okay to have a vision. The Shambhala tradition talks of creating an enlightened society, and the Great Eastern Sun view offers ways to uplift our situation. Also, warriorship as it is understood in this tradition never denies suffering, and we are constantly reminded not to shy away from working with our world. Therefore, when we say that hopes and fears are meaningless, we are saying that it is fruitless to try to go against the natural way of the world. We can work with our world, and we can especially work with our mind, which is the whole point.

Hoping for this, hoping for that, fearing this, worrying about that—all those habits don't do us any good. We all know this, but we're caught in wanting or trying to push things away. We want what's going to be good and yummy, and we want to push away what's going to be yucky. But "yum" and "yuck" cannot alter the natural way of the world.

We can allow the basic laws and principles of this world to unfold, and we can appreciate what we have. As a warrior, we can feel that what we have is wonderful. We can also rest in the knowledge that it *will* change and we don't even know in which direction. The warrior's way is to be with whatever is happening.

» Awaken the genuine heart of sadness.

This is an interesting one because it goes against the conventional ways of viewing warriorship. As Trungpa Rinpoche writes,

> Awakened heart comes from being willing to face your state of mind. The sitting practice of meditation is a means to awaken this within you. When you awaken your heart, to your surprise, you find that it is empty. If you search for awakened heart, if you put your hand through your rib cage and feel for your heart, there is nothing there—except for tenderness. You feel sore and soft, and if you open your eyes to the world, you feel tremendous sadness. It is not the sadness of feeling sorry for yourself or feeling deprived. It is a natural situation of fullness. The genuine heart of sadness comes from this feeling that your nonexistent heart is full. Your experience is so raw, tender and personal that even if a tiny mosquito lands on you, you feel its touch.[3]

If you want to be a warrior, your senses will open. As your senses open, your sensitivity increases. As your sensitivity increases, you feel the pain and sadness of this world more and more. But since you're a warrior, there's a fearlessness about this. It doesn't get you down, and you are willing to be with that sense of sadness.

Earlier in the book I mentioned that once, when someone asked Trungpa Rinpoche how he was feeling, his reply was, "Cheerful, but strange." I suppose it is the same idea.

This genuine heart of sadness can be awakened, and it is what connects us with others—not just human beings; all beings. It is from that connection, rather than from some big macho warrior thing, that we can actually be of benefit to ourselves and others. In other words, the key to true warriorship is making contact with that genuine heart of sadness rather than trying to create anything artificial.

» To experience fearlessness, it is necessary to experience fear.

We discussed this principle in chapter 13. We can't run away. There is no place to go, no haven, though we try as hard as we can to avoid confrontation with that which scares us.

As Trungpa Rinpoche said, "The essence of cowardice is to not acknowledge the reality of fear."[4] By comparison, the warrior acknowledges fear—and from that, fearlessness can arise.

We experience all sorts of fear. We fear death. We're afraid that we won't be up to the task; that we're somehow not qualified to live as we should or could. There's abrupt fear, when unfamiliar situations occur. We also express fear through our constant search for entertainment and general restlessness. It shows in how we move and talk: We may constantly pull up our phone, stroke our beard or play with our hair, button and unbutton our jacket, or something else altogether. Whatever form it takes, we must acknowledge our fear and reconcile ourselves with it.

If we understand and apply this slogan, then acknowledging fear is not depressing. Quite the contrary. When we truly experience fear, fearlessness becomes possible. It's the only way it becomes possible. Which leads us to the next slogan.

» Go beyond fear.

If we examine the nature of fear, if we look below the veneer of our nervousness, what we'll find is that sense of sadness mentioned earlier. If we're nervous, we're always trying to crank up, vibrate, or avoid the situation somehow. When we slow down and relax enough, we can be with the sadness, which in fact is calm and gentle. In the warrior tradition of Shambhala, the discovery of fearlessness comes from being willing to work with that sore and soft spot. Put another way, fearlessness comes from genuineness.

We may feel that it's a mix of good and bad news. Perhaps we think that if we acknowledge our sadness, we are giving in to depression, or something akin to that. That's not at all how it works. If we're actually willing to just be who and what we are—which includes that sadness—then the openness that comes from it almost has a quality of bliss, even though it is tinged with the sadness. It's not tinged in a bad way, however. It's part of the flavor, if that makes any sense. It's all of one taste. Happy and sad come together. It's authentic and beautiful.

» Synchronize mind and body.

If we're mindful in the present moment, our body and mind are synchronized. Things aren't off. This naturally comes about when we develop fearlessness. Conversely, when we're too caught up in ourselves, too caught up in our own ideas, our mind and body disconnect. If you practice martial arts, you clearly notice if you're heavily involved in your thought process. It is also the case with flower arranging, tea ceremony, and various artistic pursuits. If the mind is too busy, a separation or a lack of sync occurs between mind and body.

As we develop fearlessness, we develop a sense of accuracy, which is in direct relationship to the phenomenal world. Our mind and the phenomenal world come together. In Buddhism, this is described as the unifying of the *ayatanas*. Simply put, there is the perceiver, or the organ of perception; the process of perception; and that which is perceived. Generally, in our life, there is a gap between the three. However, when they are all unified, that's enlightenment, from one point of view, because we have entered into the realm of nonduality. Our current habit is to have a dual world: percept and perceiver, me and you, this and that. We reinforce this duality habit, this sense of separation, over and over. The synchronicity that this slogan points to implies that this sense of mistaken duality is forgotten.

We can uplift ourselves as human beings and get a glimpse of the Great Eastern Sun, the sun of human dignity, of human power. Even if we've only felt it once—and each of us has already felt it once—sometimes our little idea of ourselves gets out of the way and then things just come together. There's no separation between what we're doing and who we are. The training of the warrior involves this synchronization of body and mind. Again, sitting meditation is the key to that.

» By the dance of the setting sun, the entire world becomes cowardly.

This is a bit of a social commentary. The setting-sun world, as opposed to the Great Eastern Sun world, fears death, hides death, and is caught in the idea of being on vacation. It is caught in degradation, and it is opposed to life. Strangely enough, the setting-sun world of nihilism is the world that we find ourselves in most of the time. It's a horrible situation.

Because of habit, the setting-sun world is that which makes us depressed, repressed, or distraught. But there's a different way, which is leading a sane and dignified life in the brilliance of the Great Eastern Sun. Trungpa Rinpoche says that this vision is based on celebrating life.

Subjectively, for example, we may think, "When I die, it's all a done deal and all is going to disappear." The setting-sun approach is based on trying to ward off death by having this nihilistic outlook, which is really based on fear. As Trungpa Rinpoche says,

> In the world of the setting sun, we are constantly feeling afraid of ourselves, ashamed of who we are and what we are.[5]

The warrior's approach is to fight this tendency toward nihilism. It takes effort. You have to rouse yourself. We'll come back to this in the next chapter when discussing windhorse and the four dignities. We don't just go with the flow of the setting-sun world. There's something bigger than just going down the drain!

» The food of the setting sun fills everyone with grease and fat.

As Trungpa Rinpoche says,

> In the setting-sun, or degraded, approach, you have a giant vision, beyond anything you can consume, and you get bloated and end up throwing things away.[6]

This points to our constant tendency toward materialism. In other words, the setting-sun world is the world that gets caught in all kinds of materialism, whether it's physical, psychological, or spiritual. It can be quite literal. For example, there are many beautiful countries, such as Australia and Canada, that are for the most part empty of human beings, yet think of all the junk that exists all around. We human beings put the junk in stacks over here, but then we get more junk, and where are we going to put it? Well, we'll put it over there—and on it goes. Even though this planet is incredibly vast, it's polluted. It happened because we're used to wanting more and more.

The restaurant experiences in America are also quite something. Unless we go to some fancy places, we're often given about twice as much as we should or could eat. We think, "Oh, that's good." Well, it's probably good if it's good food, but generally the places that give us the largest quantities mostly give us big stacks of French fries!

The Great Eastern Sun approach is different; it's a sacred view of the world. And it is ultimately the ecological view, but without the politically correct, self-righteous attitude that often goes with it. We can appreciate our world, yet we don't have to overindulge in it, and we don't have to leave a mess.

» Always return to the primordial ground.

Regardless of what has gone wrong with our world, regardless of all the cowardice and grease and fat that we've discussed, there's always the possibility of reconnecting with original purity. As Trungpa Rinpoche explains, this is because the world is clean to begin with. Since the world is originally clean, if you make a mess, you can clean it up again. As Rinpoche puts it, "Dirt never comes first." It comes on, you clean it.

When I was a kid, my mom would say, "Go bathe," and I would retort, "Why? I'm going to get dirty in a little while!" That's cute, I suppose. But it's noble to clean. It's part of warriorship. Trungpa Rinpoche describes it like this:

> If you use clean towels, they become dirty, but you can always wash them and return them to their original state. Similarly, our physical and psychological existence is originally clean.[7]

Sometimes we feel like we're a real mess. That mess isn't inherent; it is an extra. Even though we may be a psychological mess, a physical mess, a total wreck—and I know we sometimes think of ourselves that way—we can go back and clean up. About this Trungpa Rinpoche says,

> [Our] existence is all good, and it is totally launderable. This is what we mean by basic goodness: the pure ground is always there, waiting to be cleaned. We can always reconnect with the primordial ground.[8]

I lived with Thinley Norbu Rinpoche for many years. Earlier in the book, I mentioned how he liked everything perfectly clean. That didn't mean we cleaned up his mess; we cleaned up *our* mess. But this man, one of the great meditation masters of the world, enjoyed vacuuming more than anyone else I've ever met! Now, was he just a clean freak or was he trying to show us something about our own mind?

Interestingly, this teacher was considered by Tibetan Buddhists to be a manifestation of Vajrasattva. Vajrasattva is a buddha that is all white and can clean up any mistake or sin. It's the absolute absolver. Any mess you make can be cleaned up by Vajrasattva, but that Vajrasattva is not separate from your own mind; it's the buddha that exists within you. You mess up, Vajrasattva will clean the mess. But where is Vajrasattva? He is your own mind. This is very profound.

This touches to the Vajrayana, which we will come back to. But if we spend time with this slogan, we may see the connection and realize that the primordial ground that it points to is truly basic.

» All-victorious, you have nothing to conquer.

This is the warrior's way. Warriorship is not about going out and conquering anything. We are all-victorious to begin with. As Trungpa Rinpoche explains in the commentary associated with this slogan, this is not about talking ourselves into believing that everything is okay. It's not any baloney like that. Just look. Look, look at your own mind, look at your own being . . . Take a good look: You are good, and you are genuine. The whole of existence is good and genuine. Yes, there are constant challenges and aberrations. "But for the true warrior," Rinpoche says, "there is no warfare. You are never at war with your world."[9] That's not to say that we won't take care of our world, but we're never at war with it. We can deal with whatever comes our way, whether it's terrorism or anything else. It all has to do with how we conduct ourselves. All-victorious, we have nothing to conquer.

The Shambhala Warrior Slogans contains fifty-three aphorisms. We have just covered the first fifteen, which summarize some of the core principles. They are simple ideas, but if we can remember them and put them into effect, they will reveal their power. There's not all that much to remember. If we can simply remember basic goodness, we basically have the whole thing; likewise, "genuine heart of sadness" or "all-victorious," every one of them contains the whole thing. It's up to us what we do with it.

In the next chapter, we will explore more of these slogans. But in order to make the most of them, we will also discuss how to engender the energy that cuts through hesitation and how to cultivate the four dignities of the warrior.

16
Authentic Presence, Windhorse, and the Four Dignities

In this chapter, in addition to presenting another selection of the Shambhala warrior slogans, we will discuss the various ways and styles of the warrior, the essence of which has to do with the development of *lungta*, a Tibetan word translated as "windhorse." A lot of animal names will come up, as this approach comes from a nomadic culture. But essentially what we will be dealing with are fundamental, elemental principles. These principles are quite powerful and inspiring.

Windhorse is the steed of the warrior. It has to do with the energy that comes from confidence, particularly the confidence of fearlessness. Being a true warrior in this world and riding the majestic "horse of the wind" invokes both freedom and the capacity to cut through hesitation. It is also connected to what are called the four dignities of the warrior. Getting into those dignities presupposes that we have a basic understanding of the warrior's view, the foundations of which are both simple and profound. Therefore, a brief recap might prove useful.

THE WARRIOR AS BODHISATTVA

As explained, a warrior is someone who is willing to go beyond aggression and be victorious over war. It's about creating a good and decent world for ourselves, our family, and anyone that we meet, whether in our neighborhood, city, country, or planet. The only way to create an enlightened society of any kind in this world is for us, as individuals, to take responsibility for our own body, speech, and mind. The warrior's way is precisely this: It is the way of taking responsibility and not putting blame elsewhere. It begins right at home.

As we know, it's very difficult to help anybody if we don't help ourselves. But the warrior's approach is a bit tricky. How do we help ourselves? By putting others before ourselves. This warrior's path is the path of egolessness. The warrior can thus also be a bodhisattva, and that is where Mahayana Buddhism and the Shambhala teachings meet. The only way to truly help ourselves is to begin to forget ourselves and to put others before ourselves. Strangely enough, that is the best solution to egomaniacal problems. It is also the best solution to put our own house in order. We don't have to constantly fixate on *me*, *mine*, and "what do *I* get out of this?" That approach to reality is awfully limited. We may get something out of it, but ultimately it leads nowhere. The other approach—being kind, putting the concerns of others before ours—is a much better way of living our life, and it provides a much better result altogether. But it's up to us to find out if that is in fact true.

In a previous chapter, we discussed the mythological history of Shambhala and how it applies in this world. The underlying view is that everyone in the kingdom could be a king or queen. It's the imperial view. Not *imperious*; it is caring for all beings, including animals in the kingdom and the general environment altogether. In fact, the Shambhala vision is a precursor to a genuine ecological perspective that everything matters.

The specialness of the Shambhala approach is that it teaches us this imperial view and shows us how to carry it into the world. The idea of caring for others is natural. It doesn't come from a wretched place or naïve place, or a place of poverty; it comes from the richness that exists in ourselves. It comes from basic goodness, which is the ultimate vein of richness that runs through our being. As pointed out by the slogans "Goodness is the ground of all" and "Always return to the primordial ground," the warrior is always returning to that basic goodness, touching into that vein of gold that underlies our common humanity.

To do that, the practice of sitting meditation is essential. Yet since the warrior's way is above war, in learning to meditate we are not waging a war with ourselves. We allow discipline to become natural. However, this requires some exertion, as it won't just happen by itself. You have to at least sit down and take a good posture—and not all that much more. But it's difficult to sit down because we're used to our busy mind. And it's difficult sometimes to have a good posture because we're used to slouching. And it may be difficult to be quiet because we're used to being noisy. But a little effort will make it happen. From that little exertion comes great virtue—more than we can imagine. It seems like nothing to just sit down and be mindful of our body, breath, and mind. In fact, it's immeasurable how worthwhile it is. The repetition of it is even more worthwhile. But there's no big payoff in the sense that it is not about just having some little experience and then whoopee! This is an ongoing situation that we put into our life.

From that, like the Buddha, we can become a universal monarch. "Universal monarch" doesn't mean big shot. It means that, like the king or queen at the center of the palace of wakefulness, we are inseparable from all aspects of the mandala. It means that everything can be seen and cared for.

WANGTHANG: AUTHENTIC PRESENCE

The practice of meditation and other virtues, like putting others before ourselves and paying attention to our world—paying really good attention and actually caring—produces something that in Tibetan is called *wangthang*. It means "field of power," but Trungpa Rinpoche liked to translate it as "authentic presence." It's not power over anybody; rather, it's a genuineness that actually can be seen by those who'd like to see it or have the sensitivity to see it. The virtues reflect in our being.

Some people naturally have charisma. I remember meeting a few well-known politicians in my life. Bill Clinton was one of them. The earliest president I met was Dwight D. Eisenhower, although I'm afraid that few of us are old enough to remember him! I also met other presidents of the United States. As a young man, I was very involved in politics, and I had the opportunity to meet these charismatic figures. They had a kind of "outer wangthang," or outer authentic presence, somehow based on who they were and what they did, whether they were good or bad. Even George W. Bush had some weird wangthang, whether you liked him or not. The same can be felt with some actors and actresses. For example, if you see Tom Cruise, say what you will, but he's got something going. Such people have this outer charisma, or outer wangthang, which comes somehow from the power in their being that's built up from their activity. However, when we're talking about the warrior's way, we're not talking about that kind of so-called authentic presence, which doesn't last. In fact, these people usually get on top of their world and then fall down—big time. Think of many of the presidents of modern Korea: such a big deal when they get elected, and then within eight years they end up in jail. Billionaires in jail—it's the strangest thing. But all these people have a certain charisma. They believe in themselves, and because they believe in themselves, it seems that a lot of people believe in them, too. That is not what we're talking about here.

We're discussing *inner* authentic presence. It is based on primordial space, a sense of real spaciousness rather than glad-handing and good looks.

The inner authentic presence comes from egolessness. It's the kind of presence that a real spiritual person has. For example, I liked Pope John Paul II, even though he'd said a lot of bad things about Buddhism. I know who his Buddhist advisor was, and I think he misinformed him. In any case, that pope had an authentic presence that was the charismatic outward kind along with something special—a spiritual power and a kind of lovingness.

You will meet so many people in all aspects of life that have this authentic presence who are unknowns. They're just wonderful people. They can be your aunt, grandfather, spouse, boss, or employee. It's surprising where you find these people, because they're sort of everywhere. Even if they've never heard a word about Buddhism or Shambhala, somehow they embody that approach, because in fact they do put others before themselves. And they don't make a big deal about themselves either. Because of that virtue, there is something special about them.

The inner wangthang has to do with genuineness, truth, and honesty rather than just charisma. Each of us, if we simplify and practice the most basic of these warrior virtues, can be like that. Not so that we can feel we're a bigwig but so that we can actually be of benefit to others and ourselves. That kind of authentic presence comes about if we can let go of our ideas about ourselves and others while allowing ourselves to be mixed with the magic of this world.

What does "magic" mean in this context? It means not getting caught in the logics and lies of this world. It involves letting go of fixed mind. There's the magic of the natural world; the magic of the fact that this existence is even here; and the magic of all the karma, all the causes and effects that bring us to the point where we are. It's amazing, in fact, that we can even read this book and discuss these teachings. An intricate set of circumstances has brought us together through the medium of a book, to say nothing of the opportunity and willingness to contemplate and practice these teachings.

Part of our approach is letting go into this way of looking at things and then mixing our mind with the magic of the moment. We don't do this once. Nor twice. It's about letting go and mixing with the magic *constantly*. But we have to begin with once. And then we have to begin again with twice—on and on until it flows uninterruptedly.

It takes exertion because even though we may be inspired at one moment, we may become depressed in the next and experience doubt or fear. But we can begin again. We may forget about our meditation practice: Even though it's a wonderful thing, we create some psychology of all the reasons we don't have the time to do it while we busy our mind with every possible entertainment. We can make up all kinds of storylines. We don't have to believe them. Remember, magic is not getting caught in the logics and lies of this world.

LUNGTA: WINDHORSE

There is a spontaneous process that brings about the manifestation of this authentic presence, and that is the raising of lungta, or windhorse. In the Shambhala tradition and the Tibetan tradition as a whole, there are teachings related to this, which Trungpa Rinpoche describes as "rousing the energy of basic goodness into a wind of delight and power."[1] The four qualities, or four ways of the warrior, that we will explore below—meekness, perkiness, outrageousness, and inscrutability—are also based on the development of lungta, the spiritual power of being able to ride the horse of exertion, bravery, and cheerfulness. Regardless of our age, health, and overall situation, it's possible for us to ride the windhorse.

The way we ride this horse is by casting out any depression that comes our way, on the spot, in the moment. Not giving in to depressive thoughts or heavy emotions that come our way, we take a good posture. This good posture includes our body and mind. We can rise above all the things in this world that we feel are pressing us down. It's not necessary to go down with those depressing thoughts. We can ride the horse of lungta—not that it's going to hurt any less. But we don't have to fall prey to that dark world.

Windhorse is associated with a special symbolism. In Tibet and elsewhere in the Himalayas, on mountainsides and in temples and monasteries and people's homes, you'll see colorful flags. They usually have a horse with jewels on its back: That is a representation of the lungta. In the corners of the flags you will see four animals: the tiger, the lion, the garuda, and the dragon.[2] So that's one animal that actually inhabits this earth, and three "mythical animals." (The lion is a snow lion; I don't know if anyone has actually seen one.) It's a special mythology because it is connected to instructions on how to be a warrior. The key to it all is the windhorse in the middle. The flags usually have text as well, often an invocation of windhorse composed by the great Nyingma master of the late nineteenth and early twentieth centuries, Mipham Rinpoche. Mipham wrote many such texts that contain instructions on how to raise windhorse into our being.

It is believed that the flags spread goodness through their interaction with the elements, wind in particular. It should be noted that lungta is connected not only to the outer element of air but also to the "inner winds" or energies that circulate in our body.

If we're going to raise lungta and practice the ways of the warrior that are symbolized by the tiger, the lion, the garuda, and the dragon, it means that we have acknowledged the Great Eastern Sun; that we have seen the possibility of going beyond depression and this little idea of *me, me, me*; and that we are willing to take it further.

Taking it further means developing the various virtues that include sitting meditation, putting others before ourselves, paying attention, and generally caring for the environment that we live in, which includes our own body, clothes, house, space, public spaces, and so forth. This part, by the way, is literal. This teaching is very interesting because it's both literal and figurative; sometimes it's hard to discern which parts are figurative and which parts are literal. But being a simpleminded person, I look at all of it as literal. Sometimes we are better off being a little bit innocent and finding out what happens when we just do it. It's okay to be a little bit like a child in the beginning. We're given these teachings, so we might as well test them out.

Connecting with Lungta

The idea of windhorse refers to this combination of symbolism, gallantry, animal power, and wind. The horse symbolizes a sense of majesty: There's weight, speed, exactness...

Have you ever ridden a horse? It is not necessarily easy to learn, but if you make a relationship with the horse and a relationship with riding, at some point there's no separation between rider and horse: It's one movement. Likewise, we can learn to make a wholesome connection with lungta. If we do, it's like the vault of the biggest bank in the universe has been opened to us, and it's ours. Lungta refers to a life force—life in its fullest sense—and it is something that actually exists in our being.

We can connect to that lungta at will. Part of this lungta is cheerfulness, upliftedness, gentleness, gallantry—all at once, all bundled together. It's extremely powerful in that way. It's connected with a kind of primordial confidence—a sense of genuineness and clarity that cuts through hesitation because it is unaffected by physical awkwardness and intellectual speculation. Riding this windhorse makes us almost superhuman—or rather fully human. It is the ultimate antidote to fear because if we can bridle this powerful force, then we can always reach the other side of fear.

The Shambhala teachings contain many techniques created by the masters of the past to connect with lungta. I'm going to share the simplest one. It has four parts.

First, in any situation, we consciously—with a joyful mind, free from doubt—take our stance, either sitting or standing. We make a definite connection with where we are. It is the equivalent of sitting on a horse. There's energy and power that comes from that seat and being in that seat.

Second, we allow the genuine heart of sadness by simply opening up and noticing that tenderness in our being. It is our connection with this world, with all that lives. We should understand why sadness exists in this life, and why, when describing power, we talk about sadness: It connects us with others. It's the opposite of egotism, and it is devoid of arrogance. Therefore, though our posture is robust in the warrior's seat, it doesn't come out of any kind of aggression. It comes from this genuine heart, this sense of connection to the world.

Third, we touch in with a sudden sense of vastness in which the mind is totally free from any fixations. Being "suddenly free from fixed mind," as Trungpa Rinpoche put it, is allowing our usual ways of thinking to not arise. We just drop everything. So, we take our seat. We connect with the rich bank of power through our genuine heart of sadness. It enters into our being, and through being suddenly free from fixed mind, there's a spark—the spark of primordial confidence.

Fourth, instead of just holding on to that power and confidence, we reflect that out in harmony with the imperial perspective, or the universal monarch's view. We share that confidence and dignity, like a sun that shines out. But again, this is not done with any sense of arrogance but with a sense of brokenheartedness. It's actual compassion.

To summarize, we start by taking our seat. Then we allow the genuine heart of sadness to just be—we bring this richness into our being. Suddenly we're free from fixed mind—we just are, simply. And finally we reflect out.

This is one way to connect with primordial richness, primordial confidence. If we open our heart, we can let confidence and richness come into our being and reflect it out. Then we can rest simply in that clarity. We can do this anytime: sitting, standing, or through any situation, including difficult ones. We can do it when we feel stuck, inadequate, or somehow lacking; when we feel bound by a limited view or entangled in negative feelings about ourselves. We can do it when we need to summon strength and courage before tackling a challenge or being of service to others. We can do it before any artistic practice. At one point in my life, I oil-painted and found it helpful to raise lungta beforehand. It is accessible to us anytime.

Lungta is described as being physical *and* psychological. When the sense of windhorse is present, mind and body are synchronized. We feel wholesome and real. We feel, as per one of the Shambhala warrior slogans, that there is nothing to conquer. Being all-victorious is our birthright.

THE FOUR DIGNITIES

The process of casting out depression and raising windhorse is further detailed in the teachings on the four dignities, or the four ways of the warrior, which are related to the four animals mentioned earlier.

Each of us has experienced a version of each one of these four dignities. All beings do. However, the usual way we experience them is tied to our habits: It's just part of our habitual way of perceiving. It is different when it comes from the perspective of the warrior riding the windhorse. We can then actually put the energies of the tiger, lion, garuda, and dragon into play. They represent stages on the path of warriorship and different qualities that we can tap into.

Let's look at each of them.

Meekness

The first way of the warrior is that of meekness, represented by the tiger. In this context, it means that there's humbleness and gentleness in our state of being. We are not puffed up but open and attentive. The warrior of meek is uncomplicated, approachable, resting in simplicity. They are approachable with others, not hostile, but rather friendly, extending kindness to themselves and mercy to others.

Another slogan is particularly connected to the meekness of the warrior:

» Don't cause the Great Eastern Sun to eclipse.

As Trungpa Rinpoche says,

> Developing meekness is one of the disciplines or dignities of the warrior. Meekness is not feebleness but strength and brilliance that come from resting in a state of simplicity, being uncomplicated and approachable. In that state, simple awareness allows you to refrain from activities that dim the vision of the Great Eastern Sun.[3]

In other words, the warrior of the meek doesn't fall prey to the setting-sun world but remains with the Great Eastern Sun, which is the vision of wakeful sanity. The warrior of the meek doesn't allow their mind to just be filled with ordinary preoccupations. Trungpa Rinpoche continues:

> When you are not seduced by trivial situations, there is a natural sense of uplifted mind and vast vision.[4]

This vast vision has to do with awareness. The awareness, for example, that comes from sitting meditation; the awareness of others and the environment, where we are, what we do, cleaning up after ourselves, and so forth. All that awareness is what prevents us from falling prey to the setting-sun world. When we fall prey to that world, we get depressed. It *is* seductive, I have to say. It can look pretty good! Think of those hazy sunsets over Los Angeles that you see in movies. It looks good from a distance, but then as you get closer and closer, it's grittier and more depressing. It's dirty and messy. And then it has an underbelly that's even worse! Metaphorically, this is the sort of depression that can drag us down. The warrior of the meek doesn't fall for that, as seductive as it may appear.

One of the Shambhala warrior slogans seems connected to this idea:

» The warrior is not afraid of space.

Only cowards are afraid of space—afraid of vastness, silence. In the setting-sun approach to the world, we're always trying to do things and put on a protective pseudo-armor to protect ourselves from space—in other words, from the way that things are. As Trungpa Rinpoche says,

> The challenge of warriorship is to step out of that cocoon, to step out into space, by being brave and at the same time being gentle.[5]

The meekness of the warrior has three stages, or three aspects.

The first is modesty. We don't become overcome with arrogance, because we have a sense of modesty. That modesty comes from being true and genuine. Along with that, we take an interest in the world. We're actually paying attention. We also join that with exertion. In fact, the symbolism of the tiger is a sure-footed exertion. It's about stepping out with confidence.

Meekness also means that we don't have to make a big deal about anything. The symbolism of the tiger also connotes a sense of discernment. We can identify what to accept and what to reject. We can see what's worthwhile and what's not worthwhile. It is easier to make decisions.

The second stage or aspect is the expression of unconditional confidence. Imagine a tiger in its prime. It is slightly self-satisfied and modest at the same time. Its body is so relaxed that there are no problems. But at the same time, there's an attentiveness that comes with it. Confidence is natural, and the warrior of the meek moves through the world with awareness and mindfulness.

The third aspect is the absence of hesitation. There is no hesitation because our mind is so vast and we're willing to jump into the ocean of magic, power, and delight that is this world. We're not afraid to get into this vast world. We're not just stuck in the world of our own habitual discursive thinking—talking to ourselves and convincing ourselves about this and that, with little storylines and endless variations on the themes.

Meekness brings fruition because there is tremendous exertion, and from that tremendous exertion we have the ability to accomplish everything. Yet we accomplish it not from busyness but from a sense of relaxation that is energized.

As you will see, in each of these warrior ways, *relaxation* is a key word. It is an easily misunderstood idea because culturally we've come to think of relaxation as a beach chair or a chaise longue. Although we have nothing against beach chairs or chaise longues, that's really not what's being spoken about here. Relaxation, in this context, has to do with allowing our busy mind not to just automatically do all the stupid things that we habitually do. We can relax—and if we like, sure, it can be in the beach chair, but it can also be in any chair, or on the ground, or as we walk, or in any other situation. We can allow our attention to go beyond our blah, blah, blah, blah, blah. That busy, dizzy little mind? We can break free and extend out.

The only way to do this is through exertion. If we go to the swimming pool and want to do laps, we have to move our arms and legs, right? Likewise, the approach here is that relaxation requires doing something—not much but *something*. We need a sense of exertion to at least stop the train of discursive habits. If we can do that, then everything becomes possible. We can accomplish anything. Not only can we become accomplished ourselves, but we can also inspire others around us to do the same.

What we find out if we are in business or an artist, a writer, or whatever is that it takes a lot to get to the piece of paper, to the phone, or to whatever it is. We have a whole psychological buildup to work and artistic endeavors. The act itself is almost effortless, but the buildup is so painful! Writer's block, artist's block, worker's block, meditator's block—it's all the same. We have to *get there*. Once we're there, things change. So, we need exertion to get there, and then we need the relaxation of just being there, and then we need to repeat and get experience. When we have experience, we have confidence. When we have confidence, we can accomplish everything. But if we don't begin at the beginning, then there's no confidence. If there's no confidence, there's no accomplishment. It all goes together.

However, we don't do it in a heavy-handed way. This is called the path of meekness. It's exertion that has a gentle quality to it—but still it's exertion. Each of us knows what that is. It's that force that we can use to make our life worthwhile.

The meek warrior also leaves gain, victory, and fame behind. We don't accomplish things for those reasons. We're not dependent on the feedback of others. We're just willing to have the confidence to do what we see is worthwhile to do while respecting ourselves and our own point of view. There's no need for us to be devious to others or to lie to ourselves. We can just be simple. Our dignity doesn't ever have to be diminished.

In short, the warrior's meekness comes with a vast vision and a sense of confidence, and these come from the development of virtue and exertion.

Perkiness

We are now meeting the warrior of perky, which is illustrated by the snow lion.

With the warrior's perkiness, there is a vibrancy and an uplifted, inquisitive energy that's always youthful regardless of the age of the warrior. This youthful quality is a state of being, a state of mind; it has nothing to do with, say, decaying skin. There is also a willingness to act. Yet this is not about pouncing or aggression.

The snow lion is a highland animal. In Tibetan arts, you'll see the beast jumping from peak to peak and enjoying the wildflowers in an elevated setting with the occasional small trees, but mostly with the big boulders and rocks. The symbolism is quite telling: The highland approach is full of freshness and newness.

Thus the warrior of perky is good and cheerful, and their perkiness is unconditional. Whatever comes to the warrior, they can always find something cheerful about it, as painful as the situation may be, because the cheerfulness literally does not depend on conditions—it is not based on outside influences of any kind.

That cheerfulness comes from the ongoing discipline. You may notice that these teachings talk a lot about discipline, exertion, virtue . . . However, these are not meant to be heavy-handed. It's about repetition and a light touch. When you've forgotten, you come back and repeat. Exertion can always begin anew. You can be a beginner right from any moment. You can also begin with meek, then go to perky, outrageous, inscrutable, and go from one to the other. In fact, we naturally do so.

The warrior's perkiness has two stages.

The first is experiencing upliftedness and a joyful mind. This naturally comes from the meekness of the previous dignity: The warrior of perky now has artfulness in whatever they do because the cheerfulness is mixed with attention. It is mixed with discernment, clear seeing. When there's that mix, things come out artfully. The way the person lives their life, how they manifest in the world, always comes out beautifully. It is always dignified, even if it's crumpled, so to speak. There's a certain elegance that exudes from the warrior.

The second aspect of perkiness is that the warrior is not caught in the trap of doubt, which is crucial. In fact, the slogan that goes with this particular path of warriorship is:

» Precise and perky, you are never caught in the trap of doubt.

According to Trungpa Rinpoche, the fundamental doubt we have is doubting ourselves. We doubt our perceptions, our minds, and so forth. When body and mind are unsynchronized, we doubt. When they are synchronized, we don't doubt; everything is precise and clear. Thus, the continuous discipline here is joining body and mind, and that joining of body and mind brings cheerfulness. If we are stuck in one extreme of being just body-oriented, or in the other extreme of just being mind-oriented, depression happens. There can be physical depression if we are just stuck in our mind, or psychological depression if we feel trapped in or overly concerned with our body, or any other variation. But when body and mind are in sync, an unconditional cheerfulness arises. Then discipline is a pleasure rather than a demand. Trungpa Rinpoche says that we then become free of the unfavorable states of existence in which we are either always fighting for survival or obsessed with trivial pursuits—trivial at least from the vaster point of view. The warrior of perkiness possesses the goodness of the higher realms: clearness and preciseness, which is free from doubt. Trungpa Rinpoche adds,

> At this stage the warrior is always aware and never confused as to what to accept and what to reject.[6]

In the traditional teachings of Buddhism, the phrase "what to accept and what to reject" is generally associated with discipline and karma. For example, we'll prioritize actions that contribute to happiness and spiritual fulfillment, and avoid those that fuel confusion and suffering. But here the approach is not dogmatic. Knowing what to accept and what to reject becomes more intuitive, as the warrior is fully attuned to situations. The discernment is complete. Because of that, there is no doubt at all. This absence of doubt should not be confused with being ego-puffed, however. We must remember that this is all based on egolessness, gentleness, and goodness. In this way, each dignity builds on one another.

Outrageousness

The third dignity is illustrated by the garuda. A garuda is a bird that hatches fully born, fully grown. In other words, when the egg cracks—voilà!—the garuda is fully developed; there's no childhood. The symbolism of the garuda is also that it never touches the earth. The mythic bird immediately flies into space and never even needs to land on the ground. There is a sense of outrageousness: Though it is born in a worldly existence—the egg, of course, has to be on the earth—the garuda flies out into the open as soon as it hatches, and this involves tremendous freedom. There's no issue of mommy or daddy helping it along.

This symbolism also reflects a willingness to be daring and enter situations without hope or fear—and without any stupidity either. Yet it involves the willingness to make a mistake. In this way, the outrageous warrior possesses tremendous strength, yet there is no sense of being unreasonable or wild. We are not outrageous in the manner of a fool. The outrageousness of the warrior is based on the achievement of absolute fearlessness. We just dive right into phenomena, right into space, without fear.

How do we overcome fear? Not just through meeting fear, as we have already discussed; we also have to overcome hope. The outrageous warrior has overcome both fear and hope. There's no roller coaster ride of wanting something and being frustrated, elated, or excited at first then disappointed. We're all familiar with this going up and down. Here there's an evenness that develops because there's no hope at all. There's no need to desire anything because everything is complete as it is. There's no ambush of hope to come and get you.

The garuda, the warrior of outrageous, has an extremely vast mind. Mind is extended beyond any of the fetters that could bring them down. There's a sense of complete freedom, of fathoming all of space, all of reality.

Because of that, the outrageous warrior doesn't need to hold anything back. There's no obstruction, no need to measure, no need to compare. There is also no anxiety about how far they can go—they just go. What this means is that the outrageous warrior can accomplish things in this world that are extraordinary because there's no notion of limitation. The warrior can go beyond the cages that trap most of us—our little doubts, fears, social norms, and so forth.

Another symbol for this outrageous way of the warrior is that of a "good self-existing sword." In fact, here is the slogan that's associated with the warrior of outrageous:

» A good self-existing sword: desire to sharpen it will make it dull.

Often, either out of hope or fear, we try to measure, compare, compete, or apply some kind of rivalrous logic. There is nothing of the sort here—nothing better, nothing worse. That self-existing sword, if we try to make it better, it's only going to make it dull. The sword is complete as it is. The sharpness of one's mind is complete. As Trungpa Rinpoche says,

> Have confidence in your awareness, and relax in your ability to connect with the larger vision, the experience of vast mind.[7]

In this way, there's no notion of having to go get anything extra to make ourselves better. As we'll see, this naturally leads into the inscrutability of the dragon, the last of the four dignities.

Another slogan that goes along with this outrageousness is:

» Overcome both hope and fear.

This is a crucial slogan, and it is quite explicit. If we are caught in the constant carousel of trying to avoid and trying to seduce, we're going to be unhappy, disappointed, upset—you know, excited and elated one day, depressed the next. Who needs this? As Trungpa Rinpoche says,

> With nothing to hope for and nothing to fear, fearlessness is achieved.[8]

That's the key.

Inscrutability

The dragon has to do with inscrutability. Not inscrutable in a Charlie Chan–movie sort of way, if anyone remembers that fictional Honolulu police detective. We are also not talking about having a good poker face. Here, inscrutability has more to do with a sense of fulfillment, achievement, and uncontrived spontaneity.

The warrior of inscrutable, which is illustrated by the dragon, is thus energetic, powerful, unwavering.

Like the garuda, the dragon is a mythological being, and here it refers to the Asian dragon, not to the Western one. They may look similar, but the symbolism is different. We'll use the imagery of the Chinese or Eastern dragon: a serpent with wings, if you will. This dragon appears in the sky in the summer and hibernates in the ground in the winter. It also appears in the spring, causing lightning and thunder. It has this regular pattern.

The warrior's inscrutability is based on fearlessness. There's no inscrutability in any conventional sense. It's not about just being quiet, a blank wall, or devious in any way, but rather from fearlessness, gentleness, and sympathy. There's a noncommittal approach that can actually be quite helpful when working with others, because they can listen and have a sense of humor about everything. No one knows what the warrior of the inscrutable really is thinking because there's a sense of being removed. Don't misunderstand: It is not a lack of caring; in fact, it is *based* on caring. However, there's a sense of being removed because there's no necessity to control.

This inscrutability is not something you can force onto yourself because it is not a static state. You can't simply say, "Oh, I'm going to be inscrutable and noncommittal." Rather, inscrutability, in the warrior sense, is built on meekness, perkiness, and outrageousness. It comes from the three other dignities very naturally.

The warrior of inscrutable involves a funny paradox. Although no one knows exactly what the warrior is thinking or going to do, that unpredictability is within total predictability, because there's something very solid about that being. Think of the symbolism of the dragon: It's in the sky in the summer and in the ground hibernating in the winter; and in the spring it rises and sends out breaths of lightning and roars out thunder. The amazing twist is that rain comes. The dragon sends out thunder and lightning; it doesn't make the rain, but rain comes. That's the inscrutable part. From the lightning and thunder comes rain—it's not so obvious that it's all about rainmaking.

The warrior of inscrutable is absolutely genuine, and there's no need for any confirmation about their genuineness. There's an unyieldingness that never gives in, doesn't change its mind. It has deadly accuracy. "Doesn't change its mind" doesn't mean that if there's a mistake, the warrior won't acknowledge the mistake. However, when something is seen, it's seen clearly, and from that clarity is definitiveness—no wishy-washiness at all. It's not about being stubborn but rather being clear, precise, and deadly accurate, just right on the point. It is the apex of the warrior's path.

The warrior of inscrutable is never interested in being the center of attention. Sometimes they don't even care about being noticed. But they're loyal to others. Such warriors can always accomplish everything because they have sympathy for others. It's very strange: The warrior of inscrutable can do everything, and you might not even know that they're doing anything. That's the best kind of leader—the leader that makes you believe that you did it and had the idea! I'm jesting, but the inscrutable warrior really is the best kind of leader any of us could be. It's not about taking center stage.

Moreover, the warrior of inscrutable is extremely methodical and extremely elegant.

The slogan that goes with this inscrutability is the following:

» Don't spell out the truth.

As Trungpa Rinpoche comments,

> When you spell out the truth, it loses its essence and becomes either "my" truth or "your" truth. By implying the truth, it doesn't become anyone's property. When the dragon wants a rainstorm, he causes thunder and lightning. That brings the rain. Truth is generated from its environment; in that way it becomes a powerful reality.[9]

The idea is that the truth doesn't need a handle and an authority to say, "This is the truth." It can just be referred to. You don't have to make it THE TRUTH. No one believes the truth anyway! Everyone says they want the truth, but it's a funny world. Therefore, we are advised to imply rather than spell out.

There's an enlightened confidence in the warrior of inscrutable. That confidence helps to create power and good things in this world. It's the enlightened leader point of view that is not about *me*, *me*, or *me*. In fact, none of these dignities are about *me*. It's about benefiting others so that we can live in an enlightened way and contribute to an enlightened society.

Embodying the Dignities

The full realization of any of these dignities only comes when the warrior is able to realize in their being an unshakable conviction in basic goodness. In other words, if we can't touch into that basic goodness any time or place, none of this is going to help us. That vein of gold is what the warrior's approach to the four dignities is based on. Without it, all we have are just a bunch of words and drawings of animals on a flag. The dignities also come alive if we have already seen the Great Eastern Sun being reflected in the sacred world. They come alive when we effectively see that the truth of wakefulness is a possibility for everyone, ourselves included.

The four dignities unfold when we fully plug into the power of the windhorse. Windhorse invigorates the energies of the tiger, lion, garuda, and dragon. The authentic presence that comes from virtue is the vehicle that allows these energies to manifest. Interestingly, Trungpa Rinpoche, in explaining this particular approach, presents us with a wonderful paradox. He says that the tiger, lion, garuda, and dragon—the meek, the perky, the outrageous, and the inscrutable—are the process of developing authentic presence. But then in the next sentence, he says that authentic presence is what allows the path of the tiger, lion, garuda, and dragon to unfold. Therefore, it is coemergent. It happens all together.

It's nice to deal with paradoxes because we have to totally jump in. It's not about something happening later. These teachings have a "path is the goal" quality. Actually practicing the teachings is the goal of the teachings, and that is wonderful. In fact, the same also applies to all Buddhist teachings. Developing the virtues is virtuous. This is a similar point of view.

Karma is a very important issue here. None of this works if we're a nihilist. If we think that we're just going to live this life, do what we please, and then be buried and that's the end of it—that's a strange and sad idea. I know that in the West we tend to believe that everything ends with death. It's a very odd kind of wishful thinking. At least from the Buddhist perspective, the view is that the body and personality die, but mind is continuous. Not *my* mind. Not the mind with my name. But mind is continuous, therefore, it is not nihilistic. But it is also not an eternalistic position where we would have some kind of permanent self. We are not talking about anyone's mind per se but mind itself as continuous.

In this way, egolessness is both the beginning view and the fruition of this teaching. Egolessness is where we begin. Our paths are described in these ways of the warrior, and the result is egolessness. Why bother then? It's good to take a moment and ask ourselves that question.

The whole thing is about openness, and it's also about living life fully. Let's face it: This life is stupidly short. Some of us may have noticed, and as we get older, we notice more. As pointed out, "Death is real, comes without warning; this body will be a corpse." That applies to every single one of us. And we have no idea which day is going to be that big day for us.

So, when are we going to put these teachings into practice? Tomorrow, right? Or next week, when this is done, or when I go to this next place, or when I can set up my room to do this or that... We have all these ways of keeping our mind busy and putting things into this future that we assume is always going to be there.

These teachings—and all genuine spiritual teachings—have to do with *this* moment. They have to do with how we could be a warrior—a genuine, real person—in this very moment. And then in this moment again. And in this moment again. It is not about the *next* one, and it is not about kicking ourselves about what we did or didn't do yesterday or the year before. The karma that brings us to this moment is complete. Then everything that we do from this moment creates further karma. Ultimately karma is only gone when there is complete enlightenment—or, in the Shambhala terminology, when we become a complete master warrior, a universal monarch. The potential for that exists in every one of us.

The approach here is not complicated. We rest in the sense of warriorship. We don't try to fight it or push it; we rest, and we begin to become comfortable with it. Becoming comfortable in this warriorship, we don't have to struggle. Rather than us trying to manufacture something out of ourselves, our being unfolds like a flower. We can't push that unfoldment.

As we navigate the spiritual path, windhorse circulates; it comes and goes. The four animals symbolize experiences that actually happen to us and dignities that we can—through our exertion and virtue—imbue into our being. It's not about getting stuck and saying, "Oh, I am now a warrior of the perky," or whatever, and trying to classify ourselves. The symbolism of the tiger, lion, garuda, and dragon is to remind us of what's possible. Each of us can make a connection to every one of these dignities because we've experienced some of their aspects.

The warrior's way is to create the basic situation through the practice of meditation; through putting others before ourselves; and, again, through caring about our environment and the world, and developing the confidence that arises from those virtues. As we develop that confidence, the four dignities, or the four ways of the warrior, become open to us.

ADDITIONAL SLOGANS

Before we end this section on the Shambhala teachings, I would like to share a few more of the slogans. They help us cultivate the ways of the warrior in our daily life.

» To join heaven and earth, go beyond selfishness.

As mentioned in chapter 14, heaven connotes vision and sanity, while earth refers to practicality. When they both come together, we have the opportunity to appreciate what is, quite simply, and we are in harmony with our world. But to experience that, we must transcend our usual ways of thinking and our egotistical habits. Put another way, selfishness creates disharmony in our experience of the world. Focusing too much on our idea of ourselves throws everything off balance.

It's not about showing off in any way or pointing to *me*, *me*, and *me*. Always watch out for those kinds of people. Including yourself.

The penultimate slogan counters any potential misunderstanding of the previous one:

» Give yourself time to be.

Give yourself a break. You don't have to be hard on yourself and push yourself all the time. Enjoy your day, enjoy normal existence, enjoy this life. We can be kind to ourselves—much, much kinder. We can smile a lot if we're so inclined. We can even smile when no one's watching. It's all right! It's fun. It's sweet. We can listen to our own music, so to speak, that comes from our being and echoes to ourselves.

So many of our problems come from hating ourselves—hating what we do, hating what we've done, or being at war with so-called issues, whatever they may be. That can all be put aside. It's possible to let go. We can be real, genuine people. We don't have to continuously play that game, which is not even fun. We don't have to create all kinds of entertainment to hide from ourselves. We can give ourselves a break from all of that.

I miss Trungpa Rinpoche a lot. He passed away many years ago, in 1987. Strangely enough, the ultimate teaching that he gave is the last slogan, and it is the mantra that he taught us all:

» Cheer up.

This is at the heart of the warrior's path: "Cheer up." We don't have to attack ourselves with our own aggression, misery, and pain. Even in the darkest of the dark, dark night of our most painful day, there is some light. We can cheer up anytime. Really!

Trungpa Rinpoche gave the perfect example. He's someone who had lost his country and many of his friends, who had been chased by Chinese Communist troops across Tibet. He was on "wanted" posters because he was a religious leader... Yet he never said a bad word about those people. It's amazing! He would simply make Mao Zedong jokes. That was his idea of a good time: making Chairman Mao jokes. Because, yes, it was a horrible situation; but it happened, and you have to go on. So you can make Chairman Mao jokes and cheer up.

Of course, cheering up is not about suppressing our emotions or letting people walk all over us. It's about cultivating contentment, developing the warrior's resilience and sense of humor, and appreciating our own inner richness and dignity. We can always uplift ourselves and bathe in the Great Eastern Sun.

We have provided an overview of the different ways of the warrior, but it was just the tip of the iceberg. These teachings are incredibly deep. But if we get it all too fast, too easily, then our own mind can't fathom it. These teachings only work if we put our mind to practicing them. This can be done in a cheerful manner, and the best way to cheer up is to practice meditation. If we practice meditation, we're not going to be so attached to everything that comes and seemingly attacks us. If we practice meditation, we can develop fearlessness. We can go beyond hope and fear. It's been done by hundreds of thousands and millions of warriors before us, and we too can do it. Tiger, lion, garuda, and dragon are not myths; they are just a way of explaining how we can *be*. We can take our good windhorse and ride it.

The cheerfulness that we will then develop is, in fact, what we call the Great Eastern Sun. It is unconditioned. We're capable of smiling beautifully, utterly, extraordinarily. We can always cheer up. Even if you don't remember any of the other teachings, please remember this one: "Cheer up." I can see Trungpa Rinpoche's face as a bright sun—or a bright moon—always with that smile. He was the kindest and gentlest person, no matter what you read in the popular media or from jealous people. This is a person that was totally kind and gentle, and this is the heart of his teachings. *Cheer up.*

PART FIVE

THE INDESTRUCTIBLE VEHICLE

In part five, we will discuss the Vajrayana, or tantric Buddhism. Though esoteric, it is based on an extremely refined and sophisticated understanding of reality. The Vajrayana is also a natural extension of the Mahayana: Motivated by great compassion, we feel the urge to learn and apply expedient means so as to cut through delusion and reach enlightenment for the benefit of all beings.

In a sense, all parts of the book are connected in one way or another to Vajrayana. In effect, my root gurus presented even the foundational teachings with a top-down perspective, subtly imbuing even basic sitting meditation with an incredibly vast and profound view. Now is the time to take a closer look at this "Indestructible Vehicle" that is the Vajrayana.

Chapter 17 will touch on general principles, while chapters 18 and 19 will discuss the particulars, using a simple practice text to explain important elements found in most tantric practices.

17
Secret and Shocking

My editor will probably tell me to be nice. But I'm afraid I have to be a little bit mean.

I don't know if you really are interested in this. You're here, holding this book... But you're not supposed to even hear or read about the topics we are about to discuss. This is supposed to be a big secret.

Yet because the times are as they are—with a darkening of sorts—teachings that were extremely secret are, well, a little less so. Currently we are facing all kinds of problems, with our minds being captured by physical, psychological, and spiritual materialism.

We obviously have a big problem with simplicity. If we're talking about the Vajrayana, and especially if we're talking about Dzogchen, or the Great Perfection, we have to simplify our minds. There's no purpose in learning anything about it if we want to be complicated or become someone special based on it. That just doesn't work.

In a way, there's no niceness here. It's—*bam!*—about *this* life. If we believe that everything just ends with death, falling over and that's it, we're mistaken. We're stuck in our materialistic mindset and our obsession with external science.

I've watched the development of Buddhism in the West for half a century. I suppose I've played a part in it as well. Yet "observer" feels more honest because for most of my life, I've been a skeptic, someone who was merely hoping that the teachings of the Buddha might in fact be real. At some point I stopped being a skeptic. The only reason I'm writing this book is because I'm not skeptical in the least.

This part of the book found its first iteration when I was asked to go to Australia by Venerable Traleg Kyabgon Rinpoche. I didn't want to go. I was quite ill, and there was no way I felt like going across the world to talk about real things with real people. But at his insistence, and then with the insistence of my root teacher Thinley Norbu Rinpoche, I had to overcome my illness and many other challenges so that many years later *you* could potentially overcome your skepticism, your illness, your death; so that you can replace busy mind with the mind of Dharma, with the mind of the Great Perfection.

But as always, it's up to you. I don't know what your background is. I just hope none of this is too much of a shock for you.

But then again, it should be a shock.

THE THREE VEHICLES

As we have seen, the teachings of Buddha and his spiritual sons and daughters are often divided into three vehicles. In the early Hinayana teachings, the basic view is that if we simplify enough, we can get ourselves out of the system of samsara, out of the viciousness of cyclic existence. In that specific vehicle, we do that through various modes of abstaining: abstaining from activities that harm others, abstaining from activities that harm ourselves, abstaining from any of the passions and conflicting emotions. Through such discipline we are able to achieve the state of an arhat, someone who has gone beyond the ordinary confines of the passions. Once that is achieved, there is a continuity of what's called *samadhi*, "meditational absorption." There have been many arhats in history, and countless people have benefited greatly from that spiritual approach. It is one of the forms of Buddhism, and it has its own profundity.

The Mahayana school developed from that. The basic view of the Mahayana is that there is no enlightenment if we do it for ourselves. The bodhisattva ideal emanates from the Mahayana, with the understanding that in order to reach liberation, it is essential to have compassion for others. We then take the bodhisattva vow, which is that we will help all beings to liberate, even if that means that all beings found liberation before ourselves. That's the genius of the Mahayana. Furthermore, in this approach, we view the world *as if* it is a dream, a mirage, or a bubbling brook—there are many poetic ways of describing it. Unfortunately there is often some misunderstanding about this. It says *like* a dream; it doesn't say it *is* a dream. The analogies point to the empty nature of existence, the empty nature of any idea that we have of a self and an other. Based on that, great compassion arises because when we give up the constant reference to ourselves, we can see the suffering of beings clearly. Even though we know that the suffering of beings is empty, that doesn't mean we don't pay attention to it. We still see it and feel it, and a relationship takes place. Just because it's empty doesn't mean it hurts any less—which applies both to our personal pain and the pain of others.

The Mahayana teachings also speak of the buddha-nature that is inherent in all beings. Basically it says that the seed of buddhahood is in our heart, and it is latent. The Mahayana then provides many different types of skillful means to allow that buddha-nature to unfold and blossom fully into buddhahood.

Thus, while the goal of the Hinayana practitioner is individual liberation and nirvana, the goal of the Mahayana practitioner is the liberation of all sentient beings, which is also known as complete enlightenment, as opposed to just nirvana as the cessation of all samsaric, desire-realm activities.

Then there's the extension of the Mahayana: the Vajrayana, or Tantrayana, or Mantrayana. It has many names. While it builds upon the previous approaches, its special quality is that it views the world as *already* enlightened; the only problem is our own obscurations.

There are different classifications of the Vajrayana. What we're going to be discussing is mainly informed by the ultimate point of view known as the Dzogchen, or Great Perfection teachings, also known in Sanskrit as Mahasandhi or Ati. According to these teachings, the universe is primordially pure, everything is perfectly enlightened, and all beings are buddhas. Not only are all beings buddhas, but they are also in a constant dance of female and male buddhas joined together. The Vajrayana practitioner is encouraged to look at the world in that way—to adopt the ultimate sacred perspective, if you will—with the understanding that buddha-nature is not merely a seed that needs to be nourished but rather an already fully blossomed wakefulness that naturally contains all enlightened qualities and wisdoms. The difference is in the acknowledging (or lack thereof), and in the cognitive and emotional veils that obscure buddhahood, like clouds covering the sky but never dimming the sun itself and ultimately never separate from the vast expanse of the sky.

There are many special practices in the various forms of Vajrayana that, as is said in the texts, make it possible to attain enlightenment in this lifetime—"or in the next," which is an interesting twist. But either one is viewed as quick. By comparison, the Hinayana is viewed as "slow" because even if we become an arhat and stay in meditative absorption, Mahayanists and Vajrayanists will say that someday, others will have to be taken into account; that there is really no enlightenment if there is only personal liberation. Just because we cut all ties to passions and experience complete absorption into the meditative state while alive and beyond doesn't mean we've reached the end goal.

A central element of Buddhism is the theory of continuous mind. There is no idea that anything ever comes to an end as such. There is constant rebirth—from moment to moment. *Tantra*, which is a general term associated with Vajrayana Buddhism,[1] literally means "warp and woof," but what it refers to is continuity. Warp and woof, in weaving, is how the threads go together. If you look at a piece of fabric closely, it has all kinds of holes in it. But it looks solid, doesn't it? *Tantra* refers to the continuity, but the continuity it's referring to is the continuity of discontinuity. It's not referring to the continuity of ego or any identification with anything solid. It refers to the continuity of openness—the ever-presence of the gaps rather than the ungaps, if you will. It also refers to the indestructibility of enlightenment.

What does this have to do with us? And how can we benefit from any of this?

BELIEF SYSTEMS

Each of us has a belief system, whether we're aware of it or not. From the Buddhist point of view, belief systems are generally classified into two main categories that we've discussed at length in this book: eternalism and nihilism. Regardless of whether we're interested in the Hinayana, the Mahayana, or the Vajrayana, and regardless of which specific school or tradition we belong to, the teachings make it crystal clear that as a Buddhist, we should not get stuck in either polar extreme.

Simply speaking, as we know, eternalism implies a belief in an ongoing God or identification with any form such as a soul that's going to last. Now, this may sound like it contradicts the idea of continuous mind. However, when we say "continuous mind" in Buddhism, we're not talking about continuous *me*, continuous Samuel, or continuous Jane; we're also not talking about a kind of "reincarnation" where we would fundamentally remain the same life after life. Continuous mind goes beyond this life, into future lives, but it is just like the continuous mind of our everyday life of waking, being in the world, sleeping, and so forth. It goes from thought to thought. Are these thoughts real? We must find out. Are they continuous? Well, if we practice meditation, we find that each thought has a beginning, a middle, and an end; that we can't think two thoughts at the same time; that, in fact, there's a gap between each thought. Whatever our idea of a self is, it's like sewing patches onto something that is not as stable as it seems.

If we can simplify our busy mind, we see that this idea that there is something continuous that is ours, is totally dubious. What's continuous is the gap. Indeed, at some point, thoughts can miraculously stop, and still there's something left—bare awareness.

Our ordinary concepts and limitations are so deeply ingrained that transcending them typically requires a lot of hard work. However, it is different for everyone. Take the passions, for example. From the Hinayana point of view, they are viewed as poisonous. When we're completely under their sway, it may be more effective simply to avoid them. The Mahayana point of view is that we should see passions as empty and having no substance in and of themselves; we can then turn them toward positive qualities through the training of our mind. The Vajrayana takes this a step further: In passion or any of the emotions, there are buddhas—*they* are buddhas in fact, but misinterpreted by our mind. Through the skillful means of the great tantric teachers, we can begin to see these passions as enlightened qualities and deities. It's because our perception is impure that we see things impurely; it's not because things are tainted in and of themselves.

Discussing Vajrayana is dangerous. I have no idea why I'm doing this with you, other than that I was asked to. I'm trusting the enlightened mind of my teachers that we can discuss these things in an open manner. Somehow you must have a connection with this. It is said that we can establish a connection with an enlightened teacher through either attraction or aversion, and I believe it is the same with the Vajrayana. In other words, we can have a connection to the tantric teachings even through a strong repulsion. If we experience some kind of emotional response, that means we're not indifferent to this. Therefore, with repulsion or any variation thereof, it's still possible to make a connection with the teachings because there's something that stirs us. It may not happen this week—but then again, maybe it will. It's simple—there's no lukewarmness in the Vajrayana. Hot is very hot, cold is extremely cold. Tepid just doesn't cut it. Our inherent buddha-nature can manifest like ice melting or like a flame expanding, either way.

A NOTE ON BUDDHISM IN THE WEST

The presentation of Buddhism into the West is less than one hundred years old, and the main presentation of the Buddhist teachings into the West happened in the last fifty years or so. There are many legitimate Western Buddhist teachers, male and female, who have been trained in the Zen tradition; the Theravadan tradition; various Mahayana traditions; and various traditions of Indo-Tibetan, Japanese, and Chinese Vajrayana. Unfortunately, a big problem has arisen. People of our generation often think that they're smarter and savvier than those who have gone before them and held the Buddhist teachings for over 2,500 years. Many Western Buddhist teachers and students aren't willing to accept the whole of the Buddhist teachings; they only want the parts that they like. And they want to replace certain parts with modern psychology, modern philosophy, or modern sociological movements because they perceive a cultural problem in the planting of buddhadharma from East to West. It is difficult to see how stupid it is. Yet it *is* inane, because these things have to be fully tested to see if they're true. Also, as hard as the Asian teachers have worked to present Buddhism in the West, they have only been able to present a fraction of it. It all can't happen at the same time.

It seems that most of the fully realized teachers come from the East—from Tibet, China, Nepal, Bhutan, Japan, Korea, Vietnam . . . That's because Buddhism is still young in the West and the first generations of Western practitioners and teachers didn't have the same level of training. Most came with a lot of baggage—beatnik baggage, hippie baggage, yuppie baggage, hipster baggage, or the baggage of various forms of eternalism and nihilism. That's not to say that as time progresses, there won't be great Western teachers in the same way that there are great teachers from the East. It is possible to find pure wisdom anywhere. Wakefulness and buddhahood are in no way limited to any particular cultural background. Here, however, we're not talking about buddha-nature or fundamental dignity; we're talking about the way certain teachings are preserved, actualized, and transmitted at certain times.

Many of the modern practitioners and scholars hold problematic views because they are tending toward the extreme of nihilism under the name of Buddhism. In addition to that, the most profound teachings are being touched upon in a happy-go-lucky way. Even *Mahamudra* and *Dzogchen* have become buzzwords for many Western Buddhists because these approaches seem to not involve all the trappings of the other vehicles of Buddhism. Presumably you can just be in the present and have pure perception! Isn't that wonderful? You don't have to do anything! If you read the most profound Mahamudra and Dzogchen texts, they talk about simply being with the moment, with the natural light, and so forth. They say there's nothing to do, no place to be; that you should just rest in the natural state. However, what many people seem to forget is that those things come from great discipline and great faith; that they are the fruition of discipline and faith, and that there is a path. The path includes the goal—it's not separate from the goal—but there *is* a path. And not only is there a path, but there is also *ngöndro*, a whole set of ordinary and special preliminaries[2] for learning any of the tantric texts and practices. Basically these preliminary practices present the essence of the Hinayana teachings—as Trungpa Rinpoche liked to say, "Never forget the Hinayana"—the essence of the Mahayana teachings, and then the special instructions for seeing everything as deity. (Again, here we don't mean deity in the usual eternalistic sense; we mean the enlightened qualities that naturally exist in all beings, all emotions, and all phenomena.) The ability to develop that pure perception without falling prey to naivety, delusions, or philosophical extremes, and the capacity to recognize the nature of mind and remain in it, depends on discipline and faith. They also depend on our relationship with a wisdom teacher.

THE DECEITLESS TEACHER

The Vajrayana provides powerful means to wake up and cut through delusions. The special quality of this approach relies on a relationship with a deceitless, qualified teacher. This is something that we will discuss at length in the next section, but I wanted to write a few words on this topic before we go any further.

In *A Cascading Waterfall of Nectar*, Thinley Norbu Rinpoche goes to great ends to show us what it means to find a qualified teacher. He does not provide a list of teachers. "Qualified teacher" means someone whom we can see as not separate from the Buddha; someone whom we can see as being the Buddha either in the full sense or in the sense that this person contains the quality of the Buddha, along with human qualities. Regardless, we need to learn how to identify the deceitless teacher. Conversely, it's impossible to fully connect with the tantric teachings if we don't have a relationship with a teacher. Vajrayana is not a do-it-yourself kit.

We need somebody to point out our faults—that is, not just someone who's going to be mean to us or nice to us because they want something. The genuine teacher's only intention is for us to realize the truth of the way things are and become buddhas ourselves. They hold the methods that allow us to achieve that, and they have the ability to transmit these methods to us. Take the example of empowerment, which is the gateway to the Vajrayana. In a tantric empowerment, the teacher gives us a glimpse of the enlightened world and typically welcomes us into the mandala of a specific practice deity. Such empowerments often take place during elaborate and colorful ceremonies, but there are also unelaborate ones. In a sense, it is a huge deal, extraordinary beyond conception, and not something to be taken lightly in any way. But in another sense, it isn't exactly a big deal, because what we are shown, ultimately, is not something added on top of our nature but our nature itself. The actual empowerment can take place when the practitioner has simplified their mind enough so that a true and thorough meeting of hearts and minds occurs. In fact, all the teachings of the Vajrayana basically are forms of guru yoga. *Guru yoga* means "union with the teacher," and ultimately it is the same as "union with the Buddha," or with buddha-nature being fully blossomed.

Many texts say that we should establish a relationship with a teacher only after having observed the teacher for a very long time. It's not something to just jump into. However, when we have observed for a long time, and if we have made a heart connection with that teacher, the relationship changes, and the teacher becomes like a benevolent dictator.

I've had the good fortune of living with two of the greatest tantric masters of their time. I have talked a lot about the first one, Trungpa Rinpoche. The second one, Thinley Norbu Rinpoche, had a very different style. For instance, toward the end of his life, he enjoyed teaching children most. Depending on the time of year, the community around him was a group of anywhere between a dozen to as many as a hundred students. What did it mean to be his student? It basically meant that you were willing to live in an X-ray machine. And it meant that you were willing to practice Dharma, as much as you possibly could. He would let you know everything that's screwed up about you, and it hurt. But he would never deceive you, and his love for his students was boundless. The same could be said of any true teacher: A true wisdom teacher is one that is truly caring and that will not lead you astray.

THE LEAP INTO FAITH

Earlier we discussed Buddhism in the West. Here, however, we'll use *Western* to refer to a mentality or mindset that can apply regardless of birthplace. The truth of complete enlightenment is no more a myth for Americans than it is for Tibetans. The biggest hurdle we have has to do with faith—with crossing over into believing the Buddhist teachings. It's a mystery, but people are willing to believe all kinds of Evangelical Christian ideas, Hindu God ideas, and other eternalistic ideas. Everyone's willing to be saved by hatha yoga! There's nothing wrong with hatha yoga, by the way; but we're willing to be *saved* by it or Pilates or a suchlike system. A lot of my Buddhist friends have more faith in those exercises than they do in Dharma because they're only thinking of this physical body and this short life. Don't get me wrong: It's *excellent* to have a healthy body. I wish that all of us die healthy! (That's supposed to be a joke!) But truly, the only thing that's going to comfort us in any way through pain, sorrow, and even death is the truth of Dharma. There is really nothing else that delivers. Everything else, at one level or another, is foolish.

However, there is no way in the world that we can develop faith if we don't put the teachings into practice. Also, in terms of the Vajrayana, and most especially in terms of Dzogchen, without devotion to a deceitless guru or lama, there is no Great Perfection. It doesn't work. With faith and devotion, everything becomes possible. Without the Buddhist view, there is no way to practice Dharma.

Now, what does it mean to have a teacher? It depends on our individual circumstances. For example, Thinley Norbu Rinpoche had probably tens of thousands of people that would say that he's their teacher. But he lived in a community of just a couple dozen people, who were a mixture of Americans, Europeans, Himalayans... Yet all over Bhutan, Tibet, Nepal, India, America, even Australia and elsewhere, there were people who considered themselves to be his student, and he treated them with great care because they had made a heart connection with him. Some might only have seen him from a distance. But they heard what he had to say, they put it into practice, and their connection was from one mind to another. There are many people like that in Asia who had that connection with him, who maybe only met him once or twice. But they've been practicing what he taught, and occasionally, through messengers or some other way, they would receive further instructions from him. For example, there was a group of lamas that came from Bhutan who requested the transmission of *A Cascading Waterfall of Nectar* so they could bring it back to all the people who wanted further instruction, and the instruction is in this book.

For some, the relationship with the teacher is that you live with the person, for a long time or a short time; or you come to classes, or whatever the situation might be. There are no rules and regulations. The relationship with the teacher is this heart-to-heart communication that happens. Then there's faith, which is to put the teachings into practice. Entering the world of the Vajrayana then becomes a possibility.

THE DAWN OF VAJRAYANA

I am not particularly interested in discussing how the Vajrayana appeared and evolved in this world from a purely historical perspective. Of course, the life stories of the early masters are extremely precious and inspiring, packed with the most profound teachings. But I don't know whether it is useful or even possible to pinpoint a specific time frame according to ordinary perceptions. In many ways, the magic of it transcends calendars and concepts.

What seems more useful is to understand that Vajrayana dawned when Vajrasattva dawned. We alluded to Buddha Vajrasattva earlier, when discussing "cleaning" and the launderability of our existence, which is fundamentally good. This "adamantine being" (which is one way to translate Vajrasattva) personifies indestructibility and primordial purity. He is therefore invoked for confession, purification, and healing. But ultimately Vajrasattva is not separate from our own mind. He represents its naturally pure quality. If it wasn't for Vajrasattva, there would be no enlightenment. If you made the wrong move, then you would have blown it, with no possibility of going back to enlightenment. But Vajrasattva's presence makes it possible for any of us to become enlightened. This includes every single one of us, including the worst of us. Vajrasattva isn't just a character in a painting, and he isn't just a machination of the mind; ultimately, he is the primordial purity itself. This purity is truly basic.

While I'm at it, I want to make clear that the way I presented the earlier chapters were aligned with Trungpa Rinpoche's teachings, while the present section is in tune with Thinley Norbu Rinpoche's style. I'll try not to mix my metaphors, and so should you. Yet essentially, the view is the same, which is that of pure perception, and that *anything* in our being can be cleansed. And when it's cleansed fully, that's buddhahood.

In the tantric teachings, there is also another related buddha referred to as "the primordial buddha," known as Samantabhadra, who is indistinguishable from his consort Samantabhadri. It's two buddhas, male and female, yet they are not separate. As soon as you say "Samantabhadra," there is Samantabhadri, and vice versa. Their names mean "All good"—that is, there is absolute, complete goodness, with no sense of separation whatsoever—like space copulating with space. The all-good is primordial and sacred in every sense. It is said in the Dzogchen teachings that Samantabhadra simply never fell into delusion; that as soon as the very nature of mind started to unfold, he recognized that radiance for what it is rather than solidifying his world and blindly following thoughts. He never experienced any fear, nor any clinging to fictions of any kind. The wonderful message of the Vajrayana and Dzogchen teachings is that we can always return to that primordial ground of Samantabhadra-Samantabhadri, which is the basic sacredness of this world, unaffected by concepts and delusions. We can always return to original purity.

THOUGHTS AND THE GAP IN BETWEEN

Earlier in this book, when introducing basic sitting meditation, we discussed the gap between the thoughts. It is important to note that at this level, the practice doesn't *exclude* the thoughts. It's warp and woof, just like the Vajrayana, which doesn't leave anything out. In Vajrayana, all samsaric activity becomes the activity of the enlightened play of the mind. It's only samsaric from the impure perspective, not from the purified perspective. In other words, thoughts are only viewed as a problem from the point of view of confusion, not from the point of view of enlightenment.

Therefore, at this level, the gap itself is not necessarily seen as *superior* to thoughts. It's like when you first look at Zen calligraphy, for example. All you might see is the ink, and you miss the space. Or you might be the other kind of person: All you can see is the space, and you miss the ink! Regardless, it's from the play of form and emptiness that the calligraphy arises. We tend to fixate on one or the other. However, from the enlightened perspective, both are of the same nature.

Some people equate pure awareness with the space between the thoughts, but pure perception is nondual. At some level, it makes no distinction between the eyes that view and what is being viewed. Clouds are included as part of the sky. We might acknowledge that clouds come and go and enjoy the vastness and constant presence of the sky, sure, but they are not separate. They both share the nature of our mind; and from pure perception's point of view, that's not a problem at all. In addition, from this point of view, the whole display of the light from the sun, the blueness of the sky, the passing of the clouds are all pure buddha phenomena, involving infinite fields of enlightened realms and qualities.

Therefore, between saying that the clouds come and go, and saying that the clouds are not separate from the sky whose nature is everlasting, there's no contradiction. However, our mind likes to classify—me, you, hot, cold, sun, moon, day, night, male, female, like, dislike... Classifications can certainly be useful, but our perception is currently tainted. Not only do we not see phenomena correctly, but we also don't even see that we don't see correctly. That's a two-part problem. When both parts are reversed so that the process of perception and the objects of perception are clear, then that is pure perception.

Different traditions speak of nonduality, such as Zen and Advaita Vedanta. Ultimately they are pointing to the same reality. The special quality of the Vajrayana, however, is the aspect of luminosity. Not only is the nature nondual, but it's also luminous. Not luminous in the sense of a light bulb or any kind of physical light but in a nonmaterial way. That's something that the tantric teachings generally, and the Dzogchen teachings particularly, work with: not only the reality of emptiness and nonduality but also the luminous quality, which is all phenomena viewed from the eyes of a buddha.

MAKING LIFE WORTHWHILE

My first teacher, Trungpa Rinpoche, whose teachings we've discussed abundantly in the other sections of the book, passed nearly forty years ago. I am now sharing some of the teachings of Thinley Norbu Rinpoche, who passed in 2011. Their teachings aren't separate in any way. And their wisdom mind hasn't passed. In fact, I feel both of them at my neck at this very moment! What I mean is that I don't want to lie to you, because they never lied to me. They were kind enough to tell me the truth, which is the truth of Dharma, and that knowing the truth didn't make any difference if I didn't practice it. But people like me are very stubborn. It may be that you and I are very similar. My resistance was so extreme that to practice, I had to put myself in situations where I had no way out. For example, in our community, whether you were a toddler or an elder everyone got together every evening and practiced meditation, chanting, and sadhanas.

The practice of Dharma makes our life worthwhile. As far as I'm concerned, it is the ultimate worthwhile. Everything else is absolutely secondary. If we put the Dharma into practice, it permeates our life fully—our family, our friends, our vocation, all situations. I am not saying everything gets rosy, far from it. Even my enemies—I don't know who they are, but I'm sure I have some, as everyone does—are part of my practice. It's not always easy, and I still occasionally experience resistance, but I now enjoy Dharma for the nourishing and delicious nectar that it is. It is such a joyful and fulfilling journey, which has been made possible through the kindness and blessings of my teachers.

Thinley Norbu Rinpoche taught his students through his example. Every night we practiced together, and he was there with us because he knew we were particularly hard cases. I've never known a teacher quite like this.

If none of this made any sense to you, you should stop reading. If you don't have a connection—through either attraction or repulsion—toward this approach, there is no reason for you to make any further effort because it isn't going to be of any benefit. I apologize: I was told to be seductive, but I can't!

18
The Great Exaltation, Part 1

There are many types of spiritual practices in the Vajrayana tradition, but they boil down to formless practices and practices with form. The first category mostly consists of nonconceptual meditation; the latter includes offerings, rituals, and sadhanas. A sadhana, literally a "means of accomplishment," is a text that presents a specific spiritual practice. It is chanted by the practitioner, who performs various visualizations, mantras, gestures, inner yogas, and contemplations so as to engender the enlightened view and experience. In this chapter and the one that follows, we will discuss practices with forms as a convenient way to survey some of the elements that are found in most sadhanas.

THE RAISON D'ÊTRE OF SADHANAS

Before we get into the specifics of tantric practice, we should understand the context. Why would people like us practice sadhanas? What is the mind that would sit down and chant something, perhaps even in a foreign language? That's an important issue: how we relate to a spiritual method that comes from another culture.

This conversation is geared toward those who are new or somewhat new to Vajrayana; yet perhaps those of us who are more experienced can gain some insight into why we are practicing.

The various Vajrayana rituals—their formal aspects, sounds, visualizations, all the various instructions—exist for only one reason: We have a bevy of negative emotions, conflicting feelings, and duality habits of all kinds. Deep down, we think that we exist separately from everything else. That's delusion. We separate ourselves out from our lives, from our emotions, and so forth. Also, one day we think we're great, the next day we think we're pathetic. We come up with all kinds of ideas to get excited about. We come up with all kinds of ideas to get depressed about. We torture ourselves, we titillate ourselves. We want to be entertained, we're tired of entertainment—ad nauseam. Then we want to do it *all over again*. Again and again, our whole life, and one lifetime after another—infinite numbers of lifetimes. We want to repeat the same patterns since beginningless time. We certainly know better. We know what causes us pain; we know what excites us; we know that what goes up must come down. But we keep fueling the fire.

The sadhanas come from the compassion of the great realized teachers to offer us a different approach. They engage our mind with the positive qualities of wakefulness, the boundless qualities of the enlightened state of mind, the blessed qualities of deity phenomena. This can be done through a panoply of both peaceful and wrathful manifestations. Some situations require us to rest in tranquil qualities, but our sleepiness and tendency to take things for granted sometimes need a shock. There are countless skillful means that make our mind—if we are open to it—go in an extraordinarily positive direction. These tantric sadhanas, if practiced, allow us to become one with the qualities of buddhahood, all the way until we are fully enlightened.

The basic view of these ritual practices is that they allow our awakening mind to mix with our ordinary material world so that we can see the world in a sacred manner—the way it actually is rather than in the deluded way our habits have created. This typically involves offerings of all kinds, an important topic that we will look into. Practices like feast offerings (which we will explain in more detail in the next chapter) offer us a way to not deal with "ordinary" issues as separate from our spiritual life. For example, food is seen not only as sustenance for this physical body of ours but also as an offering so that this body can be transformed into the positive qualities of wakefulness and deity phenomena.

As we practice, we use concepts to cleanse conception. We use the material to free ourselves from materialism. Is this all a trick? Not exactly.

We trick ourselves constantly. We tell ourselves lies every day. That's our habit. By creating positive habits that are connected with the positive qualities of buddhas, we enter into the primordial realm of truth, the realm of *dharmata*—the unborn space from which everything arises. Gradually we train ourselves to let go of that which makes us suffer so much.

Vajrayana is way beyond positive thinking. It's not a simple matter of "think yourself to buddhahood!" the way you might think yourself to good salespersonhood or any kind of materialhood. These tantric practices are about seeing, hearing, smelling, tasting, feeling beyond just the materialistic, conditioned way that we have constrained ourselves in.

The exact content of tantric practices varies. Vajrayana itself is by no means monolithic. It includes an infinite array of approaches, depending on our inclinations and capacities. For example, our focus can be on cleanliness, visualizing an external deity, visualizing ourselves as a deity, formless meditations, and so forth. All these approaches are to help us transcend our duality habit. And all of them involve not falling prey to either the extreme of nihilism or the extreme of eternalism. Therefore, we don't fall prey to believing in any gods or God that are purely external, with no relationship whatsoever with the nature of our own mind. We don't fall prey to believing in any simple materialistic ideas that "easy come, easy go, there's nothing beyond these five senses." It is on the ground of the Middle Way view that we can practice Vajrayana.

THE SO-CALLED PRELIMINARIES, OR *NGÖNDRO*

Sometimes a group will practice one particular sadhana together, and then individuals might practice different ones on their own, depending on their faculties and what the teacher views might be helpful and important at that stage.

However, before all that—before we enter any of the inner yoga practices—we go through preliminaries. These preliminaries typically contain the following parts: contemplating the four topics that turn the mind toward Dharma (the preciousness of a human life endowed with freedoms and advantages; impermanence and death; karma; and the suffering and unsatisfactoriness of samsara), taking refuge, paying homage through prostrations, engendering and strengthening bodhicitta, accumulating merit and wisdom through mandala offerings, purifying obscurations and obstacles through the practice of Vajrasattva, and uniting our mind with the wisdom mind of all buddhas through the quintessential practice of guru yoga. The main parts are normally recited one hundred thousand times so as to imbue the mind of the practitioner. These preliminaries help protect our mind from errant views, and they provide an actual path that we can follow.

For example, the preliminary practices are described wondrously in Thinley Norbu Rinpoche's *A Cascading Waterfall of Nectar*. This is worth studying, whatever preliminary practice we're involved with. The one that's commented on in the book is the *Dudjom Tersar ngöndro*; however, the nature of all preliminary practices in Vajrayana is basically the same, and the guidance that the author gives applies to any ngöndro that one is doing.

Interestingly, if we have keen faculty, we find that within the preliminary practices, everything in fact is included. Nothing is left out. So even though it's called "preliminary," it's complete in and of itself. It's not just about a carrot at the end of a stick. So, we shouldn't view the ngöndro as simply part of a checklist, with the intention of just collecting stuff and ending up with a big sack full of deities and pretzels. That's a very primitive point of view. And by the way, we don't have to be a Westerner to have that primitive point of view; that materialistic approach is also frequent among Asians. The point is, it's not about making collections. It's about allowing the positive qualities of the awakened state to permeate our life completely, not only for our own benefit but especially for the benefit of all beings.

CHANTING AND VISUALIZING

As mentioned, in Buddhism, as in most religions, there is chanting—the idea of enunciating the words of the teachings. Their recitation helps put our mind into the positive point of view that's being presented. But in the tantric approach, something else is added: the process of visualization.

There are descriptions of deities; mandalas of deities; palaces and their detailed architecture; the protection boundaries and charnel grounds around the palace; the central figure or figures that rule the palace; the bevy of dakas and dakinis, enlightened male and female qualities that are the retinue of the central figure, along with guardian deities. There are also descriptions of the innards of the deities. But we must understand that deity, in this sense, has nothing to do with bodies like ours. The teachings give us anthropomorphized forms so that we can identify with wakefulness. However, deities don't have livers and intestines; they have bodies of light. And depending on the sadhanas, within these bodies of light are different primordial *bijas*, or sacred syllables, that vibrate with the very sound of enlightenment. As well, depending on the practices, special attention is given to certain light phenomena within deities, or circling phenomena in different parts of the body if we visualize ourselves as the deity. A sadhana can be utterly simple or most elaborate.

Whatever we visualize, whether it's the simplest or the most complex form, the whole of the Dharma is included within that. Every buddha, every bodhisattva, every protector, every sound, every syllable is a living exposition of the Dharma.

All the elements of the visualizations invoke positive qualities and as such constitute our process of becoming just like the deity—or in other words, just like Buddha. It's said that in inner Vajrayana practice, there are even changes in this material body of ours, because the subtle bodies are connected with our karmic, material body. But the details of that are something that we work out with our teacher and through study.

Many practitioners are baffled by the visualizations. Even the simple ones can be very confusing because of our materialistic habits. We may have noticed that some texts make a big deal about the fact that our visualization should be perfect. But this notion of "perfect" seems often misunderstood. According to Thinley Norbu Rinpoche, visualization is extremely simple. You say it, and by saying it, it's there. Done! You don't have to try to recreate it endlessly. The power of the enlightened word is that it creates exactly what it says. So, we begin from the simple mind of meditation, having allowed our busy mind to subside, and we enter the practice by remembering that this is not just for ourselves but for the benefit of all beings. Then we just sit there simply, and the seed syllable emanates from our throat. HRIH, or AH, or OM, or HUM, or whatever it might be. Sometimes the text says to visualize that syllable. We can visualize it in its Sanskrit form or in its Tibetan form. If we have a problem with that, then the Roman or Cyrillic alphabet is fine.

While we're on the subject of sacred syllables, we should note that *mantra* means "mind protection." When we chant something like this, the very sound of it protects our mind. It protects it from its idiot self; from egomania, self-centeredness, duality habit, and so forth. We learn through sacred speech that all sound is the sound of the sacred, the sound of Buddha.

There is a certain magic that's incorporated in seeing and hearing these syllables. This applies to both longer mantras and the seed syllables that are found at the very beginning of sadhanas and from which the sound of enlightenment resonates. It is even said that for those of keen faculty, everything is included within the opening syllable. In fact, everything that comes afterward is an elaboration.

That elaboration might include the deity, the palace, and the surrounding universe; and it might be described in a particular way. The mindful recitation of the very description creates the visualization. Recitation + description +

awareness *is* the visualization. By uttering it, we can hear and see it. But don't confuse it with something material. If we're visualizing an enlightened palace described in a sadhana, it's not like an ordinary palace. The symbolism might resemble an ordinary palace, and we can even build physical symbols, but it points to nonmaterial truth.

Over time, as we familiarize ourselves with the recitation, we become familiar with what we're doing, where our deluded mind meets the Mind of the true meaning. It will open up to us. We don't have to worry. We don't have to create comic book deities, or two-dimensional deities. We don't have to create anything contrived or difficult. We are simply relaxing with the description. We are being with it.

As a personal footnote, I found that one of the most helpful teachings from Thinley Norbu Rinpoche was how to visualize—that is, in the way we've just described. It was such a relief. In fact, one of his priceless pieces of advice to his students was very simple: "Think of Buddha." That's it. That's really it.

19
The Great Exaltation, Part 2

Regardless of how we may categorize sadhanas, "practice with forms" is not ultimately separate from "formless practice." Indeed, practices with forms include sounds, images, and the insight that comes from the meditative mind. Thus, with all practices, we begin with simple sitting meditation. That part is initially a formless meditation: We begin by just sitting down, and there we are. We don't have to contrive anything. There is no methodology.

Many practice texts then start with a seed syllable, such as HRIH, HUM, or AH. From the boundless, unborn space comes the uncontrived sound of enlightenment. It is said that these seed syllables essentialize the sound of dharmata—the sound of enlightenment. These seed syllables are beyond our usual idea of what sound and speech are.

Now, the enlightened state can be synthesized as having five basic sets of qualities. Of course, Buddha is beyond characteristics and categories. But for our sake, classifications are made, hence the "five buddha families." Each family is connected to a direction, a color, an element, a specific symbol, and so forth; but it is especially described in terms of primary emotions and their wisdom counterparts. For example, the Lotus (or "Padma") family is associated with the western direction, the color red, the element of fire, the energy of desire, and its enlightened counterpart that is the wisdom of discriminating awareness. It is also associated with boundless compassion and a delightful nonattachment. In any case, the buddha families are the natural display of the qualities of buddhahood.[1] The tantric teachings also talk of vast buddha fields of the five lights that permeate all of space, including both the material and immaterial worlds.

What we usually think of as difficulties, all the things that fetter us, are based on our distorted, dualistic, materialistic habit. When that is cleansed, then the pure wisdom light manifests as these pure qualities of buddhas.

A sadhana will typically be connected to a particular buddha or buddha family. But a sadhana represents the synthesis of all immeasurable buddha qualities, bodhisattva qualities, and protector qualities. In other words, all the various aspects of the mandala of awakening are included within the five buddha families; all are included within each family; all are contained within the seed syllable.

THE MEANING OF "GREAT EXALTATION"

The term *great exaltation* occasionally shows up in tantric liturgies. For example, *The Assembly Palace of Great Exaltation*, extracted from a longer sadhana, was composed by Dudjom Rinpoche, Jigdrel Yeshe Dorje, one of the greatest Nyingma masters of the last century, a peerless yogin and scholar, and a tertön who was widely regarded as Padmasambhava's regent.

Generally speaking, Buddhism explains the truth of *duhkha*, or "suffering," and it also explains the truth of *sukha*, or "bliss." Looking for happiness in the ordinary sense is legitimate. But it could be said that ultimately the practitioner aims for *mahasukha*—that is, "great bliss" or "great exaltation"—which should not be misconstrued as some kind of temporary elation. It is enlightenment itself, and thus it is unconditioned and unaffected by our usual highs and lows. Therefore, the "palace of great exaltation" mentioned above is the palace of full, radiant, boundless awakening.

Someone asked me what "great exaltation" meant to me. I'm afraid I'm a bit of a religious fanatic, but my answer: being with my teacher. In a way, all of these practices are forms of guru yoga. Being with our teacher is the same as being with our innate wisdom deity. That's regardless of whether the teacher has passed or is alive. We don't have to be in the same room. Of course, spending time together is nice, but all conditioned phenomena are impermanent, and that includes karmic bodies. Regardless, mahasukha, to me, is just being with the wisdom manifestation of the guru.

"Great exaltation" can also connote being with our lover. There's a notion of "desireless desire," a union that goes beyond ordinary desire. Our mind wants to go that way, just out of habit, but it's not that. Having a "wisdom consort" means going beyond duality, up to the cessation of duality. We may find a wisdom consort and dance with that wisdom counterpart either externally or internally. That's also a form of guru yoga. But again, it's not necessarily about sexuality and ordinary desire, and it's definitely not frivolous. Guru yoga is also not a union with this or that personality but a union with wisdom mind, which is the mind of all buddhas.

GANACHAKRA, OR THE FOURFOLD GATHERING

Ganachakra (Skt.; Tib. *tsok*) is an important part of Vajrayana. It's a feast offering but of a special kind. Ganachakras are a powerful means to accumulate merit and wisdom, and to purify our obscurations.

Ganachakra means "gathering." It is fourfold. First, it involves a gathering of practitioners. Following up on the example given above, *The Assembly Palace of Great Exaltation* speaks of "great yogis and great yoginis." We can be one of them. A yogi or yogini in this case is someone who is practicing to become a buddha. So, *mahayogis* and *mahayoginis* are those practitioners that fully take the teachings of Buddha to heart.

They practice in an "assembly palace," this being the palace of wherever we are. Sometimes it may be a shrine room. But it's more than a specific room; the assembly palace is the great, unobstructed space of dharmata—the space of suchness. Within that space we practice the ganachakra very simply, by chanting a liturgy; and by chanting it we invoke wakefulness.

The Great Exaltation Palace, or whichever palace is described in our practice text, is not something that is created or visualized once. It's something that we can make constant in our life. That's why these sadhanas are called practices. We're not just aiming for some kind of instant satisfaction—this isn't a Burger King approach. The great exaltation comes from continuously overcoming our laziness, and being simple and singing, or simply sitting and doing nothing, just being in the space of where we are, of not having to exercise the busyness of our mind. Instead of accomplishing work, gossip, or fantasy, we're accomplishing the great wisdom exaltation.

The second aspect of the fourfold gathering is that of offerings. We create an environment, and within it, we make numerous offerings—material offerings, sense offerings, imagined offerings, and so forth. They can include food, drink, flowers, incense, music, and whatever is pleasing to the senses. We make offerings that are inherently pure, as well as impure offerings that are purified through our practice.

The third type of gathering is that of deities. In the case of *The Assembly Palace of Great Exaltation*, for example, we invoke the buddhas of the Lotus family—Amitabha, Avalokiteshvara, Padmasambhava—as well as Yeshe Tsogyal and her retinue of enlightened dakinis. Each is part of an enlightened mandala. Within a ganachakra, whatever deity we are referring to, and everything within the larger context of the ritual, becomes of the nature of a single enlightened intention. So, when we are consuming edible offerings at the end of the ganachakra (and we will get back to that), we're eating beyond the duality of eater and what's being eaten. Everything is meant to be approached with a sacred outlook. Our thinking, speech, and action are made sacred in the primordial sense of how it is in fact emanating from the dharmata, in the same way as the Buddha manifests.

This naturally leads to the fourth gathering, that of merit and wisdom, both of which are essential on the path to enlightenment. The accumulation of merit propels us by providing us with strength, positivity, and inner resources; the accumulation of wisdom contributes to our learning to see things as they are. It is said that one of the most positive aspects of the Vajrayana is to make constant ganachakra offerings, which is considered extremely powerful and easy to do, and it comes with a delightful sense of celebration.

DAKINIS

Dakini is an important and precious term that we should look into.

In the usual way of thinking, *dakini* refers to the enlightened feminine, or an enlightened female. For example, many sadhanas of the Nyingma tradition have Yeshe Tsogyal, or Mandarava, or Vajrayogini as the main dakini, and there's often a mention of infinite displays of dakinis. In the tantric teachings particularly, women and in fact all feminine qualities are honored. There are many kinds of dakinis: young maiden dakinis, wrathful dakinis, and various displays of every aspect of femininity. But we shouldn't confuse this with our ordinary way of thinking about people. That being said, every woman has the potential to be a *yeshe khandro*, a wisdom dakini. When there's purification, positive phenomena unfold and the ordinary female becomes a wisdom dakini.

It's also said that our spiritual consort should be a wisdom dakini or daka, which is the male equivalent of dakini—that we should mix our minds with the wisdom of the "sky dancer." It can also be internal. For example, monks and nuns don't have sex, but they have ways to practice the union of daka and dakini internally. However, this is a tricky topic because even though everybody likes sex, we've often disconnected it from spirituality, and there's a lot of confusion about it.

Any yogic practitioner, whether male or female, can take on the qualities of a dakini or daka—that is, the female and male qualities, respectively—or the combination of both male and female qualities. For example, it is very common for practitioners of the Kagyu lineage to take on all the qualities of Vajrayogini, which is the ultimate dakini. But whenever there is the enlightened feminine, there's also the enlightened masculine. Even in the visualizations, the enlightened beings are either in union or there's a symbol of the union. In the Nyingma tradition, we take on the positive qualities as they're synthesized as Padmasambhava or Yeshe Tsogyal, who is ultimately no different than Vajrayogini. But regardless of how they are depicted, they are always in union.

When it comes to enlightenment, there is no separated, male-female duality. Biologically there is, obviously. No one is saying that there's no biological difference. There can even be a difference emotionally, although that can be quite subjective. For example, the other day I was feeling very vulnerable, and for some reason I viewed that as a female quality; but it could be a male quality, for all I know. In any case, in our practice context, we're not overly concerned about that sort of ordinary duality and biology. The amazing thing about the inner Vajrayana is that it takes into account all of samsara and nirvana, including biology. Our fixation on biological duality—along with our fixation on light and darkness, day and night, and all the various dualistic tendencies and views—are all brought into union. We don't have to fixate on anything. Some schools view the male birth to be superior to the female birth. Others, like the inner Vajrayana schools, say that inherent wisdom dakinis see things clearly and that rest of us idiot men don't have much of a clue! There are many different views. In any event, buddhahood is available to, and easiest for, human beings. That's the point of all these practices, the ganachakras, the visualizations, and so forth: to cure our reality habit; to cleanse our duality habit so that we can go beyond habit.

Generally speaking, in the inner Vajrayana, the feminine qualities are connected to wisdom and the masculine qualities are referred to as skillful means. Think of it as a dance, which is the union of wisdom (dakini energy) and skillful means (daka energy).

Said like that, it sounds like there's a clear-cut distinction. But again, enlightened qualities go beyond all dualities. We live in this world that is based on all these duality habits, but the teachings show us that we don't have to get stuck in one extreme or another. And it is not only about eternalism and nihilism; *any* duality is problematic. If we identify one way or the other and experience fixation and a sense of a separate self, we are going to get trapped. Buddha-nature only ripens into buddhahood when duality is transcended. Enlightenment is beyond our usual ideas, and it is not a gender issue. We have within us the capacity to allow constructs to drop away and to be in the natural state, which is perfectly pure from the beginning.

Ultimately all buddhas, dakinis, and deities are contained within each buddha, dakini, and deity. Enlightenment, of course, is complete; but for the sake of beings, it manifests in many ways. Some texts speak of "one hundred thousand dakinis" or even millions of dakinis: Dakini energy manifests in infinite ways to accommodate the needs of beings. The accommodation is sometimes peaceful, sometimes wrathful, and there are all kinds of variations. "One hundred thousand" is a number that means a lot. These numbers are not literal; the dakinis are numberless. It's a way of expressing the fact that there is *nothing* within samsara that cannot be enlightened. That is beyond thought—there is no way to conceive of how every aspect of being can become enlightened. It is through the accommodation of the countless dakinis that every aspect of life is marked with enlightenment. In whatever occurs, there's a dakini dancer that can enlighten the situation. It is, as Thinley Norbu Rinpoche calls it, a magic dance.[2]

By dropping away constructs, we allow that magical dance to occur. Currently we allow a strange dance to occur through our addictions: the dance of ignorance, passion, aggression, greed, jealousy. They constantly pass through our body and mind. In practice, we purify through simplification, devotion, and clear seeing. All those negative emotions are then seen in their natural way, which is the wisdom display of the five families.

In any case, our aspiration is to be just like Yeshe Tsogyal so that our mind activity and all of our activities become like hers: a source of benefit for all beings. Her intention is that all beings be liberated, and we join with that intention.

THE THREE KAYAS

Another essential aspect of sadhana practice is the three-kaya principle: dharmakaya, sambhogakaya, and nirmanakaya. The three kayas are aspects of enlightenment. The dharmakaya is its boundless, empty, utterly pure, and nonconceptual aspect. Thinley Norbu Rinpoche writes,

> As is said, in general, all Buddhas have perfectly purified the two obscurations of passions and cognition, including all residual habit, so therefore it is great Dharmakaya.[3]

Unlike dharmakaya, which is beyond form, the sambhogakaya has a subtle form with a luminous quality. The nirmanakaya is an embodied manifestation with which we can interact physically. Both sambhogakaya and nirmanakaya have form; the former is completely pure, while the latter is a mixture of pure and seemingly impure qualities. Nirmanakaya (or *tulku* in Tibetan) implies a pure mind but also a human body and all the things that come with it, including lungs, intestines, and so forth. The so-called impurities of the nirmanakaya are for our benefit—we fools who believe in the reality of compounded phenomena. They are so that we can relate to enlightenment. In any case, the formless and form aspects of a buddha are not separate. All three kayas have the same essence. This principle of the three kayas being unified is known as *svabhavikakaya.*

In *The Assembly Palace of Great Exaltation*, for example, the personification of the dharmakaya is Amitabha, buddha of boundless light; its sambhogakaya is Avakokiteshvara; its nirmanakaya is Guru Padmasambhava. They are all of the Lotus family. Each one manifests in countless ways. Each reflects all the qualities of buddhahood, including an unceasing compassion.

The dharmakaya is formless, but it is not separate from its vibrant radiance—the sambhogakaya—nor from its more embodied, relatable manifestation that is the nirmanakaya.

From dharmakaya, the form aspects come as the natural expressions of compassion. But it's not that Buddha *needs* to be compassionate; it's a natural, spontaneous manifestation. All the buddha field qualities come into play from the unborn space. They naturally come into nirmanakaya form to benefit beings, without any intentionality per se. It's not like God is going to take care of God's children. Rather, there's Buddha, total wakefulness, and buddhahood permeates all of space.

FULFILLING THE WISHES OF THE GREAT BEINGS

Liturgies often depict all sorts of great beings. This includes bodhisattvas, who are often represented as anthropomorphic beings who from sambhogakaya have an effect on the world. The bodhisattvas are the embodiment of the highest aspirations. As we put the teachings into practice and engender the bodhisattva aspirations within ourselves, we fulfill the unconditioned wishes of the bodhisattvas by being just like them. This involves offering in the way that they offer: through our practice of the four boundless attitudes[4] and the six perfections, and through realizing the essence of emptiness and compassion.

While some sadhanas describe a vast array of deities, sometimes there is just one. For example, a given practice may involve visualizing only Guru Rinpoche, also known as Padmasambhava. But even then it is said that all buddhas are contained within Padmasambhava, and so through Padmasambhava, we can accomplish all enlightened qualities. We use duality to annihilate duality. Guru yoga is completed through seeing Guru Rinpoche, seeing ourselves as the dakini, and then joining in union with Padmasambhavaness.[5] When we've really "joined in union," we see why it is said that nothing really happened, because that is the primordial state of how things actually are. It never has been any other way.

Guru Rinpoche manifests countless forms, including both peaceful and wrathful ones, for the benefit of beings like ourselves. He promised that he would appear to anyone who sincerely called upon him. However, the edge between theism and nontheism, partly because of the limitations of language, always becomes an issue. Guru Rinpoche appearing is not something material appearing and coming to save us. First of all, "us" is not solid; and Guru Rinpoche is not solid either! Guru Rinpoche is the embodiment of the three kayas—in no way separate from any of their aspects—and our basic nature is not separate from that.

What makes this different from theism? The substancelessness and nonduality of it all. It is not that theists necessarily believe that a material being will manifest if they pray. But basically, the eternalist view implies that even if it's not a solid form, there's something outside of us that's going to save us. When we talk about Guru Rinpoche or any of the buddhas, we're talking about connecting to the enlightened mind, and that is our own wisdom mind. They're not separate, and there's not even an outer/inner distinction.

But there's a twist. It is going to be so contrary, but it's the truth anyway. We can have the correct view, we can practice until the cows come home, and still, without blessings, there is no enlightenment. What's that about?

It comes back to giving up. There's no guarantee. But even if we have and practice the view, devotion to the lineage of enlightenment is what allows the enlightenment to become manifest. That seems very dualistic, but the blessings really don't come from someplace *over there*, and they don't come from some someplace *in here*, either. That's part of our faulty way of looking at things. The "middle," in a sense, the place of being a yogi or yogini, is the realm within which all of it could happen. If we just continue with our ordinary deluded mind, we'll just continue to experience our ordinary deluded life. But if we become yogis and yoginis—those who have faith, basically—and practice the great exaltation, then we are in the deity's palace: We are one with the blessings of the enlightened mind.

Many sadhanas also mention dharmapalas. In the tantric traditions, they are protectors of the Dharma, protectors of the mandalas of wisdom. It is said that many of these dharmapalas are energies that were subdued by the buddhas, notably Buddha Shakyamuni and Guru Rinpoche, and became allies of the Dharma. Various gods and demons were thus transformed.

"Gods and demons" are manifestations of the mind of beings in forms that personify particular qualities. Many—and ultimately all—of these demons can and have been transformed into dharmapalas. From the pure perspective, demons don't really exist. They are all manifestations of our dualistic mind. However, because of our dualistic way of thinking, they exist within the realm of duality.

THE SIMPLICITY OF PURITY

As we know, making offerings is an important part of Vajrayana. We bless the offerings from the point of view of purity. In other words, purity itself makes everything pure. It may sound simplistic, but in fact we are so attached to confused logic and the busy machinations of our mind that it is very difficult for us to understand the simplicity and power of the enlightened view. It permeates space.

There's a difference between compounded and uncompounded. Everything in samsara is a construct, but the basic *nature* of everything is unconstructed. Dharmata, *dharmadhatu*, dharmakaya, however we want to call it, is uncompounded, unborn, and utterly pure. But we have to gain confidence. The practice of meditation, both formless and with form, is not to build a super kind of ego: "I'm such and such a practitioner, I've achieved this and that, I've been practicing meditation for years!" Or it could be, "I'm new to this. What's wrong with all these people?" Whatever the situation might be, the point of the practice is not to construct a new identity to which we keep clinging ever so dearly.

This is tied to the crucial issue of deluded mind. As Thinley Norbu Rinpoche writes,

> To sentient beings with ordinary deluded mind, appearances are reversed, and also the way of seeing is reversed, which comes from thinking that all phenomena truly exist in reality. Like this, children see a circling torch as a wheel of fire.[6]

Ordinarily we see things as solid, real, permanent, and independent. From afar, a swirling torch seems like a solid, unitary ring of fire. There is something analogous here to our not noticing the gap between our thoughts, nor their insubstantiality, if we don't meditate.

Rinpoche continues,

> To practitioners, appearances are reversed, but the way of seeing is not reversed.[7]

As we become practitioners, we are readjusting our own cognitive awareness. We start to understand that we see things backward.

> [This] comes from recognizing that all phenomena are unreal and like magic, without true existence. Like this, the wise see a circling torch as what it is.
>
> Whatever the case, to synthesize a description of all appearances in the three categories, there are the impure appearances of sentient beings [first], [then] the appearances of the experience of yogis and yoginis [second], and [then] the stainless appearance of Buddhas.[8]

The reason that even yogis and yoginis don't have wholly pure perception is because of the karma that is carried, the habitual tendencies that continue and haven't been purified. The difference between that situation and buddhas is that in the latter case, all karma has ceased and all dualistic perception has been cleansed.

It all comes back to replacing bad habits with good habits until there are no habits. It also always comes back to not falling prey to either extreme of nihilism or eternalism. However, having an intellectual understanding of these principles is not enough, due to habits of innumerable lifetimes. Enlightenment itself is uncompounded, but our ego is compounded. When that's purified . . . Ah!

This is connected to the Dzogchen approach, which goes right to the heart of the matter. This approach teaches that everything is primordially pure. But there's a practicality that comes with that. Yes, it's primordially pure—when we can see it that way! So, we train in seeing that way. By training, we purify residual habits. Up until now, we've trained ourselves through laziness, delusion, reality habit, and so forth. Therefore, our training is a reversal training. It's the quick path, but it's also the slow path. But it's slowly quick, or quickly slow, as the case may be.

For the time being, despite the fact that the practice is in fact in the realm of pure perception, karma still has an effect on us, which is why there's still a training process. There are insights that are clear, and there are moments that are lived from the perspective of pure perception, but then habits come back. We've made them come back by repeating them continuously. Habits are always latent—until the alaya is fully cleansed.

SAMAYA AND CONFESSION

The cleansing process is rendered explicit in confession practices, which constitute a crucial aspect of Vajrayana. Sadhanas typically have a section where we can confess our misdeeds and obscurations. We can have the noblest aspirations, and we can think we can subdue ego artfully, but we make errors continuously, out of habit. A special characteristic of the Vajrayana—aside from devotion and pure perception—is that all the horrendous errors that we have made, if confessed, can be cleansed. However, if we try to hide the lies, bad habits, and negativity, they fester. For example, we might develop negativity toward our co-practitioners or even our teacher. These things happen. But if we confess them, part of the wondrous power of the Vajrayana is that these mistakes can and will be cleaned; and they can be cleaned continuously, until buddhahood. If we are a yogi or yogini, it means we are somebody who makes mistakes and then cleanses them.

We can have all sorts of storylines about why we don't want to confess. We can be embarrassed about this, that, or the other... But without confession, our relationship with our teacher, our relationship with the enlightened state of mind, becomes miserable.

Generally we ask for forgiveness within our own personal practice, and then we learn from our mistakes. Sometimes, however, if something is really off, festering and affecting our practice to the point that no amount of confession works, then it's time that we actually confess to our teacher and allow our teacher to help. Then we never know how it's going to be resolved. Sometimes it can be as simple as, "Don't worry about that." Sometimes this can be as complicated as "You have to do this, that, and the other to cleanse this properly." It all depends on karmic circumstances and other factors. But it's very practical. Our mind likes to obfuscate the stainless reality as it is with all kinds of nonsense. That habit too can be cleansed away.

Within our practice, it's our aspiration that all obstacles be purified. There are obstacles of different kinds, which is why we often see the phrase "outer, inner, and secret obstacles" mentioned in texts.

Our most difficult obstacles are said to be secret. They are, as Thinley Norbu Rinpoche writes, "the five passions of desire, anger, ignorance, pride, and jealousy, which are the demons that obstruct the state of liberation."[9] The reason these are called "secret" is because they're insidious. For the most part, we don't notice them. For example, pride and jealousy may seem to us that they are well founded, but they take us away from the primordial state, and they can affect our practice in a very adverse way.

But if these obstacles are secret, how do we even know? It is a question worth asking ourselves. It has to do with *us*. And though this may be merely alluded to in just a few lines in some sadhanas, it is of extreme importance.

That's when the deceitless teacher comes into play. Yet even the deceitless teacher can't clean for us; they can only illuminate our blind spots. When an issue is brought to our attention, we must go through the karma and cleanse it ourselves. I don't know much about Catholicism, but my first girlfriend was Catholic, and I know that when we made out she had to go and tell the priest in the confession booth! I'm teasing my Catholic friends here, but the point is it's not like that.

This life is very short. We also don't know how long the teacher is going to live. If we make a connection with a wisdom guru, it's important to use that time in a precious way. We don't know how long it's going to last, but within that time, we can accomplish so much. However, we can't do anything if we just allow all these obstacles, all these excuses, to hold us back. The secret obstacles are the most difficult to overcome, but they *can* be overcome. As a friend, my suggestion is that it is best to do it while your teacher is alive. It's not impossible to take care of it afterward, however. But it's also best to do it while *you* are alive! Since it is said that enlightenment is possible at the moment of death, some of us think that we're going to put it off until that day. Out of wishful thinking, we believe that we can get it together then—even if we haven't been able to get it together throughout this whole life. At that point, we like to believe we'll have full presence of mind. But when death comes, there is no time to contrive anything, to suddenly get it together.

Through establishing a regular practice, we learn to die every day. In actuality, our identity is born and it dies every day—in fact, between every thought. At some point, of course, our identity with this body will actually cease. But if we practice in this life, all that pain and suffering take on a different quality. Within that pain and suffering, within that transition, there is clarity and blessings. The blessings come when we open ourselves to practice. The clarity comes when we open ourselves through practice.

REQUESTING ACCOMPLISHMENTS

At the end of ganachakra practice, we request accomplishments. We're opening ourselves to the same state as Padmasambhava and Yeshe Tsogyal, or whichever buddhas and deities the practice is focused on, so that the accomplishment of enlightenment and the various accomplishments that benefit beings become an indivisible part of ourselves.

We also consume some of the offerings. Thinley Norbu Rinpoche describes this process in the following way:

> When having tsok, since all practitioners with wisdom are free from dualistic mind, the offering substances are consumed as wisdom nectar free from conceptualization about ordinary substances. As said, "From wisdom, having wisdom."[10]

When we practice tsok (*ganachakra*), we present many offerings, including sense offerings and food offerings. Through our practice we think of these things as being immaculate, pure wisdom ambrosia. Therefore, when we consume these offerings, it's wisdom consuming wisdom, not animals eating apples. Rinpoche continues,

> Also, the offering of tsok is said to excel beyond the offerings of the lower vehicles in three ways. The visualized deity is recognized as Buddha. The substance offerings are recognized as the wisdom nectar of siddhi [accomplishment]. The mind delights in the manifestation of sole dharmata. These three ways of excelling mean that whoever stays within deity phenomena is abiding in dharmata, so there is no clinging or attachment of mind.
>
> Also, one's own body is fulfilled from the mandala. The mandala is fulfilled from the offering. The yogis and yoginis are fulfilled from the offering substances. All spirits are fulfilled by torma. All the deities of the senses are fulfilled by vajra songs and vajra dance. These are said to be the benefits of the six fulfillments.[11]

When we partake of the food and beverages at the end, we do so with the same sacred view. This has an element of joyful celebration. We enjoy the blessings mindfully, with a vast motivation, pure outlook, and relaxed, even mind—not discriminating between offerings.

In summary, there is the enlightened display, the practice, and the celebration that comes with them. All these elements are of the nature of great bliss. The place where we practice is a palace of wakefulness. What we are practicing, ultimately, simply comes back to the union of our being with the wisdom deity that is innate within ourselves and that is not separate from our deceitless teacher.

LIFE AS RETREAT

It is said that the more purified the mind of the practitioner, the greater their ability to perceive the sambhogakaya and dharmakaya. This purification process is a great gift. We should understand that what's being purified is not buddha but rather obscurations. Instead of just experiencing the interplay of confusion, we start to see a magical dance—infinite manifestations of wisdom.

Usually we're too busy, and instead of an infinite display of buddha fields and buddha qualities, we experience an infinite display of bullshit. It's constant, and we're comfy with it. In fact, we want more of it! "More, give me more!" Through discipline, honing our mind with the view, and then taking the view and putting it into practice, everything unfolds. It is then that we can experience true, great exaltation.

However, we must be careful. You can be someone who goes away on retreat, where you do your sadhana and whatever your teacher has presented to you... You sit down, and you do the retreat, and wondrously enough, what the teacher and the lineage say turns out all to be true. Then your retreat is over. You don't really want to leave, but it's time to go. You come back into the world, and then you forget the truth of all that, and here you are again, in the same mess. So what are you gonna do? Go on retreat again? Oh, okay. So you go on retreat again, and you see the truth of it again, and then you come back...

That doesn't work. I'm not saying that retreat doesn't work. Retreat is wonderful. But one of the lessons we could learn from retreat is how to make *all* life a retreat. The dance of the wisdom energy is not something that just happens when we are away. The practices are pointing to how to live our daily life. Of course, we like the high of something special. But what really benefits us is letting the highs go away, letting the lows go away, and being in this very life, in this very place, and not making big distinctions. It is delightful to be able to practice *here* in simple ways. Then, of course, retreat becomes a natural part of life. But if we try to separate, with some special part where we supposedly see the sambhogakaya, blah, blah, blah, and then come back to a mess, we're missing the point. It's an easy error to make. I have done it dozens of times. Everyone has. You can read about it in the biographies of the great masters.

The real effort is putting the view into practice in our daily life. Of course, in a retreat situation, you can have a large opening to see how things actually are. But when you come back, instead of letting everything close back, find a way—and there is a way—to sustain the sacred outlook. Life is much more cheerful that way. Really! It comes down to how attached we are to things. With the letting go there's a cheerfulness that comes in, and as we become more serious, we become more lighthearted. It's a contradiction, but that's the way it is. As we become simpler, we become more cheerful. We're not talking about becoming a simpleton; rather, it's an intelligent happiness.

We should look at our busy mind and its constant hammering. We're creating more versions of busy mind, filling every space that we have with more dreams about tomorrow, with how we're going to be, with how this is going to be that, with regurgitating the past, mixed with "I'm going to practice this and then maybe this and that will happen, but at the same time, I would really like to get laid—oops—but oh, I'm hungry, and darn, my stupid computer just broke down and it's going to have to spend hours at the store..." *All that isn't separate from enlightenment.* However, we create so much extra, so many unnecessary problems. There's no problem with food, clothing, sex, having a computer—any of those things. It's how we relate to them. Enlightenment does not exist separately from this life. There is no place to go to be enlightened.

The basic attitude of inner Vajrayana practice is a "no big deal" attitude. We simply just sit down and practice. There's no big preparation. We don't need a big pep talk, except sometimes. It's very simple: We sit down, and instead of arguing with ourselves about what we're doing, we just begin. "HRIH! In the Palace of Great Exaltation...," or whatever our text says. Here we are.

A LITTLE SECRET

I'm not exactly going to give instructions on how to practice Dzogchen; that's outside of my domain. If you want to learn the actual practices of the Great Perfection or any of the tantric sadhanas, there are tried-and-true ways of doing that, which, as mentioned again and again, involve making a relationship with a deceitless wisdom teacher. Under those circumstances, we can learn these things. But I should tell you a little secret. And maybe it's the only secret that I'm actually going to tell; all the rest is "self-secret" anyway.

Here it is: You will receive nothing unless you ask. No one is going to force it upon you, and no one's even going to exactly offer it to you. If you feel a connection to this approach, you have to overcome hesitation, and you have to actually make the request. In the beginning, that might be daunting, because you don't even know what you're asking for! Yet you still have to use your intelligence.

At the beginning of this section, I suggested that we shouldn't study these things if we don't have some affinity with them. If there is some karmic affinity, then it's possible that it may be for you. The Vajrayana is not for everybody. You don't need to feel bad if you find that it's not for you. The wondrousness of the Buddhist path is that there are approaches and teachings and ways to practice that are appropriate to each person's faculties. Out of kindness, the Buddha presented many, many different skillful means to allow beings' buddha-nature to ripen.

We mentioned that in the Eastern astrological systems, our current era is considered to be a dark age, the *kaliyuga*. By circumstance, these sorts of teachings, which have been kept secret for centuries, are gradually being openly transmitted to more and more people to counteract the overpowering effect of materialism on this world. We have this situation where, historically, Mao and his troops took over Tibet, the place that was home to these teachings. The core of these teachings originally came from what we call Greater India, but they were specially preserved in Tibet. In fact, *preserved* is a funny term; they were preserved from our point of view. From their point of view, they were practiced and perfected. In Tibet, Bhutan, and the various places where enough people didn't have to worry about their day-to-day jobs and were not particularly attached to work habit, making-money habit, and suchlike habit, they were able to live a simpler kind of existence. We're not saying that we should all go to a cave like so many of the great yogis did. Sure, if you have cave-dwelling fantasies, feel free! But the world is different these days. You're going to need money for the cave. Someone still has to pay the piper! What makes these teachings so applicable to those who have an affinity for them is that we don't have to go anywhere to practice. These teachings are not based on a specific temple. They're not based on any special circumstance other than the one that we create. There are highly elaborate forms, mildly elaborate forms, and unelaborate forms of practices. Everything can be done in our own space, in our own home. We don't have to go to a cave; we can bring the cave to ourselves.

The Tibetan diaspora was an incredible phenomenon. Because of it, many of the great teachers ended up in India, and some ended up all over the world. What was hidden before in the high Himalayas is now hidden in all sorts of places. Yet it's hidden and open at the same time. How we can truly make a connection with it is the subject of part six.

PART SIX

LINEAGE AND TRANSMISSION

Regardless of the types of teachings you feel drawn to, Buddhism is a living tradition, and this constant freshness involves an actual transmission. Therefore, in part six we will take a look at the issues of lineage and transmission, which are key to genuine practice and accomplishment.

In chapter 20 we will discuss the student–teacher relationship in general, using words such as *teacher* in a global sense.

In chapter 21 we will define how this relationship evolves in the context of the different vehicles—Hinayana, Mahayana, and Vajrayana.

In chapter 22, we will take a closer look at the notion of lineage, retelling some illuminating stories from the lives of the Indian and Tibetan masters, and we'll see how it can propel us along the path to spiritual awakening.

20
Entering the Student–Teacher Relationship

The student–teacher relationship is an important aspect of the Buddhist approach, and it has been so since the beginning. What is it that would make us want to have a relationship with a spiritual teacher, or a spiritual friend? What is it within our being that would like to invite someone like that into our life?

In Western culture especially, there is a notion of self-sufficiency, and an idea that asking for help, at least in the spiritual realm, is chancy. We read about all the charlatans who pick people's pockets—or people's panties, as the case may be. There are all kinds of issues in the press. The very topic is often approached with a sense of distrust.

It is important to know why we would want a relationship with a teacher. It begins with the simple truth that every individual, every single being, has buddha-nature; that this nature lies within our own heart. But for it to fully awaken, it needs nurturing, like a plant that requires sunshine, water, and fertilizer. It is not enough to say, "I have buddha-nature and everything's going to be okay." Nor is it an object of pride—as it's been pointed out, even rats have buddha-nature. Yet buddha-nature needs to be cultivated.

There is an aspiration that comes from our own sense of insecurity—from our basic misery, if you will. How can we provoke, or awaken, that aspiration? All of us have certain parts of our being and life that are miserable. We have pains that we go through, pains that our friends and families go through, and so forth. But it turns out that the various miseries and pains *provoke* buddha-nature. Something has to happen, and it is that very sense of provocation that invites a spiritual teacher into our life.

As we saw in part two and the discussion of mind training, the Sanskrit term *bodhicitta* is often used to refer to a "mind set on awakening" for the benefit of all beings. But in some context, it is connected to the very notion of buddha-nature. In fact, the term *bodhicitta* could just as well be translated as "awakened heart." In both cases, it is imbued with love and compassion, and connected with naturalness, openness, and intelligence. There is, however, a twist: Buddha-nature, or *bodhicitta*, is not particularly a peaceful state. It's not particularly disturbing either. Our very state of being, and our wanting to make a relationship with something more than just our own pain or simple satisfaction, is our intelligence. Bodhicitta is more akin to intelligence than it is to any peaceful or disturbing state; it is intelligence itself. We find out that we can question our life and the meaning of our life. We have so many unanswered questions, and that is a healthy situation. If we had all the answers, what would we need a spiritual life for? What would we need a spiritual friend for?

THE FULL CATASTROPHE: BEING FRIENDS WITH OURSELVES

To begin with, if we are going to make a relationship with something bigger than ourselves, we must make a little bit of peace with ourselves. That is called *maitri*, a Sanskrit word that is often translated as "loving-kindness." In our context, however, it refers to a sense of friendliness toward ourselves, something we've been discussing on several occasions. It allows us to ease up on the expectations we have about ourselves. Maitri also helps us ease up in the various things we do to avoid a direct experience of life—to avoid going out and having a genuine relationship with the world.

When we come to the place where we feel we need a teacher, something has already happened within our being so that we're prepared to invite someone into our life who is going to mess with it a bit. If we're ready for that, it is crucial that we use our intelligence—and again, bodhicitta *is* intelligence itself. As well, if we're going to invite a teacher into our life, it is vital that we find a genuine teacher.

How do we do that? It comes down to the intelligence in our own heart. There is no reliable guidebook that will tell us, "This teacher" or "That teacher." It is a difficult issue. When we experience the longing to get out of our little trap of who we are and allow our bodhicitta to blossom, it is scary. It is akin to getting into a romance and not knowing what is going to happen. Having a relationship with a spiritual friend is actually more intimate and more intense than a husband and wife or any suchlike situation. Therefore, it is worth repeating that we should use our intelligence as well as the power of maitri.

Think of the family, for instance. We may have positive or negative feelings about our family—"the full catastrophe," as Zorba the Greek put it. But we're *familiar* with those feelings. Regardless of whether we hate our brother or love our sister, it is known territory. Something different happens when we invite someone into our life who's going to have such a close relationship with our emotions, with the way we think and perceive things, and so forth. It's very different, letting someone see our neuroses as well as our sanity. We are asking for an all-encompassing friendship.

But it has to begin with ourselves. If we are going to invite a spiritual friend in, we must be friends with ourselves. There is no other way. First, we must completely accept our own sense of being and settle down to our own situation. If we don't, there's no reason to have a spiritual friend, because we're going to run. No question about that.

So, the first step in awakening our potential, embryonic enlightened mind is to begin to trust in our own fundamental sanity. If we don't trust our own heart, how can we trust somebody else? It is just going to wreak havoc. We can trust in ourselves without having to categorize, philosophize, moralize, judge, whatever. We can simply have a direct realization of our own being and be with that. If we can do that, then there is room.

The thing is, we are predictable. We are going to have ups and downs. We will have upsurges of energy. We will want change. We will grasp, seek pleasure, experience constant unrest—all those things. First, we can begin to see what that's like, and then we can appreciate the contrast provided by somebody who is *not* so affected by all the ups and downs of life.

THE SPIRITUAL FRIEND AS ANOTHER HUMAN BEING

"Okay," you may ask, "so how do I relate to a spiritual friend? And how do I know that this is worthwhile?"

The spiritual friend is another human being just like us—with a few differences. They speak the same language—and I don't mean English, or Sanskrit, or Lithuanian. The spiritual friend understands our world. The spiritual friend eats breakfast, and they might like the same stupid television show that we like. So, there's a sense of familiarity, but there's also the quality of being *deceitless*:

The spiritual friend is not going to tell you foolish lies and lead you up the garden path.

When you make a relationship with a teacher, you're making a relationship with someone who, through their very being, will love you, and perhaps insult you as well; someone who's not going to play games with you, though you may view them as games.

Also, as we will see in chapter 22, every teacher is somebody's student. That is so important. It is an ongoing relationship and always a two-way street.

NO SUCH THING AS AN IMPERSONAL SPIRITUAL RELATIONSHIP

In the beginning, when we make a relationship with a spiritual teacher, it's all hunky-dory, because we're open to the situation and everything is quite nice.

My friend Matthieu Ricard told me the story of when he first met Dilgo Khyentse Rinpoche, who passed away in 1991. Matthieu was so happy because Khyentse Rinpoche was always totally cheerful and wonderful. He taught him about absolutely everything, and Matthieu was always delighted to be around the great lama. It was the most amazing experience. Then he asked Khyentse Rinpoche to be his teacher. His Holiness agreed. From then on, as Matthieu says, *everything changed*. This person who was nothing but sunshine now always seemed to emit black air when Matthieu was around him, and the poor guy couldn't figure out what he was doing wrong. He said it was a nightmare: "This completely enlightened being, a sun to me and to the world, is always on my case and I can't do anything right . . ." He was in shock—for years! He said it kept going and going, and he couldn't figure out what had gone so wrong.

Nothing went wrong. Perceptions change. Situations change. It's not that the spiritual friend is purposefully on our case 24/7, it's just that they are a complete mirror of our being. That is their job. But it is only because we are letting them be that person for us. This comes from that sense of maitri that we mentioned: We've opened ourselves up to this friendliness. It just turns out that being with this particular friend has funny edges. Fortunately Matthieu said that the black air didn't last forever. It only lasted for a few years; and then on and off over time.

I will add a story of my own. Once, I was particularly stressed about a situation, so I went to Bhutan to visit Dilgo Khyentse Rinpoche. I also had only experienced the most benevolent and magnificent manifestation. In any case, it was very hard to find him—he was hidden away somewhere in the back forty of the country of Bhutan. But I finally made my way to him. I was distressed about things that were happening—political issues, but awful ones. I needed insight. So I went to the same person that in my eyes was always the sunshine of the world.

It was like walking into a dungeon of coal. I asked him my questions and all I got was this stare: "Why are you asking me to explain what I've already explained many times?" Really, it was dark. With hindsight, I can't help but think of this notion of a black sun: There's still something radiating, but it's black. In any event, it was powerful. And boy, was I depressed—because my questions weren't answered in any way that I wanted them to be. On top of that, I felt that my hero was not exactly a nice guy! I was confused, in a state of shock.

I went back the next day. There was a line of hundreds of people waiting to see Khyentse Rinpoche. Strangely, because I was a Westerner in Bhutan, I was brought to the front of the line; sometimes there is a reverse prejudice. In any case, I was invited in. His Holiness was sitting there. He invited me over and asked, "Why do you think all these people are waiting to see me?" I said, "Well, of course, they want spiritual instructions from you." This was through a translator. His Holiness explained, "That's what you think? This one wants to know which are the best days to smuggle gold over the border. That person is asking about that child and what they should do to discipline them. This other person is asking this and that..." And he's smiling—no problem with what they're asking. I guess he just wanted to disabuse me of my concepts and to show me a bit of his world. But he was cheerful as can be. The black sun had become a brilliant, shining sun, and my question was answered by the strange pointing out of what people were asking about. And there was no judgment of any kind about their requests. For each person there was a response and an interplay, because they had a relationship with him.

Here is another story. Sometime thereafter, I ran into another teacher, at an airport. This person turned out to be Thinley Norbu Rinpoche, who would become one of my root teachers. I was at this airport waiting to meet a well-known lama, when someone whispered to me, "This person over there is another famous teacher. Would you like to meet him?" I said, "Sure." I held out my hand, met this person, and bowed or something—and he began shouting at me at the top of his lungs. What was he shouting about? It was about asking Khyentse Rinpoche stupid questions about American Dharma politics! So this goes back to the last bit—it is a continuation of the story, just with a different person! This is quite telling, because the whole thing about spiritual teachers is that there's a lineage. The qualities of wakefulness don't exist just in one person. In Buddhism, it's not about a personality cult but rather lineage and realization. And it is uncanny how it all works. It can also be extremely claustrophobic, but in a positive sense—the kind of claustrophobia that can help us wake up.

There is no such thing as an impersonal spiritual relationship. It is not necessary to see the other person all the time; but it *is* personal. They know our name, it works both ways. On top of that, we're open enough that we've let them into our world. Likewise, they're open enough that they've let us into their world—that's part of the two-way situation. The spiritual friend helps us awaken buddha-nature by their care, their seeming non-care, their friendliness, and their wrath. It all goes together. Anything to wake us up. But it is up to us if we want to invite that into our being. It's not a decision to be made in a fickle, facile manner.

FROM FRIENDLINESS TO COMPASSION

Some seem to believe that there can only be one spiritual teacher. I doubt it. Again, it is not a personality cult. Yes, there's probably one person that opens our mind so that we can begin to see clearly. However, we can learn from many teachers. It's not about making a collection, having a little trinket with what's-her-name and what's-his-name and this tradition and that tradition. Rather, it is the natural flow of events. This natural flow allows our friendliness to ourselves and to others to grow to be something different, which is called *karuna* in Sanskrit, or "compassion." It allows us to get outside of our personal situation and begin to care for others, because someone is making the effort to care for us. It's amazing how that happens. It works on the inside of our situation.

At some point we may want to up the ante with the spiritual friend—if the person is qualified for the ante to be upped.

In particular, in the Vajrayana tradition, the kalyanamitra may take on the role of guru or lama: someone we actually ask to tell us what to do so we can be of benefit to others through achieving or working toward enlightenment. That is a huge step. The problem is, anytime we ask a question, we should commit ourselves to living with the result of the answer. I learned over the years: Don't ask too many questions! Really, as the saying goes, you're just asking for it! Sure, at some point, you may need to ask in order to find out how things work, but what the guru can show you is the skillful means to quickly burn your karma and cut through your obscurations. That's what the Vajrayana is about.

We will discuss the role of the spiritual teacher across the different vehicles and in tantric Buddhism more specifically in the next chapter. For now, know that it is also said that a guru per se is not always necessary; that a relationship with a kalyanamitra can be enough. The Vajrayana, as wondrous and powerful as it is, is not for everyone, and a simple spiritual friendship in the general Mahayana sense may be all that you need.

TRUSTWORTHINESS IS THE ISSUE

Now, how do we actually find a spiritual teacher? By making friends with ourselves and being open. Then, it is said, the teacher will appear; it's a natural progression. What do we do when the teacher appears? Again, there's no guidebook. It's a mind-to-mind situation, and we must play it as it goes.

There's an unbroken lineage from the Buddha to our genuine teacher. The closest thing we have to a guarantee that things will work out is if the lineage is unbroken. But there are no guarantees, really. We still have to go into this with eyes wide open, based on our personal experience. We don't have to go on a caricatural "guru hunt." Naturally there might be some searching involved, but we should stay genuine. We simply must have some responsibility to our own awakening first—and then there's room.

It is important to remember that what the Buddha taught, and what all Buddhist teachers teach, is how to be like them. They are the exemplars. If you don't like a teacher, and you don't like their life, you'd better stay away because, really, what you're asking is how to become like them. Remember, however, that it's not about their personality—their "Matt-ness," their "Carolyn-ness," or whatever the case may be. It's also not about their specific cultural background. It's not even necessarily about their specific lifestyle. It's about wakefulness.

Yet the wonderful thing about the Buddhist teachings and teachers is that there's a panoply of enlightened styles. We can find someone—if our heart opens—that we can click with. That's the way it works. It's not important if the person is male, female, famous, or unknown; all those issues are tossed away. What matters is whether the relationship is genuine. Sometimes we like to think we have a relationship with someone who's well known and there's no actual relationship. What good is it to have a little credential, "I'm a student of this and that person" but no relationship with them? It's in your imagination.

Also, it helps if the person is enlightened, I suppose, but how do we know what "enlightened" is? *Trustworthy* is the issue. The teacher should be deceitless, caring, and extremely knowledgeable. That all works. I've also heard from great teachers that part of the relationship and enlightenment go together. Often a teacher needs students so that they can become enlightened together, so to speak. Again, our ideas of this hierarchical structure, of someone who's going to save us—it doesn't work that way. It's much more fluid than that. And it is that fluidity that we can make a relationship with. As we will see, there are many different levels and types of teachers, but if they are genuine and hold an authentic Buddhist lineage, it's all tied together. We don't just jump into it. Then again, if they're truly wise, they don't just jump into it either. Beware of someone who tells you right off the bat that they would like to be your teacher and immediately accepts you as their student.

THE KEY IS OPENNESS

Many things can happen in life. My first Buddhist teacher was a vaudeville singer, an old guy whom I met in a Chan temple—a Chinese Zen temple in San Francisco. What he was doing there is beyond me. He was interested in Buddhism, and somehow I made a mind connection with him.

At this temple, there was a great Chan master, one of the great teachers from China, and he really was the master, while this other fellow, Joe Miller, was just any old Joe, so to speak. Except that he wasn't just any old Joe. This person opened my eyes and mind to a much larger world. He was not famous at all; he just happened to be teaching the *Sutra of Hui-Neng*[1] on Tuesday nights. We made a connection and a whole world opened. So, I'm deeply thankful to Joe—a Joe that none of you will ever know, and that's not important. But to those who met him and had a connection, it was good.

Joe was married to Guin. Once you got to know Joe, you got to know Guin. Sometimes you would be learning about Buddhism, and he would go into a spontaneous song, singing about the five buddha families and other topics. He would make up these fantastic melodies on the spot, but then his false teeth would click off! There was something truly wonderful about that! Guin would play the piano as he was singing... But here is something I learned from her.

She told me that after her son had died during the war, she sat in a room and smoked cigarettes for fifteen years and barely left those walls. She shared all these personal stories with me, and I found out that the most cheerful, most amazing person I had ever met had created the most horrible, claustrophobic life for herself, and had come out of it. There was something very important to be learned from that—from her self-imposed nicotine retreat. It really was a wonderful thing.

I'm not sure how she came out of that hellish situation. At some point, the maitri must have developed and turned into compassion. When things turn to compassion, our life changes. I believe that the biggest change that can happen, in a Buddhist context, is that once we see the emptiness of ourselves, the emptiness of others, we can actually reach out. We see the pain of others as it is, and we can be compassionate, and there's nothing more joyous than that. It is genuine and real. I don't know if that's what happened to Guin, but I'll tell you something: I knew her for another fifteen years and until the day she died, she was terminally cheerful. Nothing could flap her. And it wasn't that she was being "positive" based on anything.

In a way, that chance meeting with Joe and Guin opened my world so that I could eventually see and meet my root gurus. I didn't have the slightest idea of how it worked. But through meeting these two persons, everything worked out. They're not famous people. They're not in anybody's annals, except for those who were fortunate enough to meet them.

We can make this kind of relationship if our heart opens. We have the process of being concerned with ourselves; then starting to open to others who are part of ourselves, like family and friends; and then starting to open to something bigger than just what's *me* and *mine*. When we can do that, friendliness turns into compassion, and there's room for a spiritual teacher. It all starts with the simple truth of buddha-nature, but at some point, meeting the teacher is what allows the blossoming to truly begin.

In any case, there are many kinds of student–teacher relationships, and as we will see in the next chapter, it can evolve along the path or across the different vehicles. It is not a one-size-fits-all situation. It's so individual, so specific to the person. But the key is openness: If we're open, it appears.

21 The Evolution of the Student–Teacher Relationship

In the previous chapter, we explored the teacher–student relationship in general. I would now like to address some of the specifics, including how the role of the teacher evolves at different stages on the spiritual journey. I will start with some finger painting, then we will take a closer look at some of the nuances.

THE TEACHER ACROSS THE THREE YANAS

The different schools of Buddhism have different ways to discuss the relationship with a teacher. What we'll discuss presently—a helpful way to understand how this relationship evolves—is found in Kagyu writings, but I believe it applies to other systems as well. Basically the approach here is based on the full view of Hinayana, Mahayana, and Vajrayana.

The Hinayana has to do with trying to understand the pain in life and how to assuage this pain.

The Mahayana has to do with the notion of ambition and how to deal with ambition in our life.

The Vajrayana has to do with looking for the subtleties of life and how to work with those subtleties.

In our relationship with a teacher, we work with each of these aspects. This includes the frightening pain of life, which refers to the Hinayana view—the basic understanding that the nature of our ordinary life is not satisfactory; that there's wanting, longing, and all sorts of problems. Sometimes this is translated as "suffering," but that may be a little extreme. Rather, there's this unsatisfactoriness about our whole situation. The foundational teachings present the truth of that pain—that it comes from grasping and desire; that it's possible to liberate ourselves from that; and that the way to find liberation is the eightfold path, the various correct ways of meditating, behaving, and so forth.

The Mahayana view, as mentioned, has to do with the ambition of life. The specific ambition of the Mahayana is what's called the bodhisattva path, the path of compassion—putting others before ourselves. It has everything to do with reversing the dualistic habit of "me first." It is the ambition to live our life for the benefit of all sentient beings, not just for our own benefit.

The Vajrayana view is associated with the subtleties that we normally miss because of our busyness and lack of clarity. Our mind is so crowded by preconceptions that we don't see the magic and sacredness of this world. The tantric teachings are skillful means to show us this sacredness and the subtleties of mind, body, and phenomena altogether.

The relationship with a teacher implies working with all these things that we are trying to find: the truth of pain in life, the ambitions of life, and the subtleties of life. In this context, the approach has a threefold pattern. It generally follows an order, though not always, and it can flip back and forth. In other words, it is not a solid, fixed A-B-C pattern. It can be A, B, C, B, A, as the case may be.

The Hinayana Teacher, or the Elder

The "A" part: At the beginning, our relationship with a Buddhist teacher or guru is very simple. *Guru* is just a Sanskrit word that refers to the teacher, much like the Japanese word *sensei*. Although the term has a different meaning in a Vajrayana context, at this point we are simply talking about our Buddhist teacher. Since this person has more experience and maturity than ourselves, we often use the term *thera*, which means "elder." In fact, at the beginning, we relate to our teacher as just a highly accomplished human being who has more maturity than ourselves—someone who has much better understanding than we do about the nature of reality, the truth of Dharma, and the Buddhist path.

To make a relationship with someone like that, it's important that we feel that the person has achieved some higher goal and that their understanding is good. In any event, we must use our intelligence. As we mentioned in the previous chapter, that intelligence is the intelligence of bodhicitta, our innate buddha-nature. It's not about going on some exuberant teacher hunt. It has to do with our heart, and our heart has everything to do with our intelligence. It's also about a meeting of minds. But it can be very simple and straightforward.

At the beginning, we might view our spiritual teacher a little bit like Wonder Woman or Superman: still human but with some superpowers or wonder powers—you know, special armbands that ward off samsara, or something of the sort.

The basic idea, from this point of view, is that the elder—or whatever we want to call them—can save us from a lot of unnecessary problems because they have much more experience than we do. They can help us by pointing out what is worthwhile and things that may be a waste of time. It's a simple guidance system.

The thera can save us from a lot of those unnecessary problems because they have solutions. These solutions are based on their own experience and the experience of the lineage. From the time of the Buddha, one thing is truly amazing with lineage: Although our own situation is unique, variations on our situation have been happening forever.

Whatever our particular situation, it is as we mentioned in the last chapter: For there to be a relationship with a teacher, first there must be an opening within ourselves—feeling the dissatisfaction in our own being—and then the willingness to make friends with ourselves, which is the development of maitri. From there, there's further opening: We are willing to deal with other people in a different way. And at some point we might be open enough to allow somebody in—that is, to allow a spiritual teacher into our life.

In essence, the first part of the threefold pattern is a relationship that is simply based on someone who has gone a bit further than us, someone who can help us through their knowledge. Thus, "elder" refers to someone who is wiser and more accomplished than we are. The idea is that we can have some faith that this person can guide us the right way.

The Mahayana Teacher, or the Spiritual Friend

The second approach is that of the Mahayana. In Sanskrit, this type of teacher is called *kalyanamitra*, or "spiritual friend," as we learned in the previous chapter. A spiritual friend is more than just someone who gives us a little advice. It is more than just someone we can talk to about issues in our practice and life. The spiritual friend, like a true friend, is *concerned* about our life, inner and outer. They are willing to make a direct link with us, and we're willing to make a direct link with them. We can communicate directly with a spiritual friend, as a friend. It is not that the kalyanamitra is someone up on a pedestal, while we're down in the subbasement. There's a meeting of minds, and we can actually relate to that person. Sure enough, from the Mahayana point of view, when we make a relationship with a spiritual teacher, it's friendship on different terms than just drinking or gossip buddies; it's a different level. Nonetheless, even though the other person is in fact superior, we're coming together as two human beings.

The kalyanamitra listens to our problems, both spiritual and ordinary. They care enough that they can be helpful in that way. So, the relationship with a spiritual friend requires a lot of trust, a lot of opening—and this, as we discussed, is a two-way street.

We must understand, however, that the spiritual friend doesn't *need* the relationship. The kalyanamitra is someone who has taken the bodhisattva vow to be of benefit to others. They take this vow seriously and live their life that way. When we also want to put others before ourselves and to actually wake up from the dream of samsara, that is when the meeting of minds and hearts happens.

As a side note, it seems that my dear, dear friend, the late Traleg Kyabgon Rinpoche, and his line of tulkus were renowned in the Tibetan world as representing the epitome of the spiritual friend. To my Dharma brothers and sisters in Australia: Think about it—how the paragon of the kalyanamitra ended up in Melbourne is beyond me. But by circumstances, I was looking into lineages in preparation for a course several years ago and realized that his particular lineage represents a prime example of what the spiritual friend is. Isn't that extraordinary? I guess the moral of the story is you never know what opportunities come up if you're brave enough—or stupid enough, or open enough.

The Vajrayana Teacher, or the Master Warrior

The third aspect of the threefold pattern is sometimes referred to as a "master warrior." The more common term is *dorje lopön* in Tibetan, or *vajracharya* in Sanskrit. In English we would say "vajra master." *Vajra* is a term that is omnipresent in tantric Buddhism. It refers to complete indestructibility. It can also refer to an implement or scepter that symbolizes compassion and skillful means. In any case, the master warrior is someone that we can implicitly trust. The Vajrayana point of view is therefore the most challenging aspect of this threefold pattern. That relationship is based on this vajra master teaching us as their student, apprentice warrior, apprentice master, apprentice bodhisattva, or apprentice buddha.

The ante is upped and no-holds-barred. Basically when we apprentice ourselves to the vajra master or master warrior, we are requesting the same training that they had, so that we can become like them. I must tell you: That is a huge commitment that should *never* be taken lightly. It's also not for everybody—far from it. It must be something that we feel very deeply about and can be committed to, because it's going to hurt. It's also going to be blissful. But pleasure and pain are not the issues. It's about being brave enough to have our neuroses, psychoses, whatever we want to call it—chicken shit in our minds, and chicken-shit habitual patterns—messed with, big time. This is major. We will be angry, we will cry, and we will laugh and feel every possible emotion.

The Vajrayana approach has to do with the quickening of karma. It brings seeds to their natural fruition. Thus, all the karma of our past, whether it's positive or negative, will come into play. Our health, wealth, family—everything—will be affected. *Warning!* This is like playing with fire. In the best situation, we can handle it and we've chosen a deceitless guru. In the worst situation, either we can't handle it or we've got ourselves a charlatan. Either way, we're screwed! It's an awful deal. Therefore, we have to be extremely intelligent, extremely mindful, most careful. You don't do it with a blindfold on.

In this threefold pattern—thera, kalyanamitra, vajracharya—the Kagyu tradition especially emphasizes the spiritual friend, or kalyanamitra, which we alluded to in the previous chapter, and it should now make more sense. Yes, sometimes we need the cutting edge of the vajra master, but the vajra master is sometimes vajra master, sometimes spiritual friend; and the main relationship, from the Kagyu point of view, is with the spiritual friend. However, over time it deepens, and as we develop, there is no difference between spiritual friend and master warrior.

If we make that relationship, we must commit to living our life with a warrior attitude. As an apprentice master or apprentice warrior, our commitment—*samaya* in Sanskrit, or *damtsik* in Tibetan—is that we make an inextricable pledge, until complete enlightenment, to live with that attitude of constant bravery, being willing to accept whatever comes our way, and with constant openness, not trying to block anything out. This even includes being open about trying to block things out—it's a bigger view. It is a combination of bravery and openness, at the same time.

When we enter this kind of relationship with a teacher, we don't have any choice but to deal with any situation that arises in our life and practice. That's the indelible seal, the commitment aspect of it. We commit ourselves, and it's the real deal—thoroughly, absolutely. We commit to live our life clearly.

A Special Case: The Crazy Wisdom Teachers

In parallel to the threefold pattern, I want to briefly mention another aspect of the guru–disciple relationship that is specific to a certain kind of teacher, especially a certain kind of Vajrayana teacher: the "crazy wisdom teacher," which is often connected to the Sanskrit terms *vidyadhara* and *mahasiddha*. This type of teacher has very particular qualities and is available to those who need that sort of extreme wake-up call.

The crazy wisdom teacher has an absolutely penetrating intelligence that knows no limits. Because it is uncontrived, their outer manifestation can sometimes go against the usual constraints of social norms. But it's always open and warm. It's not abusive in any way. Some people do all kinds of abusive and stupid things and declare themselves crazy wisdom yogis—the word for that is *bullshit*. I'm not talking about anyone in particular here. But in the tradition, especially within the Kagyu and Nyingma traditions, there are genuine crazy wisdom teachers, and their characteristic is that they have no allegiance to ego at all—none whatsoever.

I just wanted you to be aware that there are teachers like that. If we have a relationship with such a teacher, it isn't just about being with them. It is like having a 360-degree mirror, where everything is reflected penetratingly, constantly.

Our relationship with a crazy wisdom teacher is also marked by the fact that when we are relating with ourselves, we are relating with our teacher—there's no separation between outside and inside. Some of this, of course, crosses over with normal teacher–student relationships, but in a crazy wisdom situation, the social norms can be ground to dust. And, again, such vidyadharas are people that ripen the student's karma very quickly. But be careful that you don't get burned. It's hot, very hot! So much so that it should come with warning signs! Actually, it does, but we don't want to pay attention to the signs...

Anytime you read about this in the texts, it always has warnings. You should take heed.

A RELATIONSHIP WITH WAKEFULNESS

As the Japanese Zen master Ekai Korematsu Osho Roshi once said, some people are not made for the Vajrayana; they're made for the Mahayana. However, those of us who are Vajrayanists, we don't view the Mahayana as inferior, because Mahayana, the Great Vehicle, *includes* the Vajrayana. The latter is an extension of the Mahayana, from which nothing is missing. *Maha* means more than just "great"; it means "that which there is no greater than." We just say "great" for short. So, we can have a relationship with a spiritual friend in a Mahayana sense. It doesn't have to be in the sense of a vajra master in the tantric vehicle. That type of relationship is based on "whatever the master says, I will do," and that level of trust is something that no human being should ever ask for in any light way. That's as heavy as it gets. But know that it exists and that it's not for everybody.

However, if we acknowledge ourselves as being Buddhists, then we need a spiritual friend. It comes with the territory. I don't think there's any way for any of us to progress along the path, let alone attain enlightenment, without a spiritual teacher. It's exactly the way it was for all the disciples of the Buddha: You make a relationship with wakefulness through the spiritual friend.

Without that relationship, it's very rare to progress along the path. In the history of enlightenment, you sometimes hear that this or that master achieved buddhahood without a human teacher, and I'm sure that's true. But then if you actually look at their biography, you find out that in fact they had many teachers, just no one that they would call a root teacher; their realization came through their own efforts. But it's rare. For example, it seems that Tilopa made a direct relationship to enlightenment, as his autobiography says, "by storming the palace of the dakinis and going right to the heart of the matter." The truth is that he had four, maybe five great teachers who helped point things out, but it is said that it was through his own efforts that he was able to "storm the palace." They didn't tell him to; in fact, they probably told him, "Don't! That's not how you do it! That's dangerous." But it's a tricky issue.

For those of us who make a relationship to the Buddhist teachings, the natural thing is to make a relationship with a Buddhist teacher. The teacher gives us the Dharma and allows our ego to get out of the way. It's so hard to see our own situation clearly, and so easy to have all kinds of blind spots related to our egotistic attachments, our pride, or whatever binds us. By inviting in a spiritual friend who is 100 percent trustworthy, we can then work with dissolving those blind spots so that we can see clearly.

TESTING THE WATERS

In the Kagyu and Nyingma traditions, the relationship with a teacher is very much connected to our relationship with our own buddha-nature. We develop the trusting attitude of the Hinayana, the friendliness of the Mahayana, and the warrior quality of the Vajrayana. Part of the relationship with a master warrior is to develop the same attitude as the teacher: trusting, friendly, and complete warriorship. This is a big order. But we proceed *poco a poco*. We don't have to bite the whole thing off. It's best to start with Superman or Wonder Woman—that is, with the thera approach. If that works, we test the waters with the kalyanamitra. Later, if (and only if) we have a heart connection with a teacher in a Vajrayana sense, we can follow through, though never in a flippant or offhanded manner.

As far as testing the waters is concerned, it involves testing our own mind to see if we're ready, and then seeing if we have the fortitude to actually make a relationship. Sometimes we're not ready, because we haven't been able to make friends with ourselves. If we can't make friends with ourselves, it's almost impossible to make a spiritual friend—it is too painful, too irritating, too foreign. It's like a love affair, in the traditional sense, with a little tease here and there. All of us know what courting is, whether we've experienced it or not. Well, it's something like that: a whole process. And it requires both shyness and boldness, touch and go. It's amazing to watch our mind and being as we go through the courting. This is part of the opening process.

Of course, we're not totally naïve, and we need to ask questions. How do we know when we should ask those questions or when we should refrain from doing so? In the courting process, we know when it's the right time for the kiss. It's *there*, and it is at that moment—the situation is ripe. But we have to be willing to make mistakes—and lots of them! It's okay, you know. There are consequences, but we have to be willing. That's part of the right attitude, the right view. We must be willing to be a fool. In almost anything we do in life, just holding on to some idea of ourselves doesn't do us a lot of good. Sometimes we just do something really stupid. Some of the stupidest questions I've ever asked, the responses provided some of the most brilliant lessons I've ever learned.

FORMALITIES

Now, if you wonder about the progression from one type of teacher to the next and how that change actually happens, I am afraid that I don't have any set answer. In a way, entering a relationship with a spiritual friend is just like making an ordinary friend. It just happens naturally and with a little bit of awkwardness.

From a formal perspective, at least in Indo-Tibetan Buddhism, the moment we take the bodhisattva vow with a preceptor, that person has committed themselves to us and we have committed ourselves to them, until enlightenment for all.

Before that, there is refuge, in the Buddha, Dharma, and Sangha. This is formally the connection with Dharma, and sometimes the connection with our teacher. The bodhisattva vow, traditionally speaking, is when we make a *full* connection with a teacher. But sometimes it doesn't work that way. It's more a play of how our Dharma path progresses.

At some point, the vajra master relationship can happen, if it does at all. Often that type of relationship is acknowledged in a formal way. We could learn the formal ways—the exact process may vary according to the specific teacher or school—but don't put the cart before the horse. The acknowledgment must come from a real understanding of why we're doing it. If we have that understanding and want to enter into that type of relationship, the traditional way is to make a symbolic offering of our body, speech, and mind to the teacher. This triple offering can take different forms, and there is also a formal request. But we only do that *after* it has already happened in our being. So, it's an outer formalization, and it's not ultimately necessary. For the time being, if I had to give advice to a younger friend, it would go something like this: Begin your practice, and trust that the teacher will appear. If a connection is made, find out how to acknowledge this connection. Someone will let you know. It's a bigger decision than marrying someone; you should really feel that you can learn from this teacher and have complete trust in them.

ON ALONENESS AND LOOKING FOR MORE HEAT

The other day, a friend mentioned that she has a formal relationship with a teacher, lineage, and community, and yet she occasionally feels that it's a lonely path. This is an interesting observation that we should discuss.

For some reason, it makes me think of Marpa and Milarepa. We will talk more about them in the next chapter, but here is one of the most poignant anecdotes from Milarepa's life. After he had been with his teacher Marpa for a long time, Milarepa longed to see his mother, his family, and the place where he grew up. So, Marpa sent him: "Go see Mom. Go check out your homeland." When Milarepa arrived home, it was basically a ghost house, with his mom's skeleton lying there: She had passed, and so had the father. The cousins were also angry. Milarepa basically walked into a haunted house—the loneliest place you could ever visit.

There is something akin to that in our own experience, because the teachings of Dharma all have to do with learning how to live without grasping. That's the most difficult, because we want things to be some ideal that we can hold on to. For better or worse, there's just nothing to hold on to. You may call this "loneliness," but Trungpa Rinpoche made a point of calling it "aloneness" because it's not a negative quality; it's the truth of the way things are. We can view that in a sad-sack way, but it's simply the truth of what is. It doesn't mean that warmth or love go away, not at all. But ultimately there is nothing we can hold on to. This body goes, everyone we know goes, our concepts go, everything goes. That's true even on a conventional level. But we don't even believe the conventional view of it. We are so attached.

Some people also wish they had more "heat" in the relationship with their teacher. You may wish you could get closer to the lama and wonder how to do that. I'm afraid there are no formulas. It either works or it doesn't. Perhaps you would like to get more involved but can't, for some reason. I have low energy all the time—I'm old, you know. But I've learned to drag myself around a bit, despite my low energy. Likewise, we can do things that we don't think we can do. There's an element of decision. Sure, even when we make a decision, it doesn't mean that it's going to work out; but at least we made the decision. So much of the Buddhist path is about aspiration and view. If we have the correct view and the aspiration, precisely how it works out is not all that important. The aspiration and view fulfill themselves in their own way rather than in the way *we* think they're going to be fulfilled. Truth be told, we have no idea what is actually happening with us. But if we have the aspiration and the view, something is bound to happen.

ESTABLISHING A MIND CONNECTION

I visited Bhutan in the early 2000s. I went there with my teacher, Thinley Norbu Rinpoche. I had no idea what his relationship with that country was and no idea what to expect.

Wherever he went, thousands of people came to receive his blessings—on the sides of roads, all across the country. There were perhaps 650,000 people living in Bhutan at the time, and I would think that perhaps 250,000 of them have made their way to him. I had no concept of this at all. Compared to our society, Bhutan was a so-called primitive society. Of course, there are a few cities, but there are all these people, yogis and yoginis that live in simple structures or even caves, and even *they* had heard that Rinpoche was in the area. They would make their way to whatever he was doing that day, and they would receive instructions. Then they would go back home, perhaps never to see him again. But their mind connection was so strong that they would follow through on everything he had taught.

As mentioned earlier, things are fairly different in the West, as we don't necessarily have that same faith. But contexts change. Regardless, the idea is that if we make a true, personal mind connection with a teacher, we don't need to see them very often. Some people need to see their teacher quite often. Some people need to live with them, but it's not necessary. There is so much to be learned through that mind connection. Once there's that connection, it's not about bodies. What the teacher is showing us is that they are no different than our own enlightened being. It's up to us to develop the discipline and practice.

Of course, wherever we live, we should make a relationship with a living teacher and check back occasionally. But the most wonderful thing happens when we find a genuine lineage—something we will examine in the next chapter. When there's a connection with a lineage, then it's not dependent on just one person. It's amazing how mobile it can be. I don't mean "mobile" in any frivolous sense, only that the mind connection with a lineage continues through *all* genuine teachers within that lineage.

First, as we know, we must begin with maitri and so forth. But then there's a secret. Sometimes—it's rare—we can have a connection with a teacher without a human contact. However, it's very tricky, because we can fool ourselves. Still, I believe that we can have a connection with any of the great lineage holders, including Buddha himself. In the Nyingma tradition, for example, we all believe that our relationship with any teacher is a relationship with Padmasambhava and Yeshe Tsogyal. There's no separation. From the Nyingma point of view, every relationship that we have is a relationship with the founder of the Nyingma school and his main disciple—our connection is directly with them. Our human connections through our teachers are no different from that. It is also understood that if we make the request, Padmasambhava and Yeshe Tsogyal will be present in whatever our situation is.

This may sound like a fairy tale, but it's not. It's how it works. It's a little bit on the magic side of things, but you know, Vajrayana is a little bit on the magic side of things. Mahayana is a little bit on the magic side of things, too, because the basic Mahayana view—with which the Vajrayana is included—is that the world as we see it is like a magic show. It doesn't say it *is* a magic show; it's *like* a magic show. Like a bubbling brook, if you prefer. And given the way that we try—culturally and ego-wise—to solidify our sense of the world, Buddhism tries to point to the fact that our view is askew. Sometimes—most of the time—it is 180 degrees askew. That has to do with the fact that there's no direct continuity between our objects of perception, the sense perceptions, and what we observe, hear, taste, touch, and so on. There's a disconnect. All the various teachings are about being 100 percent unimpeded, without any disconnect. Part of what the teacher does is to show us the places of disconnect and give us the teachings on how things are when they're *not* disconnected, when they're *not* out of sync, and when body and mind are synchronized. This transmission can occur in countless ways.

It's a difficult subject, especially when we relate it to the impression that there is some kind of distance between ourselves and the teacher. There's something sad and raw about the whole thing.

WRATHFUL SITUATIONS AND FEELING OUT OF SYNC

If you put yourself in a relationship situation because you read in a book that it's important to have a guru, it might not turn out the way you wanted it to turn out. That is why the emphasis, especially in the Kagyu tradition, is on the spiritual friend. If you're going to establish a relationship with the benevolent dictator that is the vajra master, you better trust that person 100 percent. This is easier said than done, therefore that type of relationship is slightly de-emphasized, unless it develops naturally. Regardless of what type of relationship is spotlighted in your tradition, that relationship can change. Sometimes you can handle it, sometimes you can't. It doesn't make any difference because, ultimately, you can handle it. But don't be foolish. Really, if you remember one thing from these pages, it's this: Don't be foolish. Use your intelligence. There's no getting burned if you use your intelligence. You will get burned if you act like an idiot. Because enlightenment is compassionate—it always is—but it's not just *nice*. In Vajrayana Buddhism, if you look at the deities and buddhas, each deity has both a peaceful and a wrathful aspect. Some people have no problem with the peaceful aspect; they can make a connection through that. We can make a peaceful connection to compassion through Avalokiteshvara, for example. But some people can't, so they need Mahakala to shock them into compassion. Avalokiteshvara, Mahakala: two sides of the same coin—peaceful, wrathful.

The teacher is the same because from the Vajrayana point of view, all deities reside within the teacher. They don't reside anywhere other than that. The nature of the teacher is the nature of all buddhas. Therefore, the teacher manifests in the ways of buddhas. The guru manifests as Avalokiteshvara as well as Mahakala. Either way, it's still compassion. We look peaceful and act peacefully, and the other can be wrathful as hell, but both are ultimately for our benefit.

Some people may wonder what to do on those occasions when the teacher manifests a wrathful aspect. No one gives out any rule book on any of these things because it is entirely of the moment. On the one hand, if we see the teacher as a buddha, we know that a buddha has no ego; so, they're not really doing anything. On the other hand, sometimes it can be hard to maintain the sacred outlook. We may get furious because the teacher hit a nerve. But it all comes back to the maitri-karuna issue: Whatever happens, we still have to be kind to ourselves. Reacting too strongly is not ideal, but sometimes we can't control ourselves. There's a reaction, and the reaction is part of the whole display. However, we should heed the warning about *rudra*, which refers to our ego where we think we're smarter than the teachings. When we're under the power of rudra, we may want to kill the teacher, figuratively or literally. That's a tricky zone, to say the least. One actual, historical story about this is that of

Devadatta, Buddha's jealous cousin. Thinking of himself as superior, he tried to attack the Buddha, and he instigated a schism in the monastic community.

There are also occasions where we may feel out of sync with the teacher or inadequate. As Trungpa Rinpoche once told me, if that happens, don't take it too personally. It's not about your ego, nor the teacher's ego; it's just the way it is. We always want to make everything about ourselves. That's an insidious quality of the *maras*, so-called demons—that is, whatever psychic tendencies divert us from sanity and the path to liberation. Whether we're bloated with pride or always referring to how we're a mess, we're thinking that it's all about *me*. That's questionable. It may be about us, but it isn't always. It can also be about direct perception and sacred view, I suppose. If it's a vajra master situation, and if you are a real student of a vajra master, it's about pure perception, not about ego. And part of the magic of the Vajrayana world is that the teacher manifests in both peaceful and wrathful ways, just like the deities. That, again, is solely for the benefit of beings, because sometimes we just can't get the message in a peaceful way, and sometimes we just can't get it in a wrathful way. There's the interplay of peaceful and wrathful. It's not just about pointing out our faults.

That being said, we are very lucky if we have a teacher who points out our faults. That's the best fortune.

ALL THE WAY THROUGH

In the next chapter, we will discuss lineage, which is linked to the notion of devotion.

Devotion, from the Buddhist point of view, particularly in the Mahayana and Vajrayana, has to do with seeing the teacher as a bodhisattva or buddha. We relate to our teacher in the same way we would if we were a student of the Buddha, Padmasambhava, or Yeshe Tsogyal. It's not a formula. But there's a connection and a sense of blessing. And devotion is acknowledging that connection and that blessing.

Devotion is not something you can make up by modeling movements, positive thinking, or anything of the sort. It is what wells in your heart. There's no need to create any fake kinds of devotion. It does you no good, and it does the teacher no good. Devotion is the real connection, mind to mind, heart to heart, master to apprentice master. It is real. And not only is it real with the teacher, but it's also real with all the lineage holders that have come before the teacher, which is why it is important to know where you come from. Once you hold that lineage, you have a connection all the way through. You're not separate from those who came before you.

When you become an actual practitioner, you are one of them; you're no longer one of you. There's a change.

It's a wonderful change.

22

Lineage and Devotion

Let us continue exploring the issues of lineage and devotion, and how they fit into the Buddhist path. You may wonder, "The teachings of the Buddha and the great masters are available through books, videos, recordings . . . We can read them, study them, and even try out the techniques on our own. Do we really need a teacher?"

Without a teacher, without a guru, there's no spiritual gift. We could call this "blessing." Unfortunately, that word is so loaded in our culture, because of Abrahamic ideas. Regardless, without a teacher, there is no blessing, no spiritual learning process, and no one to help correct us. Learning involves corrections—sometimes blatant and often subtle. The relationship with a teacher allows that to happen. It's not that the teacher will chase you and tell you, "You do this wrong and that wrong." Rather, by being in the presence of your spiritual friend, your awakened mind speaks to you. Sometimes it does so through the teacher, through their speech or actions; sometimes it is through what they say to somebody else, if you happen to hear and understand it; sometimes it arises as insight in your own being. It is not a formula that inevitably goes from A to B in a fixed manner. There is a lot more subtlety to the whole situation, and it has to do with the sense of spiritual gift.

If, in our being, we're unaware of our own pain and confusion, it's the teacher's job to ignite the pain and confusion so we can see them and experience them fully. Therefore, there might be some strange effects, because through avoidance—which we have to agree is fairly common—we can block out our real pain and real confusion. The teacher can activate that process just by being with you. This process can be confusing and painful at times, but it's cleansing, healing, and ultimately, liberating. And if we lack confidence, the teacher can even help manufacture it for us—they can give us *their* confidence, somehow. It's amazing! The relationship with a teacher is an extraordinary phenomenon because something rubs off. That is another aspect of the spiritual gift. A totally unconfident idiot can become a totally confident being. It happens all the time, and it is extraordinary.

As well, if we've lost faith in the subtleties of our own experience, being caught up in the ordinary samsaric view—the run-of-the-mill SOS (as in, "same old shit")—the guru can introduce us to the subtleties of life, from the tantric view. Within our day-to-day, there are extraordinary subtleties—so many colors and shades, for example, and so many opportunities to see the sacredness of life. However, through various forms of avoidance, carelessness, and lack of mindfulness, we have limited our perceptions. A relationship with the teacher presents or re-presents that richness to us. That is yet another aspect of the spiritual gift.

But that simply doesn't work with self-proclaimed charlatans. You may think it does; they may be very good at making you believe that it does, but it really is not the same thing. The key to establishing a relationship with a deceitless teacher is that they have a real lineage. They are not making things up. The teacher had a teacher, who had a teacher, who had a teacher, who had a teacher. There's continuity. When we make a relationship with a teacher, we're not just making a relationship with that particular person; we're making a relationship with the lineage of that teacher. So, don't do it blindly. Find out what that lineage is and whether it resonates with you. If it does, go with it. Yet you must still be extremely careful.

STUDY, CONTEMPLATION, PRACTICE—AND FAITH

Some years ago, I was sitting with my friend Orgyen Chowang Rinpoche discussing the Kagyu and Nyingma lineages in this day and age. He had an interesting observation that both these lineages historically have stressed practice and study as being the complete path, the idea being that a person studies, contemplates, and then practices, with practice bringing realization. Study, contemplation, practice. He pointed out that by a set of unfortunate circumstances, the tradition of contemplation and realization is becoming secondary, while so much emphasis is being placed on just studying, debate, and intellectual understanding.

If we as practitioners become part of these streams, it is important that we maintain the integrity of this threefold approach of study, contemplation, and realization through practice. Intellectual understanding is not nearly enough, and it's not important that we can just *discuss* Dharma. Dharma has to do with realization. The relationship with a genuine teacher is very much connected to that. It really is all about realization.

However, we must study so that we can develop the correct view. Once we develop that correct view and work with it, we can reflect on Dharma, we can reflect on our lives. Then from contemplating Dharma, we can put it into practice and actually realize it. In this respect, this threefold process is linked to what Buddhism actually calls "faith." It's faith in the Buddha, faith in the Dharma, and faith in the Sangha. It is what brings things together, completely. Without faith, there's no reason to be a Dharma practitioner or to call ourselves a Buddhist. As well, faith means that we follow through: from hearing the Dharma, to contemplating the Dharma, to actualizing the Dharma. That's faith. If we just hear it, or if we just hear it and contemplate it, that's a complete lack of faith. Yet by now it should be clear that faith is not based on any kind of blindness. True faith means that once we have an intellectual understanding, we contemplate it, and then we put it into practice.

When we are looking for a genuine, deceitless teacher, it is important that we find someone who presents the whole threefold process of study, contemplation, and realization. Beware of those who only present the intellectual point of view.

That's an aside—but not a throwaway.

THE PRACTICING LINEAGE

In the context of our discussion of lineage, I would like to present two schools more specifically: the Kagyu and the Nyingma traditions.

The Kagyu tradition is one of the four main schools of Tibetan Buddhism, and it is of the New Translation schools. The Nyingma tradition is referred to as "the Old Translation school." Thus, the Kagyu tradition comes from a later period. It is also known as the practicing lineage: Kagyupas emphasize the actual practice of meditation, and putting the teachings into practice, rather than being satisfied with a mere academic study of spiritual topics or any kind of mechanical involvement in rituals.

In fact, one of the great scholars of another school, the Sakya Pandita, complained that the Kagyupas were like pigs, because they just sit around and breathe! But Kagyu practitioners are proud of the fact that they're like pigs. They have no problem with just sitting around and breathing—that is, practicing sitting meditation. It is not at all an issue. It turns out that all that sitting produced countless extraordinary beings, each with their own unique life story.

THE KAGYU ROSARY

It is sometimes worthwhile to look at historical figures. By examining the past we can see the uniqueness of personal situations and how they worked out. In particular, when we look at lineage holders—people who received and practiced the teachings, and especially those who achieved enlightenment—we get a taste of what it is to turn ordinary, neurotic experiences into complete wakefulness. We also catch a glimpse of the nature of the relationship with the teacher.

Typically when we introduce Buddhism or discuss its history, we start with how Siddhartha Gautama became the Buddha. There is already a lot of material available on this subject, including Sherab Chodzin Kohn's book *A Life of the Buddha*, which I highly recommend. If you read a life of the Buddha, I invite you to pay attention to some of his disciples, such as Ananda, Shariputra, and Maudgalyayana. There were women, too, such as Mahapajapati Gotami, Yasodhara, and Khema.* There is a lot to learn from the different disciples. I personally think of Ananda with great fondness, because my friend Traleg Kyabgon Rinpoche was considered an emanation of this direct disciple of Buddha Shakyamuni. It is through the kindness of such spiritual friends and lineage holders that the rosary of transmission remains unbroken to this day.

Through studying the life of the Buddha, we also discover that just because a person is a disciple of an enlightened being doesn't mean that there's any guarantee that things are going to work out. One example given earlier was that of Devadatta. There is much to learn from his delusion and pride.

So, even if the reality of enlightenment is unquestionable, it doesn't mean that everything's going to be hunky-dory. All kinds of stupid things can happen based on ego. It doesn't really mean anything that we have the best teacher; it is up to us how we actualize the teachings. It's up to us not to try to compete

*To learn more about some of the early Buddhist women, see Wendy Garling, *Stars at Dawn* (Shambhala, 2016).

with the teacher. In the Kagyu tradition, it is sometimes said that the grandson's accomplishment is better than the grandfather's, so evidently there's no problem with having good accomplishment. We only have a problem when there's ego involved and a sense of always watching, criticizing, and thinking we are better.

In any case, let us do a time jump from the time of the Buddha and get to the forefathers of the Kagyu tradition. I found it really helpful over the years to make a connection with these lineage figures and their stories. In fact, I blame reading *The Life and Teachings of Naropa* for changing my life totally. Once I read that, I could only go in that direction! It made such an impression on me.

In the tantric tradition, we have the *namthars*, or life stories of people like ourselves. Through their fortitude, the opening of their hearts, the development of their buddha-nature, and their willingness to accept the teacher, we were able to attain enlightenment. It is interesting that these various stories are all unique. The circumstances and attitudes are so diverse! Each situation is personal. But we can learn something from each of the styles that are presented in these life stories. It is particularly helpful to read those of the key lineage holders, when we involve ourselves or feel an attraction toward a particular lineage. If we are attracted to the Soto Zen lineage, for example, it's important for us to find out about Eihei Dogen's life and teachings. If we have a connection to Rinzai, it's important to find out about Linji Yixuan's life and teachings. In the Kagyu tradition of Tibetan Buddhism, we will pay particular attention to Tilopa, Naropa, Marpa, Milarepa, Gampopa, and the Karmapas. As we understand how the transmission occurred directly from one to the other, right down to us, we will feel inspired, and it will deepen our relationship with our own teacher—and our own wisdom mind.

Tilopa

The first human teacher, it is said, of the Kagyu tradition, is Tilopa (c. 988–1069). In this Indo-Tibetan tradition, some of the early figures are Indian. In this case, Tilo is a Sanskrit name, to which the Tibetans customarily added the *pa*.

Tilopa came from a Brahmin family. After spending his early years as a monk, he eventually renounced the monastic life to practice in secret and lead the life of a hidden yogi, working at ostensibly defiling jobs. By day he crushed sesame seeds to extract oil; there he perfected patience. By night he assisted a prostitute, and thereby learned compassion.

At some point, and as mentioned in the previous chapter, it is said that through his own inner understanding he was able to break into the "palace of the dakinis." What is that place, exactly? Well, as we know, "dakinis" refer to female buddhas, or to the enlightened aspect of the feminine. The palace of the dakinis would thus be a full manifestation of enlightenment. But we don't really know what that means; it's figurative, I suppose. It may be that there was an actual palace somewhere and the guards were female. There are stories like that, and they are not necessarily gender specific. Regardless, it was not an easy place to get into because dakinis are very tricky—and potentially dangerous. What's being pointed to is that Tilopa accessed enlightenment through his inner understanding, but also through his bravery.

In the center of that specific palace was Vajradhara, a primordial buddha, the tantric manifestation of Buddha Shakyamuni. Sometimes Vajradhara is seen as just masculine. But as is always the case with Samantabhadra and Samantabhadri, the masculine side always implies its feminine counterpart, and vice versa. Vajradhara is therefore in union with his consort. All of the tantras view the absolute state to be one of union of the masculine and feminine. So Vajradhara, from this Kagyu point of view, is the truth of the primordial essence.

Yet even Tilopa had human teachers. But because of his own gutsiness—or whatever you want to call it—he broke into enlightenment directly and could meet Vajradhara face-to-face. That actually exists as a possibility.

Naropa

Tilopa's main disciple was Naropa, who also came from a Brahmin caste. He became a great scholar and taught at Nalanda, a Buddhist university in India, near Bodhgaya. He was an expert at debate and logic. You had to be learned at Nalanda; if you lost a debate, you had to become a student of the person you lost the debate to! And Naropa wasn't going to lose the debate to anyone, because he was smarter than any of the rest of them. But by becoming so intelligent, he really wasn't going to attain enlightenment through study and debate. It just wasn't enough. At some point, he ran into an old hag with one tooth, and she asked him if he understood the teachings—the meaning, not just the words. Naropa thought about it and realized that he only really understood the words. But why would he confide in this old hag? He wanted to impress her, so he said, "I understand both the words and the meaning." She became very upset and berated him. She told him to seek out Tilopa, who understood both the words and their deeper meanings.

So, he went searching for Tilopa, hoping to study with him. As the story goes, he'd ask people as he was going around, and they kept pointing to him: "Tilopa lives over here," "Tilopa lives over there." He went through many trials in his search for Tilopa, sometimes even coming across Tilopa in disguise.

In any case, they finally met, and Tilopa took Naropa on as his disciple. The latter had to go through twelve major hardships and twelve lesser hardships to purify his understanding and receive the teachings. Tilopa was constantly testing him! Once, they went up to a temple and Tilopa said to Naropa, "If I had a devoted student, he would be willing to jump off this temple." Wanting to be the ideal student, Naropa immediately stood up on the roof and jumped. It was pretty high—and a moment later, there he was, bones broken, just a mass of pain. Tilopa healed him and showed him the extent of his ignorance. On another occasion, Tilopa asked him to steal a woman away from a wedding, with the result that poor Naropa ended up being chased and beaten by the family. There was also the penis incident—let's just say that poor Naropa got hit pretty hard with a rock. He fainted, but he got teachings on passion and desire, and Tilopa healed him. Then there are other stories where Tilopa tells Naropa to go get a wife, but then Tilopa takes the wife away and lives with her—bringing up issues about attachment and jealousy.

All these various stories sound extreme, but it was India, and it was a long time ago, and I bet they are true. Each episode points at our various delusions and misunderstandings. Each episode also points at the role of the teacher in showing us the nature of our confusion and in healing that confusion.

The resolution of the final hardship is quite telling. At some point, Tilopa takes off his sandals and slaps Naropa across the face—and at that moment Naropa has realization. Consider this for a moment: It's a sudden realization that came gradually. The sudden realization was at that moment, but he had to go through all twelve hardships to get to that sudden realization. After that, Tilopa gave him the remainder of the tantric teachings.

As a side note, there was a yogini named Niguma, who was affiliated with Naropa, whose teachings became part of a distinct sublineage, the Shangpa Kagyu.

Marpa

The next person in the lineage is Marpa. He was a Tibetan farmer. To better his life, he decided that he would become a translator, go to India, and bring back all the Buddhist teachings to Tibet. There had been a long initial period of transmission of Buddhism to Tibet, and then there was a lull, because the government of Tibet of that era was oppressing Buddhist practitioners. Marpa wanted to initiate a fresh start with new translations of the texts and new relationships with Indian teachers.

The story implies that some of his main sources of motivation were money and fame. He probably wanted a good situation for his family as well. In any case, he gathered as much gold as he possibly could, made his way down into India, and collected all kinds of texts that he could translate from Sanskrit into Tibetan—all the various tantras and material that he believed hadn't been translated during the first great transmission of Buddhism to Tibet. But he was in for a big surprise because he ran into Naropa, who would become his teacher. We already told the story of their meeting—that of Naropa tossing Marpa's precious offering of gold dust all over the place, stomping his feet, and adding that, to him, everything was absolute gold.[1] Through that, Marpa's eyes were shocked open to enlightenment—the real gold.

There are also fantastic stories of Marpa, during a dream, meeting with Saraha, an important Mahamudra teacher who had lived in far earlier times. It's of a very different style. In any case, Marpa's initial approach to Dharma was about pride and money and becoming somebody, and it still worked, because he was able to make a genuine relationship with his teacher.

Milarepa

Then we have the curious case of Milarepa. Before he became interested in Dharma, he was interested in magical incantations and black magic, and involved himself in strange Tibetan occultism. We hear about his harming and even killing people. But he became repentant and wanted to learn about Dharma.

His first meeting was with a Nyingma master, but because of his karma, Milarepa couldn't really make a connection or understand the teachings. The Nyingmapas like to point out that it wasn't the teacher's fault! Regardless, by circumstances, Milarepa was able to find another teacher—that is, Marpa—and asked him to become his disciple. Marpa was lukewarm, but Ms. Marpa,

Dakmema, believed that Milarepa was sincere, and she was able to convince her husband that he was worthwhile.

One of the famous stories is that Marpa asked Milarepa to build him a towered house. Milarepa built it, and when he finally showed it to Marpa, the latter retorted, "You built it *here?*" Milarepa had worked and sweated, building the whole thing by hand. Happy as he was to be able to do this for his teacher, his body was wrecked... And Marpa just told him, "No way. You were supposed to build it over *there*, see? Tear it down and build another one." So, Milarepa tore it down. He didn't have much to eat, except for whatever food was sneaked to him by Dakmema. It took him a long time, but he built another tower and finally showed it to Marpa. The teacher told him, "This is really stupid. I must have been drunk when I told you that!" Marpa's love of *chang*—barley beer or wine—was no secret. "There's no way this thing should be there. Get rid of it and build me a proper one right *here*." As the story goes, Milarepa built the tower once again. It turns out that all these hardships were to purify his being.

Previously we had the brash Tilopa, the scholar Naropa, and the farmer-translator Marpa; we now have the repentant Milarepa who became a great practitioner through his ascetic practices and fearless devotion to exactly what his teacher asked him to do, as each of the lineage figures did before him. Milarepa is extremely well respected by all Tibetans for his absolute diligence of putting his butt to the stone and actually practicing meditation until enlightenment, meeting all his demons, and being able to make his way through whatever arose.

For the Tibetan people, he's considered the paradigm of the best disciple, the best practitioner. He personally wrote what's translated into English as *The Hundred Thousand Songs of Milarepa*, his collected songs of realization, which is extraordinary and considered a masterpiece of Tibetan religious poetry. Trungpa Rinpoche calls him the original Tibetan blues singer!

Gampopa

Let us mention one more figure in the lineage: Gampopa. He was a successful and learned doctor. To this day, Gampopa's formulas are still used in Tibetan medicine. A khenpo told me that he recently had all kinds of stomach problems and that he ended up going to the hospital of the University of California to try to get it figured out, then went to Chinese medical doctors, and so on... Somehow, although he's Tibetan, he didn't necessarily have much faith in Tibetan medicine. These days, Westerners seem to have more faith in Tibetan medicine than Tibetans! In any case, he finally decided to go to a Tibetan doctor, who gave him "Gampopa's black pills," a formula that Gampopa made for stomach problems, probably in the first half of the twelfth century. The khenpo said that it cured him.

Before he met Milarepa, the well-respected Gampopa was married and had a child. His child and bride died during an epidemic. Gampopa became remorseful, extremely upset, and realized that he had to make a change in his life since everything that mattered to him had washed away.

He made a particularly strong relationship with Milarepa, followed his instructions, and attained enlightenment. He then established the Kagyu monastic order. His most famous work is *The Jewel Ornament of Liberation*, which is a complete manual of meditation and liberation for practitioners in the Kagyu lineage. You may remember that earlier in this book, I shared stories featuring His Holiness the Sixteenth Karmapa; the very first Karmapa (1110–1193) was one of Gampopa's foremost disciples.

What Does All of This Have to Do with Us?

We have seen all these different styles—an intellectual professor, a farmer-translator, a weird occultist, a grieving physician... All these lineage holders have their individual stories, and each can help us look at our own relationship with our teacher. If we have a connection with the Kagyu lineage that passed through Vajradhara, Tilopa, Naropa, Marpa, Milarepa, and Gampopa, we can make a connection with a current lineage holder. For example, if you have made a connection with Traleg Rinpoche, it is as pure as the earlier links in the lineage. It's a direct connection to Vajradhara, a direct connection to Buddha. That's a golden rosary—unbroken and direct, with everything included in it.

In centers of that specific tradition, the supplication to the Kagyu gurus is often chanted, and part of that supplication is, "I hold your lineage." That's the most important thing about our relationship with teachers: With actual connection and actual practice, we become a lineage holder and enlightenment flows through, directly. The student–teacher relationship also is student–teacher lineage. That proclamation "I hold your lineage" is an important aspect of being a student. It's taking responsibility for a complete legacy.

Enlightenment isn't something that can be earned. It is not just a matter of doing certain things, certain practices, and then adding everything up, paying the bill, and being handed realization in return. Naturally, we have to have discipline and the connection. But it's not just an earning situation; there's something else that goes on. And for lack of a better word—it's a loaded word—that something else is the *blessings* of the lineage, the blessings of the enlightenment, which has nothing to do with our ego or anybody else's ego. It comes from the sense of openness. But, again, there's no guarantee about that, no dues you can pay to receive these blessings. It's a gift, if you will.

As mentioned, the relationship with a teacher is also a relationship with the lineage of that teacher. Therefore, it's good to know what that lineage is, what that heritage is, and how we fit into it. We are just like those who have gone before us. We have our confusion and our devotion. The combination is what can propel us forward. It is good ground for the rain of blessings to descend.

From the Vajrayana point of view, we have to believe a little bit in magic. There's the magic of that pure transmission, that pure lineage. It's extraordinary. It really has to do with faith in the teacher and the lineage. If we're faking it, the blessings won't come. So, if we are in the wrong lineage, we should get out. If we are in the right lineage (the "right" for us, that is), we should push ourselves further into it.

COMMITMENT AND PRIDE IN THE MISHAP LINEAGE

When I'm asked for a good book on the history of the Kagyu school, I often recommend *The Mishap Lineage* by Trungpa Rinpoche. It is a hidden gem—one of his least-read books and yet one of his most profound. But it is not your typical history; it's the inside scoop.

"Mishap lineage" is one of the ways to speak of the Kagyu tradition. "Mishap" refers to the constant surprises that appear as we follow this practicing lineage. Whatever the surprises are, they're actually brought to the path.

The Kagyu tradition is committed to the thorough development of peace, clarity, and insight. It rigorously goes through shamatha, vipashyana, and Mahamudra, the "Great Symbol" itself, which is complete realization.

This lineage came from India, made its way into Tibet, and then by a set of circumstances, spread to various parts of China, Ladakh, Nepal, Bhutan, all kinds of places. Now it is present all around the globe. This did not happen through deliberate efforts to convert others; it just happened by its presence. It is not a proselytizing religion trying to get numbers. There is simply a commitment to those who somehow make a connection to this idea of the practicing lineage.

Furthermore, three characteristics of the mishap lineage are worth mentioning.

First, it involves commitment to a particular teacher. As we explained at length in the previous chapters, there is a relationship, human being to human being. That mutual commitment is at the heart of the sense of lineage.

Second, this commitment brings about a surrendering—of our individual, stubborn ego, that is. It's not about surrendering to someone else's power. It's surrendering our sense of disproportionate pride about ourselves, which can also include how bad we feel about ourselves. Along with that surrendering, there's an openness and a sense of devotion to the teacher and to the lineage.

Third, the lineage works with a commitment to the rest of the world and all sentient beings. It's not just about its little membership, composed of those who identify themselves in this particular way.

Whether we follow this lineage or any other genuine Buddhist lineage, the very notion of lineage involves respect for and knowledge of the forefathers and foremothers. If we look at them, we can identify with their struggle and their enlightenment. The sense of lineage has to do with that connection. It's important that we feel connected to our teacher and those that came before them. It is integral to the education process.

Part of being a Kagyupa is that we actually have pride in our own understanding. This is not arrogance or self-centered pride but rather a kind of pride that's outside of ego. Let us not confuse the two. What we are talking about is sometimes referred to as vajra pride or indestructible pride. It's the pride of practice without any sense of grasping about it. There's also the pride of our place in the lineage—of being a lineage holder. There is no problem with that because, again, it has nothing to do with ordinary ego-clinging. It constantly inspires us to immerse ourselves in the spirit of practice, in the spirit of awakened mind, in the blossoming of bodhicitta, rather than wallowing in the spirit of confusion and negativity. This uplifts ourselves to the potential of our buddha-nature.

CLIFFS AND EDGES

The Kagyu approach always has a sense of expanding out rather than trying to impose limits.

As we know, the history of the Kagyu lineage is connected with the development of the New Translation schools. In addition to the lineage holders mentioned above—Tilopa, Naropa, Marpa, Milarepa, and so on—there's a connection with Atisha and his disciples, notably through the lojong teachings. At some point, the New Translation school split: A part branched out with its own particular view and became the Kagyu tradition, while another part became the Gelug tradition. Interestingly, a saying in Tibet goes like this: "Kagyupas are like goats, and Gelugpas are like horses." It's different from the pig remark, but it's always livestock—it's Tibet, you know! This particular saying alludes to the fact that the Kagyupas are drawn to mountains; that they are attracted to such places. Quite literally, the Kagyu tradition is one of mountains and caves, and yogis in high places. Apparently this makes the Kagyupas akin to goats, while Gelugpas are compared to horses that like to roam in the fields. As Trungpa Rinpoche explains it, our forefathers were basically called "mountain freaks," and they were fine with that. Both literally and figuratively, they were always happy to conquer new territory, unafraid of cliffs and edges. It's an important analogy.

This being unafraid of cliffs and edges also transfers to being unafraid of any kind of cultural misunderstandings. It goes beyond just the culture of India or Tibet. It's applicable beyond any cultural clashes and boundaries. In describing the lineage, Trungpa Rinpoche said that every new country that the Kagyus come through is just like a new cliff, and the Kagyus are not afraid of any foreign space. This can be seen in the ways the tradition has traveled over the past fifty years or so, with people like Trungpa Rinpoche coming to North America, Traleg Rinpoche going to Australia, and various Kagyu teachers going to Europe, South Africa, Africa, Malaysia, and elsewhere. Each new cliff is approached in a fearless manner. This applies to both individual practice and the lineage as a whole.[2]

From India, the Vajrayana was willing to go to the "monkey land." Not Disneyland, mind you. This referred to Tibet. Tibetan cosmology had it that Tibetans were the descendants of monkeys; apparently they don't have a creationism problem. In India, Tibet was also known as "vampire land," presumably a scary and bizarre place. If a spiritual tradition could make it to a region where red-faced people ate raw meat and drank raw milk and didn't have any vegetables to speak of, that's quite something, because from an Indian perspective, there's nothing more barbarian than eating raw meat and drinking raw milk with no veggies. Yet this tradition made its way to Tibet. In the same way, it has also made its way to the West.

The sense of fearlessness developed by the Kagyupas also applies in relating with our own body and minds—there is no fear of foreign situations, no fear of facing the unknown. All these elements are part and parcel of the Kagyu lineage.

As mentioned, we Kagyupas also have a healthy sense of pride, along with great devotion toward our predecessors. There's also the sense of constantly inheriting mishap, along with a willingness to accept whatever surprises come to us. This has to do with our contact with reality, our having some control about reality, and the fact that really there is no control. That's like when Marpa sent Milarepa home and there was nothing but a haunted house—constant surprise. So in addition to that devotion, pride, and constant surprise, there is fearlessness, a willingness to go out.

Thus, the Kagyu lineage is an excellent vehicle for teachings and teachers. Historically, there has been so much success over time. Through the skillful means of the Kagyu teachers and teachings, so many people have been liberated and attained enlightenment. Again, this is not about numbers or proselytizing. But one thing is sure: The realization, especially the full realization of Mahamudra, is wondrous. And thanks to the tireless efforts of our forefathers and foremothers, this connection is available to us here and now, if we are open to it.

THE RELATIONSHIP BETWEEN KAGYU AND NYINGMA

The Nyingma approach has a slightly different view of the student–teacher relationship. Of course, the Nyingma—or Old Tradition—and the Kagyu, which is one of the New Translation traditions, are very close and have historically been bound together. In fact, there has always been a history of back-and-forth between them. So much so that it is very difficult to talk about the Kagyu tradition without talking about Nyingma Buddhism.

For example, in eastern Tibet, where Chögyam Trungpa Rinpoche and others came from, there were these great Kagyu monasteries and teachers but no tradition of study centers (*shedras*) where scholar-practitioners (*khenpos*) would teach defined curriculums. So by circumstances, the main educators for the Kagyu teachers in eastern Tibet, historically, have been Nyingmapas. The usual situation is that a great Kagyu master will have had at least one Nyingma teacher, especially if they're from the areas of Kham or Golok. That is the case for people such as Traleg Rinpoche, and especially Trungpa Rinpoche, whose teachers included Khenpo Gangshar, Shechen Kongtrul, and Dilgo Khyentse Rinpoche.

There's no contradiction between the two traditions. The only odd thing is that Nyingmapas have their own pride and they typically don't practice Kagyu methods. The Kagyus also have pride, and they're happy to practice Nyingma methods, with the result that Kagyu teachers often also hold Nyingma lineages. It rarely goes the other way. But the wonderful thing is that during periods when the Nyingma tradition was waning, the Kagyu tradition kept it alive and then retransmitted it back.

The tradition we end up practicing depends on our connection. Think of Milarepa: As mentioned, his first teacher was a Nyingma teacher, and he was unable to practice under that particular person—not because of a problem with the teacher or teaching but rather because of his own karma.

GURU RINPOCHE AND THE ESTABLISHMENT OF VAJRAYANA IN TIBET

Buddhism went to Tibet over the course of two main periods of migration. It was the main religion of India up until about the thirteenth century, when the Muslims came in and destroyed the various Buddhist institutions, monasteries, universities, and Buddhist culture in general. Fortunately for all of us, most of what was in India was also practiced in Tibet, because of the foresight of a couple of the Tibetan kings.

The first Tibetan king to become a Buddhist was Songtsen Gampo in the seventh century. In some sense, he became a Buddhist because he fell in love. He fell in love with a Nepali princess, who became his queen and who happened to be a Buddhist; and he fell in love with a Chinese princess, who was also a Buddhist. They convinced him! They were very good at it and must have had something special! Indeed, Tibet was then a great warrior nation, one of the strongest Central Asian kingdoms. At times it was extremely vast. The general populace was employed in warfare, with warlords and the whole nine yards. They ruled a lot of the area that we don't think of as Tibet, all the way to various areas that end with *-stan* and toward Persia and Mongolia. There are historical maps where you can see how their influence expanded and sometimes shrank. It was a powerful kingdom at the time.

Also, the religion was a shamanistic tradition called Bön. It was heavily involved with elemental spirits, the land, the mountains, and the various gods and beings that inhabited those places. There was a lot of what we would compare to witchcraft and suchlike approaches; it was very magic-oriented in that way. Even the kings were said to be divine; they were thought to be gods that descended from heaven and then went back to heaven. Things changed when one of the kings was killed prematurely and buried on the earth—that event was a great disaster for the Bön religion because he couldn't go back to heaven! In any case, there's a whole non-Buddhist, or pre-Buddhist history of Tibet informed by this highly evolved shamanistic religion, as well as a highly evolved culture that was tied in with all kinds of spirits, demons, mountain gods, fertility gods and goddesses, and whole arrays of warrior gods. This was not uncommon in all of Asia, but the local religion was extremely strong, partly because Tibet was extremely strong.

In this context, something like Buddhism, which didn't have to do with power—contrary to the institutionalized Bön of the time that had everything to do with power—was anathema to the local culture. The idea of compassion, emptiness, and luminosity? Wrong place at the wrong time! It was "kill or be killed; rule or be ruled."

Songtsen Gampo tried to establish Buddhism in Tibet, but it was extremely difficult because ministers didn't want it, nor did the people. It messed with their power structure. Therefore, despite the king's best efforts, the little bit that he could do didn't last very long.

Later, in the eighth century, there came a king named Trisong Detsen. According to the Buddhist tradition, he was born as an emanation of the bodhisattva Avalokiteshvara. He was the living embodiment of compassion—a caring man right from the beginning, whose desire was to truly establish Buddhism in Tibet.

Trisong Detsen invited a monk named Shantarakshita to come to Tibet, teach Buddhism, build a monastic institution, and bring the various teachings of Dharma to Tibet. The king's idea was that it would be a good place for Buddhism to flourish and that it would be of benefit to the people of his kingdom. He himself was very moved by the teachings.

Shantarakshita went there, and they tried to build the monastery of Samye, but all kinds of storms and strange things happened to the point that nothing could be built. His approach was monastic and practical: Let's go build it, fill it up with monks, and start schools. But he had no relationship to the local gods.

Here it is worthwhile to mention that among all that Buddhism has to offer, there is a cosmology that is different from the one we are used to. Even today, Buddhist teachers still have this perspective that the world is not an empty place of just molecules, people, and animals. There are different kinds of beings. Just because we, with our normal eyes, can't see them, doesn't mean that these beings don't exist. Actually, Buddhism says that there are those with the eyes to see. In any case, even within Buddhism, there are different cosmological views. Most intelligent Buddhist teachers will accept the scientific point of view, but they will also say that there's another way to view things that is equally correct. If you look in some of the Mahayana sutras, for example, you'll see that this planet is just one tiny planet in one tiny buddha field within vast buddha fields. The cosmology is so rich and powerful.

However, if you look into a telescope, you're not going to see these buddha fields. That's not what this cosmology presents. It presents something based on a different kind of experience than scientism. This is controversial for us Westerners. For a Tibetan, there's no controversy at all. In fact, the high point of the Vajrayana and Dzogchen teachings involves actually seeing the buddha fields. You see them because your "buddha eye," so to speak, has been opened. That sounds quite esoteric when phrased like that, but it seems that it is an actual possibility.

In the case of Shantarakshita's attempts to build Samye, basically the land rejected everything that he tried to put there. Plus, the ministers really hated the idea of this Buddhism. Even Shantarakshita himself was a threat to them because the king liked and trusted him so much. There were the usual politics.

Thankfully Shantarakshita was not an egomaniac. As learned as he was, he told the king, "I really can't do this, obviously." He suggested to the king that he invite from Oddiyana (which is a part of Greater India that we now think of as Pakistan) Padmasambhava, this yogi from Swat Valley. Shantarakshita basically told the king, "Here's a man who is trained in all the schools of Buddhism but who also happens to be a great magician. He knows how to trick demons, make offerings to local deities, convert deities and turn them into protectors. Let's invite him. He will convert the various demons and spirits to make them part of Buddhism rather than against it. If they are for it, naturally it will flourish among the people as well."

Padmasambhava means "Lotus-Born." His numerous life histories contain many variations, but they all begin with this eight-year-old born from a lotus. "Excuse me!?" you might say. "A boy with a body like an eight-year-old born from a lotus in the middle of a lake?" That will stop a lot of people. When you read the life of Guru Rinpoche or Padmasambhava, your usual understanding of how things work has to stop, somehow. Now, if you are Tibetan, you might believe this literally—I suppose in the same way that a real Catholic believes in the immaculate conception. I'm a Buddhist, and I am a disciple of Padmasambhava. Do I believe this? That's an interesting question. I believe it, but not necessarily in the same way that a traditional Tibetan person might believe it. I believe it *mythically*, and I will accept it. It doesn't have to be proven to me that this person was born from a lotus. To me, the symbolic nature of it is enough. There's a part of me that is able to let go and say, "No problem."

Interestingly, some decades ago, many Western scholars would have submitted that Padmasambhava never existed. They would have said, "There are no documents from the time of Padmasambhava that mention him at all." To be clear, there are countless texts and teachings that refer to Padmasambhava or Guru Rinpoche, many by the greatest and most accomplished masters over the centuries; but it seems that all these texts saw the day long after his time, and so the Western scholars just assumed that he was only a mythological figure. But then those scholars got messed up some years ago because they found one such document. You might have heard of the caves in Dunhuang. One of the books that was found there was from Zhangzhung, one of the Tibetan kingdoms that I first mentioned in part four when discussing the history of Shambhala. It was a special book. It mentions Padmasambhava, and it talks about him as a "water diviner." It basically implies that he was brought in by the Tibetan king as an irrigation specialist!

The Western scientific mind is sometimes funny. It says, "If I can't find evidence, then it doesn't exist." But then they have to adjust when they find something. So, for some time, for some Western scholars, Padmasambhava was an irrigation specialist. But then another antique scroll came up in Dunhuang describing how Padmasambhava and one of his disciples tamed local Tibetan deities, so there's that. Many other manuscripts have since surfaced, including biographical fragments, but also spiritual instructions that many scholars now believe were written by Padmasambhava himself. It seems that Western academics always have to readjust their definitions of Padmasambhava. But for Tibetan Buddhists, he is Guru Rinpoche, the Second Buddha.

In any event, it is said that he was found on a lotus in the Dhanakosha Lake in Oddiyana, with the body of an eight-year-old boy. A precocious one, that is, rather fully developed. He was miraculously born, it's said, partly because of the wishes of the king and queen. They wanted a son, but the queen was barren; so they adopted the boy and brought him to the palace. Much like the Buddha, he had the good life for many years in this royal environment. However, unlike the Buddha, he was accused of murder. By a set of circumstances, some people were accidentally killed, and he was accused of murdering them. It's a dicey story. It seems that the people who died would have killed many, many others. Something got dropped and hit them... Regardless of how it all happened, the ministers and the court system were very upset, and they wanted to execute Padmasambhava. But his father wouldn't have that, and so instead Padmasambhava was exiled.

He was out on his own, no longer a prince, off into the world. Even though he was born miraculously and was a buddha, he, like other great masters, went and received all the teachings—Hinayana, Mahayana, Vajrayana. At one point he ended up in another kingdom and fell in love with Mandarava, the princess there. She became his close disciple, and they lived together. However, Mandarava's dad became really upset with the fact that they were cohabiting and with the activities they were engaging in. He sentenced both to death, her by being thrown into a pit of barbs and thorns, and he by being burned at the stake. By miraculous circumstances, he didn't burn, and she didn't die. The king and everyone were extremely moved, and Buddhism began to be accepted there.

Padmasambhava also spent a lot of time in charnel grounds. If you've ever been to India, the charnel grounds are the areas where dead people are brought to be burned. It's full of ashes, body parts, bones... and odd people who live there, including sadhus who mark themselves with the ashes, even to this day. In Padmasambhava's time especially, all kinds of dakinis and strange women used to run around the charnel grounds. Padmasambhava received a lot of the tantric teachings from these strange women. This is the life history of a buddha, mind you, yet it is quite different from the history of Buddha Shakyamuni.

Thus was the man that King Trisong Detsen brought to Tibet. Padmasambhava was fully learned and accomplished in all the various aspects of Buddhism. Put another way, according to the Nyingma classification, he was fully accomplished in all the nine yanas, including the higher and inner yogas, and Ati, or Dzogchen (which is the ninth yana).

This unexcelled master had so many names, depending on the situation. Lotus-Born (Padmasambhava) is one of the most common. But Tibetans tend to call him Guru Rinpoche, which simply means "precious teacher." From the Tibetan perspective, this is the kindest person possible because he gave them everything in terms of their spiritual life. Everything comes from Padmasambhava. No matter what school of Buddhism a person belongs to in Tibet, they all love Guru Rinpoche. Padmasambhava is common to all the Tibetan schools, not just the Nyingma tradition, which is the one he founded.

When he arrived in Tibet, various offerings were made to him with the request that he build the monastery of Samye, present the teachings of the Buddha—all nine yanas—and establish an educational system as well as a translation process and a linguistic system for the texts. His job was extremely vast: He would create a whole new culture in a country. That's why I find it funny that for a few years, a couple of scholars said that he came as an irrigation expert. He probably did that, too! He was someone who had knowledge of so many different subjects, including, obviously, the natural world.

As part of the offerings to Padmasambhava, the king gave him one of his queens. I know this is not politically correct in this day and age, but there she was: Yeshe Tsogyal. She is absolutely unique in that she became his main disciple, his main consort, and it is only through her that we know his teachings. He apparently didn't do much writing per se, but he taught a lot. She wrote down all the various teachings, including the life of Padmasambhava and his countless spiritual instructions. At some point, after she had attained enlightenment, she also attained the particular quality of being able to remember verbatim every word spoken by Guru Rinpoche and every teaching she received. She recorded all of it. It is thanks to Yeshe Tsogyal that we have this vast corpus of Padmasambhava's works.

Now might be a good time to introduce a mythic aspect.

From the point of view of a Tibetan Buddhist, Padmasambhava, because he presented all these methods, and Yeshe Tsogyal, because she embodied them, both represent *all* the teachings. Not only that, when you say Padmasambhava or Guru Rinpoche, Yeshe Tsogyal is always included, and vice versa. It is nondual; everything is complete. Even in the iconography, if you see an image of Padmasambhava, Yeshe Tsogyal is either there or depicted as a symbol. If you see Yeshe Tsogyal, Padmasambhava is there or symbolized. Their enlightenment is absolutely inseparable.

She also became a great teacher and taught throughout Tibet with Padmasambhava and on her own, including after Padmasambhava left Tibet. She's Guru Rinpoche's equal in that way, because you can't say one without the other. I think this is a unique religious phenomenon. This is partly because of the depth of her understanding and realization. She learned everything from Padmasambhava and was able to transmit it.

Tibetans consider her to be the ultimate mother since all the teachings passed through her. She's considered to be Prajnaparamita, which is the personification of wisdom and "the matrix from which all buddhas are born" (in other words, all buddhas arise from the perfection of wisdom). Yeshe Tsogyal is considered to be Vajrayogini, a female buddha in sambhogakaya form. Again, for many Western anthropologists or whatever, these are interesting little facts. For a practitioner, it has deep meaning and points to the reality of how they practice: to be like Guru Rinpoche and Yeshe Tsogyal. Interestingly enough, one practices to be like Yeshe Tsogyal more than Guru Rinpoche. The basic idea is that Yeshe Tsogyal is the perfect disciple, the epitome of what it is to be a good student: You take the teachings, you make them your own, you fully embody them, up until completion. It is complete but not superior—there's no surpassing buddhahood. The realization of teacher and disciple is the same.

In the Tibetan Buddhist perspective, and especially in the iconography of the Nyingma school, all deities are included within Padmasambhava and/or Yeshe Tsogyal; they embody every aspect of enlightenment. In this sense, it's very simple for a Nyingma or Ati practitioner. Whatever quality one would like to establish in their own being, they can supplicate Guru Rinpoche and/or Yeshe Tsogyal. (I'm going to stop writing "and/or" because when you supplicate either one, you're supplicating both!)

One of the unique qualities of Padmasambhava's teaching is that he said he would actually appear to whoever called his name with faith. This, obviously, is the Padmasambhava that is bigger than the historical one. This is Padmasambhava as *buddha*: ever-present wakefulness. This buddha is not separate from the ever-present wakefulness inherent in each being.

Thus, for the Nyingmapas, the most basic practices are the guru yogas of Guru Rinpoche. *Guru* means "teacher," and *yoga* means "union." That means mixing our mind with the mind of the teacher until complete union, in the way that Yeshe Tsogyal did. It's not mixing our deluded mind with the mind of the teacher, but our wisdom mind. Guru Rinpoche's kind promise that if called, he would appear, means that that Mind—the mind of wakefulness—is available at any time, at any place, under any circumstances.

This brings us to the Dzogchen teachings. "What does that have to do with Dzogchen?" you might ask. *Everything.* Because what it is pointing to is that the primordial purity, or the Great Perfection, is not something that is far away. It is ever-present and always—so to speak—accessible. We're speaking in dualistic terms here, but Dzogchen or Ati has nothing to do with dualism. It is the Great Perfection as it is. But these are just words. The Ati teachings can only be presented by someone who holds them, and they can only be given to a worthy vessel. A worthy vessel is someone who has faith—that is, someone who is willing to put the teachings into practice.

I haven't done this any justice and I apologize to all of you; I especially apologize to Guru Rinpoche and Yeshe Tsogyal and the protectors for talking about this subject in such a clumsy way. But if it inspires you to establish a connection with their teachings and their enlightened mind, or at least to find out more about these buddhas, it would be wonderful.

Guru Rinpoche has appeared in my life and in the lives of my family and Dharma friends through the Buddhist teachers that hold his teachings. There are many regents of Guru Rinpoche—even in these times—with whom we can make a relationship. And then, through the practices of the guru yoga, we actually meet Guru Rinpoche as a living presence.

PADMASAMBHAVANESS

As we have seen, in the Nyingma tradition, the student-teacher relationship is based on a relationship with Padmasambhava, the founder of that lineage in Tibet. It has to do with his enlightenment and his promise to anyone who has faith in him. Padmasambhava is known as the Second Buddha and was prophesied by the Buddha himself. But there is the historical Padmasambhava, and then there's what Trungpa Rinpoche coined as "Padmasambhavaness." In a way, they're not separate, but the basic approach is that Padmasambhava or Padmasambhavaness, for the practitioner who has faith, is available at any time. And each deceitless Nyingma teacher is in fact an emanation of Guru Rinpoche. Thus, the sense of being a student in the Nyingma tradition means that we have a relationship with Guru Rinpoche.

As mentioned, Yeshe Tsogyal attained enlightenment through her diligence as Padmasambhava's student and became his peer. That relationship and that level of faith is what makes a good disciple in the Nyingma tradition. There's the teacher and the student, and then the student is as enlightened as the teacher.

It goes beyond that because in this context, the wisdom teacher is not different from Padmasambhava and Yeshe Tsogyal. When we are receiving teachings from our teacher, we are receiving them from Padmasambhava and Yeshe Tsogyal. Furthermore, the teachings given by Guru Rinpoche and revealed through Yeshe Tsogyal provide infinite ways of inviting them into our space. In fact, a central aspect of many of the Nyingma practices is to invite Padmasambhava into our own being so that we can become united with Padmasambhava, which is enlightenment. That's what guru yoga is, ultimately: the inseparability of the deity (Padmasambhava, or the Buddha), our wisdom teacher (who is not different from them), and our wisdom mind. Separation is a myth. Padmasambhavaness is available to us through our practice. The magic and wondrousness of that lineage is that it's actually the way it works. If requested, as per his promise, Padmasambhava will come—in any circumstances, in any place.

Now this may sound preposterous if we are nihilists. It may also sound theistic, like we ask God to come, and God comes... Yet it's not like that. This is beyond nihilism and beyond theism. It's something altogether other. However, it is difficult to describe what that "other" is. It has something to do with faith that is not blind; connection with a genuine teacher, and the genuine teacher being no different from Guru Rinpoche. If we make a connection to our teacher, we make a connection to Padmasambhava and Yeshe Tsogyal. If we make a connection to Padmasambhava and Yeshe Tsogyal, the teacher will appear that represents them. There's this beautiful interplay, which is, from my point of view, absolutely brilliant and miraculous.

I remember Trungpa Rinpoche's description of his visit to Taktsang, which is one of Padmasambhava's main places in Bhutan—a truly special place. Trungpa Rinpoche went there for a week. He talks about each day, and first he mentions how disappointed he is that he can't feel anything. He mentions that he basically just feels depressed while he's there. He expected some big thing to happen, something to be different. Then at some point he supplicated Guru Rinpoche and felt the urge to write a text called *The Sadhana of Mahamudra*. Something *did* happen, but it required him to meet the mind of Padmasambhava in a different way than he had expected.

There is also a story about the Madman of Tsang, recounted in Trungpa Rinpoche's book *Crazy Wisdom*. This devoted practitioner called for Guru Rinpoche, reciting his mantra and prayers consistently, yet Guru Rinpoche didn't answer. The guy was extremely upset because Guru Rinpoche had promised that if called upon, he would answer. So, he says, the Madman stopped—but then Guru Rinpoche started calling *him*!

THE TERMA TRADITION AND THE MANY PRACTICES ALL POINTING TO ENLIGHTENMENT

As discussed earlier in the book, part of what makes the Nyingma lineage so unique is the terma tradition. Padmasambhava created different sadhanas that showed complete ways to enlightenment for the benefit of beings that could make a connection with those practices. He and Yeshe Tsogyal hid those sadhanas in various places, all over Tibet and Bhutan. According to tradition, Guru Rinpoche buried them in rocks, lakes, and temples, but also in the subconscious mind[3] for the sake of future generations. Over time, there have been various tertöns, who through their realization and practice found these spiritual treasures, which are written or communicated in a special language called "dakini language," to be translated by the revealer.

The amazing thing about each of these practices—whatever deity or teaching they may reveal—is that they show the practitioner a complete path to enlightenment. Practicing it is the equivalent of enlightenment, and the realization of it is enlightenment. This is the extraordinary power of the termas of the Nyingma tradition.

Of course, besides termas, the Old Tradition also has an unbroken lineage based on a more conventional form of oral transmission called *kama*. These are basically the canonical teachings that have been passed from teacher to disciple over the centuries, since the early days. But the unique contribution of the Nyingma school is the terma tradition, considered a "shorter" or more direct mode of transmission.

In this way, the Nyingma tradition contains countless skillful means, including sutras, tantras, and termas. Whether we work with a revealed sadhana or kama teachings, it always points us to enlightenment through our relationship with a teacher. At some point, our teacher gives us back our wisdom mind, which is one with the teacher, one with Buddha, one with Padmasambhava.

Both Nyingmapas and Kagyupas agree that the various guru-yoga practices are the most profound practices of all. These practices have to do with joining our mindstream with the mindstream of our teachers and the buddhas, practicing that way with devotion, and receiving blessings from our teacher visualized as Vajradhara, Padmasambhava, or another buddha. It's about being blessed by their buddha light, joining their enlightenment with our bodhicitta aspiration, and allowing our buddha-nature to blossom. This is how we practice. In the beginning, it is like pretending. But over time, through devotion and blessings, the pretending changes and it becomes real.

The reason it becomes real is because it's outside of the realm of wanting or grasping—the simplicity of mind as it actually is.

Conclusion
Across Valleys and Mountains

There's a Buddhist parable that originally comes from the *Lotus Sutra*. It is often told as a tale on compassion and wisdom. But from a Vajrayana perspective, it can also be understood as a story about Dzogchen. I'll recount it in my own way, but it's a story that sticks.

A young boy lived with his parents on the heights of a very high mountain in the Himalayas. His mother nursed him perfectly, educated him, and made sure that he ate well. Dad was always there, too, but he was a yogi who spent a lot of time meditating and doing various practices. Therefore, the young boy didn't have that much of a relationship with his father, except for the fact that the father was always there.

As the young boy grew up, he spent time out of his cabin and enjoyed the surroundings a bit, where he could see distant mountains ever so high and get a feel of the valleys in between. He yearned to explore the world.

When he wasn't playing outside, he spent the rest of his time in the same room with his loving mother. One day, he noticed that Dad wasn't around. The boy was overcome by a desire to meet up with his father, whom he hadn't seen for quite some time. He thought, "Maybe Dad went on a journey. Let's see if I can find him and make sense of what's outside this cabin." Having reached ten years old, he said, "Mom, I'm going to explore the world. Is that okay with you?" And she replied, "Feel free."

Mom geared him up with some food and a little rucksack, and different kinds of layered clothing so he could add or remove a layer if he got too cold or too hot. And off he went.

First he arrived in a valley. It was springtime, and the area offered a spectacular floral display. He became fascinated by the many colors, beautiful shapes, sweet scents wafting about. The sun would rise, and its rays would play around with the flowers, giving the petals a luminous quality—there was lavender light, ruby light, golden light... The kid made a relationship with the flowers—he tasted some of them, some sweet and some bitter, and soon understood that the flowers that sent out a particular kind of light were probably safe to eat with the barley he had in his rucksack. He was a smart kid, and he came to know the area quite well.

At some point, he thought, "Maybe I can go to the next mountain range and see what's on the other side."

Although there was still snow on the peaks, summer had arrived, and it seemed like a good time to move to the next range. The boy made his way to it—but he had no idea how far away it was! It looked as though it was close, but in fact it was hundreds of miles away.

So it was arduous to get to the next range, and going up the mountain was even tougher. The upper parts weren't just snowy but also icy. During the day, the snow started melting, turning into water, but at night it was still freezing, so ice was always forming. It was a cold and slippery ascension, to be sure!

He managed to cross the mountain pass and make his way into the next valley, where he found a village. He'd never really seen one, having always lived in a remote area. But he went into the village and asked, "Have you seen my dad, Lama Papa?" People said, "Sorry, boy, we haven't heard of this Lama Papa."

Autumn was setting in, but he estimated that by the time he reached the next mountain range, it would already be winter. So, he resolved to stay in town for a bit. As it turned out, he stayed there for a few years. He made friends and was delighted to have other kids to play with. Then he was even happier as a teenager when he discovered girls... But as a late teenager, he realized, "Oh, I forgot why I started this journey! I got caught up by these social phenomena!" The village life was pleasant, but he still had this desire to find his father because he had never really gotten to know him. The young man even fell in love and got his girlfriend pregnant, but his initial excitement was fading, and he felt as though his life was getting way too real and seemingly frozen.

He resolved that he should resume his journey. He left the young woman and their little baby behind and went further over the next peak. He spent the next few years looking through the whole region for his father. During that process he decided he needed some cash, for food and clothing. So, he created a business where he could transport things from one place to another and get paid for his journeys. He made a lot of money because he was willing to deliver things to places that were hard to get to.

His heart was still filled with this exceeding desire to know his father and be acknowledged by him. But what could he do? He decided to go back home and tell his mother that he wasn't successful in finding his father. At least with the money he had made, he bought some yaks to bring back barley and butter for his mom.

Thinking he remembered how he had gotten there, he started making his way back to where he believed his parents' house was.

His memory was off. It took him a long time even to find a mountain range that he could identify with any level of confidence. The mountain looked different because after having traveled all around, he was approaching it from a different angle. Yet he thought, "Maybe this is where home is."

The incline was ridiculously difficult—sheer cliffs. He had to leave the yaks behind and precariously climb. When he got to a certain point, he could see, after a little valley, a house sitting on a mountain. "Maybe that's Mom's house!" He scraped his way to the house, but the nearer he got, the more uncertain he felt. See, he got to the house from the back; growing up, he had always used the front door, and now his childhood memories were fuzzy. In fact, it didn't look like his house at all, which was heart-shattering. But he was hungry and lost, and so he went inside anyway.

There was his dad, sitting, doing his puja. The boy—by this time a young man—was overjoyed because by some extraordinary stroke of luck, he had finally found his father, who greeted him so warmly, so lovingly.

"What are you doing here, Dad?" he could finally utter. "Is this a retreat cabin of yours or something?"

The father opened a door, and in the next room was Mom, cooking. She was also delighted to see him. The young man couldn't believe that he'd gone all this way, crossed multiple mountains and valleys, nearly died several times, left that poor girl behind, left his yaks, too, and couldn't even bring his barley and butter—only to find himself home with Mom and Dad.

This is an analogy of the Buddhist journey, including, for those of us who are Vajrayanists, the ngöndro, the sadhanas, everything. From the *Lotus Sutra* point of view, the basic idea is that wisdom and compassion are always there. Fully blossomed wisdom and compassion are our birthright. The boy made the voyage, though ultimately there was no reason for him to make it. The Buddhist path is a little bit like that: On some level, we make this journey that need never be made. There is also a Vajrayana or Dzogchen way to consider this story: We make this journey that need never have been made *because our basic nature is awake*.

This is a way of looking at the path. In some way, it is unnecessary, yet the skillful means of it are extraordinary. The hardships, the crying, the anger, the frustrations, all these things are part of life and thus part of the path. Yet perfection has always been there. In fact, there is no need to go anywhere. Wakefulness is to be found in our own home, and we're never disinherited.

It's a simple but profound tale. Everything we desire deep down, everything we need that is important, exists right from the beginning—but it's very difficult to see. It just can't be this simple, can it? We feel compelled to look for something else. And round we go.

This is just my little version of this story. I think of it quite often. When I'm stuck in my mind about something or other, feeling bad about myself or others, or when I'm practicing and thinking I'm experiencing evenness or whatever, sometimes the story comes to mind and makes me laugh. Because I have made my way so far from home! Here I am, and I've got to make my way back!

I started this journey, I'm now—as the folk song goes—five hundred miles away from home, and I must make my way back. I suppose that we are all, likewise, on the journey of Dharma, the journey to enlightenment itself.

It's a wondrous journey.

Acknowledgments

This book came into being through the blessing and request of Thinley Norbu Rinpoche, who asked that I share what I had learned from my first root teacher, Chögyam Trungpa Rinpoche. I studied and practiced with Trungpa Rinpoche for seventeen years and with Thinley Norbu Rinpoche for twenty-one years—nearly half a lifetime spent under the guidance of their wisdom and compassion.

Before meeting them, I was gently prepared for this path by my dear friends Joe and Guinevere Miller of the San Francisco Theosophical Society. Joe was a friend of W. Y. Evans-Wentz, the translator of *The Tibetan Book of the Dead, The Tibetan Book of the Great Liberation, Tibet's Great Yogi Milarepa*, and other sacred works. Through Joe I was first introduced to the Tibetan Vajrayana tradition. He also taught the *Sutra of Hui-Neng* and the *Diamond Sutra* at the Buddhist Lecture Hall in Chinatown, San Francisco—the oldest Buddhist temple in America. Those early days of discovery were shared with my old friend Michael Fagan.

Later, I was blessed to meet many remarkable Tibetan teachers. Among them, two are particularly close to my heart: Tulku Thondup Rinpoche of Cambridge, Massachusetts, and Traleg Kyabgon Rinpoche of Melbourne, Australia. Over time, Traleg Rinpoche and I became close friends, and he invited me to teach at his centers in Australia and New Zealand. At his request, I first shared the teachings I had received from Chögyam Trungpa Rinpoche and later those from Thinley Norbu Rinpoche. I have now been teaching at Traleg Rinpoche's centers for over twenty-one years.

In a profound convergence of intention and karma, Trungpa Rinpoche also suggested that his students publish accounts of what they had learned from him. I never imagined I would be among those students, yet through this book I am honoring the wishes of both Chögyam Trungpa Rinpoche and Thinley Norbu Rinpoche.

Most of this material arose from teachings I offered at Traleg Rinpoche's

Australian centers—places filled with devotion, wakefulness, and inspiration. A few pages are also based on talks I gave at the Great Stupa of Dharmakaya at Drala Mountain Center in northern Colorado; others arose from discussions I had with friends over the years.

This book would not exist without the devotion and persistence of my Dharma friend and editor, Vincent Thibault. He gathered and transcribed years of talks, shaped an outline, and worked closely with me to bring spoken Dharma into written form. We first met when I was teaching at the Hollywood Sound Studios on Thinley Norbu Rinpoche's *A Cascading Waterfall of Nectar*. Vincent is a devoted practitioner, translator, writer, and editor, and I offer him my deepest gratitude.

My heartfelt thanks also go to my Australian friends, especially David Macadams, whose enthusiasm and generosity supported this project from the beginning, and to Matty Dawson, who transcribed some of the teachings. I am also grateful to Traleg Khandro for permission to use recordings of my talks.

At Shambhala Publications, my appreciation goes to our editor, Liz Shaw, whose clarity of vision and editorial care helped this book find its final form, and to Breanna Locke, who prepared the manuscript for press. I am deeply grateful to my dear friend Carolyn Gimian, one of Chögyam Trungpa Rinpoche's principal editors, for her careful reading and insightful suggestions. I also extend thanks to Larry Mermelstein and the Nalanda Translation Committee for permission to use their translation of the lojong slogans, and to Stuart Macdonald and Belinda Kelley, who so generously opened their home so that this work could be completed uninterrupted.

My dear friend and Dharma brother, Devendra Banhart, offered the calligraphy and artwork for the cover. I am joyous to have his elegant hand welcoming the reader into these pages.

Finally, I thank my family—all sincere practitioners—for their unwavering love and support: Amy Yuill Green, Hazel Bercholz, and my children, Sara Hamsa Bercholz and Ivan Pawo Bercholz. And I offer my gratitude to all who attended my teachings over the years. Your questions, openness, and devotion helped shape the words now held within these pages.

APPENDIX 1

A Special Time in History

Reflections on the Teachings of Trungpa Rinpoche

I would like to share a few thoughts on the extraordinary teachings of the person whom we call "the Vidyadhara" and who was one of the main inspirations for this book.

Chögyam Trungpa Rinpoche passed in 1987. Therefore, what we're going to discuss is contemporary history. But whenever we look at contemporary history, it is extremely hard to see clearly. We lack hindsight. To see Trungpa Rinpoche is very difficult because we only see this person who walked this land, gave hundreds of talks, and did some unusual things. Yet from a wider perspective on history, his arrival into North America in 1970 is equivalent to Padmasambhava's arrival into Tibet more than a millennium earlier. It's not just that some guy from Tibet arrived in America and started teaching Buddhism to a bunch of crazy hippies! Trungpa Rinpoche's arrival into America and what he did in those seventeen years is momentous in Buddhist history. Only it will take time for that perspective to be seen.

We can't really talk about an extraordinary being using ordinary terms. Buddhism speaks of different aspects of enlightenment referred to as kayas, which go from the subtlest and most indescribable to the most tangible. Of course, we like to share stories about the nirmanakaya Trungpa Rinpoche, the person that was our friend and mentor, and whoever that strange man was—the man of thousands, hundreds of thousands, millions of faces; someone who changed constantly. Even at a nirmanakaya level, it's hard to describe him. He was the least static being I have ever experienced!

Yet there's also the sambhogakaya Trungpa Rinpoche, which refers to what he gave and left so that his mind—the mind of enlightenment—could be experienced directly. Being an extraordinarily kind teacher, he left many, many such forms. The reason he left so many forms is that there are different capabilities, understandings, and ways that we can make a connection to what is true and real. Out of his extraordinary compassion, Trungpa Rinpoche displayed countless sambhogakaya manifestations, as distinct ways to communicate that mind of enlightenment.

But he wasn't interested in large crowds. One of his largest talks ever was to be held at the University of California in Berkeley. There is a huge hall in the Student Union building that can hold a thousand people; it filled up. Rinpoche was going to give a talk on the Tibetan Book of the Dead. He went in, looked at the crowd, and said, "My publisher wanted me to give a talk on *The Tibetan Book of the Dead*, but I won't be anyone's Tibetan pet. Please go collect your money back." That was the talk! He was never interested in numbers. Likewise, at various times, wealthy people approached him and wanted to give him things, but he remained quite detached. He was never in it for money or fame. The issue was Dharma and transmitting Dharma. There were no ulterior motives of any kind.

I was fortunate enough to meet him within the first hundred days of his arrival in North America. I was a very skeptical young man. To tell you the truth, I was skeptical of him every day of my life while he was alive, because I always wanted to see if he really meant what he said. I wanted to know if he really meant it when he taught on compassion and putting others before yourself, and all these nice Buddhist homilies and teachings. I watched him closely, always waiting for him to be ordinary in that way and show signs of selfishness. To my utter surprise, in those seventeen years, I never saw that man do anything that wasn't for others. Now *that* is extraordinary. It's hard to run into a being that is like that, where there is absolutely no deception, ever. Regardless of contemporary histories and our jaded views, Trungpa Rinpoche was extraordinary in the same way as the Buddha, Padmasambhava, or Yeshe Tsogyal. It's the same mind and the same intention.

MARKING THE SIX REALMS

Trungpa Rinpoche was extremely kind in the way he taught Dharma. He didn't view his Western students any differently than he viewed his Eastern students when he was young—unlike many teachers who come to the West and who then have a totally different way of presenting teachings and relating to students. I think he was unique, at least in the beginning, in giving everything that he had. And he had *all* the goods!

One of his special qualities is that he totally engaged himself in Western life. He looked at it all, including whatever was going on at the time: the philosophical basis of Western thought, theology, dress, fashion, consumerism, cars, militarism, politics, sex, drugs, rock 'n' roll—there was nothing left out. Basically he explored the six realms in their Western manifestations.[1] In essence, they're not different from their Asian counterparts, but the nuances and the way people relate to them are different. There are even differences between Scotland, Canada, the United States, and so forth. Trungpa Rinpoche was fearless in that he was willing to look at *everything*. But he did not just look. Wherever he went, he also left the mark of enlightenment. That way, if any of his students looked in those places—whatever they might be—they could connect with enlightenment because they could find that Trungpa Rinpoche had been there. He left no stone unturned. That level of kindness is astonishing.

In that way, he marked all the various realms of samsara with the qualities of wakefulness, for our benefit. Really, there is no place our mind can go that hasn't been marked with the qualities of wakefulness. But it's up to us. If we want to be dull and ignorant, that's one thing. But we don't necessarily have to continue dullness and ignorance—even though we have been playing the dull, ignorant game since beginningless time, not paying any attention, and being consistently entangled. It is not an obligation!

DHARMA ENGLISH

Trungpa Rinpoche also left a mark on our language. His curiosity and compassion created a vehicle for people who didn't understand the ordinary language of Dharma, because English, French, German, all the various European languages are all theistic languages in the very way that they're spoken. These languages, in the way in which they express ideas, create a duality of *me* and *you*, this and that. In other words, the habit of our language is a duality habit. Trungpa Rinpoche created ways for us to break through that habit.

It is truly amazing that he took up ordinary English, using words that are in the *Oxford English Dictionary*. By comparison, when Padmasambhava went to Tibet, he had to create a whole language, a Tibetan Dharma language from Sanskrit, which was a very complex endeavor. Trungpa Rinpoche took the

English language and began marking it with Dharma. He took very particular terms that had very particular meanings and marked those with special dharmic meanings. This includes psychological terminology such as *ego*, *neurosis*, and *projection*. If you look in the dictionary and compare their usual meaning to the way he used these terms, you will find that they have something in common, yet they're not exactly the same. He's created a Buddhist-hybrid-English language, an actual Dharma English. For example, he is credited in the *Oxford English Dictionary* with the first known usage of the word *egolessness*.

He created a language that we could understand. We take this for granted, but this is truly amazing. It is to the point that anyone interested in Buddhism in the West, whether they know it or not, uses his language—even those that hate him and think he's a charlatan.

SOME RECURRENT THEMES IN HIS TEACHINGS

We have discussed Trungpa Rinpoche's teachings at length in this book, so here I will simply point out a few of the recurrent themes he emphasized.

Essentially he taught what he called "basic sanity." It is a term he used from the very beginning of his teaching, all the way to the end. His corpus of teachings is mind-blowingly vast and diverse, but this is clearly one of the themes that was constantly repeated over those seventeen years and a notion that we explored in this book.

Another aspect of Trungpa Rinpoche's kindness came from his pointing at the problems of materialism, and particularly what he coined as "spiritual materialism." In fact, *Cutting Through Spiritual Materialism* is an important book. Once, I asked him, "If you were to translate the title *Cutting Through Spiritual Materialism* into Sanskrit, how would you do that?" He didn't even have to think. He said, "*Adharma-vajracchedika*," which literally means "the diamond cutter that cuts that which is against Dharma." If you had a book in front of you that had that title, you would wonder what it's about! But *Cutting Through Spiritual Materialism* had quite an impact.

As far as I'm concerned, even pointing at spiritual materialism is a terma for this age.[2] I think it is one of his greatest kindnesses to have pointed to that trend, because that is the trend of almost all religious, spiritual, and psychological traditions. Everyone wants something or they want to be somebody. It's a rampant problem.

Another characteristic of Trungpa Rinpoche's teachings is that he presented everything from the point of view of the nine yanas, or vehicles. There are two yanas that are considered part of the Hinayana; the third yana is the *bodhisattvayana*, aligned with the Mahayana; and there are six tantric yanas, which are part of the Vajrayana. From the beginning and through all his teachings, whatever part of the Dharma Trungpa Rinpoche was presenting, it was from the top down. In other words, the view of the Great Perfection imbued everything that he shared. He taught the Hinayana in the most profound way, and in a sense he's perhaps the greatest Hinayana teacher of the twentieth century. *Hinayana* means "narrow vehicle," but in this case, it is not pejorative. It provides a well-defined path that you can follow, and it will actually lead you somewhere.

Trungpa Rinpoche taught the vastest view. Even the way he presented this narrow path came with the widest perspective—that of basic sanity, without ego, and specifically without hope and fear. That's another theme that he constantly presented, regardless of the yana: Hope and fear are both extremes that are ultimately painful. This particular emphasis came from his training in the Kagyu and Nyingma traditions, in which that view was especially strong. Sometimes they speak of hope and fear, other times they use the terms *eternalism* and *nihilism*. Regardless, falling into either extreme provides nothing but difficulty.

Hope is simple: You want to be saved, and you think that if you do things in a certain way, something or someone will save you. Fear involves doing things that might be really stupid in spite of yourself, because you fear death, which you see as a black ending. Sometimes fear manifests as cavalier attitude, always having a cool, contrived style that could be fairly strange; or destructivism, not caring for others at all. Fear comes in many shades. There are also subtler kinds of nihilism, like believing *exclusively* in science, for instance. In any case, eternalism and nihilism prevent us from having a bigger view. Trungpa Rinpoche pointed again and again at that kind of self-deception, which is so unbelievably deep, in each of the yanas.

That's what hurt if we were around him. Well, what hurt was our self-deception. But Rinpoche was kind. He let us have the self-deception, and through his kindness he always offered the antidote.

That undeniable kindness comes with a degree of discomfort. He used many names to refer to the various discomforts that we experience.

Samsara is thorny, but each thorn has the quality of wakefulness in it, *right there.*

However, we want to avoid pain, and we end up creating the pain of trying to avoid pain. That's another form of materialism. In this book I hounded a bit on this materialism issue because understanding the depth of this teaching really is a key to finding genuine freedom and living authentically.

Furthermore, Trungpa Rinpoche had a unique way of describing bodhicitta. He talked about the awakened heart as a living intelligence. He also stressed that each of us—all sentient beings, all human beings—have buddhanature inherent to them, and that it's just something that's dormant and can arise. It doesn't even have to arise per se; what it needs is some cultivation. In *Meditation in Action*, one of his first books, he talked about the "manure of bodhi." He explains how important it is to keep the manure, go through it, and use it as fertilizer. That refers to the shit that we've collected through all our lifetimes—all the ego-clinging, joy, pain, the whole big mess. We've done every variation on every possible thing so many times that it's ridiculous, yet because of our habit, we do it again and again and again, as if we never did it before. Even though we know it hurts, we keep doing it because it hurts so good—or so bad. We're so deluded it's even hard to remember how painful the whole thing is!

Rather than blindly repeating this cycle, we are taught to use our experience to develop openness. Openness, as we have seen in this book, begins with ourselves and can then extend to others. When that extension to others starts to truly permeate our being, we can embark on the path of the bodhisattva.

Trungpa Rinpoche gave an interesting description of the bodhisattva vow: It is when you give up privacy. If you ever spent time with him, you know this was a person who had totally given up his privacy. He was always available, and totally free of egocentric, self-protecting attitudes.

He also described compassion as having spaciousness and generosity simultaneously. Spaciousness is an extremely important aspect of his teachings, and it is the key to the Mahayana. On this topic, too, he gave many skillful means. For example, he kindly taught us Dharma art as a means to experience and share that sense of spaciousness in a very sweet way—through flower arranging, calligraphy, and many other different art forms. If we can be spacious, generosity naturally ensues.

Trungpa Rinpoche also talked about two kinds of compassion: genuine compassion and idiot compassion. The genuine kind comes from the depths of our being, not from some concept of what it is to be kind. By comparison, idiot compassion—a term he borrowed from the philosopher and mystic George Ivanovich Gurdjieff—refers to trying to do good deeds to make ourselves feel good. There's the analogy of a doctor who is afraid to treat someone because they might hurt them. But there's often pain that comes in curing. If you're an idiot, you won't cause that pain—with the result that you won't cure the patient.

Another expression to which Trungpa Rinpoche gave a slightly different meaning is "soft spot." That's perhaps the key to the whole of the Mahayana teachings—that there is in our being this soft spot that is real. It is sensitive and it hurts, but it's what allows complete openness. If that soft spot manifests, there is the possibility for karuna (genuine compassion) and prajna, which involves actual understanding of the way things are. The union of karuna and prajna is what constitutes the Great Vehicle of Buddhism.

That was just a simple overview of some of the recurrent themes in Trungpa Rinpoche's teachings. That's just the proverbial tip of the iceberg. I cannot fathom the depth of his accomplishment, nor even describe how influential he has been and continues to be. The only thing I could attempt, in this book, has been to share some of the teachings that have completely uplifted my life—that gave meaning to it and imbued it with deep joy.

APPENDIX 2

Shambhala Warrior Slogans and Commentary[1]

By CHÖGYAM TRUNGPA RINPOCHE

Included here is the complete list of Trungpa Rinpoche's warrior slogans, as well as his commentary associated with the slogans.

1

» Don't be afraid of who you are.

The key to warriorship and the ultimate definition of bravery is not being afraid of who you are. Examine your experience to see what it contains that is of value in helping yourself and others. Warriorship is the opposite of selfishness. We become selfish when we are afraid of ourselves and afraid of the seeming threats the world presents. We want to build a little nest, a cocoon, to protect ourselves. But we can be much braver than that. Even in the face of great problems, we can be heroic and kind at the same time.

2

» Goodness is the ground of all.

Fundamental goodness is unconditional. It is there already, just as heaven and earth are already there. Imagine that you are sitting naked on the ground, with your bare bottom touching the earth. You are exposed to heaven above and earth below, sandwiched between heaven and earth. You can't reject your atmosphere, the sun and the moon, sidewalks and skyscrapers, the landscape or the sea. This goodness is that basic, that unconditional. It is not good versus bad. It is not a "for" or "against" view, just as sunlight is not "for" or "against."

3

» Goodness dawns like the sun.

It is not just an arbitrary idea that the world is good, but we can experience its goodness. The human potential for intelligence and dignity is attuned to experiencing the brilliance of the bright blue sky, the freshness of green fields, and the beauty of the trees and mountains. We have an actual connection to reality that can wake us up and make us feel basically good. Goodness *can* happen to us. In fact, it is happening already.

4

» Never give up on anyone or anything.

In the wakeful vision of Shambhala, which we call the vision of the Great Eastern Sun, no human being is ever a lost cause. We don't feel that we have to suppress or put a lid on anyone or anything. We are always willing to give things a chance to flower.

5

» To overcome uncertainty is utterly good.

Uncertainty here refers to doubting yourself or the existence of basic goodness. When you don't punish or condemn yourself, when you relax and appreciate your body and mind, you begin to contact basic goodness in yourself. So it is extremely important to be willing to open yourself to yourself. As human beings, we have a working basis within us that allows us to uplift our state of existence and cheer up fully. Because we have a mind and body, we can comprehend this world. Existence is wonderful and precious. We don't know how long we will live. While we have our life, why not make use of it? Before we even make use of it, why don't we appreciate it?

6

» Don't assume the posture of a wilted flower.

When you slouch, you are trying to hide your heart, protecting it by slumping over. But when you sit upright but relaxed in the posture of meditation, your heart is naked. Your entire being is exposed—to yourself, first of all, but to others as well. Through the practice of sitting still and following your breath as it goes out and dissolves, you are connecting with your heart. By simply letting yourself be, as you are, you develop genuine sympathy toward yourself. When you sit erect, you proclaim to yourself and to the rest of the world that you are going to be a warrior, a fully human being.

7

» Hope and fear cannot alter the seasons.

The four seasons occur free from anyone's demand or vote. The natural law and order of this world is not "for" or "against" you. Fundamentally, there is nothing in the world that either threatens you or promotes your point of view. There is a natural law and order that allows you to survive, which is basically good. We often take for granted or reject this basic law and order in the universe, but we should think twice. We should appreciate what we have. We should feel that it is wonderful to be in this world.

8

» Awaken the genuine heart of sadness.

Awakened heart comes from being willing to face your state of mind. The sitting practice of meditation is a means to awaken this within you. When you awaken your heart, to your surprise, you find that it is empty. If you search for awakened heart, if you put your hand through your rib cage and feel for your heart, there is nothing there—except for tenderness. You feel sore and soft, and if you open your eyes to the world, you feel tremendous sadness. It is not the sadness of feeling sorry for yourself or feeling deprived. It is a natural situation of fullness. The genuine heart of sadness comes from this feeling that your nonexistent heart is full. Your experience is so raw, tender, and personal that even if a tiny mosquito lands on you, you feel its touch.

9

» To experience fearlessness, it is necessary to experience fear.

The essence of cowardice is to not acknowledge the reality of fear. Fear takes many forms. We are afraid of death, we are afraid that we can't handle the demands of our life, and there is abrupt fear, or panic, when new situations occur. Fear is expressed as restlessness: how we move, how we talk, how we chew our nails, how we sometimes put our hands in our pockets uselessly. We have to realize our fear and reconcile ourselves with fear. However, acknowledging fear is not a cause for depression. Because we possess such fear, we can potentially experience fearlessness.

10

» Go beyond fear.

When you examine your fear, if you look beneath the veneer of your nervousness, you find sadness. Nervousness is cranking up, vibrating all the time. When you slow down, when you relax with your fear, the sadness is calm and gentle. In the Shambhala tradition, discovering fearlessness comes from working with the softness of the human heart.

11

» Synchronize mind and body.

When you are completely mindful in the present moment, mind and body are synchronized. Here, synchronizing mind and body is connected with developing fearlessness, in the sense of being accurate and direct in relating to the phenomenal world. That fearless vision reflects on you as well: it affects how you see yourself. You begin to realize that you have a perfect right to be in this universe. You have looked and you have seen, and you don't have to apologize for being born on this earth. You can uplift yourself and appreciate your existence as a human being. This discovery is the first glimpse of what is called the Great Eastern Sun, which is the sun of human dignity, the sun of human power.

12

» By the dance of the setting sun, the entire world becomes cowardly.

The warrior's vision of how to lead a sane and dignified life, which we call the vision of the Great Eastern Sun, is based on celebrating life. It is contrasted to the setting sun, the sun that is going down and dissolving into darkness. Setting-sun vision is based on trying to ward off death. It is based on fear. In the world of the setting sun, we are constantly afraid of ourselves, ashamed of who and what we are.

13

» The food of the setting sun fills everyone with grease and fat.

In the setting-sun, or degraded, approach, you have a giant vision, beyond anything you can consume, and you get bloated and end up throwing things away. This could be quite literal. In many countries, thousands of tons of leftovers are discarded every year. When people go to a restaurant, they are often served a giant plate of food, more than they can possibly eat. Great Eastern Sun vision is that the world is very sacred, so you have to constantly serve your world and clean it up. It's not necessary to overindulge. Also, because you appreciate the world, you don't leave a mess in it.

14

» Always return to the primordial ground.

In this world, there are always possibilities of original purity, because the world is clean to begin with. Dirt never comes first. If you use clean towels, they become dirty, but you can always wash them and return them to their original state. Similarly, our physical and psychological existence is originally clean. We may smear the situation with our conflicting emotions, but fundamentally, our existence is all good, and it is all launderable. This is what we mean by basic goodness: the pure ground that is always there, waiting to be cleaned. We can always reconnect with the primordial ground.

15

» All-victorious, you have nothing to conquer.

Being all-victorious is not a matter of talking yourself into believing that everything is okay. Rather, if you actually look, if you take your whole being apart and examine it, you find that you are genuine and good as you are. In fact, the whole of existence is well constructed so that there is very little room for mishaps. There are, of course, constant challenges. But for the true warrior, there is no warfare. You are never at war with your world.

16

» The warrior delights in heedfulness.

Heedfulness here refers to paying attention to what is taking place in your world. Shambhala vision brings natural interest in the world outside. Ordinarily, interest occurs when something extraordinary or threatening occurs, or it may be an escape from boredom. For the warrior, interest happens spontaneously. You feel that the world is naturally full of interest: the visual world, the emotional world, whatever world you might have. So interest, or heedfulness, manifests as raw delight, delight together with rawness or tenderness.

17

» Let the Great Eastern Sun illuminate the way of discipline.

When you look at the sun rising in the sky, its rays of light almost seem to provide a pathway for you to walk on. Similarly, the Great Eastern Sun, the sun of human wakefulness, creates an atmosphere in which you can constantly move forward, recharging energy all the time. However, the Great Eastern Sun is not something outside of you but a journey unfolding within. It provides the means to take advantage of your life in the fullest sense. This is the way of discipline for the warrior. By discipline we do not mean something unpleasant or artificial that is imposed from outside. Rather, this discipline is an organic process that expands naturally from your own experience. Then you don't need an architect or a tailor to redesign your world.

18

» When doubt arises, contemplate warriorship.

Doubt takes many forms. One is fear that you'll hurt yourself by going forward. Another form of doubt is feeling that you've misunderstood your life and that you're constantly making a fundamental mistake. Being without doubt has nothing to do with accepting the validity of a philosophy or concept. Absence of doubt comes from trusting in the heart, trusting yourself. Being without doubt means that you connect with yourself, that you experience mind and body being synchronized together. When mind and body are synchronized, then you have no doubt.

19

» Propagate health as a basic discipline of warriorship.

The Great Eastern Sun is wakefulness and genuineness reflected in every aspect of your being. This realization brings a feeling of being a truly human being. Physically, psychologically, domestically, spiritually, you feel a gut-level sense of health and wholesomeness in your life, as if you were holding a solid brick of gold. When you feel healthy and wholesome, then you cannot help projecting that healthiness to others.

20

» Celebrate the feast of faith and joy.

Faith is based on genuineness, trusting in yourself and your vision. You are not faking anything, and you are not trying to impress anybody. Faith inspires discipline. Here, discipline is not based on punishment or arbitrary rules and authority, but rather on becoming thoroughly gentle and genuine. Discipline guides you in the way of the warrior and shows you how to live in the warrior's world. When the warrior has unwavering discipline, he or she takes joy in the journey and joy in working with others. This joy is like music, which celebrates its own rhythm and melody. The celebration is continuous, in spite of the ups and downs of life.

21

» Daring to let go, the warrior is great in friendliness.

To overcome selfishness, it is necessary to be daring. We are accustomed to accepting what is bad for us and rejecting what is good. We are attracted to our cocoons, our selfishness, and afraid of stepping beyond ourselves. To overcome hesitation and to commit oneself to others' welfare, the student warrior has to jump. A leap is necessary. This occurs in the practice of meditation when you step beyond the ups and downs of your thinking process and let yourself go with the breath. Let it dissolve. By letting go, you develop trust in the strength of your being. Then, you also find that you have tremendous willingness to give selflessly to others.

22

» The humble warrior is supreme.

Once you have made a leap of daring, you might become arrogant. You might say to yourself: "Look, I have jumped! I am so great, so fantastic!" But arrogant warriorship does not work. It does nothing to benefit others. You need to cultivate gentleness so that you remain humble, soft, and open. Allow tenderness to come into your heart. Renounce putting on a new suit of armor or growing a thick skin. The warrior who has accomplished true renunciation is completely naked and raw, without even skin or tissue. You are able to be, quite fearlessly, what you are.

23

» You cannot possess basic goodness.

The goal of warriorship is to express basic goodness in its most complete, fresh, and brilliant form. This is possible when you realize that you do not *possess* basic goodness, but you *are* the basic goodness itself.

24

» The warrior's discipline is like the sun.

The light of the sun shines wherever the sun rises. The sun does not decide to shine on one piece of land and neglect another. Similarly, the warrior's discipline is unwavering and all-pervasive.

25

» Join the arrow of intellect with the bow of skillful means.

With the sharpness of your intelligence, the arrow of intellect, you can clearly see the setting sun, or any degraded tendencies in yourself or the world. Then, you need to harness your insight with skillful action, which is the bow. When the arrow of intellect is joined with the bow of skillful means, you are never tempted by the seductions of the setting-sun world. Temptation here refers to anything that promotes ego and goes against the vision of egolessness and basic goodness. Together, the principle of the bow and arrow allows you to say no to ungenuineness, to carelessness, crudeness, or the lack of wakefulness.

26

» Take your seat in the warrior's world.

The practice of meditation is taking your seat in the warrior's world. Then, throughout your life, meditative awareness shows you how to regain your balance when you lose it and how to use the messages from the phenomenal world to further your discipline. The practice of meditation also allows you to be completely grounded in reality. Then, if someone asks, "How do I know that you are not overreacting to situations?" you simply reply, "My posture in the saddle, my seat on the earth, speaks for itself."

27

» The warrior's awareness is like an echo.

When the warrior starts to lose track of discipline, by taking time off or indulging in a setting-sun mentality, a state of mind that is degraded and confused, awareness is like an echo that bounces back on you. At first, the echo may be fairly faint, but then it becomes louder and louder. You are constantly reminded that you have to be on the spot.

28

» The ultimate warrior protects the world.

You are willing to be awake in whatever situation presents itself to you. You feel that you can take command of your life, because you are not on the side of either success or failure. Success and failure are your journey. In this state, the warrior always maintains loyalty to sentient beings who are trapped in the setting-sun world. The warrior's duty is to generate compassion and warmth for others, with complete absence of laziness. Your discipline and dedication are unwavering.

29

» Don't confuse letting go with arrogance or indulgence.

For the warrior, letting go is relaxing within the discipline you have already developed, in order to experience freedom. Letting go is not enjoying yourself at other people's expense, promoting your ego and laying trips on others. Arrogance of that kind is based on fundamental insecurity, which makes you insensitive rather than soft and gentle. The confused, or setting-sun, version of letting go is to take a drunken vacation or to be wild and sloppy and do outrageous things. For the warrior, rather than getting away from the constraints of ordinary life, letting go is going further into your life. You understand that your life, as it is, contains the means to unconditionally cheer you up.

30

» Don't freeze windhorse into ice.

You should appreciate yourself, respect yourself, and let go of doubt and embarrassment so that you can proclaim goodness and basic sanity for the benefit of others. The self-existing energy that comes from letting go is called *windhorse* in the Shambhala teachings. Wind is the energy of basic goodness, strong, exuberant, and brilliant. At the same time, basic goodness can be ridden, or employed in your life, which is the principle of the horse. When you contact the energy of windhorse, you can naturally let go of worrying about your own state of mind, and you begin to think of others. If you are unable to let go of your selfishness, you might freeze windhorse into ice.

31

» Take delight in others, and propagate dignity.

The warrior principles of genuineness, decency, and goodness all lead us to work with others. When this occurs, basic goodness is no longer a theory or a moralistic concept. It is direct and personal experience. Therefore, you can trust in your ability to see the setting-sun, or degraded, world and trust in your ability to help those trapped in it. You are the vanguard to uplift your society—to begin with, your parents and friends. People often say that it's too difficult to work with others, that it's impossible to help them. But that is not true; it has been done, and you can do so as well. Shambhala vision is not purely a philosophy.

32

» Be without deception.

Being without deception is an extension of telling the truth: it is based on being truthful with yourself. When you have a sense of trusting your own existence, then what you communicate to other people is genuine and trustworthy.

33

» Rest with gentle patience and strength.

This slogan is connected with realizing unconditional confidence. Here, confidence does not mean having confidence *in* something, but remaining in the state of confidence, free from competition or one-upmanship. This is an unconditional state in which you possess an unwavering state of mind that needs no reference point. There is no room for doubt; even the question of doubt does not occur. This confidence contains gentleness, because the notion of fear does not arise; sturdiness, because in the state of confidence there is ever-present resourcefulness; and joy, because trusting in the heart brings a greater sense of humor.

34

» Appreciate the accomplishments of your ancestors.

We should not ignore the contributions of the past. The failure to appreciate the resourcefulness of human existence—which we call basic goodness—has become one of the world's biggest problems. However, we need to find the link between tradition and the present experience of life. *Nowness*, or the magic of the present moment, is what joins the wisdom of the past with the present. When you appreciate a painting, a piece of music, or a work of literature, no matter when it was created, you appreciate it *now*. You experience the same nowness in which it was created. It is always *now*.

35

» This very moment is always the occasion.

The principle of nowness is very important to any effort to establish an enlightened society. You may wonder what the best approach is to helping society and how you can know that what you are doing is authentic and good. The only answer is nowness. The way to relax, or rest the mind in nowness, is through the practice of meditation. In meditation you take an unbiased approach. You let things be as they are, without judgment, and in that way you yourself learn to be.

36

» Let your wisdom as a human being connect with the power of things as they are.

There is no fundamental separation or duality between you and your world. This discovery may arise as an extraordinary smell, a fantastic sound, a vivid color, an unusual taste. Any perception can connect you to reality properly and fully. If you are able to relax—relax to a cloud by looking at it, relax to a drop of rain and experience its genuineness—you see the unconditionality of reality, which remains very simply in things as they are. There is some principle of magic in everything, some living quality. Something living, something real is taking place in everything.

37

» Without arrogance, see the brilliance of the universe.

We can't ignore the phenomenal world. We should always take the opportunity, seize it on the spot. Appreciate the world, which is so vivid and beautiful. Arrogant people are so involved with themselves and competing so much with others that they won't even look.

38

» A warrior never needs to take time off.

Trying to relax by slouching or indulging in habitual patterns only produces schizophrenia. You are such a nice person at the office, but the minute you come home you turn on the television, argue with your spouse, and send your children to their rooms, telling them you need peace and quiet. Such habitual patterns are dangerous and destructive. They prevent you from seeing the Great Eastern Sun, the experience of human wakefulness. Uplifting your head and shoulders may sometimes give you back pain or a strained neck, but uplifting yourself is necessary. The journey may be demanding, but there is no way of avoiding it.

39

» Always think only of the good of others.

The point of warriorship is to become a gentle and tamed human being who can make a genuine contribution to this world. The warrior's journey is based on discovering what is intrinsically good about human existence and how to share that basic nature of goodness with others.

40

» Cultivate natural decorum.

In the warrior's world, a sense of order or hierarchy is based on allowing things to flower. This comes from the discovery of wakefulness, or the Great Eastern Sun, reflected in everything. You see possibilities of order in the world that are not based on struggle and aggression. This understanding of hierarchy manifests on a personal level as natural decorum, or intrinsically knowing how to behave. Because you experience dignity and elegance that do not have to be cultivated or imposed, you see how to be quite naturally in the world.

41

» Do not wear shoes as a hat.

Some people would like to ignore the most basic societal norms. They say, "So what if I put my shoes on my head?" Yet everybody knows that something is not quite right in doing that. In the same way, if instead of winter, summer followed autumn and spring followed summer, the whole order of cosmic principles would be violated. Crops wouldn't grow, animals wouldn't reproduce, and we would have devastating droughts and floods. When natural order is ignored in society, it is like disrupting the order of the seasons: it weakens society and causes confusion. This does not mean paying lip service to these principles. You begin by appreciating your world, by taking a fresh look at the universe. In that way, you can discover what order or natural decorum really is.

42

» Join survival and celebration.

There appears to be a conflict between survival and celebration. Survival, taking care of your basic needs, is based on pragmatism, exertion, and often drudgery. Celebration, on the other hand, is often connected with extravagance and doing something beyond your means. For the warrior, ruling your world means that you can live in a dignified and disciplined way, without frivolity, and at the same time enjoy your life.

43

» Apply the seven principles of richness.

To cultivate harmony in your life or household, view yourself as the ruler of your world. Then, the ruler's first richness is to have a mate, a *king* or *queen*. This represents extending yourself and cultivating decency. Whether you have a partner or live by yourself, you develop decency and reasonability in relationships. The second richness is the *minister*, representing friends who provide counsel or advice. Third is the *general*, representing fearless protection, a companion who will actually take care of you. Then, you need exertion and energy in your life, the richness of the *horse*. Next, the principle of the *elephant* is that you are earthy, steady, not swayed by confusion. The sixth richness is the *wish-granting jewel*, connected with generosity. You are open and hospitable to others. Finally, you hold the *wheel of command*. You take your seat properly in your life so that all these principles work together.

44

» The warrior is not afraid of space.

The coward lives in constant terror of space: afraid of darkness because he can't see anything, afraid of silence because he can't hear anything. The setting-sun world teaches you to wear a suit of armor to protect yourself. But what are you protecting yourself from? Space. The challenge of warriorship is to step out of the cocoon, to step out into space, by being brave and at the same time gentle.

45

» Cultivate authentic presence.

Authentic presence is genuineness that radiates both gentleness and brilliance to others. Cultivate inner authentic presence by letting go of selfishness and regarding other people's welfare as more important than your own.

46

» Don't cause the Great Eastern Sun to eclipse.

Developing meekness is one of the disciplines or dignities of the warrior. Meekness is not feebleness but strength and brilliance that come from resting in a state of simplicity, being uncomplicated and approachable. In that state, simple awareness allows you to refrain from activities that dim the vision of the Great Eastern Sun, the warrior's vision of wakeful sanity. Then your mind is not filled with ordinary preoccupations. When you are not seduced by trivial situations, there is a natural sense of uplifted mind and vast vision.

47

» Precise and perky, you are never caught in the trap of doubt.

The fundamental doubt is doubting yourself, which occurs when body and mind are unsynchronized. Continuous discipline joins body and mind and brings unconditional cheerfulness. When discipline becomes a pleasure rather than a demand, you are free from the lower realms, which is living purely for survival. You possess the goodness of the higher realms. This refers to being clear and precise, free from doubt. At this stage, the warrior is always aware and never confused as to what to accept and what to reject.

48

» A good self-existing sword: desire to sharpen it will make it dull.

When, out of hope and fear, you apply a competitive or comparative logic to your experience, trying to measure how much you have fathomed, how much is left to fathom, or how much someone else has fathomed, you are just dulling your sword, the sharpness of your mind. Instead, have confidence in your awareness, and relax in your ability to connect with a larger vision, the experience of vast mind.

49

» Overcome both hope and fear.

When you hope for something in your life, if it doesn't happen, you are disappointed or upset. If it does happen, then you become elated and excited. You are constantly riding a roller coaster up and down. With nothing to hope for and nothing to fear, fearlessness is achieved.

50

» Don't spell out the truth.

When you spell out the truth, it loses its essence and becomes either "my" truth or "your" truth. By implying the truth, it doesn't become anyone's property. When the dragon wants a rainstorm, he causes thunder and lightning. That brings the rain. Truth is generated from its environment; in that way it becomes a powerful reality. From this point of view, studying the imprint of the truth is more important than the truth itself. The truth doesn't need a handle.

51

» To join heaven and earth, go beyond selfishness.

To bring together vision and practicality, you need confidence and trust in yourself. Beyond that, you have to be without selfishness. If someone thinks, "Now I have it! Ha-ha!"—that doesn't work. Joining heaven and earth happens only if you go beyond an egoistic attitude. The master warrior is extremely humble.

52

» Give yourself time to be.

Give yourself a break. Enjoy the day, your normal existence. We have to learn to be kinder to ourselves, much kinder. Smile a lot, although nobody is watching. Listen to your own brook, echoing yourself. A lot of problems come from self-hatred. Let us let go of that; let us let it go away. Let us *be* as real people. Let us be genuine people.

53

» Cheer up.

A lot of us feel attacked by our own aggression and by our own misery and pain. However, even in the darkest of the dark age, there is always light. That light comes with a smile, the smile of Shambhala, the smile of fearlessness. That cheerfulness is what we call the Great Eastern Sun. We are capable of smiling beautifully, utterly, extraordinarily. We can always cheer up.

Notes

1. EMBARKING ON THE PATH TO LIBERATION

1. Ati, or Dzogchen, is generally associated with the ancient (Nyingma) tradition of Buddhism, which considers it the pinnacle of all spiritual approaches, while Mahamudra is generally considered to be the highest approach in the New Translation schools (such as Kagyu). Trungpa Rinpoche's style of teaching even basic sitting meditation was informed by these special approaches.—Ed.
2. At the 1986 Vajradhatu Seminary, one of a series of three-month residential programs, the last one Chögyam Trungpa Rinpoche conducted, he woke up people in the middle of the night and called them into the shrine room for a spontaneous talk. It was brief: roughly two paragraphs, with an exhortation at the end: "Never forget Hinayana." He explained, "The Hinayana teaching should not be regarded as something that you can just carry out and then get rid of, or discard. The Hinayana teaching is the life force that carries out our own practice and discipline, which goes on continuously. From that point of view, the Hinayana should be regarded as life's strength." (Details kindly provided by Carolyn Rose Gimian.)

2. LIVING AN ARTFUL LIFE

1. For more on the topic of sadhana practice, see part five.
2. More on this in part four, especially chapter 13.

3. EXPRESSING WAKEFULNESS

1. "In Buddhism, emptiness is not mere nothingness or some kind of nihilistic void. In fact, some teachers explain that the Sanskrit term *shunyata* could just as well be translated as 'fullness' or 'openness.' Essentially, emptiness means that, no matter how much we believe that phenomena are unitary, permanent, independent, and autonomous, these imputed characteristics are illusory and not at all inherent.... The teachings on emptiness are meant to challenge our false assumptions about the nature of things. They are designed to dismantle the ramshackle complex of our ordinary conceptions, which is bound to provoke all sorts of reactions.... Things are ultimately 'empty,' or 'boundless,' in the sense that we cannot define their identity by pointing to strict borders that isolate them from the rest of the world." Vincent Thibault, *Overflow: A Buddhist Guide to Navigating the Chaos of the Digital Age* (Shambhala Publications, 2026). As we will see later, the wisdom that realizes emptiness is also connected to an experience of vastness.—Ed.

4. KEYS TO MIND TRAINING

1. Not to be confused with the seventh-century Indian master of the same name who is famous for his treatises on epistemology and ontology. The tenth-century lojong master referred to here is often called Dharmakirti of Suvarnadvipa.—Ed.
2. Traleg Kyabgon (1955–2012) was a great master of the Vajrayana, Mahamudra, and Atiyoga. As the ninth Traleg Tulku, he was enthroned as the abbot of the Thrangu Monastery in eastern Tibet. A pioneer of the transmission of Tibetan Buddhism in Australia, he was renowned for his erudition and deep understanding of comparative philosophy and the Western psyche. He has authored many books, including *The Essence of Buddhism*, *The Practice of Lojong*, *Mind at Ease*, and *Moonbeams of Mahamudra*.—Ed.

5. BOUNDLESSNESS AND COMPASSION

1. Composed in early 1974 by Chögyam Trungpa Rinpoche to help his students who were beginning the Kagyu *ngöndro* practice.
2. Often translated as "transcendent actions" or "perfections," the paramitas constitute the sixfold training of a bodhisattva: generosity, ethical discipline, patience, diligence (or joyful effort), concentration, and wisdom. To be called paramitas, the first five must be connected to the sixth; in other words, paramitas are virtues that are informed by wisdom and that transcend dualistic concepts such as those of "I" and "others."—Ed.
3. To simplify, there are two types of alaya. Generally speaking, the alaya as the eight consciousness, or *alayavijnana*, though neutral, subtle, and inactive, is still predisposed toward samsara inasmuch as all the seeds that it carries involve a "split," or a subject-object duality. There's also the "higher" alaya, which is the source of all (as in all phenomena, rather than just all dualistic consciousness), which is connected to nondual wisdom. Here, we start the discussion with the eight consciousnesses, but as we will see, rather than training ourselves to remain in samsara through ordinary, dualistic consciousness, we are more interested in finding a "bridge" to actual nondual wisdom, be it through finding a temporary resting place where the compulsion of duality loses some of its power. As Trungpa Rinpoche once said, "To teach ordinary beings, any higher or more awakened form must be reached through the lower level of alaya." See Nalanda Translation, "kunshi," accessed October 23, 2025, https://nalandatranslation.org/offerings/translations-and-commentaries/glimpses-of-alaya/.—Ed.

6. CEASELESS OPPORTUNITIES

1. See above, under "Rest in the nature of alaya, the essence."

8. THE DAILY GRIND

1. See Chögyam Trungpa, *Work, Sex, Money*, in *The Collected Works of Chögyam Trungpa*, vol. 10 (Shambhala Publications, 2017), 53–65.

9. SEX AND THE SACRED

1. Typically the four *dhyana* stages are presented as levels of meditative concentration that, though refined, are still egocentric experiences and therefore still part of samsara. However, here they are approached from a different angle, that of sexuality

and communication. For more on this, see Chögyam Trungpa, *Work, Sex, Money*, in *The Collected Works of Chögyam Trungpa*, vol. 10 (Shambhala Publications, 2017), 89–91.

2. From the glossary in the *Collected Works*, vol. 10: "In yogic practice, which focuses on an inner or esoteric path of unifying mind and body, *bindu* may often refer to semen in men and to the sexual essence or essence of life in human beings generally. . . . [It] is more broadly associated with mind or consciousness. In *Journey Without Goal*, Chögyam Trungpa says, 'So consciousness or *bindu* is journeying through the energies of the world. Consciousness is the awake quality that doesn't have to refer to immediate reference points alone, but has greater scope, like a radar system. . . . The radar system is called *bindu*' (128)."
3. For more on dakinis, see chapter 19.
4. To reach its destination, a bird needs two wings. Likewise, to fully actualize buddhahood, we need the twofold accumulation of merit and wisdom. All Buddhist practices are connected to either (or both) in one way or another. Merit is our inner wealth, so to speak, generated through virtuous acts. It propels the mind in a positive direction and helps us tread the spiritual path with favorable circumstances and fewer obstacles.—Ed.

10. THE ENERGY OF MONEY

1. This quote is frequently attributed to the American writer Beatrice Kaufman (1895–1945).—Ed.

11. BUSINESS ETHICS AND MEDITATIVE DISCIPLINE AT WORK

1. Typically, Vinaya refers to one of the three *pitakas*, or traditional collections of Buddhist scriptures. It is primarily concerned with monastic discipline, but here it is used in a wider sense.—Ed.

12. THE ORIGINS OF THE SHAMBHALA TEACHINGS

1. For more on Padmasambhava and his tradition, see chapter 22.
2. For more on the dakini principle, see chapter 19, under "Dakinis."

13. BASIC GOODNESS, WARRIORSHIP, AND THE GREAT EASTERN SUN

1. The axiom is famously associated with Franklin D. Roosevelt's 1933 inaugural address, but similar phrasings had been used before by other authors, including Henry David Thoreau (1851) and Michel de Montaigne (sixteenth century).—Ed.
2. Chögyam Trungpa, *Shambhala: The Sacred Path of the Warrior* (Shambhala Publications, 2015), 3.

14. WORKING WITH ONE'S WORLD

1. The three main books are *Shambhala: The Sacred Path of the Warrior* (Shambhala Publications, 2015); *Great Eastern Sun: The Wisdom of Shambhala* (Shambhala Publications, 1999), and *Smile at Fear: Awakening the True Heart of Bravery* (Shambhala Publications, 2009).

2. Chögyam Trungpa, *The Collected Works of Chögyam Trungpa*, vol. 9 (Shambhala Publications, 2017), 540.

15. THE WARRIOR SLOGANS

1. See Carolyn Rose Gimian's general introduction to *The Collected Works of Chögyam Trungpa*, vol. 9 (Shambhala Publications, 2017), notably pages xv–xvii, as well as her introduction to *The Shambhala Warrior Slogans*, starting on page 287 of the same volume.
2. See *The Shambhala Warrior Slogans*, in *The Collected Works of Chögyam Trungpa*, vol. 9, which is an important source of inspiration for the current chapter.
3. Chögyam Trungpa, *Shambhala Warrior Slogans*, 296–97.
4. Chögyam Trungpa, *Shambhala Warrior Slogans*, 297.
5. Chögyam Trungpa, *Shambhala Warrior Slogans*, 298.
6. Chögyam Trungpa, *Shambhala Warrior Slogans*, 298.
7. Chögyam Trungpa, *Shambhala Warrior Slogans*, 298–99.
8. Chögyam Trungpa, *Shambhala Warrior Slogans*, 299.
9. Chögyam Trungpa, *Shambhala Warrior Slogans*, 299.

16. AUTHENTIC PRESENCE, WINDHORSE, AND THE FOUR DIGNITIES

1. Chögyam Trungpa, *Shambhala: The Sacred Path of the Warrior* (Shambhala Publications, 2015), 160.
2. A garuda is a mythical birdlike creature that has several meanings in both Hindu lore and Indo-Himalayan Buddhism. For more on its significance in the context of the four dignities, see below.
3. Chögyam Trungpa, *The Shambhala Warrior Slogans*, in *The Collected Works of Chögyam Trungpa*, vol. 9 (Shambhala Publications, 2017), 309.
4. Chögyam Trungpa, *Shambhala Warrior Slogans*, 309.
5. Chögyam Trungpa, *Shambhala Warrior Slogans*, 308.
6. Chögyam Trungpa, *Shambhala Warrior Slogans*, 309.
7. Chögyam Trungpa, *Shambhala Warrior Slogans*, 310.
8. Chögyam Trungpa, *Shambhala Warrior Slogans*, 310.
9. Chögyam Trungpa, *Shambhala Warrior Slogans*, 310.

17. SECRET AND SHOCKING

1. It should be noted that *tantra* is a term that is also used in other religious and spiritual traditions, most notably Hinduism. Though there are *some* overlaps, it is also quite different. Naturally, what we will be discussing in this section of the book is tantric Buddhism.—Ed.
2. For more on this, see "The So-Called Preliminaries, or *Ngöndro*" in the next chapter.

19. THE GREAT EXALTATION, PART 2

1. For more on this subject, see "The Five Buddha Families," chapter 9 in *Journey Without Goal*, in *The Collected Works of Chögyam Trungpa*, vol. 4 (Shambhala Publications, 2003).

2. See Thinley Norbu, *Magic Dance: The Display of the Self-Nature of the Five Wisdom Dakinis* (Shambhala Publications, 1999).
3. Thinley Norbu, *A Cascading Waterfall of Nectar* (Shambhala Publications, 2009), 263.
4. Loving-kindness, compassion, empathetic joy, and impartiality.
5. For more on that principle, see "Padmasambhavaness" in chapter 22.
6. Thinley Norbu, *Cascading Waterfall of Nectar*, 264.
7. Thinley Norbu, *Cascading Waterfall of Nectar*, 264.
8. Thinley Norbu, *Cascading Waterfall of Nectar*, 264.
9. Thinley Norbu, *Cascading Waterfall of Nectar*, 277.
10. Thinley Norbu, *Cascading Waterfall of Nectar*, 281.
11. Thinley Norbu, *Cascading Waterfall of Nectar*, 281.

20. ENTERING THE STUDENT-TEACHER RELATIONSHIP

1. Also known as the *Platform Sutra*. Hui-Neng (638–713), a beloved figure in Zen Buddhism, was an illiterate woodcutter who became the Sixth Patriarch of Chinese Zen. He is regarded as the father of the "Sudden Enlightenment" school. See also chapter 8, under "Oryoki."

22. LINEAGE AND DEVOTION

1. For a more detailed retelling of that encounter, see "When Marpa Met Naropa" in chapter 10.
2. To learn more about this, see Chögyam Trungpa, *The Mishap Lineage: Transforming Confusion into Wisdom* (Shambhala Publications, 2009).
3. As Tulku Thondup Rinpoche puts it, "Guru Padmasambhava concealed the teachings in the essential nature of the minds of his realized disciples through his Mind-mandate Transmission power." See *Hidden Teachings of Tibet* (Wisdom Publications, 1997), 61.

APPENDIX 1: A SPECIAL TIME IN HISTORY

1. The six "realms" or "classes of beings" are the major modes of existence within samsara. We could be born among hell beings, hungry ghosts, animals, human beings, demigods, or gods. Each one is dominated by a particular emotion (anger, greed, etc.). While these realms are often depicted as existing externally, Trungpa Rinpoche liked to present their internal, subjective counterpart. On some level, all six modes can be experienced as a human being in this very life. See "The Six Realms," in *Cutting Through Spiritual Materialism* (Shambhala Publications, 1973).—Ed.
2. For more on the terma tradition, see chapters 12 and 22.

APPENDIX 2: SHAMBHALA WARRIOR SLOGANS AND COMMENTARY

1. Chögyam Trungpa, *The Shambhala Warrior Slogans*, from *The Collected Works of Chögyam Trungpa*, vol. 9 (Shambhala Publications, 2017), 294–311.